The Taming of
Fidel Castro

Every step and every movement of the multitude, even in what are termed enlightened ages, are made with equal blindness to the future; and nations stumble upon establishments, which are indeed the result of human action, but not the execution of any human design.

ADAM FERGUSON, *The Essay on the History of Civil Society*, 1767

The Taming of

FIDEL CASTRO

Maurice Halperin

University of California Press

Berkeley / Los Angeles / London

University of California Press Berkeley and Los Angeles, California
University of California Press, Ltd. London, England
© 1981, by The Regents of the University of California
Printed in the United States of America

1   2   3   4   5   6   7   8   9

Library of Congress Cataloging in Publication Data

Halperin, Maurice, 1906–
  The taming of Fidel Castro.

Continues the author's The rise and decline of Fidel Castro.

Includes bibliographical references and index.
  1. Cuba—Foreign relations—1959– 2. Castro,
Fidel, 1927– 3. Cuba—History—1959–
I. Title.
F1788.H26   972.91'064'0924   80-18581
ISBN 0-520-04184-4

To the memory of
Ethel and Philip Halperin
exemplary mother and father

Contents

Preface   ix

Prologue   1

1. The Second Visit to Moscow   11

2. The First Trial of Marcos Rodríguez   26

3. The Trial Annulled   32

4. The Second Trial: Act I   38

5. The Second Trial: Act II   45

6. The Second Trial: Act III   55

7. The Second Trial: Act IV and Epilogue   61

8. Toward a Rational Economic Strategy   71

9. The Great Debate   78

10. The Power to Disrupt   86

11. Castro's Peace Offensive (I): The Eder Interview   93

12. Castro's Peace Offensive (II): The Speech in Santiago   101

13. Castro's Peace Offensive (III): Rationale and Response   107

14. The Hard Line Restored: Ché Guevara at the United Nations   112

15. The Hard Line Implemented: Ché Guevara in Africa   120

16. Agriculture and the Cult of Grass   132

17. A Digression: The Case of Oscar Lewis   141

18. The New Strategy   152

19. Growing Tensions   159

20. Gestation and Innovation   166

21. The New Communist Party   172

22. Two Revolutionary Spectaculars   180

23. The Tricontinental Conference   185

24. The Great Sino-Cuban Quarrel   195

25. Concerning Revisionism, Yugoslavia, and Power   208

26. Concerning Money, Ice Cream, and Dogma   217

27. The State of Revolutionary Consciousness   222

28. The Conflict with the Venezuelan Communist Party   233

29. Fidel Castro and the Jews (I): Before the Break with Israel   237

30. Fidel Castro and the Jews (II): 1973 and After   249

31. "De l'Audace, Encore de l'Audace, Toujours de l'Audace"   256

32. The Death and Resurrection of Ché Guevara   261

33. Escalation of Dispute: Soviet Pressure and Domestic Treason   269

34. "The Profound Revolutionary Offensive"   277

35. A Precarious Situation   286

36. The Complexities of the Dilemma   295

37. The Management of the Dilemma   302

38. The Dilemma Resolved   307

39. The Tenth Anniversary   318

Epilogue   325

About the Author   339

Index   341

Preface

THE PRESENT VOLUME, primarily concerned with the years 1964 to the end of 1968, is a sequel to *The Rise and Decline of Fidel Castro* (Berkeley and Los Angeles: University of California Press, 1972) which dealt with the previous five years. It thus completes my account of the first decade of the Castro regime.

As in the first volume, the main narrative is developed chronologically, but with digressions where they seem to be appropriate, as in the treatment of certain topics and observations which permit the reader to keep abreast of events in later years.

Since it is anticipated that many readers may not be familiar with the period covered in the first volume, a Prologue has been provided by way of background and introduction. For those who have read the first volume, it should be noted that the Prologue contains some new material not previously included.

By an unanticipated coincidence, the end of the first decade of Castro's rule approximately marked the end of the Cuban Revolution and the beginning of what can properly be defined as the postrevolutionary era. It was during this latter period that the "taming," which Castro fiercely resisted during much of his first decade in power, was finally accomplished. Hence the book concludes with an Epilogue to provide the reader with a summary of the process of change which occurred during the 1970s.

As the reader will become aware, the book reflects my personal experience in Cuba, where I spent close to six years (1962–1968), following a period of three years in the Soviet Union. In Havana I lectured on economic geography at the University and also served as a consultant to the

Ministry of Foreign Trade. This experience undoubtedly affected my perceptions and may have added a subjective element to my treatment of some of the materials I dealt with. If so, I can say that I tried to describe and evaluate empirical data and observed evidence, as Margaret Mead once put it, with "disciplined subjectivity."

I wish to express my deep gratitude to my friend and colleague Dr. F. Quei Quo, who served as Chairman of the Department of Political Science at Simon Fraser University during a major part of the period in which I was engaged in writing this book, and who in that capacity provided me with all the facilities I required to complete my work. At the same time, I was able to draw upon his specialized knowledge of Far Eastern affairs as they related to Cuba and to benefit from materials from Japanese sources which he brought to my attention and translated for me.

I also wish to thank the editor of *Worldview* for permission to include, in Chapter 16, a slightly modified version of "Looking Back on Fidel," an article of mine published in the October 1976 issue; and similarly *Queen's Quarterly* for permission to include, in Chapter 10, "Fidel Castro in Retrospect" (No. 4, 1974), and, in Chapter 17, "Oscar Lewis and the Cuban Revolution" (No. 4, 1978/79). In Chapter 15, I have incorporated material from my essay "The Cuban Role in Southern Africa," in *Southern Africa Since the Portuguese Coup*, ed. John Seiler (Boulder, Colorado: Westview Press, 1980).

Finally, I am grateful to Paul Weisser, of Berkeley, California, for his skillful and painstaking editing of my manuscript.

Burnaby Mountain, British Columbia
May 1980

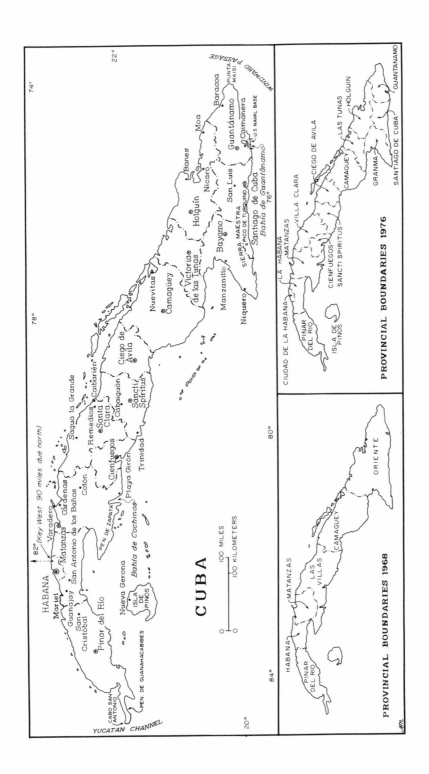

CUBA

100 MILES

100 KILOMETERS

82° (Key West 90 miles due north)

HABANA
Mariel
Guanajay
San Cristóbal
Pinar del Río
Nueva Gerona
ISLA DE PINOS
PEN DE GUANAHACABIBES
CABO SAN ANTONIO
YUCATAN CHANNEL

Varadero
Matanzas Cárdenas
San Antonio de los Baños
Colón
Playa Girón
Bahía de Cochinos
PEN DE ZAPATA
Cienfuegos
Trinidad
Sagua la Grande
Remedios Caibarién
Santa Clara
Cabaiguán
Sancti Spíritus
Ciego de Ávila

Nuevitas
Camagüey
Victoria de las Tunas
Manzanillo
Niquero
SIERRA MAESTRA
PICO DE TURQUINO
Bayamo
Holguín
Nicaro
San Luis
Santiago de Cuba
Bahía de Guantánamo

Bánes
Moa
Baracoa
PUNTA MAISÍ
Guantánamo
Caimanera
U.S. NAVAL BASE
Bahía de Guantánamo

WINDWARD PASSAGE

22°
74°
78°
80°
84°
76°
20°

PROVINCIAL BOUNDARIES 1968

HABANA
PINAR DEL RÍO
MATANZAS
LAS VILLAS
CAMAGÜEY
ORIENTE

PROVINCIAL BOUNDARIES 1976

CIUDAD DE LA HABANA
LA HABANA
PINAR DEL RÍO
MATANZAS
VILLA CLARA
CIENFUEGOS
SANCTI SPIRITUS
ISLA DE PINOS
CIEGO DE ÁVILA
CAMAGÜEY
LAS TUNAS
HOLGUÍN
GRANMA
SANTIAGO DE CUBA
GUANTÁNAMO

Prologue

A Revolutionary Instinct

FIDEL CASTRO, son of a Spanish immigrant who had become a prosperous landowner, was born in 1927 (erroneously recorded as 1926 when he was first enrolled in school) in Oriente Province, some 600 miles east of Havana. As a child he already exhibited the temperament of a rebel and a leader, which he later displayed in his student days at the University of Havana law school, then as a radical lawyer and politician, next as the organizer of two armed uprisings, and finally as the charismatic creator and supreme authority of the Cuban Revolution.

"I was evidently born with a calling [*vocación*] for politics and revolution. . . . I had a political and revolutionary instinct," Castro explained in a tape-recorded memoir some five or six years after taking power. "Why do I say this? . . . When I was eighteen years old, I was politically illiterate, not having come from a politically-minded family or raised in a political environment. The fact that I was able to develop into a revolutionary in a relatively short time . . . would not have been possible for a person without a special calling." Fidel described his headstrong character as a schoolboy, his striving for prominence among his peers, his refusal to submit to unjust treatment, and his physical conflicts with his teachers. At one point, exasperated by his conduct, his father decided that Fidel should leave school for good. "It was a decisive moment in my life," Fidel recalled. Moved by an overwhelming feeling of injustice, he threatened "to burn down the house, . . . it was made of wood, . . . if they didn't send me back to school. As a result, I returned to school."

Later in the tape recording, he remembered that in the sixth grade his classes bored him. "I didn't do a bit of studying," he confessed. "How did I occupy my mind? My imagination was attracted by problems of history, . . . [especially] war. . . . I invented war games for hours at a stretch." By the time he was twenty-one, he was actively involved in the political and social struggles of the day. "At that time," he noted, "I was a mixture of a quixotic idealist, a romantic and a dreamer, with scanty political under-standing and a great thirst for knowledge . . . and for action. . . . I had visions of Martí, Bolívar, and of utopian socialism." [1] And somewhat later, it would appear, of Robespierre and Napoleon, for whom he expressed great admiration. [2]

Castro's genetically determined "calling," according to his own quite plausible estimate, in due course blossomed into a lifelong mission of epic proportions. In 1952, a bloodless military coup by General Fulgencio Ba-tista, one-time president of Cuba, set in motion the events that would cul-

1. The quotations are from Carlos Franqui, *Diario de la revolución cubana* (Barcelona: Ediciones R. Torres, 1976), pp. 9, 13, 15, and 17, respectively. The re-cording was from a conversation between Castro and Franqui, and was the begin-ning of a projected biography of Castro that was never completed. Franqui left Cuba toward the end of the 1960s. The 28-page transcript takes Fidel through his experiences during the Bogotá riots in April 1948. The rest of the book consists of transcripts of recordings by other important participants in the struggle against Batista, as well as previously unpublished correspondence and documents which Franqui collected when he was in charge of Castro's radio and press operations in the Sierra Maestra. The book, which also contains Franqui's personal recollec-tions, is an invaluable source of information concerning the prehistory and history of the guerrilla war that toppled Batista.

For a systematic account of Castro's career prior to taking power, viewed in the context of the political climate in which he operated, the reader should consult Ramón L. Bonachea and Marta San Martín, *The Cuban Insurrection 1952–1959* (New Brunswick, N.J.: Transaction Books, 1974). A revealing analysis of Castro's personality can be found in Juan Arcocha, *Fidel Castro en Rompecabezas* [The Jig-saw Puzzle of Fidel Castro] (Madrid: Ediciones Erre, 1973). Arcocha was Fidel's classmate in law school and, until leaving Cuba in the late 1960s, had frequent contact with him as a translator and journalist.

2. In correspondence from prison on the Isle of Pines, he wrote on March 23, 1954: "Robespierre was an idealist and an honorable man until the day of his death. . . . In Cuba we need many Robespierres." And on the following day: "I never get tired reading about [Napoleon]. . . . I always considered him to be great-er . . . than Alexander . . . Caesar . . . Charlemagne . . . and Frederick II. . . . Napoleon [unlike the others] owed his success entirely to himself, to his own ge-nius and will-power." Franqui, *Diario*, pp. 94, 96.

minate in Fidel's conquest of power and the ensuing Cuban Revolution. On July 26, 1953 (subsequently a red-letter day in the revolutionary calendar), he led a small band of disaffected urban youth in an attack on the army barracks in Santiago, Cuba's second largest city, located at the eastern end of the island. It was a disaster that nearly cost him his life and did result in his capture and imprisonment, but it was the prelude to his second, and successful, effort to overthrow Batista's government.

The Successful Insurrection

Released from prison by an amnesty in the spring of 1955, he departed for Mexico, leaving behind the nucleus of a clandestine organization known as the Movement of July 26. After a period in late November 1956, during which he prepared for an armed invasion, for which Cuban history provided many precedents, he embarked with some eighty followers aboard a leaky yacht with the unlikely name of "Granma." (Years later, the boat was salvaged and enshrined in a specially built museum in Havana.) Unable to reach their prearranged destination, they landed on December 6 in a mangrove swamp on the southeastern coast of the island. Immediately spotted by Batista's air force, all but a handful were mowed down by machine gun fire from the air.

Among those who miraculously survived and made their way into the nearby shelter of the Sierra Maestra wilderness were Fidel Castro, his younger brother Raúl, and Ernesto Guevara, a footloose Argentine physician with a strong revolutionary disposition. Such was the improbable beginning of a successful guerrilla campaign. Had Raúl and Ché, the nickname by which the Argentine came to be known, been killed, in all likelihood Fidel would have managed without them. Had Fidel perished, then beyond a reasonable doubt the guerrilla band would have collapsed and history would have taken a different turn. This was another of a number of providential accidents that led to the birth and survival of the Cuban Revolution.

By mid-1958, with the help of his underground movement, Fidel had assembled a band of some three hundred followers, fought a number of successful skirmishes against Batista's reluctant soldiers, and sent his "army" into the lowlands for the decisive struggle. Moving westward toward Havana, gathering recruits on the way, they met little resistance until they reached Santa Clara, about 200 miles from their goal. Here, in mid-December, they fought and won the only pitched battle of the war. During the night of December 31, Batista fled the country; and on the next day,

January 1, 1959, a small contingent of Castro's ragged troops, now numbering three thousand, entered Havana unopposed and amidst a pandemonium of celebration at the defeat of the "tyranny," as Batista's regime was henceforth to be known.

It was more than a defeat. It was the total collapse, as much self-imposed as inflicted by armed force, of a government undermined by corruption and brutality, lacking both mass and class support, and defended by military and police establishments which literally disintegrated in the face of a determined challenge. Thus, when Fidel took over, he moved into a power vacuum which he quickly filled, promising restoration of constitutional government, respect for civil liberties, substantial social and economic reforms, and effective national independence vis-à-vis the United States. It was a radical program but framed within the context of "humanism" and nationalism as its guiding philosophy. Under these circumstances, with his philosophical credibility enhanced by the Cuban Communist Party's early assessment of his guerrilla struggle as "petty bourgeois adventurism," and with the Cuban economy intact, since there was practically no destruction of property during the war, he had two years in which to consolidate his rule and distribute the fat accumulated under previous regimes. By the end of 1960, Fidel's honeymoon was over, and humanism had given way to socialism.

Cuba before the Revolution

The Cuba which Castro at first set out to reform radically, rather than transform totally, was not a typically underdeveloped or Third World country, a misconception which Castro later assiduously promoted as a justification for the poor economic performance of his regime. Close to 60 percent of Cuba's more than six million people (in 1980 numbering about ten million) lived in urban communities. There was poverty in the countryside, but nothing comparable to the destitution which afflicted large areas of Latin America, not to mention Africa and Asia. A strong trade union movement had secured decent wages and many modern benefits for urban workers, and a large middle class had attained fairly high standards of living. Some three-quarters of Cubans were literate; and in the realm of popular and high culture, Cuban poets, novelists, artists, musicians, and ballet performers enjoyed international esteem. While there was room for considerable improvement in the distribution of wealth and social services, neither an economic crisis nor a great social upheaval were imminent in Cuba on the eve of Fidel's insurrection.

Nevertheless, Cuban development had been distorted by a number of historically conditioned factors. The most important were Cuba's dependence on the export of sugar (and sugar's fluctuating prices) for the great bulk of its foreign exchange, and dependence on the United States as a market for its sugar and the source of most of its imports. These constraints interlocked, and, combined with large American investments in important sectors of the economy, including sugar, they maintained Cuba in a state of highly restrictive economic and political dependency. In addition, they tended to retard the diversification of agriculture and native investment in industry. Hence the inevitable growth of nationalism among educated and reform-minded Cubans who associated the corruption in Cuban politics with the country's excessive dependency on the United States. Nationalism, in effect, became a decisive element in uniting Cubans of various ideological and political beliefs behind Fidel Castro.

The American Confrontation and the Soviet Presence

A radical, though not yet socialist, agrarian reform and other limitations on property rights and business operations, affecting both American investments and native entrepreneurs, set the stage for both a deterioration in relations with the United States and the rise of counterrevolutionary activity and repressive measures to contain it. The problems were exacerbated by a stubborn refusal of both the Eisenhower administration and Castro to explore the possibilities of a reasonable accommodation on such issues as the size of Cuban sugar quotas and prices in the American market, and the manner of determining them; Cuba's concern about levying higher duties on American imports to protect and encourage local producers; and American insistence on prompt and equitable compensations for American property affected by the agrarian reform. The ensuing polemic was heightened by Fidel's inflammatory anti-American rhetoric and by premature charges from the United States that Castro had installed a brutal Communist dictatorship in Cuba.

A new and what turned out to be a critical and determining element in the confrontation was the visit to Havana of Soviet Deputy Prime Minister Anastas Mikoyan in February 1960. This at once led to a Soviet-Cuban trade and loan agreement, and then in May to the opening of diplomatic relations between the two governments (followed shortly by a similar, and even more provocative, Cuban-Chinese agreement). At the end of June, the Cuban authorities seized the American and the British-Dutch Shell oil refineries for refusing to accept a quota of Soviet petroleum, purchased by the Cuban government, to replace part of their own Venezuelan crude. Apparently in consultation with Washington from the start of the controversy, the companies, in addition to refusing to comply, retaliated by placing an embargo on further shipments of oil from Venezuela and by placing pressure on independent oil tanker operators not to charter their vessels to the Russians. The expectation was that the Russians would not be able to transport sufficient oil to meet Cuba's requirements. As a result, the Cuban economy would be paralyzed for lack of energy in a few months, and the Castro regime would collapse.

This proved to be a gross error of judgment, comparable in importance to the miscalculation over the Bay of Pigs invasion less than a year later. The Russians managed to overcome the transportation difficulties, and thereafter Cuba's survival was irrevocably linked to its dependence on the Soviet Union. The refinery crisis, in effect, marked the point of no return in the process which led Washington, in July, to impose a crippling reduction in the Cuban sugar quota. Castro's response, with no delay, was a series of expropriations of American property, which resulted, by the end of October, in the nationalization of all American holdings on the island, with a book value of close to one billion dollars. For good measure, Fidel nationalized a major part of Cuban nonagricultural private enterprise, including both industrial and large retail establishments. Hence, the "commanding heights" of the economy had passed from private to state ownership by the end of October 1960, and Cuba for all practical purposes had become a socialist state, although this was not acknowledged at the time. Then, in mid-December, Washington eliminated the entire Cuban sugar quota; and in early January 1961, the two countries severed diplomatic relations.

The Bay of Pigs and Socialism

Less than four months later, the first—and last—American attempt to overthrow the Castro regime by an armed invasion ended in abysmal failure. Some fourteen hundred Cuban exiles, trained and equipped by the CIA, were put ashore at the Bay of Pigs, 100 miles southeast of Havana. They were at once engaged in battle by a hastily assembled but highly motivated government militia, and at the end of seventy-two hours were thoroughly defeated. It could not have turned out better for Fidel, who was himself in command of his troops. His international prestige zoomed upward. Cuban national pride soared, and with it popular confidence in his leadership. Shortly before the invasion, which was known to be imminent, thousands of real and suspected dissidents had been rounded up, with the result that counterrevolution on the island suffered a setback from which it never recovered. In later and more difficult years, the memory of the victory—kept alive in speeches, in print, and in annual commemorations—would serve to bolster a sometimes lagging spirit of patriotism and enthusiasm for the Revolution among the Cuban people.

On the eve of the invasion, Fidel for the first time proclaimed his regime to be socialist. Faced with a crisis when national unity was of supreme importance, it seemed the wrong moment to appeal to Cubans to defend socialism, a term to which most of the population was either allergic or indifferent. Thus it was in all probability a message addressed to the Kremlin and designed to remove any hesitation it might have to come to Cuba's rescue. Although Khrushchev for months had been publicly threatening nuclear reprisal against American imperialism if it attacked "progressive" Cuba, Castro had reason to suspect that the Russians might back off if it came to a showdown. However, they could not so easily abandon a "socialist" Cuba—that is, a member of the "socialist family," of which the Soviet Union had assumed the obligation of supreme leader and protector.

As it happened, the showdown was avoided by the lightning victory at the Bay of Pigs. However, Castro's suspicions were reinforced by the fact that even after the crisis there was no response from Moscow to his claim that Cuba was a socialist country.

As the year wore on, Cuba began to look more and more like a country whose socialism deserved Soviet recognition. A rough copy of the Gosplan was set up to direct the Cuban economy, and something resembling a Communist Party had begun to function, in which the "old"—that is, pre-Castro—Communists loyal to Moscow played a leading role. Marxist-Leninist literature filled the bookstores, and translations of Soviet textbooks were introduced into the universities. Trotskyists and anarchists were put in jail. When eventually the Soviet press coyly spoke of Cuba as "building socialism," it was something less than acknowledgment that Cuba was a socialist state, which Fidel interpreted to mean that the military security which he required still eluded him.

Marxism-Leninism and Economic Decline

On December 1, 1961, Fidel made the celebrated speech in which he declared that "I am a Marxist-Leninist and shall remain a Marxist-Leninist until the day I die." It was a farfetched effort to establish the ideological

credentials which he hoped would admit him to membership in the socialist'"club." However, the response in Moscow, and even in Peking, was silence. Paradoxically, the news of his speech was greeted with enthusiasm
in Washington. Several Latin American governments were dragging their
feet in getting on with the project of removing Cuba from the Organization of American States (OAS), and Fidel's profession of faith made the job
easier. Accordingly, at a special OAS meeting in late January 1962, Cuba's
membership was suspended. This, in effect, amounted to expulsion from
the organization.

Less than two months later, the rationing of food and other consumer
goods in Cuba began, and was destined to continue indefinitely. The rationing was a reflection of the precipitous decline of production in all sectors of the economy. This was due to a number of factors, including the exodus of Cuban technicians and the disruption of trade with the United
States. Mainly, however, the cause was the incompetence and mismanagement of the new bureaucracy, compounded by Castro's constant and erratic intervention in matters affecting both planning and administration.
Meanwhile, tension between Cuba and the United States, aggravated by
Fidel's defiant rhetoric, was growing, leading to fears both in Cuba and the
Soviet Union that a new, and this time full-scale, American invasion was
being prepared. How to meet this potential threat then became the subject
of urgent consultation between Moscow and Havana.

The October Missile Crisis

The result was the missile crisis of October 1962, of harrowing memory,
which came within a hair's breadth of unleashing a nuclear holocaust. A
minor consequence would have been the obliteration of Fidel Castro and
the Cuban Revolution. What prompted Khrushchev to take the enormous
risk of surreptitiously introducing strategic atomic missiles in Cuba will remain a matter of speculation until the archives in Moscow and Havana are
open to inspection, an unlikely event in the foreseeable future. It would
appear that two interlocking motives were involved: (1) to improve the Soviet position in the strategic "balance of terror" on which depended the
credibility of the Soviet military and political posture in the cold war with
the United States; and (2) to dissuade any further aggression against Cuba.
Cuba would thus be converted from a liability to an asset.

Khrushchev expected to present the United States with a *fait accom-
pli*, apparently hoping that, as a result of the advantage gained, a lethal
American response would be irrational. There is some evidence that Cas-

tro had reservations about Khrushchev's plan but was persuaded to go along. In any event, U-2 reconnaissance flights over Cuba discovered the emplacement of the missiles before they were operational. After a week of "brinkmanship" between Kennedy and Khrushchev, the latter agreed to dismantle the weapons and ship them back home. In return, Kennedy promised not to invade Cuba. Thus ended the American-Soviet confrontation, with the happy by-product of setting the stage for later détente between the two superpowers.

Crisis in Cuban-Soviet Relations

Another and more immediate by-product of that confrontation was a crisis in Cuban-Soviet relations. Khrushchev had not consulted Castro when he had agreed to remove his missiles from Cuba. It was both a personal affront and a violation of Cuban sovereignty that Fidel could not afford to ignore. With a great display of wrath and indignation, he in effect accused Khrushchev of cowardice and betrayal, and he refused to give permission for a United Nations inspection team to come to Cuba to verify the removal of the missiles. As a result, the weapons had to be counted after they were loaded aboard Soviet vessels and were on the high seas. In addition, he rejected as worthless Kennedy's promise not to invade Cuba. All of this was despite a hurried visit by UN Secretary-General U Thant, followed by Mikoyan's arrival in Havana, where he spent three unrewarding weeks trying to soothe Castro, who for most of the period ostentatiously ignored his presence.

The Reconciliation

Nevertheless, too much was at stake for both Cuba and the Soviet Union, so that they had no choice but to patch up the quarrel. The initiative came from Moscow, and subsequently Fidel and his entourage arrived in the Soviet Union on April 27, 1963. In Moscow he was given a hero's welcome, the likes of which had never been seen there before or has been seen there since. During his three weeks in the Soviet Union, Fidel was personally attended by Khrushchev and otherwise celebrated and flattered beyond measure.

On his return home, Fidel gave the Cuban people a glowing report of the virtues and might of the Soviet Union and the sterling qualities of its magnificent leader, Nikita Khrushchev. There had been a joint Soviet-Cuban declaration which contained the unequivocal recognition of Cuba as a member in full standing of the "great socialist community" and of its party as a genuine Marxist-Leninist "vanguard." The declaration had also included a solemn commitment by the Soviet Union to "defend the liberty and independence of the Republic of Cuba." In addition, it had recorded Cuban acceptance of the unity of the socialist camp as defined by the Soviet Union (and disputed by China), and of the principle of peaceful coexistence between socialist and capitalist states as upheld by Moscow (and rejected by China).

There was also a section on economic relations which projected a brilliant future for Cuba, including a large increase in Cuba's sugar production and exports to the Soviet Union, for which a guaranteed and generous price would be paid. It was in this connection that Fidel, admitting the flaws in Cuba's economic performance, admonished the Cuban people that the time had come to turn over a new leaf, to give priority to an efficient and rational development of the economy, taking as a model the methods and achievements of the Soviet Union.

In his speech on January 2, 1964, commemorating the fifth anniversary of the Revolution, Fidel spoke with unbounded optimism about the prospects of the Cuban economy, predicting that ten million tons of sugar would be produced in 1970 (less than four million had been produced in 1963). He also spoke about Cuba's indestructable fraternal relations with the Soviet Union, "the power behind all the countries of the socialist camp and all the countries that are struggling on all continents against colonialism and imperialism." He praised the Soviet Union's policy of peaceful coexistence, declaring that on the basis of "fullest respect for the sovereignty of all countries, we can live in perfect and absolute peace with any country and any government of Latin America, and with the United States, independently of the social regime in these countries."

The first reconciliation between Cuba and the Soviet Union appeared to be all-embracing and irrevocable.

1

■

The Second Visit to Moscow

"A Gigantic Greenhouse"

ON THE EVENING of January 24, 1964, the day after his return to Havana
from his second visit to the Soviet Union, Fidel Castro spoke to the Cuban
people over a nationwide hookup of television and radio.[1] As on the occasion of the return from his historic journey of reconciliation nearly eight
months earlier, the Prime Minister spoke from a studio, electronically projecting the magic of his extraordinary personality and amazing capacity for
extemporaneous and convincing exposition. It was as effective as if he were
physically present before the living multitudes in reach of his high-pitched
voice and bearded image.

Once more he was in a state of high optimism as he told his fellow
countrymen about the fabulous Sugar Agreement which he and Nikita
Khrushchev had signed in Moscow. And now a new vision of the great
prospects which lay ahead transformed optimism into euphoria. It was a
vision of a bountiful nature which had endowed Cuba with unequal resources for producing not only sugar but also meat, milk, fruit, and vegetables galore. Yesterday he had boarded the TU-114 under leaden skies in a
land covered with snow and ice and had disembarked in a land that was
green under blue skies, bathed with the warmth and light of the sun.

"You have to go through the experience," he said, "of seeing that country covered with snow, the land underneath asleep for many months. . . .
Right now a large part of the world is covered with snow, where not a blade of
grass can grow, and where tomatoes and lettuce and the like are produced in
greenhouses—think of it, señores [it was more than five years after the Revolution, but Fidel would still at times lapse into the bourgeois form of ad-

1. Citations below are from the verbatim stenographic report published in
Política Internacional, 5 (January–March 1964), 103–123.

dress], with artificial light and heat, . . . and then arrive here . . . and see what can be done in this country, . . . in the middle of January grass growing in the pastures and being harvested for fodder, . . . this countryside green as far as the eye can reach, and you look at what can be done with a little cultivation, a little water and some fertilizer, practically even when it doesn't rain. . . ."

There was much truth in what Fidel was saying. I had also been struck by the comfort of the Cuban climate, the verdure of the Cuban countryside and its potentialities, after experiencing the rigors of the long and dreary Russian winter. There were other contrasts which Fidel did not mention. After my three-year sojourn in Moscow, the ordinary amenities of urban living in even the less favored quarters of Havana were impressive. The fact that practically all Havana was supplied with potable water, while in most sections of Moscow (as in Mexico City or Rio de Janeiro) it was still not safe to drink the tap water without boiling, was unexpected. Everywhere men and women on the streets of Havana wore better fitting and more tasteful clothing and were better groomed than the residents of Moscow, to say nothing of the less favored Russian cities. Riding the crowded buses of Havana in the heat of the day, it was obvious that even the humblest Cubans bathed frequently, and that many passengers used deodorants, a much needed but unknown luxury in the Soviet Union. It was in the smaller Cuban cities and towns that the contrast with their Russian counterparts was sharpest. Urban Cuba, slums and all, was incomparably more attractive and comfortable and had better sanitary and recreational facilities than most of urban Russia. It was a bewildering and enviable form of "underdevelopment" for the Soviet technical experts who were now coming to Cuba in ever greater numbers.

Clearly, Fidel was not stressing, as he had done on less happy occasions in the past or would do again in the future, the scourge of underdevelopment and other iniquities imposed on Cuba by a ruthless capitalism and criminal imperialism. "This country gives the impression of being a gigantic greenhouse," Fidel went on to say. "It is as if the natural treasures of our country had just been discovered, had all of a sudden been revealed. Many who live in this paradise . . . are completely unaware of . . . the treasures we possess." Moreover, he added, the "paradise" also had mineral resources, but his emphasis was overwhelmingly on agriculture, and especially sugar. Ironically, in the years to come, it would be a mineral, nickel, whose production would grow slowly but steadily while the "gigantic greenhouse" would by and large produce less and at greater cost than before the Revolution.

The Role of Sugar

Fidel went on to explain to his fellow countrymen the Sugar Agreement which he and Khrushchev had just signed in Moscow, and which was to provide the fundamental guarantee of Cuban prosperity. From 1965 to 1970—that is, over a period of six years—the USSR, at a fixed price of six cents per pound, would purchase approximately twenty-four million tons of Cuban sugar, starting with two million in 1965, increasing by a million tons in each of the following two years, and then leveling off at five million per annum in 1968–1970.[2] The price of six cents a pound, it turned out, was the same which he and Khrushchev, at their first meeting in Moscow the previous May, had agreed upon for sugar shipped in 1963 and 1964. Fidel could present the deal as something of a bonanza for Cuba, since six cents was considerably higher than the free market price level of the preceding few years (although very close to the preferential rate paid by the Americans before the elimination of the Cuban quota). However, at the very moment that Fidel was talking, sugar was selling at close to eleven cents a pound,[3] so that to justify the six-cent rate to his listeners he had to twist and turn a bit and stress the long-term advantages of a stable price for a commodity which had historically always had violently fluctuating prices. "Socialism," he declared, "above all means a planned economy, and in order to plan . . . we have to know what resources we can count on. How can we do this if today we have one price and tomorrow another?"

It was a convincing argument, and Fidel was right about the price of sugar. As it turned out, it averaged less than 2.5 cents a pound on the free market during the six-year period of the Agreement.[4] However, it also turned out that Cuba's "planned economy" required more than a guaranteed socialist market for six-cent sugar. It required planning, the kind that could produce the amounts of sugar "planned," and here Castro was to be

2. For the Spanish text of the Agreement, see *Cuba Socialista*, 30 (February 1964), 165–166. The amounts are in metric tons and refer to raw sugar. The USSR imports only raw sugar from Cuba and is an exporter of refined sugar. Unless otherwise indicated, all further mention of Cuban sugar tonnage will be in metric tons, raw value. It generally takes 106 units of raw sugar to produce 100 units of refined sugar.

3. The average (mean) price for January 1964 was 10.64 cents a pound; *Economic Survey of Latin America 1964* (New York: United Nations, 1966), p. 230.

4. Annual averages for spot prices of raw sugar, calculated in accordance with the International Sugar Agreement Rules, in U.S. cents per pound: 1965—2.08; 1966—1.81; 1967—1.92; 1968—1.90; 1969—3.20; 1970—3.68. See *Sugar Year Book 1971* (London: International Sugar Council, 1972), p. 357.

a dismal failure. About one-half the amount of sugar stipulated in the Agreement was delivered to the Soviet Union,[5] the high cost of producing the sugar impoverished the whole Cuban economy, and the accumulative trade deficit with the Soviet Union rose to staggering heights. When a new long-term agreement was announced at the end of 1972, the Cuban economy would be firmly mortgaged to Moscow.

It was easy to fall under the spell of Fidel's rhetoric. Not only was the deep and genuine conviction with which he spoke contagious, but his vision of the new Cuban economy carried with it an aura of plausibility and rationality. If Cuba was not quite the natural "paradise" which his enthusiasm had invoked, it was true, as he said, that "no country in the world is so well endowed by nature to produce sugar." Nor did any country in the world have greater experience than Cuba when it came to producing and marketing sugar.

Fidel did not remind his listeners that the production record of his regime thus far was not good. In 1963, Cuba produced 3.8 million tons of sugar, an amount considerably less than the average production in the decade preceding the Revolution, and far below the more than seven million tons produced in the peak year of 1952. However, for any but the most skeptical listener who momentarily gave thought to the recent decline, this could be discounted as the price paid for the errors committed during the difficult period of transition. Fidel and Cuba were turning over a new leaf. In the revolutionary calendar, 1964 had been proclaimed to be the "Year of the Economy." True, it was the third such "year" under different names, but this time it was serious. There was the Agreement, just signed in Moscow, which "ends a whole stage in the economic life of the Revolution and provides the foundation for . . . the ideal, . . . the optimum development of our economy." Given the assurance which the Agreement gave Cuba for "an annual market of as much as ten million tons of sugar"—five to the USSR and the rest to the other socialist countries and Cuba's traditional customers in the capitalist world (excluding the United States)—given "our land, . . . our sugar mills, . . . improving our agricultural technique, . . . we must declare our goal of producing ten million tons."

A Mechanized Harvest and Sugar By-Products

However, one important innovation was required, the mechanization of work in the cane fields. "Without machines to cut the sugar cane," Fidel

5. The exact amount was 54.1 percent. See *Sugar Year Book 1971*, p. 53.

declared, "it is inconceivable to think of a harvest of eight and nine million tons." But he passed over this rapidly. He had already explained in some detail after his first trip to Moscow how he and Khrushchev had studied this matter and discussed the design of the machine with the Russian experts, and how Khrushchev had promised to produce and deliver the machines in two years. It was a foregone conclusion that in the harvest of 1966 the machines would be cutting a good part of the cane. There was no need to dwell on it this time.

Fidel did not overstate the importance of the cane-cutting machine, but he failed to heed the wisdom of his own caveat. Nikita's machine did not materialize, contributing to Fidel's major planning errors and the larger mismanagement follies which by 1970 nearly wrecked the Cuban economy. Curiously enough, when Fidel next visited Moscow—it was after his great quarrel and the second reconciliation with the Russians—the Cuban press noted that he was taken to the Okhtomski agricultural machinery factory, on the outskirts of Moscow, "where the cane-cutting combines for Cuba are being built." It was July 3, 1972, a great day for the workers of the factory, who, according to the newspaper, "since 1964 . . . have been working constantly to solve the problem of the mechanization of Cuba's sugar cane harvest."[6]

As Fidel continued expounding his grand design for the development of the Cuban economy, the role of sugar became clearer. What are we going to do, he asked, with the "millions of tons of bagasse" which the grinding of sugar cane will give us? We can turn them into "cellulose, . . . paper, . . . wood, . . . including many products for export. . . . And what shall we do with the molasses?" The answer was "sugar chemistry," with which the nation can establish an industry to process "all these by-products. . . . Here we have one of the fundamental sectors in the future development of Cuba." (Only fifteen years later would a small experimental

6. *Granma Weekly Review*, December 10, 1972. As part of a continuing and massive pro-Soviet propaganda campaign under way since the end of 1970, the review printed a large illustrated "Special Feature" on the factory. One worker was quoted as having told Castro that "we'd make our greatest effort to have . . . 50 combines ready this year." They would have to be tested in the fields before large-scale production could be undertaken. At an international sugar conference held in Geneva in May 1973, Marcelo Fernández, Cuba's Minister of Foreign Trade, explained that he expected "300 or 400" combines to be put in service every year "until 80% of the harvest is mechanized by 1980" (*Granma Weekly Review*, May 20, 1973). That would be sixteen years after the project was initiated. As it turned out, the minister was overly optimistic. Only 40 percent was machine cut in 1978.

plant be set up.) More important, however, sugar exports would generate Cuba's foreign exchange. "That's where our foreign currency will come from" that will provide Cuba with "the means for developing our industry."

The Importance of Optimism

Here Fidel digressed to refute the "imperialists" who claimed that by reverting to sugar production after earlier plans for rapid industrialization had been abandoned, "we are giving up our illusions." On the contrary, he exclaimed, "we are more *ilusionados* than ever before. . . . Only now our illusions have such a real basis that they are no longer illusions but realities, and very serious realities." Who could anticipate that most of the "realities" would turn out to be illusions, or at best realities that would have to be postponed for a generation or more? The guidelines for economic development which Fidel expounded, stripped of their rhetorical ornaments, seemed to be reasonable enough. And at the moment when Ché Guevara, the minister of industries, was stressing the virtues of "moral incentives" as opposed to "material incentives" in the difficult task of creating a work ethic among the Cuban masses, it was comforting to hear Fidel declare that while henceforth farmers would be paid long-term stable prices for the cane they produced, "stable" did not mean "equal." Prices would vary according to the amount produced. "Because it is not correct," he explained, "to pay exactly the same rate to the person who makes an effort . . . to produce more as to the person who does not make the effort. The one who goes on increasing his production is helping the country's economy."

Thus, Fidel had his feet on the ground, although, as the charismatic political leader that he was, he sought in his appeal for performance to invoke an enthusiasm for a national goal that transcended personal interests. Summing up the "incredibly good outlook" for the Cuban economy, he expounded the higher morality which it inspired. "I believe," he went on to say, "that when we have this outlook, the very outlook itself constitutes a mobilizing force, a force which generates . . . enthusiasm for work; it is also a force which creates *conciencia* [social consciousness], because the people will see that any person who does not accept his responsibility, who does not do his work wholeheartedly, . . . is a person who is conspiring against the interests of the entire nation."

Thus, Fidel's unfailing and often unfounded optimism was not only deeply engrained in his subconscious mind but was also a conscious instrument for mobilizing the population to perform the tasks which he imposed on it. Such optimism was a characteristic apparently shared by all charismatic leaders, from Mohammed to Mussolini. At the same time, his appeal for *conciencia* was something less than Ché's obsessive goal: the transformation of the Cuban worker, conditioned by the sordid values of the capitalist system, into the new "socialist" man (thus far a rare creature in any socialist society). It was rather a call for patriotism, the same patriotism which he so effectively mobilized when the country faced external danger, as at the time of the Bay of Pigs invasion in the spring of 1961 and the missile crisis in the fall of 1962. Later he was to discover that, as far as the great bulk of the population was concerned, the willingness for self-sacrifice and heroism in war could not be transferred to peacetime pursuits. There would be unconscionable abuse and neglect of equipment, slothful response to exhortation, and persistent absenteeism, which Fidel would be compelled to control with classical carrot-and-club procedures.

A Model for the World

Toward the end of his long report—it lasted more than three hours—Fidel turned his attention toward the world scene, where, as he saw it, Cuban prestige was now a glowing beacon in the darkness of imperialist exploitation in which the underdeveloped nations were submerged. With Latin America uppermost in his mind, he was confident, he said, that the example of the Sugar Agreement with the Soviet Union set a precedent which would shatter the pretensions of [Kennedy's] Alliance for Progress, "which is nothing more than a swindle. . . . [The poor countries] now have the great opportunity of proposing a similar kind of commercial exchange to the United States . . . and saying 'No, what we need from you is not . . . money, but a fair and stable price for our products. . . .' Soon there will be an international meeting in Geneva, and the agreement between Cuba and the Soviet Union will certainly be the kind of commercial policy which all the underdeveloped countries of the world will demand. . . ."

The issue of fair and stable prices for the raw material exports of the nonindustrialized countries—an issue of exasperating complexity—had been debated ever since the close of World War II, but Fidel's speech stirred no excitement in Latin America or among the underdeveloped nations attending the Geneva conference.[7] To the disgust of Ché Guevara, who headed the Cuban delegation to the meeting, even the Russians failed to perceive the Soviet-Cuban deal in the glowing terms with which Fidel

7. This was the first United Nations Conference on Trade and Development (UNCTAD). It met from March 26 to June 16, 1964.

described it, and, like the industrialized capitalist countries, dragged their feet when it came to making any real commitments to alleviate what they called the "unequal exchange" between rich and poor countries. The fact of the matter was that the Russians could not afford another deal like the one with Cuba, even if it would be politically profitable, while no Latin American government would remotely contemplate paying Moscow the political price which Castro had paid for the Soviet-Cuban sugar agreement.

Concerning Panama

Shortly before Fidel's arrival in Moscow, a serious riot had occurred in Panama, an event which provided unexpected grist for his mill. On January 9, several hundred Panamanians, led by militant students, marched on the Canal Zone in order to raise a Panamanian flag on what they claimed to be national territory illegally occupied by the United States. Confronted by American troops, twenty-two Panamanians were killed and many more wounded in the ensuing fracas, while four Americans also lost their lives. It was the first foreign policy crisis of the Johnson administration. At issue was an escalating nationalism keyed to recurrent demands over the years for a new Panama Canal treaty to replace the pact signed in 1903 by the infant Republic of Panama, a piece of territory wrenched from Colombia for the express purpose of granting the United States a secure strip of land for the inter-oceanic canal which it was to complete in 1914.

It came as no surprise that the Joint Cuban-Soviet Communiqué, which Castro and Khrushchev signed in Moscow on January 21, carried a paragraph condemning the "massacre" and supporting the "people of Panama in their just claim of sovereignty" over the Canal Zone.[8] Now, as Fidel spoke to his people—and indeed to listeners outside Cuba, for his major pronouncements were customarily broadcast by powerful shortwave radio throughout Latin America—he could take full advantage of the godsend which had fallen into his lap.

This he did with his customary skill, but adding a new wrinkle which the particulars of the Panama situation offered him. The OAS, he declared, as always subservient to the United States, is sitting on its hands, even when aggression strikes a people whose government is not Marxist or socialist but simply nationalist and which "includes many representatives of the Panamanian oligarchy." But his main purpose was not so much to

8. *Cuba Socialista*, 30 (February 1964), 162. The full text of the communiqué is printed on pp. 157–165.

discredit the OAS—denouncing the OAS had become a matter of routine for him following Cuba's exclusion in January 1962—but to assume the role of leading supporter of a small Latin American republic, irrespective of ideological considerations.

"What should be the position of the Latin American countries?" he asked. "To back up Panama. . . . Among other things, immediately offer Panama economic aid." Why? Because the United States is exerting economic pressure against Panama to bring it to its knees. The United States threatens to suspend economic aid to Panama. How much aid have they given? Nine or ten million dollars, a mere pittance. The Latin American countries can supply Panama with much more economic aid than it has been getting from the United States. And Cuba is ready to contribute to a common Latin American fund for this purpose.

A Dramatic Offer

Having wound up his argument, Fidel was now ready to spring his dramatic offer: "And let me add that if they [the Latin American countries] don't want to join in some kind of collective aid, Cuba is ready to help Panama unilaterally. . . . If Panama needs our economic aid, Panama can count on economic aid from Cuba. And to start with, in the same amount which it has been getting from the United States. And, of course, with absolutely no strings attached, with no conditions of any kind, not even the reestablishment of diplomatic relations." Fidel reworked the formula several times for maximum effect, finally converting the offer into a challenge to the Latin American community. "Because what the imperialists do today to Panama," he exclaimed, "tomorrow they can do to any Latin American country. One day they shed Cuban blood, the next day it's Panamanian blood, the following day . . ." and so on, concluding with a random list of possible future victims.

Fidel had everything to gain and nothing to lose with his Panamanian gambit, for he could be sure that his offer would not be taken up. What he was mainly aiming at, it would seem, was to impress Washington with his bargaining power. For as we shall presently see, he was already committed to seeking a settlement with the United States, the loss of Panamanian blood notwithstanding.

Some years later, Panama was again on the Cuban agenda. Following a coup d'état in Panama City early in October 1968 by the National Guard, Panama's commander-in-chief Brigadier General Omar Torrijos emerged as the country's new strong man. He turned out to be the product of an increasingly aggressive nationalist mood which grew out of the riot of 1964 and the continuing deterioration of relations between Panama and the United States. In the early 1970s, when Castro had exchanged his role as the firebrand leader of the Latin American revolution for that of the veteran exponent of Latin American nationalism, he and Torrijos found common ground on the issue of Panamanian sovereignty over the Panama Canal. Diplomatic relations between the two countries were restored in August 1974; and in mid-January 1976, Torrijos paid a state visit to Cuba. Now the sober elder statesman, Fidel advised Torrijos to be prudent and persist in negotiating a settlement with the United States rather than risk a confrontation.[9]

It was, moreover, self-serving advice, since Fidel at that very moment was fighting a war in Angola that had set back discussions under way for normalizing relations with the United States. Moderation on the Canal problem would prove that the military intervention in Africa was no precedent for Cuban behavior in Latin America. It could also be perceived as support for President Carter, for whom an amicable settlement with Panama was, at the time, an urgent matter. Thus, history provided an unexpected epilogue to Fidel's Panamanian gambit following his second visit to Moscow.

Support for Soviet Foreign Policy

Having finished with Panama, Fidel was ready to wind up his speech. His concluding remarks, however, can be better understood if viewed against the background of the Joint Cuban-Soviet Communiqué which he and Khrushchev had signed on the eve of his departure from Moscow. It was a lengthy document of some 2,500 words, of which less than ten percent was devoted to the sugar agreement. Leaving aside the elaborate declarations of mutual admiration, climaxed by the invariable stereotype of "unbreakable friendship," of more than routine interest was the fact that the communiqué spelled out Cuba's full and unequivocal support for Russian foreign policy. In this respect, two major points stand out. One was Castro's acceptance of the Soviet position vis-à-vis China. Although China was not mentioned by name, the target was unmistakable when both parties "rejected the factional and sectarian activity in the ranks of the Communist and Workers' Parties and in the international communist movement" and

9. Lester A. Sobel, ed., *Castro's Cuba in the 1970s* (New York: Facts on File, 1978), p. 157.

agreed that the "revolutionary movement must make use of both the pacific and nonpacific road [*camino*] in the struggle for the liquidation of the capitalist regime." There was further agreement that the "unity [of the] international revolutionary movement" required acceptance of the Soviet-imposed "general line" established at the 1957 and 1960 "meetings of the Communist and Workers' Parties held in Moscow."

The other point referred to Cuban-American relations. "The Cuban Government," the communiqué stated, "is ready to do whatever is necessary to establish good neighborly relations with the United States of America, based on the principles of peaceful coexistence between states with different social regimes." In this connection, the document added that "Comrade N. S. Khrushchev affirmed the full support of the Soviet Union for this orientation [*rumbo*] by the Revolutionary Government of the Republic of Cuba, an orientation which corresponds to the interests of the consolidation of peace and the relaxation of international tensions."

There was, to be sure, the admonition that Cuba would brook no "intervention" in its internal affairs, and that in case of American "aggression" against Cuba, the Soviet Union would come to its defense "with all the means at its disposal." But this was essentially window dressing: "good neighborly relations" and "peaceful coexistence" were principles which did not envisage "intervention" and "aggression." Thus, the message to the United States—and to Latin America, for that matter—was clear: Castro offered to negotiate an accommodation with Washington, Khrushchev approved, and the unavoidable inference for Latin America was that Castro was prepared to abandon the Latin American revolution for the sake of an accommodation.

Addressing his fellow countrymen, Fidel betrayed some embarrassment about the communiqué, the text of which he did not mention. After declaring that he "found no words" to express the "deep affection with which he was received by the Soviet leaders, especially by Comrade Khrushchev," and his own ever increasing "admiration and gratitude" with respect to the Soviet Union, he scornfully rejected "imperialist claims" concerning what motivated his support for Soviet foreign policy. "They are always explaining that when we go to the Soviet Union we exact payment from them for the [political] backing we offer them," he said, but "this is so completely absurd that we won't even bother to reply." Then, without a pause, he went on to reply: "Because the Soviet Union from the first moment has given Cuba unlimited and unconditional aid. Never, not once, has the Soviet Union placed any conditions on its aid to our country."

It was a sensitive point, but he could not avoid dealing with it because it was obvious that, however he explained it, his endorsement of the Soviet "line" both in his first visit to Moscow and even more so in his second visit was a matter of importance to the Russians in their confrontation with the Chinese. After all, Castro had become a worldwide symbol of revolutionary integrity, and thus his commitment to what the Chinese and their international following denounced as "revisionism" was a valuable ideological and political asset for the Kremlin.

Looking back from the vantage point of history, it could well be that Fidel was uneasy about his commitment, not only because its motivation was under suspicion but also because of a deeper psychological discomfort. He had not, so to speak, "internalized" the ideological rationalization of Soviet foreign policy which Khrushchev had persuaded him to accept; and once the restraints of Moscow and the text of the joint communiqué were behind him, and he was again in Havana performing as the Leader of the Revolution, he was subconsciously reassuring himself that he had not compromised his deepest convictions. For Castro, as we shall see, was soon to change his tune, and some years of *Sturm und Drang* in his relations with the USSR would follow. It would not be until his next visit to Moscow, in 1972, after the Kremlin had finally achieved his domestication, that he would truly assimilate the ideological content of the communiqué which he had signed in January 1964.

A Position of Strength

It will be recalled that the text of the communiqué referring to a change in Cuban-American relations was straightforward. Understandably, Fidel felt the need of embellishment when speaking directly to his Cuban constituents—and by shortwave radio to his following in other parts of the world—about his offer to the Americans. His offer, he explained, was made from a position of strength. The Yankee "economic blockade" (it was properly speaking a trade embargo), he announced, "has been completely demolished, . . . and their contradictions with the countries which want to trade with us are steadily growing. . . . The increase of Cuban trade with the rest of the world can't be stopped. . . . The only complete idiots who don't want to trade with us are the Yankee imperialists. . . . When we say that we can live in peace with all countries, including them, they think we are up to our necks in deep water and are about to go under. But I am going to see what they say now. . . . Do they want to discuss matters with us? We'll discuss. Do they want to have better relations with us? We are willing."

In a sense, Fidel was in fact speaking from a position of strength. The price of sugar had risen dramatically, which more than compensated for Cuba's dismal harvest of 1963. Foreign hard currency reserves were plentiful.[10] Trade with capitalist countries, such as France, England, Spain, Japan, and Canada, was beginning to boom, and with trade came credits. The "economic blockade" was largely a failure, and this time Fidel was speaking truthfully, although later he would time and again blame the "blockade" for his own mismanagement of the Cuban economy. And, of course, it turned out that the United States had completely misjudged Castro's capacity to withstand American economic and political pressures.

Seated in the studio, Fidel fiddled with the microphones, as was his custom. Yes, he went on to say, we can do very nicely without trading with the United States or having any kind of relations with them. In fact, we would just as soon leave things as they are. Then why bother discussing anything with them? He had an answer to his question: "We are interested in peace, yes, and peace is not a Cuban interest but something in which the whole world is interested, and therefore, for the sake of [world] peace, we are ready to improve our relations with them, but apart from this we have no economic or political interest of any kind. They have been defeated; we are the ones who have come out the winners in our struggle with them."

You could almost hear the cheers in a million Cuban households, for this was a posture that flattered the self-image of a people whose country had just emerged from the backwash of history into the limelight of world affairs. As for "world peace," Fidel was less than candid. Not that he was opposed to it, but this was not his "only interest" in offering to negotiate with the Americans. To begin with, it was to satisfy Khrushchev, whose major foreign policy objective was a global settlement with the United States. At the same time, for all his dedication to the anti-imperialist struggle of the peoples of Latin America, Africa, Asia, and so on, Fidel was sufficiently realistic to conclude that he could scarcely afford to sit idly by while the two superpowers were, as it seemed, successfully moving toward a broad agreement on the major outstanding issues between them, one of which was Cuba. In fact, he was at that very moment waiting for President Johnson to resume the secret exchange of messages which had been under

10. According to Castro's speech on January 2, 1964, "when the Revolution took power, our reserves totaled less than 70 million [dollars]; at this moment, [they] are above 100 million." See my *Rise and Decline of Fidel Castro* (Berkeley and Los Angeles: University of California Press, 1972), pp. 366–367.

way between Kennedy and himself, and which had been cut short two months earlier by Kennedy's assassination.[11] Whatever his expectations were—no doubt he believed he could drive a hard bargain—he would meet the problem of "explaining" his coming to terms with the Colossus of the North if and when the problem arose. His rhetorical resources would be equal to the task.

Fidel ended his speech with a glowing tribute to Khrushchev and a final reminder of the "undreamed-of opportunities" that lay ahead for the Cuban people, since all that remained to be done was "to get to work" and "to take advantage intelligently of all of this; for all the conditions are right for us to do so." Alas, it was easier said than done.

A Television Trap in Moscow

In contrast to his first visit, Fidel's second visit to Moscow was a quiet affair dedicated to business. One part of the business probably did not require Fidel's presence in Moscow: the economic agreement, the principles of which were actually laid down during the earlier visit, could have been completed through other channels. Another part of the business no doubt did require face-to-face discussion with Khrushchev: an evaluation of the intentions of the new Johnson administration and coordination of Soviet and Cuban policy in the light of the evaluation. Still another part of the business certainly required that Fidel show up in Moscow, at least from the Russian point of view: the endorsement of the Soviet "line" vis-à-vis China was enormously strengthened by Fidel's signature on a document enjoying the status of a joint communiqué. Finally, there was another item of business which one could easily imagine was high on Khrushchev's list of motives for inviting and, one would suspect, urging Fidel to return to Moscow so soon after his first visit.

On the eve of his departure for Havana, Fidel appeared on the Moscow television network, where he was interviewed by a Soviet journalist. As was to be expected, the questions put to Fidel were designed to elicit replies which would reassure the viewers that, thanks to the magnanimous and decisive support of the USSR, the Cuban Revolution was now a solid and secure achievement (hence with no further risk of war or shortages of consumer goods, such as cheese, which Russian housewives attributed to shipments to Cuba), and then to heap praise on the virtues of the Soviet

11. Ibid., pp. 287 ff. Kennedy and Castro were in the early stages of exploring the possibility of normalizing relations.

system, its Communist Party, the wisdom of the leadership, and so on. Fidel could do no less than play his part gracefully and with his accustomed skill.

At the climactic point in the interview, Fidel was asked: "During your visit you have had many discussions with the leaders of the Party and the Government of the Soviet Union, and with Comrade Khrushchev. What impressions do you have about your discussions with Nikita Khrushchev?"[12] Fidel appeared to be embarrassed, as if polishing the image of the Chairman in full view of his constituents might be a performance that could easily be misinterpreted. "I'd really prefer to go into these matters after I leave the Soviet Union," he said apologetically, "but since you asked for my opinion, I am going to give it to you in all sincerity." Then he launched into a eulogy of the Chairman which, including the translation into Russian, must have lasted some twenty minutes: Nikita the "modest, simple, lovable man"; an "extraordinary leader of extraordinary intelligence"; a man "young in spirit, . . . great hunter, . . . in wonderful physical condition," and so on. All of this he had said in Havana when he returned from his previous visit to the USSR. It had the ring of sincerity then, although it also served the special purpose of rehabilitating Khrushchev's image, which had been severely damaged in Cuba at the time of the missile crisis.

Now his praise was something else again. It is conceivable that the question put to Fidel was an innocent one, but this is hardly likely. For some time, Khrushchev had been building his own "personality cult." Moreover, he was in trouble, as the world discovered several months later when he was unceremoniously toppled from power. The Soviet public had been given massive exposure to Fidel's charisma during his earlier visit. The dashing young "national hero" of the "island of liberty" had truly captured the imagination of the great masses of people. Thus, Fidel had permitted himself to be exploited by the Chairman for his own personal ends, and the memory of it must have rankled him when he heaped abuse on Khrushchev after his fall.[13]

12. Castro's interview was featured in *Cuba Socialista*, 30 (February 1964), 1 ff.

13. As, for example, when he told the French-Polish journalist K. S. Karol, "He was a man who really had no principles" (*Les Guérilleros au pouvoir* [Paris: Robert Laffont, 1970], p. 342).

2

■

The First Trial of Marcos Rodríguez

The Setting of a Political Storm

IN THE WEEKS THAT followed Castro's return from Moscow, the mood in Havana was one of high optimism and confidence. An incident enlivened the early days of February. On the third day of that month, four Cuban fishing boats operating off the Florida coast, in "international waters," according to Havana, were held up by U.S. naval vessels, boarded, searched, and escorted to Key West. In reprisal, Cuba cut off the water supply to the U.S. naval base at Guantánamo three days later with much fanfare, thereby also cutting off some $5 million in annual revenue and forcing the United States to transport water via tanker, and later to install a seawater desalinization plant at the base. What was perhaps more noteworthy than the incident itself was that Fidel was relatively relaxed about it. Imperialism, he said, is becoming simple piracy. "This event," he further declared, "is most irritating, especially since it occurs at a moment when international tensions are diminishing."[1]

On March 4, Castro attended a gala reception at the Moroccan embassy. The occasion was the third anniversary of the ascension to the throne of King Hassan II. Fidel's presence turned a sumptuous but nonetheless routine affair into an "event" given major coverage in the Cuban press. The message was clear: Fidel was fully committed to a policy of peaceful, even cordial, coexistence, not excluding a repressive monarchy.[2]

1. *Revolución*, February 7, 1964.
2. Among capitalist countries, Morocco was Cuba's most important sugar customer after Japan. This fact alone would not account for Castro's presence at

In the middle of the month, the traditional spring carnival was in full swing. For several days, great throngs applauded the gaily decorated floats, fanciful costumes, dancing groups, and competing beauty queens as they passed in parade. At the sports Coliseo, a visiting Soviet circus was performing before overflow audiences. The baseball season was under way. An element of sport was also injected into the sugarcane harvest as the media reported the "scores" of competing individual and group cane cutters.

Such was the scene in Havana—festive, hot, and sultry—when suddenly a great political storm blew up, reviving deep and suppressed antagonisms between post-Revolution and pre-Revolution Communists. Memories of betrayal and assassination, the thirst for revenge, and the integrity of revolutionary justice were issues which gave emotional depth to the conflict. For Fidel it created an extremely awkward situation. But it also presented an unusual opportunity for an ever astute Fidel to enhance his role as the supreme source of virtue, wisdom, and power in the nation. Both the political and human aspects of the drama deserve to be examined in detail, although it would require the talent of an Arthur Koestler to do justice to all of its fascinating complexities.[3]

The Opening of the Trial

On Monday, March 16, *Revolución* (the government's semiofficial daily) reported that at a trial which had begun on Saturday, and would continue for another day, a certain Marcos Rodríguez had confessed that in April 1957 he had informed the police concerning the whereabouts of the hideout of four participants in the "attack on the palace," as the event came to be known. The action occurred on March 13, 1957, and was a spectacular but unsuccessful attempt by the Directorio Revolucionario, a largely student organization, to kill President Batista in his quarters and seize the government. After the fall of Batista, March 13 became a red-letter day in the revolutionary calendar.[4]

---

the reception. His rare visits to foreign embassies in Havana always had political significance.

3. The subject is understandably taboo for the historian living in Castro's Cuba. Elsewhere many writers have referred to it, but only in a cursory manner. A notable exception is an article by Robert J. Alexander, "Old Quarrels in Havana," *New Politics*, 3:3 (Fall 1964), 65–75. It had the virtue of recognizing the importance of the affair, but, written immediately after the event, lacked the perspective which the passage of time could provide.

4. At the time of the attack, the Directorio had no connection with Castro's insurrection, which had barely gotten under way some 500 miles southeast of Havana. In fact, the Directorio had been a rival of Castro's organization and for a

The hideout was an apartment at 7 Humbolt Street, in the center of Vedado, Havana's modern "uptown" business and residential section. The police, clearly tipped off by an informer, had raided the apartment and killed the four youths. After the triumph of the Revolution, the massacre was commemorated by a plaque at the entrance to the building, and the victims became known as the "martyrs of Humboldt 7."

The news about Marcos was a front-page story in Monday's *Revolución*, which told of "a dramatic public trial which began on Saturday." It was normal for the daily, which did not appear on Sundays, to report the event on Monday. But the other government daily, *Hoy*, did appear on Sunday and made no mention of the trial. Although *Revolución*, born in Fidel Castro's mountain headquarters during the guerrilla war, and *Hoy*, venerable organ of the former Partido Socialista Popular (PSP, that is, Communist Party), had been integrated in Fidel's new ruling party, the Partido Unido de la Revolución Socialista (PURS, the United Party of the Socialist Revolution), *Hoy* was edited by Blas Roca, former secretary general of the PSP, and still reflected the views of the "old" Communists.

Thus, seven years after the crime, the mere news of the trial and confession at once stirred up excitement, to which an unexpected element of tension was added by the account of what transpired at the trial and by the failure of *Hoy* to report on the trial. The central figure, 26-year-old Marcos Rodríguez, as described by *Revolución*, spoke in a scarcely audible voice. Of slender build and pallid countenance, his eyes shielded by dark sunglasses, his body limp and head bowed, he must have been both a loathsome and pathetic figure to those in the courtroom, as if he were crushed by guilt and the knowledge of his impending doom, sealed by the written confession he had given before the trial. Guided by the state prosecutor, he related the events which led to the death of Juan Carbó, Fructuoso Rodríguez, José Machado, and Joe Westbrook.[5]

---

few days after the flight of Batista unsuccessfully disputed Castro's claim to power. In due time, Castro incorporated the Directorio's heroic attempt to overthrow Batista into the common revolutionary heritage, always featuring the exclusive leadership of Fidel Castro. Later, a strange distortion of history transformed the amply recorded anti-Communism of the Directorio into its opposite. "The men who attacked the Presidential Palace . . . on March 13, 1957," wrote *Granma*, official organ of the Cuban Communist Party, "[by taking the offensive] were faithful to . . . Marxist-Leninist principle, which has always characterized our revolutionary process" (*Granma Weekly Review*, March 25, 1973).

5. Summaries and citations of testimony at the trials are based on coverage by *Revolución* in the issues indicated in the text, or otherwise in the issue published on the day following the testimony.

In the evening of April 19, 1957, he had been to the apartment at Humboldt 7, to which the four fugitives had just been spirited from another hideout. He had known them for two years, had been involved in the political activities of the Directorio, and was one of those on the "outside" who were looking after them. He had previously had some nasty scenes with two or three of them, and that night another occurred. This time he could not contain his resentment. The next morning, April 20, he phoned the office of police Lt. Colonel Esteban Ventura (notorious for his brutality)[6] and asked for an appointment, saying "I had very important information to give him." Ventura received him in a secret apartment that afternoon. Marcos was there only long enough to give Ventura the address of the hideout, after which he went directly to a movie theatre. When he emerged a couple of hours later, he heard on the radio the news that the fugitives had been trapped and killed by the police.

Old Wounds and New Suspicions

One line of questioning, brief as it was, opened up an old wound of pre-revolutionary days: the bitter rivalry between the anti-Communist Directorio, following a line of "blitzkrieg" seizure of power, and the Communists committed to building a "mass base" from which to topple the Batista regime. Asked by the prosecutor about the nature of the "discrepancies" that arose between himself and members of the Directorio, Marcos replied: "mainly on methods of struggle." The judge intervened: "How come you kept up relations with the Directorio?" Marcos: "I wanted to change their political views." Judge: "To what organization did you belong before you informed?" Marcos: "For two years or more, I was a member of the Juventud Socialista [youth auxiliary of the PSP]." The courtroom was stunned. The prosecutor quickly jumped into the breach. How is this possible? he exclaimed. A Communist is never an informer, a Communist is not a coward, a Communist will sacrifice his own life for his ideal. "You are the negation of a Communist."

Shortly after the death of the martyrs, suspicion among the surviving activists of the Directorio had fallen on Marcos. One who played a key role in keeping alive the hunt for the informer was Marta Jiménez, widow of one of the victims. Marta was a witness at the trial. She testified that shortly after the Revolution came to power, she had located two of Ventura's bodyguards in the Cabaña prison (Lt. Colonel Ventura himself had fled

6. In a book entitled *Memorias* (Mexico City: Imprenta León M. Sánchez, 1961), Ventura gave a version of the affair that can be safely discarded.

the country). Given permission to interrogate them, she obtained from one a description of the informer that fitted Marcos. The other identified Marcos in a group picture. On the basis of this information, Marcos had initially been arrested in February 1959. However, the first bodyguard had been executed before he could be brought face to face with Marcos, after which the second refused to cooperate and was also executed. As a result, the evidence against Marcos was destroyed and he was released.

When Marta finished her testimony, a pall of dark misgiving hung over the courtroom. Was the timing of the executions mere coincidence? Was there a political motivation in protecting Marcos, who claimed to be a member of the Juventud Socialista?

Testimony Suppressed

The second, and what was supposed to be the concluding, session of the trial took place as scheduled on Monday, March 16, and was reported by *Revolución* the following day. In describing the first session of the trial, *Revolución* had given prominence to the coming appearance of Major Faure Chomón at the second session. This was understandable. Chomón was the most prominent survivor of the suicidal attack on the palace, had succeeded to the leadership of the Directorio following the death of its leader in the aftermath of the attack, had been co-opted by Castro to be his first ambassador to the Kremlin, and was now minister of communication in the revolutionary government. Nevertheless, in reporting the second session, *Revolución* curiously revealed practically nothing of Chomón's testimony, limiting itself to saying that the "most revealing witness . . . was without doubt Major Faure Chomón, who accused the informer with great vigor."

However, word of what Chomón had said in the courtroom, especially his blistering indictment of the "old" Communists, quickly spread through Havana and became a topic of heated discussion. The suppression (for that is what it amounted to) of his testimony by the press added to the excitement. In other respects, the noticeably brief report left a number of questions unanswered. It concluded with an account of how the prosecutor asked the court to impose the death penalty against the defendant, which was greeted by "a great ovation by the public attending the trial." Marcos was then given an opportunity to make a final statement. He refused, after which the judge said that he would pass sentence a few hours later. At no point was it publicly revealed that Marcos's confession had been extracted from him by the security police a year before the trial.

The final witness was Major Guillermo Jiménez, comrade-in-arms of the martyrs and now serving in military intelligence. The heart of his testimony was his opinion concerning what moved Marcos to commit his dastardly crime. "His act of betrayal was basically the result of his *formación*," Jiménez declared, "of the contradictions which arose between him and the martyrs and hence his contempt for them." The key word was *formación*, literally "formation," "training," or "upbringing," but in the context of his remarks the implication was clearly that of "political formation"—that is, Jiménez was referring obliquely to the defendant's association with the youth branch of the PSP.

Thus, at the end of the first session of the trial, not only did the Cuban people rejoice that the infamous and hitherto concealed betrayer of the martyrs of Humboldt 7 was finally brought to justice, but they were jolted by the unexpected political implications of the trial. In March 1962, they could recall, Fidel had turned on the "old" Communists for what was euphemistically termed "sectarianism"—that is, for attempting to build an exclusive power base within the supposedly integrated new revolutionary party and within the government bureaucracy. There had been a great purge. Six months later came the missile crisis, when the "cowardly" Russians pulled out their missiles without bothering to ask Cuba's permission. This did not improve the public image of the "old" Communists. But after Fidel's triumphant tour of the Soviet Union in May 1963, nothing more was heard of "sectarianism" or Russian cowardice. Now, after his second visit to Moscow only two months earlier, the further celebration of the unbreakable fraternal bonds between the two countries seemed to usher in an era of new respect for those whose ties with the Soviet Union antedated the Cuban Revolution by thirty years.

The judge's few hours inexplicably stretched into two days. It was not until Thursday, March 19, that *Revolución* announced on the front page: "Death Sentence for the Informer Against the Martyrs of Humboldt 7." The story itself was brief and to the point. It summed up the two-day trial and reported that the court-appointed lawyer for the defense had appealed the sentence. This was mandatory procedure whenever a lower court imposed capital punishment. In the case of Marcos Rodríguez, one could be confident that the appeal would forthwith be denied, after which in less than twenty-four hours, according to custom, he would be dispatched by a firing squad. In short, it would appear that the proceedings demonstrated the Revolution's new juridical sobriety: guilt established and punishment decreed in open court, according to the code of criminal law which antedated the Revolution.

3

The Trial Annulled

The "Siquitrilla" Provocation

FIDEL'S DRAMATIC CALL for a new trial came suddenly and unexpectedly, although in all likelihood it was not a hasty decision. He must have become aware as soon as the trial had gotten under way that the sensitive political issues it raised had somehow escaped control. Chomón's testimony on the second day confirmed his worst fears. The press was plainly disoriented. Censorship of Chomón's testimony was like locking the barn after the horse was stolen. What finally triggered Fidel's intervention was a short article in the same issue of *Revolución* (March 19) that had reported the end of the trial. The article was by the immensely popular columnist Segundo Cazalis, Cuba's foremost daily dispenser of wit-and-wisdom on random topics. Under the familiar by-line of "Siquitrilla," he wrote that "topic number one wherever people gathered to chat is the trial of Marcos Rodríguez, informer on the martyrs of Humboldt 7. . . . It is not only a moving story but also enlightening. Major Faure Chomón's testimony . . . is being discussed on every street corner. Will the enemy try to make use of the testimony? Obviously. Would its publication cause some disturbance? Beyond a doubt. . . . Publicizing the trial was good for the Revolution. The truth is good for the Revolution."

The column was a challenge that could not be ignored. Behind the scenes, forces for and against the release of Chomón's testimony were locked in combat. "Siquitrilla"—and of course *Revolución* as the publisher of the column—had decided to take a stand—in public. It was a bold course to take, but the issues as they perceived them were crucial: grave misconduct by the "old" Communists, once more influential in the regime, and censorship designed to cover up their misdeeds. Then there was the sheer indignation at what they saw to be the moral complicity of the "old" Communists in the revolting crime committed by Marcos Rodríguez.

Fidel's Intervention

Significantly, it was *Hoy* that Fidel selected to break the news of his great wrath and direct intervention in the escalating crisis. On Saturday, March 21, two days after "Siquitrilla's" blast in *Revolución*, the front page of *Hoy* featured a "Letter from Fidel to Blas Roca." "There is confusion concerning the trial of Marcos Rodríguez," he wrote. "There are some who dare to insinuate that the Revolution fears full public disclosure of this trial or is capable of covering up guilt." With respect to Chomón's testimony, he explained, it had not been published because "the stenographic transcript was full of errors and had to be corrected by him." This was "gleefully" seized upon by "certain elements" who never lose any opportunity to give vent to "resentment, ambition, dissension, or reactionary feeling," to which they give a "neo-revolutionary gloss designed to conceal the petty bourgeois hatred which in reality they feel toward the Socialist Revolution. And this in fact is at the bottom of the whole issue!" Then he called for the publication of the original transcript of Chomón's testimony, and without paying any attention to legal propriety, simply as "Prime Minister," instructed the Attorney General to order a new trial and "make it wide open to the public."

As Fidel had ordered, both *Hoy* and *Revolución* published the full verbatim transcript of Chomón's testimony of March 16. In both papers, the transcript appeared in the same issue that carried Fidel's letter to Blas Roca. The transcript was thus available to the public by the time the second trial opened, on the afternoon of Monday, March 23. It was to be a trial for which there was no precedent in the Marxist-Leninist world, or anywhere else for that matter. What made it unique, apart from its specifically Cuban political setting, was not the fact that it was set up in a totally arbitrary manner, that the cards were stacked, so to speak, and the outcome predetermined, but rather the candor and boldness with which Fidel risked exposing a whole collection of skeletons in the closets of the Revolution and his sheer virtuosity in orchestrating and conducting the performance, bringing it to a brilliant conclusion by his own appearance on the witness stand on the final day.

Chomón's Testimony Revealed

Fidel's explanation that the transcript had not been released a week earlier because it was "full of errors and had to be corrected [by Chomón]" could easily be discounted as an awkward face-saving device. The "uncorrected" document, as published, was a perfectly lucid and coherent statement whose only "error" was Chomón's imprudence in having made it. As recorded in the transcript, Chomón had begun by saying: "I shall deal with two aspects of the case: one which this court will judge; the other which the court should know but will be judged by the court of history." It was the second aspect, to be judged by the "court of history," that rocked Havana like an earthquake. It featured a letter written in prison by Marcos a year and a half earlier (the date was later revealed) and addressed to Joaquín Ordoqui, army quartermaster general and a vice-minister in the ministry of the armed forces headed by Fidel's younger brother Raúl.

Ordoqui was an "old" Communist who for more than a quarter of a century before the fall of Batista, and the merging of revolutionary organizations in 1961, had been in the top leadership of the Cuban Communist Party, and of the PSP after it changed its name.[1] He had come through Fidel's March 1962 purge of ex-PSP "sectarians" unscathed. Chomón did not explain how he managed to obtain a copy of the letter, but as he read from it, it was evident that Marcos had written it before he had confessed to the state security agents, but after he had spent considerable time in prison. Only after the conclusion of the second trial, as we shall see, would it become possible for an attentive observer to reconstruct, bit by bit, the extraordinary chronology of the second imprisonment and subsequent developments in the ordeal of Marcos Rodríguez.

The Letter to Ordoqui

"During the period when [the PSP] was illegal, I was assigned the task of obtaining information concerning the Directorio Revolucionario by working within that organization," Marcos had written to Ordoqui, and he went on to name members of the PSP who "worked with me" in the party's intelligence service. Among them was Valdés Vivó, an assistant editor of Hoy at the very moment Chomón was reading the letter. "I was engaged in a struggle which was strategically necessary," Marcos continued in his letter, "not only to keep abreast of steps taken by the petty bourgeois revolutionary movement [the Directorio] but also to coordinate the mass struggle as a whole." Here Chomón could not contain himself. "Vicious, . . . despicable activity by this fellow," he interjected. "This way of fighting [against Batista] did tremendous damage to the revolutionary struggle."

---

1. I recall hearing Ordoqui in New York in June 1935 (at the time he was in exile), denouncing the crimes of Batista at a mass meeting which was also addressed by Archibald MacLeish, Clifford Odets, and Carleton Beals. Fidel Castro was then eight years old.

Chomón continued reading from the letter: "The Directorio suspected me but could not undertake to expel me, because of my [close] relationship with Jorge Valls, a member of their executive committee. . . . What was the Directorio at that time? An action group containing factions [of adventurers] . . . opposed to unity [the guiding principle of the PSP] . . . and not even popular among the university students. . . . It was urgent [for us] to know in what direction they were moving." Again Chomón interjected: "He considered us a bunch of gangsters." Chomón resumed his reading of the letter. "Why do they accuse me of being the traitor of Humbolt 7?" Marcos asked. Yes, he was an informer, he admitted, but not a police informer. Then he made a distinction between two "opposite" types of informers: one engages in an activity that is "positive," because it is "political and necessary and concerned with the integrity and purity of the revolutionary struggle. . . . There is a clear distinction between a man who informs for his party and the man who informs the police."

Chomón interrupted his reading to refute the "distinction." Marcos did both, he declared, adding that "whoever is capable of spying on a revolutionary organization is capable of spying for the police." It was perhaps Chomón's most provocative remark that day, for in the context in which it was made, its implications were obvious: the PSP itself had been "capable" of informing the police.

In his letter, Marcos recalled that he had been "humiliated" by his first arrest and interrogation (in February 1959), instigated by the Directorio, and he reminded Ordoqui that after his release he had consulted him about his idea of publishing a declaration of his innocence and persecution, but "you said my proposal was not tactical or prudent because it would have precipitated a big scandal." Now, after his second arrest and prolonged detention, he turned once more to Ordoqui, asking that his ordeal be terminated either by a speedy trial or his release.

His plea was eloquent, and although in the light of his subsequent confession it could be dismissed at the trial as an unmitigated piece of self-serving effrontery, it struck at a sensitive spot in Castro's machinery for the dispensation of justice—a matter which did not go unnoticed among many to whom the text of the letter was revealed. "What has become of Marxist humanism?" the letter asked. "How is it possible that on the one hand the foremost leader of our Revolution has maintained that the more urgent a problem, the more rapidly it must be solved, and on the other hand this principle is not applied in everyday life? Can it be that we are on the threshold of the abuse of power by the department of state security? By virtue of what principle of socialist legality can such detestable methods of operation be permitted to exist? What kind of Leninist thinking justifies such procedures?"

It was a long letter, skillfully put together by a shrewd, talented, and, at the time, incredibly self-possessed writer. For Chomón to read it, particularly without "clearing" the matter with Fidel, verged on the foolhardy. Even discounting the impact of the "abuse of power" reference, its allegations concerning the informer's relations with the "old" Communists could easily be believed, the more so since the letter was addressed to Ordoqui. And for Chomón, his willingness to believe was reinforced by the memory of his own experience with the PSP during the period described by Marcos, and by the understandable need to avenge the slaughter of four of his closest and most valiant comrades-in-arms.

Truth Defended, Sectarianism Denounced

"I have brought this document here out of respect for the martyrs and in the name of truth," declared Chomón when he finished reading the letter. Nor was it a secret document, he went on to say, since "this fellow Marcos Rodríguez made copies which today are surely in the hands of the CIA. Therefore, it was my duty to analyze it before this tribunal . . . so that it can be of use for the history of our Revolution as well as the history of our party and so that nothing be hidden. . . . Documents such as these must be brought to light, for they can be useful for ourselves or revolutionaries of other countries who should know about experiences such as these."

Although by now the lesson which Chomón wished to draw from the letter should have been obvious enough, he was apparently carried away by the bitterness and intensity of his feeling, for he went on to expound the political dimensions of Marcos's treachery with a devastating indictment of the PSP. "The case of Marcos Rodríguez," he exclaimed, "was a bitter fruit of sectarianism," a term which he recalled was used to characterize the attitude of the PSP when, in 1961 and 1962, it "placed [its] old militants in all the key positions of the Revolution. Then," he continued, "after March 26, when Fidel denounced sectarianism, it was discovered that in the nuclei of [the new integrated party] there were opportunists, informers, and traitors of the working class." To underscore his point, Chomón gave two concrete examples of such individuals (not including Marcos) "who had been shielded by sectarianism, . . . brazenly living in the ranks of the Revolution. . . . It is sad and painful to realize that such things happen . . . because the truth is not told and because many fail to do their duty."

The truth and its function had been disputed concepts among philosophers and kings for centuries, not without penalties for those defeated in the disputation. In revolutionary Cuba, moreover, there was a marked tendency to measure the truth by its political consequences, as perceived by Fidel Castro. Chomón, in no sense motivated by a desire to challenge Fidel, was nevertheless aware that he had ventured into politically and ideologically treacherous territory. Thus, toward the end of his long testimony, he came back to the question of truth, as much in his own defense as in the justification of a principle. "Revolutionary truth," he concluded, "serves to defend our party . . . and the prestige of our leaders. With the truth, we faithfully fulfill our obligations to Marxism-Leninism." Then, with a final flourish: "Let us condemn Marcos Rodríguez, and when he is buried may sectarianism also be buried."

4

■

The Second Trial: Act I

The Scenario of the Trial

THE SECOND TRIAL of Marcos Rodríguez, like the first, was open to the public, but this time a fully alerted public. Moreover, following the Prime Minister's instructions, it was broadcast live over the national radio hookup. For several hours, on each of four successive days from Monday, March 23, to Thursday, March 26, 1964, all Cuba listened with fascination as more than a score of witnesses, many of them appearing for the first time, addressed the court of law and the court of public opinion. And for the public record, full transcripts of the proceedings were published in *Revolución* and *Hoy*. At the last session of the court, reserved for Fidel, the proceedings were televised the length and breadth of the island.

The four days were carefully planned. On the first day, Marcos and former members of the Directorio, including Chomón, were put on the stand. The highlight of this day was Chomón's retraction of his charges against the PSP. The next day featured former members of the PSP, among them Ordoqui and other "old" Communists still prominent in public affairs. It was a day dedicated to the defense and exoneration of the PSP. On the third day, members of the department of state security involved in the investigation and interrogation of the prisoner took the stand. They were followed by President Dorticós, who played back a tape recording of a top-level secret party meeting at which Marcos was confronted by a high official named in his written confession. It was a day of unexpected revelations designed to clear the regime of either negligence or cover-up in the apprehension and prosecution of Marcos. The final day, as noted above, was Fidel's, a day of more revelations, of summation and edification—and of judgment.

Monday, March 23, 1964

The Testimony of Marcos Rodríguez. The defendant was clearly in a state of deep depression, and for good reason. The new trial had given him a few extra days of life, with no hope of escaping the firing squad, and at the cost of once more submitting to the mental torture of confronting the details of his guilt and the humiliation of public disgrace. It was thus not remarkable that during the long and hostile interrogation, Marcos would become confused, would contradict allegations made in his written confession, or would remain silent, often on the verge of collapse, in response to a question. What was noteworthy, on the other hand, was that on some points of key importance Marcos could not be shaken.

A major objective of the prosecution was to reduce Marcos's entanglement with the PSP to an innocuous minimum. However, Marcos continued to claim that he had been a member of the Juventud Socialista and that he had passed on confidential information concerning the rival Directorio to the Communists. Marcos also again denied that he had received money from the police for informing on the martyrs, before or after their betrayal, or that he had at any time been a police informer, thus in effect maintaining his position as a PSP spy motivated by ideological loyalty. And once more Marcos affirmed that, in Mexico in late 1958, he had confessed his role in the crime at Humboldt 7 to Edith García Buchaca. Edith, wife of Ordoqui and a leading "old" Communist in her own right, was at the time of the trial in charge of cultural affairs for the revolutionary government, in effect Castro's minister of culture.

Marcos had first made this assertion in his written confession, then retracted it under circumstances which I shall explain later, but now stood by his original statement, despite the efforts of the prosecution to make him back down. The stubbornness of the witness was disconcerting. For the spectator at the second trial, the interrogation of Marcos as a whole was a disturbing experience. The defendant was suffering intensely and for the most part was led helplessly by the prosecution through a maze of incidents which, while they filled gaps in the information hitherto available to the public, left important questions in doubt. What was the true nature of Marcos's relationship to the PSP? And to the Directorio? What in fact moved Marcos to inform the police? Was Edith García Buchaca really privy to Marcos's secret? As it turned out, the answers to these and other questions would have to be reconstructed from elements of varying degrees of credibility as the second trial continued.

The Testimony of Major Guillermo Jiménez. First a few words are in order concerning two witnesses who preceded Major Jiménez on the stand: Marta Jiménez, wife of one of the martyrs and a witness at the first trial; and Major Julio García, comrade-in-arms of the martyrs. They were questioned about their role in the apprehension of Marcos on his return to Cuba in January 1959, and about their efforts to have him identified as the informer by two of Lt. Colonel Ventura's jailed bodyguards, as I have previously related. This time, Marta revealed to the public that Marcos, at the time of his arrest, was in charge of the department of education of the Rebel Army, as Fidel's guerrilla forces were known, at Ciudad Libertad, the new name for what had been Batista's military headquarters. Who was the person with sufficient influence to place Marcos in this job? Ordoqui, already assigned to the new military bureaucracy by the PSP, now working closely with the Castro regime? The question was never raised at any point during the trial. As for Julio García, he recalled learning that the confrontation between Marcos and Ventura's men had not come off as expected. "When I discovered that Ventura's men had been shot, I lost interest. I figured it would be impossible to prove [Marcos's] guilt." The prosecutor: "Was there any negligence by the authorities in handling this case?" This was the key question, and Major García did not hesitate: "Absolutely not at any time." He had been tactful and sparing of words throughout his testimony. In 1967 he served a term as Cuban ambassador to North Vietnam.

With respect to Major Guillermo Jiménez, it will be recalled that, along with Faure Chomón at the first trial, he had made the sharpest criticism of the PSP with his reference to the *"formación,"* or "upbringing," of Marcos by the PSP as the main reason for his dereliction. Thus, a principal objective of the prosecutor at the second trial, which was no secret to the witness, was to prod him to retract. Jiménez turned out to be less compliant than might have been expected after Castro's blast against the detractors of the PSP. As a result, his interrogation was lengthy and took on the characteristics of a fencing match with the prosecutor.

First came the question of "negligence," implying PSP intervention, in the interrogation and release of Marcos in February 1959. To get Jiménez to give the right answer was like pulling teeth. He had related how the Directorio had sent him to see Ordoqui and Carlos Rafael Rodríguez (the PSP leader closest to Fidel) "to explain our suspicions . . . and our interest in clearing up the question of Marcos. We proposed that while the legal . . . normal proceedings were taking their course, we discuss the matter as something of concern to our two organizations to see whether or not our views were sufficiently objective to merit support." For the prosecutor this was definitely not leading in the right direction. Abruptly moving to the main issue, he tried to get the witness to agree that the outcome of the investigation was the best to be expected, considering the understandable confusion that confronted the newly created tribunals. The witness evaded a direct answer. "Taking into account Marcos's affiliation," he replied, "we thought it correct to talk with Carlos Rafael Rodríguez and Joaquín Ordoqui."

Major Jiménez was making matters worse in general, and in particular by mentioning Carlos Rafael Rodríguez, now a minister in Castro's cabinet. The prosecutor had to abandon his line of questioning for the time being and tackle the issue of Marcos's affiliation with the PSP. "I am not the person most qualified to answer this question," the witness maintained, but as "a matter of fact, nobody at the time questioned it. . . . I have no proof that he was a member of either the Juventud or the party." Jiménez stubbornly refused to give the right answer, although the matter of "proof" was a small concession. The prosecutor then decided to go back to the unfinished business of "negligence," finally phrasing a question which the witness could not evade: "Do you consider that the revolutionary authorities at that time [February 1959] acted correctly, and as diligently as necessary?" Jiménez: "Yes." After what preceded this exchange, everybody realized that he meant "no."

Later the witness added another disconcerting detail concerning the political situation at the time of Marcos's release. "It was our moral obligation to talk to the party [PSP] through Ordoqui and Carlos Rafael," he said. "After all, they represented the Revolution in power at that moment." The PSP, he was in effect saying, was "inside" the new power structure, while the Directorio was on the outside. The PSP, he clearly implied, had sufficient influence to keep Marcos in prison and prolong the investigation, or to have him released. The prosecutor wisely decided to end the matter then and there. "So in general," he summarized, ". . . you do say that you are completely satisfied with what was done, satisfied with the investigation. That is all, your honor." It was a perfect non sequitur. The witness was dismissed.

Some weeks after the end of the trial, I was not surprised to see Guillermo Jiménez walking down the street in mufti, without holster and pistol dangling by his side. He was no longer an army officer and now had a job in the lower ranks of the civilian bureaucracy.

The Testimony of Dr. Blanca Mercedes Mesa. Several witnesses who had
been heard thus far, both at the first and the second trials, had commented
on the personality and appearance of Marcos. Marta had noted that he was
thin, wore glasses, and always had a book under his arm. Chomón had
said that "we didn't like the type, . . . the way he dressed. . . ." Guillermo
Jiménez considered that Marcos had an "evidently abnormal personality,"
and mentioned that he wore a yellow jacket and also sandals "like a Fran-
ciscan monk." Another witness spoke of his "strange, affected manner-
isms," those of a "homosexual."

Blanca Mesa saw Marcos in a different light. She identified herself as
a "doctora" in philosophy and letters who was currently working as a li-
brarian. She had been a member of a clandestine "women's auxiliary," so
to speak, helping members of the Directorio pursued by the police to find
shelter, bringing them food, and delivering messages. She explained that
Marcos contacted her on the evening of the tragedy and showed her a
newspaper account which reported that he had escaped from the apartment when the police broke in (false information very likely planted by Lt.
Colonel Ventura to shield Marcos from suspicion as the informer). Believ-
ing Marcos to be in danger, she at once took him to an aunt's house and
eventually to the Brazilian embassy, where she had arranged asylum for
him. (Soon after, he left Cuba, spending time in Costa Rica, Argentina,
and Mexico before returning to Havana after the fall of Batista.)

Blanca testified that she and some of her female literary friends had a
high opinion of Marcos. Among these was Dysis, the *novia* (steady girl-
friend) of Joe Westbrook, one of the four martyrs. None of her friends,
Blanca said, including Dysis, could believe that Marcos was the informer.
Blanca was understandably troubled about her "blindness," but she found
comfort in Karl Marx's assessment of this weakness: "I believe that, as Marx
said, the defect in a person which can be most easily forgiven is self-deception." Having invoked the protection of an indisputable source of moral
judgment, though without citing chapter and verse, she went on to proclaim "the great faith that I have in the department of state security," and so
on. Nevertheless, she continued in a great burst of candor: "In all sincerity,
if he himself did not admit his guilt and sign the confession, I couldn't believe it, because we were so completely deceived by him." Blanca, without
intending to do so, had called attention to one of the ironies, later confirmed, in the trial and conviction of Marcos Rodríguez: except for the
confession, almost certainly there would have been no trial and conviction. Blanca was a voluble and uninhibited witness. She related that Mar-

cos wrote poetry which was recited in her literary group. "I still have some of his poetry at home," she said. Question: "Romantic or revolutionary poetry?" Blanca: "Lyric, very dramatic and very tragic." Question: "Good poetry?" Blanca: "Yes, quite good."

The Testimony of Major Faure Chomón. In keeping with his status as a member of Castro's cabinet and the leadership of the ruling party, Chomón, unlike previous witnesses, was invited by the prosecutor to address the court without being subject to questioning. He spoke for an hour, part of the time going over the circumstances which led to the selection of Humboldt 7 as the hideout and explaining how suspicion for the betrayal immediately fell on Marcos. This, however, was preliminary to the real task that confronted him: to retract his previous attack on the PSP in compliance with Fidel's scenario and, at the same time, to maintain what he could of his dignity and stature as a responsible leader. One could say, when he had finished, that all in all he did as good a job as could be reasonably expected. Still, by the nature of the circumstances, he could not come out of the ordeal unscathed.

There was no way to avoid echoing Fidel with respect to the "errors" in the stenographic transcript which supposedly delayed the publication of Chomón's testimony at the first trial. "I was astonished," he said, and needed to "reconstruct it." Meanwhile, he continued, following Fidel's script, rumors spread that converted the trial "into a weapon against the Revolution," and, in the name of antisectarianism, another form of sectarianism reared its ugly head, and so on. Then, moving on to "reconstruct" his position, he explained the case of Marcos Rodríguez as comparable to the classic infiltration of revolutionary organizations by enemy agents, as for example the FBI's infiltration of the PSP, as Blas Roca had one time explained, and which the party constantly had to guard against. There had been a lack of vigilance, he declared, "an error in the revolutionary struggle which permitted an element like Marcos Rodríguez to move into one or two revolutionary organizations." The Directorio, Chomón was now saying, shared the blame with the PSP.

There was another point to be cleared up. Did anyone purposely shield Marcos when he was first arrested? Certainly not. However, Chomón added, "we thought that by exercising a certain amount of caution, it could have been possible to see to it that he remained in our country [Marcos went to Prague shortly after his release, about which more later] tied down to some kind of job until in time . . . .it might have been possible to get at the truth. . . ." It was, of course, a point well taken and phrased with

circumspection, leaving unsaid but not unthinkable that persons like Ordoqui and Carlos Rafael had sufficient influence both with Marcos and the
government at the time to prevent Marcos's departure from Cuba. This
was apparently about as far as Chomón felt he could go in expressing his
deepest feelings and those of many who shared his views. For the rest, he
adhered closely to Fidel's directive. It was "clear" in his previous testimony, he said, "that when I attacked . . . sectarianism, I was not speaking
against our old Communists but against the fakers, . . . opportunists, . . .
pseudorevolutionaries," and so on. At no time did he mention Marcos's
letter to Ordoqui.

In his concluding remarks, Chomón drew himself up to his full
height, as if to rise above the humiliation of "reconstructing" the testimony he had given at the first trial. "In keeping with my duty," he said in a
voice filled with emotion, "my duty as a comrade-in-arms of those who
were assassinated, . . . in keeping with my responsibility as a member of
the national leadership of our party, . . . as one who fought as a soldier [he
was severely wounded in the attack on the palace], . . . in accord with my
conscience as a Communist [converted after the Revolution], . . . I tried
to provide a clear, . . . revolutionary, comradely exposition at the trial
which took place a few days ago."

It was a reminder to the whole nation just what his credentials were—
and to Fidel that these credentials had best be respected. And in fact they
were. Major Faure Chomón survived, in due course moving from the
ministry of communication to become minister of transportation. In 1970,
Fidel fired him under different circumstances.

5

■

The Second Trial: Act II

Tuesday, March 24, 1964

THIS DAY WAS LARGELY reserved for rebuttal and, as it turned out, uninhibited counterattack by the "old" Communists, who comprised nine of the eleven witnesses heard. According to the account published on the following day in *Revolución*, on the front page under a banner headline, the session began at 3:25 in the afternoon, but "people came early in the morning, and all seats were taken by noon. . . . Hundreds of thousands listened by radio." It was like a Watergate hearing in Washington in 1973. When the session ended late at night, many who listened wondered whether tensions in the Havana "establishment" had not risen higher than Castro had anticipated.

The Testimony of Raúl Valdés Vivó. Secretary-general of the Juventud Socialista in 1955, and now Blas Roca's assistant editor of *Hoy*, Valdés revealed something of the bitter antagonism at the University of Havana between the Communist-directed Juventud and the predominantly anti-Communist leadership of the Directorio. He admitted having talked once with Marcos, who was introduced to him by a comrade as a member of the Directorio. He had asked Marcos a couple of questions about Directorio policy and connections, which Marcos answered. Marcos, he reminded the court, admitted on the witness stand that he had joined the Directorio because of his "affinity" for Jorge Valls (more about him later), who at the time was a "notorious anti-Communist." In short, Valdés Vivó declared, "Marcos was never a member of the Juventud Socialista. . . . He never informed us about anything at all."

There were obvious flaws in Valdés's argument. He had himself just explained that he asked for and received information from Marcos about the Directorio, and as anyone at the trial or listening over the radio might have suspected, it could have been confidential and useful information. If Marcos were indeed an anti-Communist, as Valdés claimed, some explanation was required as to why and how a "comrade" in the Juventud with access to the secretary-general—that is, a "comrade" of some standing in the organization—could arrange a meeting with Valdés, and why this anti-Communist gave information to a hostile Communist group.

The bulk of Valdés's statement was a frontal attack on Faure Chomón and Guillermo Jiménez, with a few strictures against *Revolución* thrown in for good measure. He said that he heard Chomón's testimony at the first trial "with the greatest astonishment," and then he corrected himself to say that he meant "read" rather than "heard," adding that he first learned about the trial in *Revolución* on Monday morning. No one listening to him could believe for one moment that an editor of *Hoy* had to wait until Monday morning's edition of *Revolución* to discover that an open trial of Marcos Rodríguez, charged with informing on the martyrs of Humbolt 7, had taken place on Saturday. *Hoy*, as noted earlier, had in fact suppressed the news, and now Valdés was implying that *Revolución* was motivated by more than simple news reporting in carrying the story. In this respect, Valdés was probably not far from the truth, since the competition between the two newspapers was based on something deeper than professional rivalry. Before he was finished, Valdés directly accused *Revolución* of "creating confusion," which *Revolución* answered the next day with a stinging editorial. A year and a half later, Fidel abolished both papers, replacing them with a single new daily.

Turning his attention to Guillermo Jiménez, Valdés expressed open contempt for his backtracking and accused him of reviving "anti-Communism in our country." Since anti-Communism automatically was equated with counterrevolution, Valdés was striking back with the ultimate weapon. With respect to Chomón, he was more circumspect but no less severe. "We who aspire to be Communists," he declared, a reminder that Chomón was a new convert, "should simply speak the truth and not disguise it: if an error was committed, if a lie was uttered because of being carried away by emotion or prejudice, . . . then don't get up here and say 'I was misunderstood, it was not my intention to say this.'" And in a final admonishment, Valdés ended his testimony by altering Chomón's appeal for burying "sectarianism," along with Marcos, to call for the burial of "anti-Communism."

There was, of course, no opportunity for Jiménez or Chomón to reply to Valdés, even if they had considered it expedient to do so. In these proceedings there was no provision for rebuttal or cross-examination. And both the prosecutor and Marcos's court-appointed defense attorney, who understood the political objective of the trial, asked no questions.

The Enigma of Marcos Rodríguez. Two witnesses who had had more than casual contact with Marcos spoke differently about his character, but together their testimonies revealed a complex personality which neither witness suspected to be sufficiently unbalanced to lead him to commit his monstrous act of betrayal. Jorge Valls, one of the original organizers of the Directorio in 1955, asked to appear as a witness to defend himself against charges by Chomón, at the first trial, that he failed to show up at the time of the attack against the palace although he was pledged to participate. His last-minute withdrawal was considered to be an act of betrayal and cowardice, and shortly after the disaster he was expelled from the organization. On the witness stand he was permitted to state his side of the story, which boiled down to a countercharge of breakdown in communications which left him without clear instructions on that fatal day. Apparently, he was not the only one who failed to show up, for one reason or another. Thus, old skeletons continued to emerge from revolutionary closets.

Valls testified that he and Marcos had been close friends both before and after the massacre at Humboldt 7, and he gave Marcos a clean bill of health. Marcos especially distinguished himself in finding shelter for activists of various persuasions who were pursued by the police. He undoubtedly saved many lives. It was Marcos who had actually rented the apartment at Humbolt 7 in the first place. He had never been known to betray a secret, much less a comrade. When Marcos told Valls in early 1959 that he planned to go to Czechoslovakia, Valls advised him to go to Central America instead. "I believed," said Valls, "that he needed to free himself from all ties and find himself, philosophically speaking. Marcos's philosophical views fluctuated. . . . He tried out various philosophical currents, both Marxism and other currents of contemporary European philosophy. I consider Marcos to be a magnificent poet and scholar of high quality. I have known few students as profound and serious as he."

The other witness was Alfredo Guevara, head of the official Cinema Institute from the time it was set up by the revolutionary government. He was an "old" Communist who moved away from the dogmatism of the PSP in matters of art and literature soon after Castro took power. He had not appeared at the first trial, and his presence at the second trial was motivated by the need to discredit Marcos as one who in any way enjoyed the confidence of the PSP. "I knew Marcos from way back," said Guevara (no relative of Ché and reputed to have been a personal friend of Fidel when both were students in law school), "at the time he was working as a custodian for the Cultural Society [a PSP front organization], which published *Nuestro Tiempo* [Our Times]. He created political problems. He used to hide Marxist propaganda under his pillow [he had a bed in one of the rooms], in spite of instructions of the [party] politburo not to do so. . . . It was a united front society. . . . What he did endangered the Society. He always lied, . . . but I never thought he was a person capable of [deliberate] betrayal. I came to the conclusion that he had a dual personality with a tremendous capacity for deception." Nevertheless, earlier in his testimony, Guevara had already stated that in 1958, when both he and Marcos were in Mexico, he had recommended Marcos to a friend in the Czech embassy when Marcos had first applied for a scholarship to study in Prague.

As was to be expected, the prosecutor made no effort to probe further into Marcos's relations with the Juventud or the PSP. Since Marcos "always lied," the presumption was that he lied when he claimed to be a member of the Juventud. But this was now becoming a technical matter. After the testimony of Valdés Vivó, and now of Guevara, there was no doubt that Marcos was no stranger to the PSP and its affiliates. But Marcos was also emerging as something more than a common run-of-the-mill black sheep. Shortly, more was to be added to the portrait of Marcos, who sat slouched in his chair, head bowed, for all the world not listening to what was said.

The Testimony of Edith García Buchaca. Four witnesses remained to be heard on this second day of the second trial. They were, so to speak, the "heavy artillery" in the counteroffensive by the "old" Communists, having been leading functionaries of the PSP who were now installed in the top echelons of Castro's bureaucracy. They were treated by the court with all due respect and, as can be imagined, were listened to with absorbing attention within the courtroom and by the nationwide radio audience.

Of the four, perhaps the most eagerly heard was *la doctora* Edith. As head of the government's Cultural Council, she was not only a personality in her own right and one of the very few women with authority in the regime, but she was also the wife of Joaquín Ordoqui and the ex-wife of Carlos Rafael Rodríguez, the former PSP luminary and now cabinet minister. In addition, a thick dark cloud had been cast over her. As soon as she took the stand and was sworn in, the prosecutor addressed her: "Comrade Edith García Buchaca, the defendant Marcos Rodríguez has stated that in Mexico he revealed to you the secret that he had been the one who informed on the comrades of Humboldt 7, an act which cost them their lives. I should like you to explain to the court anything that you may wish to say concerning this allegation."

She spoke for some forty-five minutes, without interruption and with considerable feeling. She was testifying, she said, "not to defend myself against . . . this monstrous accusation, . . . because my life [history] defends me, my revolutionary conduct [since the age of fifteen, she later explained, and for twenty years, she was a member of the Central Committee of the Communist Party, and of the PSP when the name was changed], my conduct always firmly rooted in the principles of a militant Communist." Her purpose, she went on, was to explain her past relations with the defendant and "also to express my views concerning some aspects of the proceedings at this trial." About her relations with Marcos she told a moving story. In 1958, she and her husband (Ordoqui) had come to Mexico after a trip to China (presumably on PSP business). Here they met Marcos for the first time. He had come from Argentina with no money at all. He was desperately poor and was receiving no help from his family in Cuba. So they fed him and found him a place to sleep, considering this to be a duty to an exile. "We considered him to be a good man, a revolutionary [presumably of Marxist persuasion]," she said. His conduct in Mexico was "irreproachable, . . . and there was never any derogatory information about him from Cuba or anywhere else." Moreover, Marcos was in training with a group planning a guerrilla invasion of Cuba, and "we never heard from any of them, directly or indirectly, anything negative" about Marcos. All in all, they had known Marcos in Mexico for nearly a year—that is, until the fall of Batista.

She said no more about the planned invasion. What the political complexion of the group in training might have been was not mentioned. Very likely it had Communist approval, which means that it was formed after mid-1958, when the PSP reversed its position and decided to support Fidel's guerrilla forces. Presumably the invasion was called off when Batista collapsed. Nevertheless, this episode in Marcos's career was not without interest. An earlier witness had testified that, shortly after the attack on the palace on March 13, 1957 (the Directorio did not consider Marcos physically or psychologically fit to participate and kept him in the dark about the preparations), and some weeks before he informed on the martyrs-to-be, Marcos and a comrade in the Directorio set out from Havana to join Fidel's guerrillas in the Sierra Maestra. They failed to make contact and in a short time returned. This was Marcos in a different character, not the frail intellectual with a book under his arm and a verse on his lips. Once again, this time in Mexico, he had tried to trade his books for a rifle.

What followed in Edith's testimony was the public exposure of a top-level meeting which had been kept a carefully guarded state secret. As soon as she learned what Marcos had written about her in his confession, she demanded a face-to-face confrontation with Marcos in the presence of the party leadership. At the confrontation, Marcos retracted: he had in fact not revealed to her that he had been the informer in the tragedy which took place at Humboldt 7 (more about the confrontation would be revealed when President Dorticós took the stand the next day). In short, Edith declared, Marcos had tried to convert his "vulgar crime" into a "political crime" in which the PSP was involved. Why single out the PSP, she asked. Marcos's slanderous fabrication should be considered not as an isolated act but linked to political trends gaining momentum in Cuba. "This slander has been planted in fertile ground," she asserted, "because during the past year we have witnessed a real campaign to defame and undermine the prestige of dedicated revolutionaries like ourselves who have devoted a whole lifetime to the cause of our people and the working class. . . . That is why Marcos once again repeats . . . his slanderous statement."

Concerning Marcos, her explanation was questionable, but she was right about the "fertile ground." Fidel himself had had a hand in creating the problem of "the prestige of the dedicated revolutionaries." He had denounced them in March 1962, during the purge of the "sectarians," and had cast a deep shadow on their ideological brethren in the Kremlin following the missile crisis six months later. Now he was faced with the need of undoing the damage, although a year later he would again be moving back to his 1962 frame of mind, to be followed, in the 1970s, by another reversal requiring a massive and prolonged reindoctrination of the population in the virtues of the Soviet Union, along with the rehabilitation of the old "sectarians."

Edith concluded her philippic, focusing her wrath on Chomón. While he claimed to speak as a Communist, she said with obvious irony, he had contributed to the creation of a "climate of anti-Communism, . . . of hostility against the old Communists," and so on. With the unfortunate Chomón safely muzzled, she left the stand in a glow of self-satisfaction. She had crushed Marcos's infamous slander, had extolled her own virtue and that of the PSP, and in so doing had reinforced Fidel's denunciation of the "pseudorevolutionaries" and "new sectarians." Nobody would have reason to suspect at that moment—or two days later, when Fidel would officially give her a clean bill of health—that she and her husband, who followed her on the stand, would be quietly placed under arrest a few months hence.

The Testimony of Major Joaquín Ordoqui. Like his wife Edith, whom he outranked as a vice-minister of the armed forces, Ordoqui was invited by the prosecutor to tell the court whatever he might wish to say about his knowledge of Marcos and related matters. A founding member of the PSP and now a white-haired figure already in his sixties, Ordoqui was conspicuously older than the witnesses who preceded him. In Mexico, he recalled, he had advised Marcos against joining a guerrilla group because he was not physically strong enough and his talents lay in another direction. Accordingly, he and Alfredo Guevara went to the Czech embassy to see about getting a scholarship for Marcos to study Czech literature in Prague. The scholarship was granted, but Marcos could not accept it because it provided only travel expenses and not living expenses in Prague, and "we couldn't spare the money from the revolutionary struggle."

Returning to Cuba, Ordoqui learned about Marcos's arrest. "I was perplexed," he went on to explain, for Marcos's behavior in Mexico had been very good. When Ordoqui discussed Marcos with the comrades of the Directorio, all they had against him were uncorroborated suspicions. For example, they said that he lived very extravagantly in Costa Rica, "but I know that he was poverty-stricken in Mexico, . . . so I wasn't impressed." When Marcos, after his release from jail in February 1959, told Ordoqui that he wanted to accept the Czech scholarship previously offered in Mexico, "I suggested that he shouldn't go with this hanging over your head." (This time, with the PSP apparently close to the purse strings of the revolutionary government, there seemed to be no problem of living expenses.) Marcos replied: "I've got a clear conscience. . . . I'll come back if they want me. . . . I can't prove my innocence, . . . it's up to them to prove my guilt."

After Marcos was extradited from Prague and imprisoned (more about this shortly), first Marcos's father and later both his father and grandfather came to see Ordoqui. They wanted him to look into the matter of Marcos's continued detention, but Ordoqui explained that it would not be proper for him to intervene. Then he received a letter from Marcos, which "Faure Chomón has described in detail." Soon after, Ordoqui discovered that a copy of the letter "is circulating from hand to hand," whereupon he spoke with the minister of the interior. "Marquitos is still in prison. What's going on?" he asked. The minister told him that he would have to see President Dorticós. When he did so, he was informed that "Marquitos confessed six

or seven months ago. . . . He has accused your wife of knowing what he
did." Edith was in Oriente at that time, at the other end of the island. Ordoqui phoned her and she returned at once. She insisted on a confrontation with Marcos, which ended with Marcos's retraction.

The high point of Ordoqui's testimony occurred when the prosecutor
interrupted him to ask a question: "While he was in Mexico did Marcos
Rodríguez apply for membership in the Partido Socialista Popular?" It was
in all likelihood intended to be an innocent question, but Ordoqui was
trapped. "As a matter of fact, he did ask me to put him up for membership," Ordoqui replied, as if it were a matter of no importance which had
slipped his mind, ". . . I sent his application to Cuba, and he was admitted." Thus, Marcos had returned to Cuba as a member of the PSP. What
the members of the Directorio had correctly assumed when they discussed
Marcos with the leadership of the PSP in Havana early in 1959, although
they refrained from spelling out their assumption in their testimony, was
now finally confirmed. Who in Cuba was responsible for admitting Marcos into the party? The question was never asked. Was his relationship with
the Juventad a factor in his favor? Was the party aware of the strong suspicions by the Directorio that he had informed on the victims of Humboldt
7? The prosecutor remained mercifully silent.

The Testimony of Carlos Rafael Rodríguez. Carlos Rafael, as he is commonly referred to in Cuba, was the only one in the top leadership of the
PSP in whom Fidel came to have full confidence. During World War II,
when the party and the Batista regime were allied in the common struggle
against the Axis, he had been a minister in Batista's cabinet, a fact that in
later years was never mentioned in the revolutionary press. In his middle
fifties at the time of the trial, well educated, something of an economist,
and politically sharp-sighted, he headed the National Institute of Agrarian
Reform (INRA) with the rank of minister. In 1972, when Fidel reorganized
the government bureaucracy according to the Soviet model, he was to become one of nine ministers promoted to the new rank of deputy prime
minister, and at the end of 1975 he became a member of the party politburo. Since then, excepting the Castro brothers, he has been the most influential person in the regime.

As could be anticipated, Carlos Rafael's testimony was well organized
and, from a political point of view, mature. He began by saying that there
were rumors that he was related to Marcos because they both had the same
surname. That he felt it necessary to deny the rumor—Rodríguez being as
common a name in Spanish-speaking countries as Smith is in English-

speaking countries—was another symptom of the disrepute in which the "old" Communists were held. He then went into considerable detail concerning Marcos's relations with the Juventud and the Cultural Society, and concluded that Marcos was no more than a "fellow traveler." He also reiterated the lack of hard evidence concerning Marcos's crime over the years, even after his extradition from Prague, which Carlos Rafael claimed was due to an unrelated matter.

Turning to the indictment of the PSP by Guillermo Jiménez and Faure Chomón, Carlos Rafael recalled some matters of past history that were conveniently forgotten by some and never known by most. After the Revolution, he explained, past animosities were put aside and relations between the PSP and the Directorio were very close. Jiménez, he said, "used to come to me as a friend for political orientation. . . . I was like an older brother. . . . Would he have come to see me if he thought the PSP produced informers?" And Chomón, among others in the Directorio, "studied Marxist texts with Valdés Vivó." Carlos Rafael then reminded Chomón that at one point in his testimony he had referred to Marcos as belonging to "two revolutionary organizations," meaning the Directorio as well as the PSP. "Those who attacked the palace," he continued, "were heroes, those who died and those among the survivors who remained good revolutionaries; but there were some who were later convicted of trafficking in cocaine, and another was shot as a traitor to the Revolution. I would never, never say that these persons were typical of the men who attacked the palace, nor that the fact that they used pistols in attacking the palace later led them to use pistols in order to assassinate the leaders of the Revolution."

It was an unexpected and astonishing disparagement of the reputation of the Directorio. The attack on the palace had been inscribed in the annals of revolutionary struggle as an unadulterated feat of self-sacrificing heroism, as a venerated symbol of the traditional Cuban resort to armed violence against a venal and tyrannical government. Though Fidel, when he took power, might well have preferred to downgrade the aborted coup —from the Sierra Maestra he publicly criticized it as thoughtless "putschism" when it occurred—the reckless attempt in broad daylight to assassinate Batista in his fortified bastion in the heart of Havana was still fresh in the memory of Cubans celebrating the overthrow of the dictatorship. Thus, Fidel incorporated the event into the official history of the Revolution, and each year on March 13 a public commemoration of the attack paid tribute to the heroes and martyrs of the Directorio. But were there really criminals, traitors, and armed thugs among them? Or were they all just "a bunch of gangsters," a charge indignantly rejected by Chomón at the first trial. It was an exceedingly hard and cruel blow that Carlos Rafael now struck against the detractors of the "old" Communists. And once more, skeletons rattled as closet doors were opened.

Carlos Rafael's defense and counterattack were the most effective of the statements made by former members of the PSP. They were also the most astute. Anticipating Fidel's call for unity two days later, he held out his own olive branch. He was "satisfied," he said, "with yesterday's clarification by comrade Guillermo Jiménez" concerning what he really meant when he used the word *formación*. As for Faure Chomón, "although his first speech lent itself to misinterpretation, . . . yesterday he clarified his meaning and I accept his intention and categorical explanation."

The Testimony of César Escalante. The final witness of the day was the director of the Committee of Revolutionary Orientation (COR), the regime's information and censorship control apparatus. An "old" Communist functionary like his disgraced elder brother Aníbal, César presented an impassioned defense of the PSP record, his "blood boiling," as he put it, at the infamous "insinuations" that the PSP was in any way responsible for the crime committed by Marcos and that the PSP "protected" Marcos after his return to Cuba. César even went so far as to defend his brother, something strictly taboo after Fidel had purged him from the party in 1962 and expelled him from Cuba. Aníbal, César conceded, made "errors," but he was always completely and loyally dedicated to the Revolution. Some people, César said, still enjoy blaming Aníbal for anything, including Marcos. "This is cowardly!" he exclaimed. "Aníbal is not in Cuba" and can't defend himself.[1]

Fidel, when his turn came to speak, said that he was impressed by César's "valor" in speaking up for his brother. What the general public did not know was that César was afflicted with an incurable cancer and had only a few months left to live. He was, as it were, on his deathbed, proclaiming something akin to a political last will and testament. Fidel could afford to be magnanimous.

---

1. At the time of the purge of the "sectarians," Fidel's main wrath fell on Aníbal Escalante, who was then de facto leader of the old Communists, and banished him, appropriately enough, to Moscow. At a later date, Fidel permitted him to return and manage a small farm. Early in 1968, Aníbal once more fell afoul of Fidel and was sentenced to a fifteen-year prison term for political dereliction. This episode is dealt with in a later chapter.

6

■

The Second Trial: Act III

Wednesday, March 25, 1964

ACTS I AND II, as it were, of the drama that Fidel was directing had been primarily aimed at one objective: to restore public confidence in the "old" Communists who had survived his purge of 1962 and whom he had incorporated into the upper levels of the administrative and party bureaucracy. However, the case of Marcos Rodríguez had also raised doubts about the integrity of the revolutionary government's dispensation of justice. Had there been negligence or collusion when Marcos was released from jail early in 1959? What in fact prompted his extradition from Czechoslovakia two years later? How was his confession obtained? What actually transpired at the confrontation with Edith García Buchaca? Why the long delay between the confession and the trial? In Act III, therefore, Fidel's scenario called for opening some of the hitherto secret files of the case to public scrutiny. It was a display of candor, typical of Fidel in those days, which despite gaps and awkward revelations would serve to bolster confidence in his regime.

The Testimony of the Department of State Security. Five officers who had worked on the case took the stand, one by one. The first had been in charge of investigating Marcos shortly after his return to Cuba from Mexico. He had placed Marcos under arrest and had taken him to the cell of one of Lt. Colonel Ventura's two bodyguards (the other by this time had been executed) who earlier had confirmed the identity of Marcos to Marta Jiménez, the widow of one of the martyrs. According to the arresting officer, the prisoner looked at Marcos and said: "'He is not the man.' . . . So I reported [to headquarters] that I was unable to obtain proof of the guilt of Marcos Rodríguez." Marcos was released two weeks after his arrest. There was no negligence or collusion, just lack of hard evidence. The explanation was credible, as far as it went, but it was not entirely satisfactory. Fidel, who was presumably listening on the radio, realized this and elaborated on the testimony the following day.

The next four witnesses revealed some important elements in the chronology and handling of the case. Marcos, it was explained, was flown back to Havana from Prague in early March 1961, on the express order of Raúl Castro. The reason given was that Marcos, who in effect had been acting as cultural attaché of the Cuban embassy in Prague, was in contact with functionaries of a number of capitalist embassies (it would be normal activity for a cultural officer, though nothing was said about this), and since he was suspected of having been the informer of Humboldt 7 (presumably Chomón and company had reactivated the suspicion, but no explanation was offered), he was susceptible to blackmail by foreign agents and could have been providing them with confidential information. At no point in the trial was it claimed that he had actually provided information to a foreign agent. Thus, it would appear that what motivated the extradition and second incarceration of Marcos was the unfinished business of Humboldt 7. In any event, it was an arbitrary decision by the Prime Minister's brother. However, it was not a matter that would disturb most of those listening to the trial. They would have no compassion for Marcos, and besides, they were already accustomed to the new socialist legality.

With Marcos safely tucked away in jail, and in the absence of any legal machinery that he—or any prisoner, for that matter—could set in motion either to be tried in court or released, there was no hurry to move on with the case. One would even imagine that Raúl Castro and the Department of State Security, busy with other matters, even forgot about Marcos. However that may be, it was not until July 1962—that is, fifteen months after Marcos's imprisonment in Havana (seventeen months after his arrest in Prague, as was to be revealed later)—that "I received orders to investigate the suspicions that Marcos Rodríguez was the informer" in the raid on Humbolt 7, according to a witness from State Security. This witness's account of the investigation, given in great detail, added nothing of significance to what was already public knowledge by this time. However, the impression gained was that the investigation was thorough. After concluding his testimony, the witness declared that "I reached the conclusion that Marcos Rodríguez was the informer."

Another witness testified that the interrogation (as distinct from the investigation) of Marcos began in January 1963, first by one security agent and then by two. It was candidly admitted that the objective was to obtain a confession, since without it there was not enough evidence to establish guilt. Put on the stand, the two interrogators described how, over a period of many weeks, they went about breaking the prisoner's resistance. "From the beginning, we tried to convince him that we had all the proof we needed," one witness explained. Applying psychological pressure—"utilizing the usual police methods," as the other interrogator put it—they succeeded "in drawing a net around Marcos" and reached "the critical moment." They made him believe, according to the witness, that a revolutionary tribunal had been set up to try him, and that, despite his denial of guilt, he would be punished because they had all the necessary evidence. "At this point," the witness affirmed, "we asked him if he was the informer. He replied, no. Immediately we asked him why he did it, that [we knew] he did it for money. He said, no, not for money, and the confession began. . . . Sobbing, . . . his head bowed, speaking slowly and pausing frequently, . . . he tried to justify why he did it."

The next day, Marcos was asked to write out his confession. It was a lengthy document which took several days to complete. Since it contained sensitive "political allegations," the head of State Security sent it directly to the Prime Minister. This must have been toward the end of April, or early May, 1963, as Castro's testimony on the following day made clear.

The Testimony of President Osvaldo Dorticós.[1] When Fidel learned that Marcos's confession implicated Edith García Buchaca in a cover-up of his crime, he "informed me and Raúl and nobody else," the President stated, "and because of the delicate political implications . . . he asked us to leave the matter in his hands." Some six months later (probably October 1963), Ordoqui went to see Dorticós, as previously related. He told the President about the letter that Marcos had written him (dated September 1962—that is, a year or so earlier) and about subsequent visits by Marcos's father and grandfather, and asked Dorticós to secure a quick decision concerning Marcos (at the time, it was some thirty months since Marcos's arrest in Prague).

"I saw Fidel right away," Dorticós testified, and obtained permission to inform Ordoqui that Marcos had confessed six months earlier and had

1. Dorticós, who was appointed president by Castro in mid-1959, relinquished his office to Castro after the new Cuban constitution was adopted in February 1976. Dorticós was also an original member of the party politburo, and as of 1980 was still a member.

implicated his wife. This led to her request for a confrontation with Marcos. "It was her idea," the President testified, "not ours, but we agreed." The meeting took place soon after, and among those invited to attend, Dorticós mentioned Faure Chomón and Blas Roca, as well as Joaquín Ordoqui. "I have the tapes with me," the witness told the court, "and I request permission to play them back at this time." It took about two hours for the tapes to unreel. Marcos's admission, in his own voice, that he had lied about Edith in his written confession was indisputable. But while for Castro's political problem of the moment Marcos's retraction was the highlight of the playback, what held the attention of the courtroom and radio audiences were Marcos's explanations of his motives and the remorse that he felt for his abhorrent behavior, and what these statements revealed of the deep emotional problems of a sensitive, highly politicized, and no doubt deviant personality.

"When I arrived at the apartment [Humboldt 7], I was very nervous because [I saw a] police car at the curb. . . . The boys called me chicken." It was the taped voice of Dorticós, now reading from Marcos's written confession. The voice continued: "I rushed out into the street like a crazy person. . . . That night I didn't sleep, the insults, incidents at the university, the way they belittled me kept hammering at my brain. What was my reaction? The most unjust, abnormal, and cruel. . . . I listened [over the radio] to the news of the assassinations. . . . I hadn't thought of this possibility, . . . only that they would be arrested. . . . I heard [on the radio] that I had escaped from the police, . . . and then I began to believe it myself. I fled, I don't know whether from the police or myself, horrified at what I had done. . . ."

At another point in the tape recording, Dorticós asked Marcos: "Why did you inform on your comrades?" *Marcos:* "I really can't find the words . . . to explain such a crime for which I deserve the death penalty. . . . They considered me to be wrapped up in theory, . . . not as a man of action. . . . I wanted to be involved in action, but they wouldn't let me. . . . Then I realized that the theoretical or political position . . . of these comrades was [not only wrong but] even harmful. . . . I considered them to be adventurers, terrorists. . . . I was a complete sectarian, . . . and a criminal one." *Dorticós:* "Why do you say 'criminal sectarian'?" *Marcos:* "At that time, my convictions were based on a single criterion: everything which did not conform to our [PSP] position was no good. I underestimated all other views. . . . This dogmatism . . . slowly led me to the conclusion that everything which was not Communist was harmful, and I found that certain events justified my ideas. . . . In addition, the comrades [of the Directorio] were constantly humiliating me. . . . And so all these things made me think at that moment that I really had a good reason [to inform the police]. . . . [*He begins to sob.*] . . . Excuse me."

Later in the recording, Dorticós asked: "Why did you persist so long in maintaining your innocence?" *Marcos*: "I wanted to spare the party the disgrace. . . ." At this point, Blas Roca was heard to ask: "But why would the disgrace fall on the party?" To which Marcos replied: "Because I was in fact a member, and the blame would be placed not only on the individual. . . . I could have been mistaken, . . . but I felt real damage to the party could be done."

The confrontation proper between Edith García Buchaca and Marcos was relatively short but tense. Marcos quickly backed down from his written confession. He had in fact not told her his "secret" but only "insinuated" something about it in connection with a discussion with her concerning China. Edith denied this emphatically and was backed up by her husband. "I did speak to him about my trip to China and how party members who made mistakes were rehabilitated," she said, "but the word *treason* was never mentioned. I could never have told him that a person who would betray a revolutionary, whoever he might be, could rehabilitate himself in any way or by whatever deed."

Marcos was silent, and the matter of "insinuation" was not pursued further. Dorticós then asked Marcos about his written confession: "Weren't you conscious you were lying [about Edith]?" Marcos explained that he had been through "a long interrogation, five or six hours" prior to writing his confession. "During that period I didn't sleep, I didn't eat. Possibly I was imagining things. . . . I don't know why I lied about Edith." The question of Marcos's letter to Ordoqui came up. What prompted him to tell Ordoqui that he was innocent? "It [the crime] was so monstrous," Marcos replied, "that I couldn't accept the fact that I had done it. . . . I even reached the point where—and I am not demented or crazy—I thought what I was writing was the truth. And now a rational person may wonder: how is it possible? Is this fellow a complete scoundrel or schizophrenic?" *Dorticós*: "And what are you?" *Marcos*: "I am a scoundrel. I'm not a schizophrenic."

Other questions dealt with matters of fact. Concerning the plentiful supply of money he was observed to have had during the time he spent in Costa Rica, Marcos explained that he was living off the earnings of a prostitute for whom he procured customers. "She gave me lots of money," he said, "but I became disgusted with this kind of life. I wrote about it to Dysis [girlfriend of one of the martyrs] in Buenos Aires, and she sent me money for the trip [to Argentina]."

The playback of the tapes ended, and Dorticós summed up for the court: "As a result of the confrontation, I decided the accusation against Edith was totally false. Everybody at the meeting, including Faure Chomón, agreed with me. We were also convinced of the guilt of the defendant. I shall be glad to answer any questions." There were undoubtedly many questions that could be asked, but nobody took up the President's offer. The court adjourned "until tomorrow at 9 P.M."

7

■

The Second Trial: Act IV and Epilogue

A Provocative Editorial

AN UNEXPECTED COMMOTION occurred on March 26, the day Fidel was to take the stand. It was created by an editorial which began on the front page of *Revolución* and carried on at length on an inside page. Entitled "Decir Siempre la Verdad" (Always Speak the Truth), it lambasted *Hoy* for suppressing the news of the opening of the trial, and Valdés Vivó and César Escalante for deliberately distorting in their testimony both the words and intentions of *Revolución* in reporting the first trial. It was Marcos, not *Revolución*, the editorial said, who claimed that he was a member of the Juventud Socialista, and this is what we reported: "*Revolución* understood and continues in its understanding that the policy of the Revolution and the declared intention of our Commander-in-Chief has been always to tell the truth." They reported the opening of the trial, they said, as a matter of news, and then the editorial added, with scarcely concealed malice, "also out of a sense of respect and justice for the four martyrs. . . ." It is precisely the "news vacuum," the editorial went on to say, "which sows confusion" and creates "insidious rumors" spread by troublemakers. We who "suffered from the aggressions of sectarianism," the editorial continued in a damning reference to the time (mid-1961) when its weekly literary supplement was censored by the "old" Communists, "cannot at this time fall into the same vicious practice which did such great damage, and still does, to the great task of promoting revolutionary unity." Echoing the editorial, "Siquitrilla" in his column (it was to be his last) in the same issue of *Revo-*

lución concluded that "giving the people the facts enlightens and educates them and never befuddles them."

Despite the ritualistic invocation of the "Commander-in-Chief," *Revolución* was taking a position which Fidel had already clearly and unmistakably condemned. In later years, this would have been not merely foolhardy but suicidal, but in the spring of 1964 there was still a margin of tolerance for dissent "within the Revolution." Nevertheless, the shock of the nearly direct challenge to the Prime Minister reverberated through the ranks of political and administrative functionaries in Havana and heightened the crisis. Fidel, on the eve of his appearance in the courtroom, was unexpectedly placed under pressure to redress the imbalance which he had created between his "old" and "new" Communists.

The Testimony of Fidel Castro

Shortly after 9 P.M. on March 26, Fidel took the stand and was sworn in. Hundreds of thousands of Cubans tuned in to see and listen over the national television and radio hookups. Among the courtroom spectators could be discerned practically the entire leadership of the party and government. Conspicuously absent was Ché Guevara, who was in Geneva heading Cuba's delegation to the first meeting of the United Nations Conference on Trade and Development. Ché's name had nowhere appeared in any of the information made public during the unraveling of events in the case of Marcos Rodríguez. It was strictly "an affair among Cubans," and in this respect Ché remained an Argentine and a foreigner even though, after the triumph of Castro's insurrection, a special decree—probably unprecedented in all the annals of history—had officially pronounced him to be a "native born" citizen of Cuba.

Continuing with the simulated procedure of a trial—the fiction now held it to be the "fourth session in the appeal [of the defendant] before the Supreme Court"—the presiding judge signaled to the state prosecutor that he could begin the "interrogation" of the witness. Whereupon the prosecutor addressed the witness with the deference due his rank: "Comrade Prime Minister, a number of important political questions have been raised in this trial. We beg you to tell the court anything which you think can throw light on these matters."

A "Double" Trial. Fidel, however, had come prepared to speak on both the criminal and political aspects of what he said had become a "double trial." Therefore, he explained, "it is necessary to speak before two tribunals: the tribunal of law and the tribunal of the people." He would separate the two and first speak of the criminal aspects of the case. Castro, it will be recalled, had begun his career as a lawyer. Thus, he went about his task with professional competence, but also with his special flair for the unexpected. Shortly after he began to speak, he explained that he had himself interrogated Marcos several days before. He would now read the stenographic record of his conversation with Marcos.

An Exceptional Interrogation. One would have wished that the meeting between the Prime Minister and the prisoner had been videotaped, for although their conversation added little of substance to what was already known in the case, a view of the setting and the faces of the interlocutors would have given all the poignancy of the human drama reflected in the words related by Fidel. "I thought of bringing a tape recorder, but perhaps the microphone would disturb you so I brought along a stenographer instead," said Fidel, opening the conversation. "Perhaps you would prefer it this way," he asked. "How do you feel? Don't you feel well?" Marcos must have been stunned, possibly turned pale or broke out into a cold sweat. "It doesn't matter," Marcos replied, "you may proceed."

Fidel then went on with remarkable patience and skill to offer Marcos an opportunity partly to redeem himself by telling the truth. *Fidel:* "Are you conscious of the great harm you did?" *Marcos:* "Yes, very conscious." (Marcos apparently began to sob at this point, because Fidel said something about keeping calm.) *Fidel:* ". . . If you could choose between continuing to do harm even after your death . . . and acting in such a manner so as to avoid doing more harm, would you choose to avoid doing more harm?" *Marcos:* "Certainly, of course." Fidel then stated that while Marcos explained some things very clearly, in his reference to other persons there were contradictions that could create much harm. "I believe," Fidel said, "that you might want to think of doing something so that all those who condemn you will have to agree that in the end you performed a good deed." Fidel had done his homework. The presence of an exalted but gentle father confessor who knew how to exploit the prisoner's feeling of remorse might unlock the truth. "It is an opportunity," the Prime Minister continued, "for you to clear your conscience burdened with all the things that have happened." Marcos replied in the affirmative.

No matter how carefully and deeply Fidel probed, Marcos seemed to be unable rather than unwilling to supply more "logical" or less confusing explanations for his behavior. Frequently his answers were simply "I don't know," or "I'm not sure," or "perhaps." However, on one important matter Fidel curiously failed to press Marcos sufficiently, although we have no way of knowing whether he had edited the transcript he was reading. When Fidel questioned Marcos as to what made him believe he would be secure when he decided to return to Cuba from Mexico, Marcos replied: "I thought, like I told Edith, and she told me: well, you have to become more faithful to the party, to continue struggling [for the cause], so I thought. . . ." But Fidel did not let him finish, nor did he ask him point-blank whether he thought the party would protect him, for this is what seemed to be in the back of Marcos's mind.

Negligence Denied, Guilt Confirmed. Putting aside the transcript, Fidel focused his attention on two important questions. The investigation by the Department of Security, he said, revealed that Marcos gave an accurate description of the apartment where he met with Lt. Colonel Ventura. "If there is a suspicion that the confession was false," Fidel argued, "Marcos could have invented some things but not describe an apartment which he had not actually seen." This effectively disposed of whatever doubts still may have lingered concerning whether Marcos was the informer. As for the seemingly hasty execution early in 1959 of the two police bodyguards who were in a position to identify Marcos, Fidel produced the records of the dates of the trials and executions and convincingly argued that there was no interference with the normal course of justice. However, this did not answer the question as to why, given the seriousness of the accusations against Marcos, the executions could not have been postponed until such time as a more thorough interrogation of the prisoners and of the charges against Marcos had been made.

Summing up the case against Marcos, Fidel declared that he was completely convinced of his guilt. "It would be a waste of time," he added, "for me to speculate about what social or family experiences created this kind of person. Perhaps those with the time and competence to analyze these matters can provide an explanation." He went on to say that he believed that Marcos was entirely sane and acted with premeditation, "grasping this opportunity to unload his hatred and urge for vengeance." Fidel seemed to imply that the motivation for the betrayal was purely personal and not political. However, the fact that he did not specifically reject a political motivation or conditioning for the crime was probably not an oversight.

Political Judgment. It was late when Fidel turned from the legal to the political aspects of the trial and unleashed a torrent of rambling and frequently impassioned rhetoric that held viewers and listeners spellbound until long past midnight. Eagerly awaited was the judgment he would pass on Faure Chomón and Joaquín Ordoqui. Faure, he said, must bear the responsibility for converting the trial into a political confrontation, but without meaning to do so. "His close ties with the victims understandably moved him deeply, . . . and there were things that were not clear," Fidel added, but the "correct thing would have been for him to bring these matters before the party leadership." (What Fidel did not say was that Faure had good reason to believe that the party leadership would have swept the whole mess under the rug.) At the same time, Fidel praised Chomón for the "positive elements" in his testimony at the second trial (when he recanted, it will be recalled). "His Marxist exposition was very firm, very clear," he said. The irony of one amateur "Marxist" approving the "Marxism" of another amateur went unnoticed, except perhaps by the "old" Communists, who would prudently suppress their awareness of it. In any event, although Fidel's reprimand was humiliating for Chomón, it was tempered with "understanding" and a patronizing pat on the back and could be interpreted as incorporating forgiveness. Thus, as previously noted, the onetime leader of the Directorio and participant in the suicidal attack on Batista's quarters in March 1957 survived the storm in March 1964.

(Of more than passing interest was Fidel's explanation of how Marcos's testimony at the first trial, claiming affiliation with the "old" Communists, happened to be published. "Dorticós was out of town," he explained, "and the people in the press had a new and unexpected problem on their hands. They had no instructions and nowhere to turn, so they went ahead and published." [Apparently Fidel was also inaccessible.] Fidel was, of course, referring to *Revolución*. *Hoy* did not need instructions to suppress Marcos's statement.)

The full force of Castro's wrath fell on Joaquín Ordoqui, who should have recognized, Fidel said, the "unreliability" of Marcos and the "confusion in his head" when he was recommended by Ordoqui for "membership or renewal" in the PSP. (Was "renewal" a slip? Fidel apparently retained the possibility that Marcos was already a member of the PSP when he informed on the martyrs, despite the vigorous denial of the PSP witnesses at the trial.) In 1959, Fidel said, Ordoqui should have seen to it that Marcos remained in Cuba, and he should have requested the Czech embassy to cancel Marcos's scholarship. In his confession, Marcos had made it abundantly clear that his trip to Prague and his subsequent function at the Cuban embassy resulted from active sponsorship by the PSP leadership, with which he maintained close liaison, but Fidel preferred not to

comment on this. As for Ordoqui's effort to intercede with Dorticós on behalf of Marcos, "I confess I became very angry," Fidel exclaimed, "because
he was so simpleminded, . . . so lacking in intelligence. . . . And this fellow [Marcos] was even trying to implicate his wife. . . ." Soon after the
trial, Ordoqui publicly admitted his errors,[1] but it was hard to imagine that
he would long retain his job as vice-minister of the armed forces or his
position in the party leadership. What could not be anticipated, as previously noted, was that in November (eight months later) Ordoqui would
be placed under arrest. But more on that later.

Concerning Ordoqui's wife Edith, Fidel explained that when he visited Marcos in his cell, he asked the stenographer to leave so as to remain
alone with the prisoner. This way he had hoped that Marcos would reveal
why he had contradicted himself concerning his original claim that he had
revealed his crime to Edith, but Fidel got no satisfactory answer. Nevertheless, if only as a matter of "principle, . . . the word of a confessed and
proven informer can never be given credence against the word of a revolutionary," Fidel concluded, giving Edith a clean bill of health. Her arrest
eight months later therefore came as an even greater shock than the detention of her husband.

Thus, with respect to the "principals" in the political confrontation—
Chomón, Ordoqui, and his wife—the score was only partially favorable to
the "old" Communists. However, with the other points that Fidel allocated to them, they ended up with a very comfortable lead. Extravagant
praise went to cancer-stricken César Escalante. And on the crucial matter
of PSP "sectarianism" in the days before the Revolution, Fidel all but con-
doned it. They were Communists in a bourgeois society, he said, and their
"sectarianism was understandable. . . . They had to defend themselves."
Then there was the rivalry among the various groups that were struggling
against the Batista tyranny. "As a matter of fact," Fidel added, "I don't believe it would have been the worst thing that could have happened in those
days if the [revolutionary] organizations . . . went so far as to spy on one
another. I say this in all sincerity." Here, in his eagerness to rehabilitate the
"old" Communists, he inadvertently opened a window on the sordid aspects of the cutthroat competition in which his own and opposing organizations were engaged at the time. Fidel's remark about spying would be the
last time during his regime that anything which might tarnish the origins
of the Revolution would be revealed in public.

1. *Cuba Socialista*, May 1964, p. 58.

The Press Rebuked. Fidel came down hard on what remained of Cuba's "undisciplined" press, promising in effect that it had had its last fling. "*Revolución* . . . has given us many headaches at different times," he confessed, but this time it went so far as "to pour oil on the fire." As for Cazalis and his column "Siquitrilla," Fidel said, "he inflamed the dispute over the movies and art [last December] when we faced . . . more urgent problems. . . . Movies and art could wait for ten years. . . ."[2] Well, it is one thing to stimulate controversy among intellectuals, but it's a much more serious matter to stir up conflict among revolutionaries. . . ." And in the name of "truth," Fidel added scornfully. Cazalis and others claim that the "truth is never harmful. . . . This is an abstract idea of truth," he said, expounding a specious argument which few of his listeners could grasp. "Truth is a concrete entity, a means [*función*] to a noble end. . . . When truth is used for an evil purpose, then it is no longer the truth." Since Fidel was the ultimate source of what was a "noble end" and an "evil purpose," in effect he was saying that he would rule on what was or was not the truth. The spectacle of Castro embracing this kind of pseudo-Marxist sophistry was indeed a melancholy one.

Fidel made it clear that Cazalis had written his last column.[3] "It is far better to do without the 'marvelous' collaboration of this señor," he exclaimed, "and to create new and brilliant journalists capable of attaining the lofty cultural goals for which our people are striving, so that in ten years our press will be better than it is today." Alas, the "goals" were achieved, and in much less time than ten years. Cuban journalism, by almost any definition, disappeared and was replaced by the deadly monotony of shrill exhortation, bombastic slogans, and pompous ritual. It was an irony that, having achieved nearly universal literacy, the Cuban people found themselves

2. A proposal by Blas Roca, editor of *Hoy* and spokesman for the "old" Communists, to prohibit the screening of "degenerate" capitalist films was denounced by *Revolución* and the "new" Communist intellectuals. For a full account of this episode, see my *The Rise and Decline of Fidel Castro* (Berkeley and Los Angeles: University of California Press, 1972), pp. 347 ff.

3. In a notable series of six articles published by the Caracas (Venezuela) *La República* (February 4–10, 1966), under the general title of "Cuba: From Popular Revolution to Personal Dictatorship," Cazalis wrote (February 4, p. 7): "One person saved me from going to jail: Ché Guevara." Six months later, Ché persuaded Castro to allow Cazalis to emigrate. At the time, Fidel was again in a mellow mood and offered Cazalis employment, but not in journalism. Cazalis preferred to leave Cuba.

in many respects among the least informed and most misinformed in the civilized world.[4]

The Prerogatives of Power. Among the various and sundry matters which Fidel disposed of that night was one which went directly to the heart of the system of governance which guided the destinies of the Cuban Revolution. The issue which led Fidel to define the nature and extent of his authority was his handling of Marcos's confession. Aware that his arbitrary "impounding" of the document had created both suspicion and resentment, he found it necessary to justify his behavior. He explained that he received the confession "about a year ago" (which would be late March 1963), at which time he was busy preparing for his first trip to the USSR (he departed at the end of April). The confession, he said, raised important questions, and besides, "there was no hurry. . . . This señor was in the hands of our security corps." He therefore informed only Dorticós and his own brother and asked them to leave the matter in his hands. "I did not believe that it would be correct to present this document to the Leadership of our Party," he declared. "It is my understanding that I had the right to proceed in this manner, . . . and [this right] is inherent in the prerogatives of a person who has the responsibilities and burdens which I bear." So that there would be no doubt as to what he meant, he made his point again in the simplest terms: "It is obvious that in the fulfillment of our [my] obligations, we [I] have the right to take the time which may be necessary, and to give the explanations which may be necessary, when it may be necessary."

4. Toward the end of 1978, something of the environment in which Cuban journalists and other writers worked was revealed in an interview given to a Spanish journalist by Roberto Fernández Retamar, poet, magazine editor, and professor at the University of Havana. Explaining that only material "which is not ideologically harmful to our peoples" was suitable for publication, he added: "In my country there is no censorship, and article 38 of the Constitution of the Republic says, 'Artistic creativity is free.' There is no restriction other than that of attacking the Revolution, which I think is an enormously broad and noble principle. And now you will ask me, 'Who decides whether a work is attacking the Revolution?' We do. When I read something that has been submitted to the magazine, I can detect it. The Revolution is not an entelechy. Like it or not, we the revolutionaries are the Revolution" (*Granma Weekly Review*, October 29, 1978). The late Chilean poet Pablo Neruda (Nobel Prize for Literature, 1971) was not far off the mark when, after an earlier encounter with the Cuban poet-editor-professor, he described him as a cultural "sergeant" and "just one more among the political and literary arrivistes of our time" (Pablo Neruda, *Memoirs* [New York: Farrar, Straus and Giroux, 1976], pp. 299 and 327).

The corollary to this principle was the need to eliminate the "lack . . . of discipline and responsibility, . . . [the lack] of a Marxist-Leninist conception of life . . . and revolutionary behavior."

Fidel wound up his discourse with a lengthy and impassioned exhortation for unity. "We have created something greater than ourselves," he exclaimed. "The Revolution must not devour its own children! . . . No faction can be permitted to annihilate another. . . . The law of Saturn must be rejected!" The truth of the matter was that the Cuban Revolution had not been, and in the future would not be, immune to the "law of Saturn," but, compared to other revolutions, its toll was much more modest. For this, most of the credit must go to Fidel's assuming and maintaining a position of unrivaled authority from the very beginning and to the uncommon skill with which he exercised that authority.

On March 30, four days after Fidel's speech, the court upheld the death penalty decreed at the end of Marcos's first trial. He was presumably executed by firing squad shortly after sentence was pronounced.[5]

Epilogue

Several months later, with the trial now all but forgotten and revolutionary "unity" firmly restored, Ordoqui and his wife suddenly and quietly disappeared from sight. The news spread in informed circles that they had been

5. The chronology of events leading up to Marcos's execution can be reconstructed with reasonable accuracy as follows: (1) Marcos informed the police on April 20, 1957. (2) He went into "exile" in mid-June 1957. (3) He returned to Cuba in late January 1959. (4) Marcos's first arrest, followed by his quick release, occurred in February 1959. (5) Marcos departed for Prague in May 1959. (6) He was acting cultural affairs attaché in the Cuban embassy in Prague during the entire year of 1960. (7) He was arrested in Prague on January 10, 1961. (8) He was extradited to Havana and imprisoned in early March 1961. (9) The investigation by the Department of State Security began in July 1962, eighteen months after Marcos's arrest in Prague. (10) Marcos's letter to Ordoqui asserting his innocence and protesting his twenty-one months of detention without charges was dated September 10, 1962. (11) Marcos's interrogation by the Department of State Security began in January 1963. (12) Marcos's confession was obtained and forwarded to Castro at the end of March 1963, twenty-seven months after his arrest in Prague. (13) Ordoqui, unaware of Marcos's confession, spoke in September 1963 with the minister of the interior concerning the long detention. (14) Marcos was confronted with Edith García Buchaca in October 1963. (15) The first trial was held on March 14–16, 1964, thirty-nine months after Marcos's arrest in Prague. (16) Marcos was given the death sentence on March 18, 1964. (17) The second trial was held on March 23–26, 1964. (18) The death sentence was confirmed on March 30, 1964.

arrested as suspected agents of the CIA. There was naturally speculation that the real reason was that they had been in fact more than negligent in their relations with Marcos Rodríguez, and that Castro had deliberately delayed their punishment until it would not disturb the refurbished image of Cuba's pioneer Communists or embarrass their sponsors in Moscow.

The years went by, with no word of the two who had vanished, until April 17, 1973, when *Granma* (successor to *Revolución* and *Hoy*) published an official statement entitled "Political Bureau's Decision in the Case of Joaquín Ordoqui Mesa."[6] According to the statement, he "had been suspended from his positions in the Party and Government . . . and placed under arrest on November 16, 1964." The reason given was that "serious evidence" had come to light "indicating that since his stay in Mexico [in 1958]" he "had been in personal contact with an enemy agent who was intending to recruit him." Because Ordoqui "denied any guilt, . . . it became clear that the investigation would take a long time." In January 1965, he was removed from prison and placed under house arrest, "a situation that has continued since that time."

Eventually, according to the statement, Ordoqui was "confronted . . . with the documents" in his case "and again denied that he had collaborated with the enemy." Nevertheless, a recommendation was sent up to the Political Bureau of the Communist Party, "expressing a unanimous conviction of guilt." But in view of the fact that "no evidence of definite juridical value had turned up to confirm the indications of collaboration, the best thing would be not to put him on trial." Acting on this recommendation, and taking into consideration Ordoqui's advanced age and precarious health (and with no expression of regret for his nearly nine years of detention), the Political Bureau decided to "file the investigation," suspend the "restrictions against him," and revoke "his Party membership and all responsibility in the Revolutionary Government."

Whatever else may be credible in this bizarre communication, it appeared that Ordoqui's stubborn refusal to confess had saved his skin, although not much else. As for Edith García Buchaca, one could assume that she shared some or all of her husband's ordeal, although no word of her fate has thus far been released.

6. *Granma Weekly Review*, April 22, 1973.

8
■

Toward a Rational Economic Strategy

The Primacy of Agriculture

THE YEAR 1964 was designated in the revolutionary calendar as the "Year of the Economy." There was reason in the beginning to be less skeptical than the experience of the previous two years would justify. The "Year of Planning" (1962) and the "Year of Organization" (1963), both of which were focused on the economy, had conspicuously failed even to approximate their objectives. What raised expectations was the new strategy of economic development worked out in agreement with, and underwritten by, the Soviet Union. Priority was assigned to agriculture, once more dominated by sugarcane as it was under capitalism. Industrial development would be limited to the needs of agriculture—for example, farm implements, fertilizer, and irrigation equipment—and to increasing production of construction materials, especially cement, and consumer goods such as refrigerators, stoves, textiles, and shoes.

Sugar production was scheduled to reach ten million metric tons by 1970, roughly double the annual average in the decade before the Revolution, and more than two and a half times the figure for 1963. Sugar export earnings would finance the import of capital goods and raw materials required for the expansion and modernization of the entire economy. They would also pay for the import of consumer goods that could not, or should not for reasons of cost, be produced in Cuba.

After sugar in the agricultural sector, emphasis was to be placed on the production of a variety of foods, including meat and dairy products and other staples that would provide the Cuban people with an abundant and sound diet. It was expected that beef would eventually even become a significant export, rivaling tobacco, traditionally in second place after sugar. The production of citrus fruit would be greatly increased and would provide another source of export income. A substantial investment in fishing was scheduled, with an eye on both domestic and foreign consumption.[1] In short, the new strategy was to be based on the exploitation of Cuba's three principal natural resources, with which it is copiously endowed: sun, soil, and sea.

In this scheme, the original dream of basic industrialization involving complex metallurgical, machine-building, and heavy chemical installations was abandoned. It was a dream inspired in part by the Soviet model, but perhaps more by the theories concerning the cause and cure of underdevelopment emanating from the then Chilean-based United Nations Economic Commission for Latin America, at the time directed by the prestigious Argentine economist Raúl Prebisch. Along with industrialization, according to the Prebisch school, a corollary requirement for overcoming underdevelopment was the elimination of "monoculture," or excessive dependence on a single export commodity—in the case of Cuba, sugar. A leading advocate of industrialization, with a corresponding downgrading of sugar, was Ché Guevara, who appropriately enough became Castro's first minister of industries early in 1961. On the technical side there was Regino Boti, a Cuban economist on Prebisch's staff, who soon after the Revolution returned to Havana accompanied by several of his United Nations colleagues. Boti in due time set up the Central Planning Board, on the East European model, serving as its director with the additional title of minister of the economy.

Experience proved, however, that a new developmental strategy was needed. What easily might have been foreseen was now clear. Cuba, unlike, for example, Brazil or Mexico or even Venezuela, lacked both the energy and other resources for the kind of industrialization envisaged by the

1. A decade later, modest success was achieved in the export of citrus and fish products, in the latter case primarily frozen shrimp and crayfish, marketed as "Caribbean lobster." Significant beef exports failed to materialize, while domestic meat rations, including beef, were still skimpy fifteen years later: one pound per person per ten days (*The Christian Science Monitor*, January 31, 1979). By the end of 1964, nickel exports had permanently displaced tobacco from second to third place. This was mainly due to a marked decline in tobacco production, with no sign of revival at the end of the 1970s.

Latin American economists in the United Nations. Moreover, "monoculture," it turned out, could play a positive as well as negative role in economic development. Nor could the prevailing Marxist theory concerning the primacy of industry, and particularly heavy industry, in the building of a socialist economy square with Cuban reality. The experience of Rumania or Bulgaria or North Korea, let alone the Soviet Union, was simply not relevant to Cuba. Thus, from a doctrinal point of view, the new strategy could also be termed "revisionist," although since it raised no public dispute in the Marxist international community, its departure from orthodoxy by and large remained unacknowledged.

Marxist Theory Revised

An exception that should be noted was a lengthy article by Carlos Romeo, "Acerca del Desarrollo Económico de Cuba" (Concerning the Economic Development of Cuba), which appeared in *Cuba Socialista* in December 1965. Romeo, a Chilean economist employed by the Cuban government, set himself the task of belatedly reconciling the new strategy with Marxist doctrine. "It is an old truth," he boldly declared, "that when theory does not fit the facts, theory must be modified and not vice versa." Thus, after a lengthy and generally sound excursion into the "facts," he concluded that the indispensable role of the "production of the means of production" in socialist economic development, according to classic Marxist prescription, had been taken over in Cuba by foreign trade, based primarily on the export of sugar. By way of theoretical support, he had to be satisfied with quoting a footnote from Paul Baran's *The Political Economy of Growth* (New York: Monthly Review Press, 1957): "Export industries can be converted into 'industries that manufacture producers' goods,' since their product —foreign exchange—can be transformed into capital goods." [2] Baran's notion, apparently an afterthought, turned out to be sensible enough, although in a Marxist frame of reference it smacked of heresy. It was perhaps more than a coincidence that Romeo's article appeared at a time when Fidel was broadly hinting at new heresies to come. Romeo quoted Fidel as saying in his speech on July 26, 1965: "In a world with different levels of culture . . . and political power, . . . it is very important—especially for small countries—. . . to develop revolutionary ideas with their own heads." [3]

2. Page 13. Baran's text is here retranslated from the Spanish.
3. Romeo, "Acerca del Desarrollo," pp. 23–24.

Impediments to Development

If the new strategy for economic development appeared to be rational, a rational implementation of the strategy would be quite another matter. By 1964, the normal dislocations to be expected in any transition from a capitalist to a socialist economy had been compounded by the reckless speed with which it had taken place. Except for greatly reduced segments of the agricultural and service sectors and the survival of a limited number of small workshops—all closely regulated by the government—private enterprise had ceased to exist. The Cuban economy—overnight, so to speak—became one of the most completely, if not *the* most completely, socialized in the world.

This accomplishment was hailed as a great revolutionary-ideological victory, and the enthusiasm carried over into the sphere of economic planning and management. If central planning and management were essential features of a socialist economy, and the inherent source of its superiority over capitalism, then it followed that the more centralization, the more truly socialist and, ipso facto, efficient the Cuban economy would be. In Havana, enormous bureaucracies mushroomed in short order, and before long they were making literally thousands of decisions per week. These concerned not only major questions of national scope such as capital investments, allocation of basic resources, national production targets, and foreign trade, but also local administrative details such as shifting the warehousing of paper from one building to another in a town two hundred miles from Havana, or scheduling the planting of beans on a state farm in Oriente province.

Later, at the height of his largely unproductive campaign against the evils of bureaucracy (which he attributed to "petty bourgeois mentality"), Fidel gave some amusing examples of administrative absurdities. "Here is a case that really happened," he said. "There was a bar in Baracoa [500 miles east of Havana]. . . . The man in charge was almost always drunk. This went on for months and months until the central office [in Havana] remembered it was running a bar in Baracoa, discovered the manager was a drunkard, and decided to appoint a new manager. Is it correct that a shop in Baracoa be supervised by the Central Government? Or a laundry, for example? Should a laundry in Baracoa, in Manzanillo, or Nicaro be run by the Central Government?"[4]

4. Speech at Santa Clara, July 26, 1965 (*Política Internacional*, 11–12 [third and fourth trimesters, 1965], 192).

Even under more favorable circumstances, excessive centralization—as was earlier demonstrated in eastern Europe—would result in an exceedingly cumbersome system slow to respond to the normal stream of fluctuating conditions and denied the timely input of experience, to say nothing of the benefits of initiative, at the middle and lower levels of management. But, in Cuba, circumstances could hardly have been less favorable. The ministries were mainly staffed with technically innocent personnel. Statistics were rudimentary and the network of communications haphazard. Thus, the quantity and quality of information, its availability, and the expertise to use it were at a very low level. Decision-making at any level frequently became a matter of intuition. Under these conditions, the Cuban version of socialist planning and management of the economy could be aptly described as organized chaos. Thus, production fell, distribution was erratic, crops frequently rotted in the fields, and imported machinery and equipment rusted on the docks. In part stemming from planning and management failures, there was an acute shortage of manpower and a considerable decline in the productivity of laborers whose incentive to work was lowered, among other factors, by the spectacle of wasted effort.[5]

Survival Factors

Living and working in this "organized chaos"—I lectured on economic geography at the University of Havana and served as a consultant to the ministry of foreign trade—I constantly wondered why the economy did not break down completely. Massive Soviet aid was the most important part of the explanation. The wastage of the aid was painful to observe. The loss was high. My guess was that, excepting what went to the military establishment, in 1964—and later, for that matter—between a third and a quarter went down the drain. However, what remained was still enough to keep the economy hobbling along. Then again, the loss varied from sector to sector. Petroleum and food imports, for example, were reasonably well handled. Oil refineries, power plants, and flour mills, limited in number, were largely manned by skilled workers who stayed on the job after the Revolution and continued to work as they always had, a matter perhaps of sheer habit.

5. For an analysis of planning and management failures during the 1960s, see B. H. Pollitt, "Employment Plans, Performance and Future Prospects in Cuba," in *Prospects for Employment Opportunities in the Nineteen Seventies*, ed. Ronald Robinson and Peter Johnston (London: Cambridge University Overseas Study Committee, Her Majesty's Stationery Office, 1971), pp. 57–76.

Given these conditions and a measure of government priority for "strategic" goods, the supplies of such indispensables as gasoline, electricity, and bread could be maintained most of the time at acceptable levels.

The rationing of food and other basic consumer goods, although a very large-scale and complex operation, was another "strategic" function of the economy that managed to overcome the worst impediments of the prevailing disorder. Here, the well developed prerevolutionary network of wholesale and retail outlets, and part of the corresponding personnel, were assets that were available and, given priority attention, could be incorporated into the new system. Finally, Cubans were no less inventive than other peoples in similar circumstances. The deficiencies of the rationing system were corrected by the gray and black markets where a large variety of legitimately and illegitimately acquired goods were bartered or bought and sold. Among others, "dealers" in automobile parts filched from government repair shops did a thriving business.

In the countryside, small private farmers concealed vegetable gardens in the middle of the sugarcane fields that they were obliged to cultivate under government contract. In the cities, vacant lots would be taken over by neighbors and planted with such crops as onions, garlic, lettuce, and bananas. Never lacking before the Revolution, these were now always in short supply and frequently unobtainable. In this case, however, there were problems with the lack of fertilizer and the control of pests, and especially with the lack of know-how. Most city dwellers in Cuba, unlike those in a number of Latin American countries, had long been thoroughly urbanized, while the experience of many recent settlers from rural areas was restricted to sugarcane.

A Tolerable Situation

All in all, it would be safe to say that until the further decline in consumer supplies in the late 1960s and the beginning of the 1970s, life for a large majority of the people was still tolerable; and for the fifteen or twenty percent of the population formerly in the lowest income group, life on the whole was better than before the Revolution. There was full employment and job security with greatly relaxed work discipline; social services had been notably expanded and improved; and with mass meetings, movies, beaches, baseball, and Fidel's speeches, there was plenty of entertainment. Even the acute housing shortage, the country's most serious social problem, was mitigated by the fact that in Cuba's benign climate people spent much time outdoors all year around.

Thus, "organized chaos" was not synonymous with crisis. However, there was now a keen awareness in top circles, including Fidel himself, that with the commitments undertaken in the new development strategy, the glaring defects in economic planning and management had to be corrected. Such was the background against which a great polemic burst upon the Cuban scene early in 1964.

9

■

The Great Debate

BEGINNING IN FEBRUARY 1964, two sharply opposed views of a major economic issue surfaced in the pages of several specialized journals and over
the course of the year developed into a formidable dispute.[1] It concerned
the question of (1) whether Cuba's state enterprises should operate under
the so-called "self-financing system," that is, with a large amount of financial autonomy, using bank credit and other quasi-commercial methods of
transacting business in the "socialist market," and thereby motivated to cut
costs and increase profits; or (2) whether they should be centrally administered as departments of a single national "super-enterprise," namely the
Cuban government, in which case their funds would be allocated peri-
odically from the national budget, which would absorb the profits and
losses incurred, as the case might be. In the latter kind of arrangement,

---

1. The most important articles appeared in *Cuba Socialista*, at the time the
de facto official monthly party organ. In chronological order, they were as follows:
(1) Marcelo Fernández, "Desarrollo y funciones de la banca socialista en Cuba"
(Development and Functions of the Socialist Bank in Cuba), February 1964, pp.
32–50; (2) Ernesto Ché Guevara, "La banca, el crédito y el socialismo" (The
Bank, Credit, and Socialism), March 1964, pp. 23–41; (3) Charles Bettelheim,
"Formas y métodos de la planificación socialista y nivel de desarrollo de las fuerzas productivas" (Forms and Methods of Socialist Planning and the Level of Development of Productive Forces), April 1964, pp. 51–78; (4) Ernesto Ché Guevara,
"La planificación socialista, su significado" (Socialist Planning, Its Meaning), June
1964, pp. 13–24; (5) Joaquín Infante, "Características del funcionamiento de la
empresa autofinanciada" (Characteristics of the Functioning of the Self-Financed
Enterprise), June 1964, pp. 25–50; (6) Luis Alvarez Rom, "Sobre el método de
analisis de los sistemas de financiamiento" (On the Method of Analyzing Financing Systems), July 1964, pp. 64–79; and (7) G. Glezerman, "Las relaciones eco-
nómicas y los intereses personales en el socialismo" (Economic Relations and Personal Interests under Socialism), November 1964, pp. 93–110.

known as the "budgetary system," financial control of an enterprise would fall under the jurisdiction of the ministry of the treasury, which administered the national budget. The incentive for good performance, instead of solvency or profitability as in the "self-financing" system, would presumably be that of contributing to the national welfare.

The chief protagonists at the beginning were, on the one side, none other than Marcelo Fernández, veteran leader of Fidel's underground support movement during the insurrection, outspoken anti-Communist during the first months of the new regime, and now minister-president of the National Bank of Cuba; and, on the other side, the indomitable Ché Guevara, who, among his other attributes, was minister of industries. Marcelo, as he was commonly referred to, argued for the "self-financing" system, at the time adopted by the foreign trade enterprises and a large number of state farms. In this system his bank played an important role as dispenser and monitor of credit. Ché defended the "budgetary" system under which the hundreds of enterprises in his ministry were operating. Ché's chief backer in the controversy was not unexpectedly Luis Alvarez Rom, minister of the treasury. Hence, the controversy had jurisdictional as well as practical and theoretical implications.

As happens when dirty linen is washed in public, some embarrassing facts came to light. Marcelo, for example, was able to show that for lack of "stimulus" either to pay for debts incurred or to collect payment for goods and services produced, the "budgetary" enterprises "failed to meet . . . an average of 20,000 commitments, totaling 20 million pesos, per week," an astonishing record of irresponsibility.[2] On the other hand, he admitted that most of the "self-financing" enterprises did little better, but he claimed that the reason for this was that these enterprises "have never really operated as economically autonomous firms."

From the point of view of common sense and the historical experience of the other socialist countries, Marcelo had much the better of the argument; but given Cuban conditions at the time, and for some years to come, it could make little practical difference which system was used. The larger planning and administrative irrationalities and the gross statistical inefficiencies meant that most of the enterprises most of the time would operate in the red. One way or another the deficits would be covered by state funds, while the aggregate national deficit would be covered by the Soviet Union.

2. *Cuba Socialista*, February 1964, pp. 45–46.

To be sure, this appraisal of the debate could only be shared in private among the more sophisticated Cuban technicians and foreign observers of the Cuban scene. One reason is that from the very beginning the practical questions of economic policy were overshadowed by their ideological implications. Which system for financing a socialist state enterprise was in keeping with Marxist-Leninist doctrine? How far could a socialist economy be decentralized, as in the "self-financing" scheme, without creating the conditions for backsliding into capitalism? What should be the role of moral and material incentives in a socialist society? It was the first time that the Cuban economy was publicly subjected to doctrinal scrutiny, and this was not entirely an accident. The teaching of Marxism-Leninism had been stepped up in recent months, both in the special schools for party cadres and in the universities. Earlier a special course of instruction had been set up in Havana for a select group of "new" Communists in the government and party leadership. For this group an Hispano-Soviet expert had been imported from Moscow.[3] Both Ché and Marcelo had attended the course, and it was said that Ché had given the professor a hard time with his irreverent probing of dogma.

As the debate grew more heated, the opponents fired ever greater salvos of scripture against one another, principally citations from Marx and Lenin but also including Stalin, and in the case of one proponent of "self-financing," Nikita Khrushchev.[4] The display of Marxist erudition reached an angry climax in Ché Guevara's rebuttal of a critique of an earlier article of his by Charles Bettelheim. The latter, a distinguished Marxist professor of political economy at the University of Paris, had spent several weeks in Cuba on two or three occasions as a consultant to JUCEPLAN (the Central Planning Board), each time preparing lengthy reports which, if they were read, went unheeded. In his article, bristling with references to Bukharin, Rosa Luxemburg, Oscar Lange, Mao Tse-tung, and others that Ché could not match, as well as Marx, Lenin, and Stalin, Bettelheim in so many words branded Ché's position as what Lenin had called "infantile leftism." Published in the April issue of *Cuba Socialista*, the party monthly, and given Ché's exalted status in Cuba, the article created something of

3. The son of Spanish Civil War refugees raised in Moscow, he also lectured at the University of Havana.
4. Joaquín Infante, *Cuba Socialista*, June 1964, p. 50. One reads with some amusement today the author's faith in Khrushchev's prediction that the USSR "during the present decade will surpass the global and per capita production of the United States."

a sensation, despite the prudence of the editors in stating that the article reflected the personal opinions of the author. It was, however, an open secret that the "old" Communists who ran the journal were sympathetic to Bettelheim's views.[5]

Ché's reply in *Cuba Socialista* two months later was sharp, as could be expected, though it also projected an arrogance scarcely justified by his limitations as a Marxist scholar. Ché's argumentation need not detain us, since our interest does not lie in the doctrinal merits of the points in dispute. At the end of his article, he dismissed the professor with less than comradely respect. Concerning Marxists like Bettelheim, he concluded, "I can only say that may God protect me from my friends, from my enemies I can protect myself."[6]

By a strange coincidence, the great debate on Marxist economics overlapped the trial of Marcos Rodríguez, with which it had one thing in common: the public exposure of serious rifts at the highest levels of government. Both events marked the end of open controversy in Castro's Cuba except on the most trivial of matters. In fact, nothing like either event was to occur again. The Rodríguez affair had accidentally slipped out of Fidel's control, and he found it necessary to intervene to bring it back under control. On the other hand, there seemed to be no accident about the lengthy polemic that broke out in the pages of *Cuba Socialista*. It is difficult to imagine that Marcelo Fernández, totally dependent on Fidel for his job and career, would take on the formidable Ché Guevara without at least an implicit nod from the "boss." Nor would *Cuba Socialista* venture into the maelstrom, however its working editors favored Marcelo over Ché, without permission from Fidel, whose name appeared on its masthead. And Fidel, in the meantime, remained discreetly quiet throughout the battle and after it ended.

What prompted Fidel's silence? One can only speculate against the

5. Later, Bettelheim turned against the Soviet brand of Marxism and embraced the Maoist version. In 1971, at the time of the arrest of the Cuban poet Heberto Padilla on the charge of writing counterrevolutionary poetry, Bettelheim publicly denounced the "degeneration of the Cuban Revolution" promoted "by their Soviet friends" (see my *The Rise and Decline of Fidel Castro* [Berkeley and Los Angeles: University of California Press, 1972], pp. 357–358). After Mao's death, Bettelheim broke with the new Chinese leadership, henceforth apparently condemned to ideological solitude (see "The Great Leap Backward," in *China Since Mao*, by Neil G. Burton and Charles Bettleheim [New York: Monthly Review Press, 1978], pp. 37–116).

6. *Cuba Socialista*, June 1964, p. 24.

background of such facts as are known. Marcelo and company were supporting the Soviet line, both in its practical and ideological implications. Fidel, following his two visits to Moscow, was committed to close economic and political collaboration with the Soviet Union. From the Russian point of view, Ché's position was a major factor in the continuing malfunction of the Cuban economy and in the enormous deficits that in turn were a burden on the Soviet economy. His position also implicitly supported the Chinese campaign against Soviet "revisionism."

In June, Marcelo Fernández replaced Major Alberto Mora as minister of foreign trade. It was one of two important changes in cabinet personnel in the summer of 1964, the other being the removal in July of Regino Boti as minister of economy and director of the central planning board. Boti was replaced by President Dorticós, who continued to hold the office of president. Fidel gave no explanations, but it was clear that he blamed both Mora and Boti for mismanaging convertible currency expenditures, which resulted in the embarrassing need to cancel a number of contracts for imports from the capitalist market. The general impression in Havana at the time was that neither man was any more to blame than the general "system" in which they were enmeshed—including Fidel, who often made decisions regarding imports without consulting anybody. The decisive external factor in the situation was the drastic decline of convertible currency revenue caused by a sharp drop in the free market price of sugar (from the then record monthly average of 11.6 cents per pound in November 1963 to less than five cents in July 1964, and under three cents in December).[7] Mora, as I learned, was summoned by Castro late one night. Without any suspicion of what lay in store for him, he was fired then and there. As usually happened to those who fell out of Fidel's favor, he moved from one obscure job to another. Eventually he committed suicide.[8]

Marcelo's shift to the ministry of foreign trade was a promotion, contrary to the assumption of some writers who were not on the scene that it was a demotion and hence represented a "victory" for Ché.[9] The ministry of foreign trade is a key ministry in Cuba and definitely ranks above the na-

7. *Economic Survey of Latin America 1964* (New York: United Nations, 1966), p. 230.

8. In 1972, as recorded by Juan Arcocha, *Fidel Castro en Rompecabezas* [The Jigsaw Puzzle of Fidel Castro] (Madrid: Ediciones Erre, 1973), p. 68.

9. For the mistaken assumption, see in particular Theodore Draper, *Castroism, Theory and Practice* (New York: Praeger, 1965), pp. 190 and 198. Draper's account of the ideological aspects of the debate, however, is one of the best.

tional bank in importance. Although Marcelo's selection by Fidel was justified by his demonstrated administrative merits in the bank, he would not have been chosen if Fidel did not have full confidence in him in all respects. Immediately after becoming minister of foreign trade, Marcelo had no inhibitions in either privately or publicly maintaining his position vis-à-vis Ché. Thus, *Comercio Exterior*, the quarterly review published by his ministry at the time, gave extensive and indulgent coverage to "revisionist" economic trends in the Soviet Union and other East European countries.[10]

Politically speaking, Ché had come out second best in the controversy, a matter of some importance at the time. Aside from Alvarez Rom, minister of the treasury, all the Cuban participants had prudently opposed Ché's position. In addition, the Bettelheim article was particularly damaging to Ché's prestige, exposing him as a pretentious amateur in Marxist economics. As for Fidel, although he ostensibly remained aloof from the quarrel, more than likely he was not displeased by the way it turned out. His own approach to questions of planning, management, and work incentives, when not subject to spells of intuition and inspiration, tended to be practical and political, not ideological. In fact, he lacked even Ché's rudimentary knowledge of the Marxist-Leninist classics to venture into doctrinal polemics. Pragmatically, in this period, he would not object to the Soviet "revisionist" line—or to any other that he thought would work—

10. Notably in the issue of October–December 1964, which carried a translation of Soviet economist E. G. Liberman's seminal article on "Industrial Planning and Management," which first appeared in *Voprosy Economiki*, No. 8, 1962, and an article of mine on the continuing debate over the Liberman and similar reform propositions in the Soviet Union. Marcelo personally complimented me on the article, entitled "Toward a New System of Economic Planning and Management in the Soviet Union," which was distinctly favorable to the "new system." Ironically, although Moscow finally introduced an industrial management reform program on an experimental basis in 1965, nearly a decade later the problems still remained acute—a tribute to entrenched bureaucracy. As reported in the *New York Times* (January 12, 1974), a poll taken by a Soviet economist revealed that ninety percent of factory managers claimed that production was impeded by their lack of authority to make decisions and the continued intervention of higher authorities in local management. This was followed by an unprecedented rebuke in *Pravda* directed against the GOSPLAN for excessive interference in the daily operations of industrial plants. On the other hand, both the German Democratic Republic and Hungary had been operating, with some success, under considerably decentralized planning and management systems. In Cuba it was only in 1971 that a serious process of rationalizing the economic system began using the Soviet rather than the more efficient German and Hungarian models.

while politically it suited his relations with Khrushchev. At the same time, by remaining silent he could keep his options open, one of which might be to swing over to Ché's line, which in his own way he actually did a year or so later.

In retrospect, Fidel's conduct in this episode had still another meaning. The relationship between Fidel and Ché was a very complex one, unlike that between Fidel and any other of his close associates. There was a genuine mutual admiration, but also an underlying tension between them. There was no question about Ché's complete loyalty to Fidel, but it was also common knowledge in higher government and party circles that Ché was the only person in the ruling elite who in private discussions would dare challenge Fidel when he did not agree with his views. Being highly allergic to anything that smacked of criticism, particularly by his subordinates,[11] Fidel considered Ché to be "difficult"; and, of course, the feeling was mutual. How to deal with Ché, in whom he had made a very large political investment, was thus a special problem for Fidel. Ché was at this time an asset that he would be loath to dispense with, nor could he easily find a formula by which this could be done without seriously damaging the image of the Cuban Revolution. Not long after Ché's defeat in the "great debate," these matters would come to a head and a formula would be found: Ché would depart first to fight in the Congo and then to embark on his fatal mission to Bolivia. Meanwhile, in 1964, it was more expedient for Fidel to have Ché harassed in an open polemic than to keep the controversy bottled up.

The last salvo in Havana's battle of the printed word was fired in November 1964. It took the form of an article in *Cuba Socialista* by one G. Glezerman, identified as a Soviet philosopher. It was an abridged translation of a scholarly and eminently "revisionist" document published short-

---

11. Western journalists who interviewed Fidel were generally unaware of this. With them he was a different person, projecting through them to the outside world the figure of a reasonable, affable, give-and-take interlocutor. It was an "allergy" of long standing. In a sharp memorandum addressed to Fidel and the executive committee of the Movement of July 26, dated Camagüey, October 1958—that is, three months before the defeat of Batista—Carlos Franqui, a member of the executive, wrote: "It is very difficult for him [Fidel] to accept . . . criticism. . . . I have noted that many of our meetings are nothing more than conversation, . . . the prodigious conversation of Fidel, in which decisions are taken without an agreement fully discussed by those present" (Carlos Franqui, *Diario de la revolución cubana* [Barcelona: Ediciones R. Torres, 1976], p. 611).

ly before in *Kommunist*, the official monthly journal of the Communist Party of the Soviet Union. The article seemed to be specifically directed against Ché Guevara, although its appearance was probably only a coincidence of which the editors of *Cuba Socialista*, with no objection by Fidel, were happy to take advantage.

Finally, early in the new year, President Dorticós, serving as Fidel's mouthpiece, signaled the end of the debate. In a speech delivered on January 24, 1965, he spoke against the disruption caused by the "useless wars between government bureaus" and against the "loss of time and waste of our human and intellectual energies in these little internal theoretical wars within the State." On matters of substance he was equivocal. "Lenin was right," he declared, "that we must remunerate each one according to his work. . . . This is indispensable." But on the other hand, "we must choose methods which . . . do not endanger the ideological future of our society and the creation of the new man." One such method, he pointed out, had already been invented by Fidel: the distribution of scarce material goods as prize awards to the workers who cut the largest quantities of sugarcane.[12] Fidel's Solomonic wisdom, it turned out, heralded the shape of things to come.

An epilogue to the jurisdictional and theoretical "useless wars" occurred soon after the end of hostilities. Once Ché was gone, Fidel abolished the ministry of the treasury and transferred its functions to the national bank, headed by Marcelo's able successor, Orlando Pérez. Left without his sponsor and protector, Alvarez Rom—and many lesser figures in Ché's entourage—vanished into permanent obscurity.

12. *Política Internacional*, 9 (first trimester, 1965), 183–190.

10
■

The Power to Disrupt

A Compulsive Urge

IT WAS DIFFICULT to measure the direct impact of Fidel Castro's personality on the day-to-day functioning of the Cuban economy, except to say that it was constant and enormously disruptive. No one who was even marginally associated with the economic process in the mid-sixties could doubt it. Except perhaps for the ministry of industries during Ché's tenure, there was no area affecting the economy—including, for example, the training of geographers and economists at the university—that was immune to the sudden intervention of the Maximum Leader, or to the near-paralysis that could follow when his attention veered to another project, resulting in the fear of making decisions if he could not be located or was not available for other reasons.

Fidel's compulsive urge for personal control of whatever undertaking struck his fancy, and at any level that he chose, was not motivated by a mere lust for power but by the great mission which destiny had entrusted to him and the conviction that he was especially endowed with the wisdom for fulfilling the mission. His intentions, therefore, were always the best: in this instance, to move the economy toward an efficient and abundant production with all possible speed. Among the obstacles he perceived to this objective were the low competence and the retarded learning capacity of most of his subordinates, which in turn fed bureaucratic inertia. In one of his midnight forays to the university campus, he was probably deadly serious when he told a group of students who quickly gathered around him —this was reported to me by a student of mine who was there—that in all of Cuba he could only count on twenty administrators with enough intelligence to handle the jobs they were assigned to do.

The Problems of Bureaucracy

Thus, while Marcelo Fernández, Ché Guevara, and others were debating Marxist economic theory, Fidel in his numerous speeches was excoriating bureaucracy as the great source of evil which he was determined to extirpate from the Cuban scene. In this respect, he set himself up as a model nonbureaucrat. According to conventional standards, he explained, as prime minister he should have an office occupying several floors in the biggest building in Havana. Instead, he practically had no office at all, just a couple of small rooms for handling correspondence.[1] To the masses held spellbound by his speeches he even appeared to be outside the government, and, like his listeners, a victim of its myriad of dull, parasitic, paper-pushing and paper-storing officials. It was almost as if he were not only outside the government but against the government. Politically, this posture—probably a genuine reflection of his deepest feelings and hence convincing—was an important element of his strength, for it helped maintain the identification of the Cuban people with his personal leadership. The Revolution was Fidel, not the idiotic creatures who filled the ministries and messed everything up.

Under pressure from Fidel, who was also responding to the manpower pressure in agriculture, a considerable pruning of personnel in the ministries eventually took place, and not always in a rational manner. The stigma attached to office work and the aura of patriotism which glorified labor in the fields prompted a number of the more able and ambitious employees to volunteer for a year or two of work in the countryside, thereby earning service merits for later advancement—in the government or party bureaucracy! The result was not only a reduction in the employment rolls of the ministries, but also a higher proportion of drones among those who remained.

1. C. L. Sulzberger, of the *New York Times*, who interviewed Castro during the predawn hours of October 31, 1964, was "struck by his unusually disorganized schedule and asked why he had no office. . . ." Castro gave an ingenious explanation: "At the start I tried to work in the prime minister's office. . . . But I rapidly learned that I had no interest in seeing ninety percent of the people who were interested in seeing me . . . so I decided to adopt a method enabling me to see those people it was necessary to see or interesting to see without being bothered by the others. . . . I have been able to establish a very wide contact with the people and with the countryside because I am incessantly visiting different places and talking with different people . . ." (*An Age of Mediocrity: Memoirs and Diaries 1963–1972* [New York: Macmillan, 1973], pp. 121–122).

In any event, of the many problems that beset the Cuban bureaucracy, the question of numbers was not decisive. Bureaucracy in all modern and modernizing states, and more particularly in a socialist state, is both an indispensable part of the machinery of the government and a major source of its imperfections. In Cuba, however, there was a special if not unique problem. It was Fidel himself whose disorganized work habits and monopoly of decision-making at the top of the bureaucratic pyramid affected all layers beneath him. It was common knowledge that at the ministerial level the fear of Fidel inhibited critical thinking and initiative, which in turn dampened initiative and prevented delegation of responsibility all the way down the line. A large part of the paper-pushing that angered Fidel was merely the moving of routine matters, which could easily be disposed of at lower levels, up through the ranks for successive approval. But who was to "bell the cat," that is, explain to Fidel that a policy of delegating responsibility and decision-making to the lower echelons would work wonders in the Cuban bureaucracy, and that the greatest obstacle to such a policy was Fidel himself?

The "Special Plans"

"I'm not a farm manager and that's not my work, but I'm interested in these problems and to put my mind at ease I felt the need of undertaking a few little experiments in growing sugarcane. . . . I don't have any farmland, so I had to plow up some vacant lots out there on the outskirts of town." It was Castro speaking in the middle of his four-hour speech at the final session of the First National Sugar Forum, held in Havana on September 19, 1964. Two months earlier, he had combined the agricultural and industrial branches of sugar production into a single new ministry of the sugar industry in preparation for the projected ten-million-ton sugar harvest in 1970. The forum, at which some 1,500 representatives from the farms, sugar mills, and the new ministry were present, was the formal opening of the six-year campaign.

However, Fidel went on to explain, he had run into a "tremendous problem" with the consolidated electric enterprise because, according to an earlier plan of which he was not aware, they were going to put up a tower and run a high-voltage transmission line right through his cane field. "Over my dead body," he told the power officials. "You're not going to destroy this cane field." [2] There was more to this amusing anecdote, but it need

2. *Política Internacional*, 7 (third trimester, 1964), 225.

not detain us. The point is that this was Fidel's quaint explanation ("to put my mind at ease") for one of his early personal ventures into "scientific research," which rapidly multiplied into scores of farming and stock-raising projects scattered through the island—projects that were euphemistically referred to in official literature as "special plans" but were otherwise not explained or described. Information about what went on in Fidel's network rarely reached the press, and even the ministries that were supposedly to benefit from the "experiments" received no systematic reports.

In time, Fidel's "special plans" tended to grow both in size and scope. Early in June 1965, Fidel casually revealed in a speech that 3,200 head of cattle had been exported to Italy.[3] This was how word reached the ministry of foreign trade that Fidel was exporting "his" beef in "his" ships to Italy. In other words, he had quietly set up a miniature foreign trade and maritime transport ministry of his own. How the financial aspects of his transactions were handled by the National Bank I never discovered, but I recall that it was impossible to incorporate any hard data from this "special plan" into Cuba's foreign trade statistics because no such data were made available.

Little in the way of positive results was achieved in the "special plans"; otherwise Cuba and the world would have been amply informed about them. The negative results were more complex than appeared on the surface. A great deal of Fidel's time and energy were absorbed by his "special plans." This might not have mattered so much if it were not for the fact that countless decisions which depended directly on him could be delayed for days or weeks while he made the rounds. Frequently it was even a problem to locate him. A related development was "influence peddling" by those he placed in charge of his projects. These people had the inestimable privilege of dealing directly and frequently with Fidel. Depending on his mood at a given moment, he could spend a great deal of time with one or another of his managers. These in turn were courted by high-level functionaries desperately trying to get a favor from Fidel, or simply to get a message to him. Thus, a bit of corruption crept into Fidel's circuit as special "friendships" blossomed and withered, depending on the tenure of the manager who had access to Fidel's ear.

There is no available record of the turnover in the management of the "special plans," but from scattered information it appears that it could have been quite high. Fidel was a hard man to work for. He was a great champion of the people collectively, but he mistreated people as individuals.

3. *Cuba Socialista*, September 1965, p. 129.

Foreign journalists who interviewed him usually found him to be, even if eccentric in some respects, a person who could be fair-minded, considerate of others, and compassionate when it came to matters of human welfare. But this was only one side, the bright side, of his character, which he shrewdly displayed to those who would report about him to the world public. The dark side was better known to those of his subordinates who had the misfortune to fall afoul of his overbearing and unrelenting ego.

The Case of Enrique Oltuski

One such case deserves mention because it deals with the experience of a onetime top-ranking and dedicated *Fidelista* who also had close relations with Ché Guevara. Thus, it provides insight into the subtleties of the Cuban revolutionary process during this period. Enrique Oltuski, son of post–World War I Polish-Jewish immigrants, in 1959 was the youngest minister in Castro's first cabinet. He was twenty-seven years old, had studied engineering in the United States, and on his return to Cuba became the leader of Fidel's underground movement in Las Villas, a key province in the center of the island. During this period he was an anti-Communist, along with other prominent members of the July 26 Movement who, like Oltuski, later went along with Fidel's conversion to Marxism-Leninism.

When Jean-Paul Sartre visited Cuba in 1960, he was much taken with the young Oltuski. In his book on Cuba, Sartre described how Oltuski had supplied weapons, food, and money to the guerrillas, and concluded that the bravery of those who faced the perils of the underground was "more difficult than military heroism: a lonely struggle without witnesses against an all-powerful enemy," with a fate worse than death if they were caught.[4] One of the highlights of Sartre's book related the first meeting of Oltuski with Ché Guevara, in mid-1958, in the hills of Las Villas. It turned into a stormy all-night confrontation on tactical and ideological issues between two very different but equally stubborn personalities. They ended up, however, convinced of each other's integrity, and later on became fast friends.

Before the end of 1960, Enrique Oltuski was literally out on the street. Castro had fired him from his post as minister of communications. It was a concession to the PSP Communists, who were moving into key positions in the wake of the close ties binding Cuba to Soviet military and economic aid. It was the beginning of the dark period of what was later euphemistically labeled "sectarianism," when Oltuski and other prominent *Fidelistas*

---

4. *Sartre Visita a Cuba* (Havana: Ediciones "R," 1961), p. 125. Translation here is from the original French edition; an English version was also published.

found themselves without jobs and friends in a political atmosphere clouded by fear and suspicion. Years later, in a moving tribute to Ché after his death, Oltuski told how, on the night his own mother died, only Ché came to the funeral home to comfort him and stay with him until dawn.[5]

In February 1961, Ché became minister of industries, and a few months later he gave Oltuski his first job after his disgrace. It was the start of another career, as Oltuski moved up the ladder in the ministry and then, following Fidel's purge of Aníbal Escalante and the "Muscovite" Communists in late March 1962, transferred with Fidel's blessing to the central planning board as vice-minister. Oltuski's "rehabilitation" was underscored in mid-December when Fidel sent him to Moscow as a member of a four-man commercial delegation.

In the late spring of 1964, Oltuski became "fed up with the bureaucratic rat race," as a friend of his explained it. In addition, it was no secret that he and the minister (Regino Boti, fired by Fidel in July 1964) were constantly at loggerheads. No doubt, he was also influenced by Fidel's major passions of the moment: against bureaucracy and for agriculture. In any case, Oltuski resigned from the central planning board and asked Fidel to assign him to a job in production, preferably in agriculture. After a lapse of several months—not an unusual delay while awaiting Fidel's decision—he was placed in charge of a "special plan," a cattle ranch some hundred miles east of Havana in the province of Matanzas. In the capital, it was the talk of the town that a vice-minister would give up his rank and the comforts of Havana and move his family to the countryside. Soon, however, the word got around that Fidel was a frequent visitor to the ranch and that he considered Oltuski to be doing an outstanding job. In a short time, a stream of new and old friends began to show up at the ranch, and many speculated that bigger things were in store for Enrique Oltuski.

Six months or so after settling in, Oltuski received a telephone call from the manager of Fidel's experimental stockbreeding farm, another one of his "special plans," on the outskirts of Havana. Feed for the cattle was running dangerously low, Fidel was incommunicado, and no relief was in sight. The herd was threatened with starvation. Could Enrique temporarily put Fidel's cattle out to pasture on his ranch? Enrique agreed, and some 2,000 head were safely transported to Matanzas.

5. "¿Qué Puedo Decir?" (What Can I Say?), *Casa de las Americas*, 46 (January–February 1968), 41–43, an issue devoted to the memory of Ché. Oltuski also recalled the night in the hills of Las Villas when "we were enemies and yet I admired him."

Crime and Punishment

Three weeks later, Oltuski was confined to a penal labor camp on the Isle of Pines, by coincidence the same island off the southwest coast of Cuba where Fidel had been imprisoned by Batista in 1953. When Fidel belatedly discovered that his prize cattle had been moved without his permission for whatever purpose, he was outraged. If he had just been an ordinary employee, Fidel explained in a verbal message relayed to Oltuski, he would merely have fired him. But as a close friend in whom he had placed his highest trust and confidence, Oltuski deserved a greater penalty. Fidel therefore offered him an opportunity for atonement by "voluntarily" accepting a six-month sentence on the Isle of Pines.

Part of the story of Oltuski's crime and punishment I learned from someone who had heard it directly from Ché Guevara. It seems that when Fidel offered Oltuski the job on his "special plan," Oltuski asked Ché whether he should accept. Ché advised him not to. "I told him," said Ché, "that knowing both him and Fidel, he was bound to end up in Guanahacabibes [on the western tip of Cuba]. I was mistaken about which prison camp it would be."

Oltuski accepted his fate philosophically. He continued to receive his "special plan" salary, and his family moved back to their old residence in Havana. Life and work in the prison camp were not too grim. After all, the Isle of Pines was not Siberia, nor was Fidel a tropical Stalin. When Oltuski was released, he wrote an autobiographical novel, the first part of which he submitted for publication. Among those assigned to read the manuscript was Alejo Carpentier, Cuba's foremost novelist and one of the most distinguished in Latin America, who gave it high praise. But the responsible book editor prudently submitted it to Fidel for his approval. The novel dealt with the period prior to the triumph of the insurrection, and apparently was the first attempt to tell the story of the underground struggle, completely obscured by the mass of literature on the exploits of the guerrillas. The novel was never published. Its author, briefly surfacing among a collection of reminiscences about Ché published early in 1968 in *Casa de las Americas* (see note 5, above), had disappeared into the rank and file of the Cuban labor force. Years later, he unpredictably emerged again in the ministry of fisheries, where, at the end of 1978, he was listed as deputy minister,[6] a remarkable case of resiliency among those who once held and then lost favor with Fidel.

6. In *Granma Weekly Review*, December 3, 1978.

11

■

Castro's Peace Offensive (I): The Eder Interview

A Surprising Initiative

IN JULY 1964, FIDEL CASTRO made what can only be described as a spectacular bid for normalizing relations with the United States. To be sure, during the preceding six months attentive observers who scrutinized his speeches and other recorded remarks could catch hints of "softness" in his references to the United States, while in diplomatic circles there were rumors, with some degree of credibility, that Cuban feelers were out with a view to enlisting the Spanish government as a possible mediator between Havana and Washington. However, during the same period, American policy toward Cuba had visibly hardened, and tensions in July between the two countries appeared to be greater than at any time since the settlement of the missile crisis at the end of 1962. Thus, Castro's bold initiative was largely unexpected and came as a particular surprise to his own people and his revolutionary following in Latin America.

Fidel's well-staged "peace offensive" began with one of those marathon interviews, combined with sightseeing, that he would give from time to time to highly placed foreign journalists through whom he wished to convey an important message aimed at a selected target. This time the medium was Richard Eder, correspondent of the *New York Times*, and the target was the United States government and, simultaneously, American public opinion. Eder's story was a front-page report on July 6 and was the product, as he put it, of "an eighteen-hour interview that took place over three days." Quite apart from the message, Fidel's method of conducting an interview provided Eder with lively copy. "Part of the interview," he wrote, "consisted of two extensive tours of farms and beaches around Havana. . . . Riding in the rear seat of a blue sedan and followed by three carloads of guards, Dr. Castro raced along the streets and highways, coming to dozens of swift stops. He jumped in and out of the car, sloshed through mud, prodded calves, talked about Cuba's agricultural future, questioned sunbathers, burst in on startled office workers. . . ." There were three night sessions in Castro's quarters, one of which lasted until five in the morning. In this connection, Eder provided posterity with a description of Fidel's uptown Havana residence. It was a walk-up apartment, he explained, "on the fifth floor of a building in a heavily guarded street in the Vedado section. . . . Halfway between the floor and the ceiling of the living room is a platform reachable by a ladder, which Dr. Castro had put in as an office."

A Proposal for Normalization

Fidel's message, boiled down, was that the time had come for the United States and Cuba to take the first steps leading to a normalization of relations between the two countries. In Eder's words, "Cuba's leaders, Dr. Castro said, were now more mature"—meaning, of course, that he, Castro, was more mature—"and the United States had given some indications —notably through the Alliance for Progress—that it was willing to accept a degree of social change in Latin America." The reference to the Alliance for Progress was a sharp reversal of Fidel's earlier and often repeated strictures that the Alliance was an unmitigated fraud. However, because of the political climate in the United States, Castro went on to say, the immediate renewal of formal relations, though desirable, would be premature. This would be possible "only when the sharp edges of the quarrel between the two countries are softened somewhat. . . ." It was at this point that Castro made the startling proposal, as Eder summed it up, that "Cuba would commit itself to withhold material support from Latin American revolutionaries if the United States and its Latin American allies would agree to cease their material support of subversive activity against Cuba." Castro returned to this theme several times so that there could be no question that he was misconstrued or that by material support to Latin American revolutionaries he meant arms and money.

Although overshadowed by his offer to abandon the ongoing revolutionary struggle in Latin America, other matters of considerable interest were dealt with by Fidel in his long interview, all of them designed to demonstrate his new attitude of moderation and conciliation. At the time, the two issues of greatest tension between the two countries concerned the U.S. naval base at Guantánamo and the continuing overflights of U-2 reconnaissance planes over Cuba. Recurring demands by Castro that the United States evacuate the base, leased from Cuba for ninety-nine years in 1903, and hundreds of incidents along the perimeters of the enclave, heavily fortified by both sides after the break in relations in 1961, culminated in Cuba's cutting off the water supply in early February 1964 (as noted earlier). This did little to restore calm. On June 11, *Revolución* ran a front-page banner headline charging that a shot fired from the base wounded a Cuban soldier; and as late as June 27, the same paper featured Castro's accusation that the United States was responsible for a similar aggression on the previous day. Hence, Eder considered it to be an "extraordinary concession" when Castro told him that the Cuban guards would be pulled back several hundred yards and placed in protected shelters, thus removing "much of the opportunity for casual incidents." Significantly, according to Eder, Castro "made a point of emphasizing that he believed Washington had nothing to do with the incidents. He attributed them to politically motivated officers on the base to embarrass President Johnson."

The continuation of U-2 high-altitude inspection of Cuban territory ever since the missile crisis—justified by the United States as necessary surveillance in the event of another surreptitious attempt to introduce offensive nuclear weapons—had been the subject of vehement protests by the Cuban government. The flights were seen as flagrant violations of Cuban sovereignty as well as a form of military and economic espionage. The matter was further complicated by the fact that the Cubans were being trained to operate the Russian SAM installations, capable of shooting down U-2 intruders, and could be expected at any time to take full possession of the weapons. Once this took place, it was anybody's guess as to what might happen.

Later it was revealed that when the SAM missiles were turned over, Khrushchev had extracted a pledge from Castro not to use them unless Cuba were actually attacked; but on the very eve of the Eder interview, tensions rose as a result of a sharp statement by Khrushchev condemning American violation of Cuban airspace. In Havana, *Revolución* carried the statement under a front-page banner headline on July 1.[1] However, speak-

1. Similar protests by Khrushchev were given prominence in *Revolución* on July 8: "We declare our total support of the Cuban people"; and on July 9: "It can lead to the most serious consequences."

ing to Eder, Castro was far from bellicose. Cuba would place the issue before the forthcoming November meeting of the United Nations General Assembly, he said, clearly implying that he would do nothing rash before then. Although he reserved the right to shoot down the planes, indicating that he had or would have full control of the means to do so, he was optimistic about a peaceful settlement. Eder quoted him as saying that "while we exhaust diplomatic means, there is time left for settlement."

The Benefits of Normalization

Prompted by Eder, Fidel cheerfully went on to paint a rosy picture of what an eventual return to normal relations would mean for both countries. For the United States, buying Cuban sugar would be more economical than expanding sugar beet production (Fidel blissfully ignored the sugar beet lobby in Washington), while both countries would benefit from a resumption of American exports to Cuba. Once trade was under way, the indemnification of expropriated American property could be negotiated. Asked about political prisoners in Cuba, Castro was quoted as saying that there were "something under 15,000" and conceding that "this is a great many." If relations with the United States were normalized, he added, there would be no need to keep most of them in jail. Ninety percent could be released and would be permitted to go abroad or remain in Cuba, as they preferred.[2]

This was the first time that Castro, or any official Cuban source, had given even a hint as to the number of political prisoners being held. The figure was large enough, and sufficiently shocking, to be credible, although estimates by unfriendly sources ran much higher. Evidently, Fidel was more interested in establishing the sincerity of his proposal for normalization of relations with the United States than in concealing this embarrassing aspect of life under his regime. In this vein he conceded that some of the methods used by the Revolution were "harsh" and the "process might have been gentler" had the United States not opposed the Revolution. However, he went on to say, with unprecedented candor on this topic, that "it is not true that these bad relations were completely imputable to either party. . . . Both sides did very little to prevent matters from getting where they did." As for the future, the prospects were for more

---

2. Some fifteen years later, under different circumstances, Castro made public a similar proposal, without strings attached except that the United States agree to accept those prisoners who opted to go there. At the time, he put the number of remaining political prisoners at under four thousand.

moderation. He could foresee the adoption of a socialist constitution by 1969, "perhaps considerably before," and the possibility at that time of holding elections (on both scores, it turned out, implementation would be delayed until the mid-1970s).

Speculation and Rejection

Finally, he made two points that helped to explain the considerable risk to his prestige which he was willing to take in making public his initiative for détente with Yankee imperialism. First, he expected that in the November elections, President Johnson would defeat the Republican candidate, almost certain to be Barry Goldwater, the implacable enemy of Cuba; and once returned to office, Johnson would resume President Kennedy's discreet exchange of views with Castro begun in the fall of 1963 and prematurely terminated by Kennedy's assassination.[3] The second point, "hinted strongly," in Eder's words, was that "the Soviet Union had been counseling a betterment of relations with the United States."

If Fidel intended his interview to be nothing more than a trial balloon, although a conspicuously large and attractive one, it would have marked the end of his "peace offensive," for the day after Eder's report was published the balloon was unceremoniously shot down. "United States officials . . . rebuffed Premier Castro's overture for negotiations," according to a Washington dispatch carried by the *New York Times* on July 7, "until Cuba ended her 'ties of dependency' on the Soviet Union and ceased to promote subversion in Latin America." The statement, reiterating "standing United States policy toward Cuba," was released by the State Department, and was said to have been prepared in consultation with Defense Secretary Robert McNamara and with McGeorge Bundy, special assistant to the President for international security affairs. The statement, taken literally, made little sense, for these were precisely the matters to be negotiated. The message was clear, nevertheless: it was a categorical rejection of Castro's overture.

Nevertheless, *Revolución* reproduced part of the Eder interview on July 9, ignoring the response in Washington. This was exceptional, since only on the rarest occasions, when some special purpose was to be served, were Cubans informed about Fidel's conversations with foreign correspon-

3. For the Kennedy-Castro "dialogue," see my *The Rise and Decline of Fidel Castro* (Berkeley and Los Angeles: University of California Press, 1972), pp. 287–297.

dents. In this case, the purpose was obviously to prepare the Cuban people for the major shift in foreign policy which Fidel had planned to announce to them before the month was over. For the same reason, the State Department's reaction to Eder's report was, in effect, suppressed by the Cuban press.

Provocation and Restraint

Two weeks later, Fidel was faced with another setback, one that he could not conceal from the Cuban people. A Cuban soldier, well within Cuban territory, was killed by a shot fired from the American side of the Guantánamo frontier. The dead soldier was given a hero's funeral, attended by 50,000 mourners. Significantly, it was Raúl Castro, Fidel's brother, rather than Fidel himself who gave the funeral oration, although what was said was undoubtedly decided by Fidel. It was apparently a way to keep open his bid for conciliation by avoiding personal identification with the harsh statement that the extreme provocation called for. Thus, it was Raúl who voiced the high indignation and the patriotic fervor expected on the occasion. President Johnson, as commander-in-chief of the armed forces, must take the responsibility for the crime, he declared, and it is up to him to investigate and punish the guilty.

At the same time, Raúl added something unexpected in his indictment of the President. "These shots," he declared, "were fired against Johnson and us." It was, he said, an extreme provocation meant to help Barry Goldwater in the forthcoming November election. Should Goldwater be elected, he continued, "we should immediately have to mobilize," because it would mean war for sure.[4] Goldwater, whom the Republican Party had nominated at its San Francisco convention less than a week earlier, had in fact called for an invasion of Cuba. Although the threat was not to be taken literally in the heat of an election campaign, it had been given major coverage in the Cuban press. The mourners at the funeral, who would normally thirst for revenge, could therefore understand what amounted to an appeal for restraint in the face of provocation.

The Problem of Ché Guevara

Meanwhile, Fidel had another problem on his hands, namely Ché Guevara. A characteristic of Ché was that when he appeared as an official representative of Cuba at an international conference, he was a disciplined

4. *Revolución,* July 21, 1964.

spokesman of his government's policies, as determined, of course, by Fidel. On other occasions, however, he was apt to speak his own mind, and this could lead to confusion both at home and abroad. During this critical month of July, Ché, in his capacity as minister of industries, made inaugural speeches at two new factories, and on both occasions took a hard line with respect to foreign policy. In particular, in a speech in Santa Clara on July 24, reported the next day in *Revolución*, he rejected all compromise with the United States. It is our duty "to struggle against imperialism whenever it appears and with all the weapons at our disposal," he declared. And then, to make crystal clear his rejection of Fidel's Johnson-versus-Goldwater thesis, he added: "It does not matter what may be the name of the señor whom the North American people imagine they elect every four years."

If there was any doubt that Ché was speaking only for himself, it was dispelled two days after his speech, as we shall presently see. Fidel must have been in a rage at Ché's insubordination, for that is what it amounted to, and at a time when Fidel was playing for high stakes and had been carefully building up public opinion at home and abroad to strengthen his hand. After all, Ché was not just another minister in Fidel's cabinet. His prestige as a leader of the Cuban Revolution was second only to that of Fidel. It was fortunate that Ché's inopportune remarks came on the eve of Fidel's momentous July 26 address, cutting short domestic disorientation and foreign speculation.

The OAS Complication

One more embarrassment to plague Fidel occurred on July 26, the anniversary of his first uprising against Batista and the very day he had chosen to broadcast his proposal for an accommodation with the United States. Only a few hours before he mounted the podium, the meeting in Washington of the foreign ministers of the Organization of American States announced that it had voted to impose mandatory economic sanctions against Cuba and to require all member states which had not already done so (Bolivia, Chile, Mexico, and Uruguay) to break diplomatic relations with Castro's government. This was the final step in a process that had begun late in November 1963, when some three hundred tons of arms secretly shipped from Cuba were discovered on the coast of Venezuela. The decision taken in Washington eight months later was based on incontrovertible evidence that the weapons came from Cuba and were destined to be used in an attempt to overthrow the Venezuelan government. Although Cuba had been suspended from the OAS in January 1962, the new measures against Cuba marked what at the time was considered an important breakthrough for United States policy.

Fidel may well have hoped for better luck at the OAS meeting, which he knew had been in preparation since the end of February,[5] in view of the steady stream of conciliatory signals emanating from Havana for many months. In that case, he had badly misjudged, since the vote was fifteen to four against Cuba, more than the required two-thirds majority. The opposing governments were those still maintaining relations with Cuba. However, after the vote, Bolivia, Chile, and Uruguay broke relations, leaving Mexico as the lone holdout. In any event, Fidel was not entirely unprepared for the setback and managed to take it in his stride, as his speech on July 26 revealed.

5. The formal announcement, convening the OAS meeting on July 21, was made on June 24.

12

■

Castro's Peace Offensive (II): The Speech in Santiago

A Militant Prologue

IT WAS ANOTHER ONE of those great speeches,[1] to a great gathering of his fellow countrymen, on a great occasion, and on hallowed ground. Oriente Province, where Jose Martí had died in battle and Fidel's storm-battered *Granma* had landed sixty-one years later, was the cradle of Cuban independence. Santiago, the capital city, was the scene of what Fidel had transformed into the most celebrated military disaster in Cuban history, the attack which he led on the Moncada barracks on July 26, 1953. Now it was precisely to Santiago, eleven years later, that Fidel delivered his annual address in commemoration of the event.

In one respect, the place and the occasion would seem to have been ill-suited for the conciliatory, and perhaps even unprincipled, proposal that he was about to announce. In another respect, there might have been some advantage in the setting, since it was appropriate for a rousing revolutionary prologue with which to smooth the way for his exceptional message. Thus, facing the 200,000 Cubans in front of him, and with the radio microphones and television cameras bringing the scene to the remote corners of the island, Fidel spent the first part of his address recalling the heroism and sacrifice of the Moncada episode and then building up the image of the Cuban people and its revolutionary leadership, struggling triumphantly against their internal and external enemies, overcoming the machinations of the CIA and the imperialist economic blockade, and so on.

1. The citations that follow are from the stenographic version in *Política Internacional*, 7 (third trimester, 1964), 151–182.

Do we have economic problems, as our enemies claim, like rationing of consumer goods, he asked. His answer was that, of course, "we don't hide it, nor are we ashamed of it. My advice to them is to have just a little patience and they'll see what socialism will do. . . . What's happening in Brazil? . . . To the best of my knowledge, imperialism has no economic blockade against Brazil, or Colombia, or Central America, and they are dying of hunger without an imperialist blockade, they are completely bankrupt. . . ." But Cuba, despite the blockade, he added, is moving ahead to a future of abundance. "And that's why our enemies hate us," he exclaimed, "our impotent enemies who thought that with one puff they could blow us off the map, but instead, after five and a half years of Revolution, you practically can't count the multitude gathered here today. And it almost makes me wonder: how is it possible for them to destroy all of this? Can they destroy the Pico Turquino [Cuba's highest mountain top close by]? There is no way they can do it. . . . Even Superman couldn't do it! And that's why our people feel secure and they [the enemy] are in a rage and frothing at the mouth."

A Change of Subject

There was a long pause, during which the spontaneous shouting and cheering of the masses swelled and subsided. Fidel could feel satisfied that they were properly conditioned. Then he abruptly changed the subject with these words: "Well, let's now turn to international politics." He began with a nonchalant, leisurely account of an interview that he recently gave to a journalist of the *New York Times*. When asked for the interview, Fidel explained, "I told him, 'sure, why not, let's have a chat.' And we talked for about eighteen hours." Fidel seemed intent on giving the impression that he had no special interest in talking with Eder other than being considerate and hospitable to a representative of a reputable foreign newspaper. If some matters of importance did come up, it was merely coincidental.

The journalist, said Fidel, asked a lot of questions, but mainly about the problems of relations between Cuba and the United States. "I spoke to him very frankly," Fidel continued, "because the best way is to be frank. Why beat around the bush? So I said to him: 'The truth of the matter is that neither of our two countries, neither the United States nor we, did very much to prevent things reaching this point [in our relations].' I was frank about this."

Indeed, he was, and it must have come as a complete surprise, not to say shock, to the Cuban people—and to the scores of "fraternal" delegates and other foreign sympathizers seated on the platform behind him—for never before had Fidel, or the Cuban government, given a hint that "el imperialismo yanqui" was not solely, exclusively, and by its very nature inevitably responsible for the break in relations. Another and bigger shock was coming, but this time he did a considerable amount of preliminary circling around the topic before coming to the point. Still ostensibly doing no more than reporting his conversation with Eder, he said that on the question of negotiating a détente with the United States, he would propose that it be based on mutual nonintervention and acceptance of the standard "norms" of international conduct. However, he interjected, this would not mean a "deal" by which Cuba would turn its back on the revolutionary movements in Latin America. After cautiously exploring the concept of "norms" and its implications for a good twenty minutes in an elaborate prelude designed to soften up his audience, he finally spoke out clearly.

A New Concept

"If there is to be peace," he declared, "if nations are to live in a civilized manner, they must comply with the norms of international law. This is necessary, no matter how great our sympathy for revolutions. . . . This is our sincere thinking on the matter, our revolutionary thinking." For Fidel, this was a new concept of "revolutionary thinking," and he at once proceeded to spell it out: "We don't believe that international norms apply to only one of the sides and are not obligatory for the other side. In a word: if we want to help a revolutionary movement, we are limited by existing international norms, that is to say, we have no right to meddle in the internal affairs of another country. . . . So the norm is an obstacle which prevents us revolutionaries from helping other revolutionaries. We would like to send them arms, . . . material aid. What prevents us? The norms which must exist between nations, . . . the respect for the principles of sovereignty . . . and self-determination of each country."

I was watching Fidel's performance on television in Havana. By coincidence, at this moment the camera had turned away from Fidel toward the thousands standing in front of him. As it focused on faces close to the platform, I thought I detected expressions of puzzlement and perplexity, though perhaps not astonishment, for these were simple people for whom Fidel was an oracle. But the oracle was giving them a strange message. Respect for international norms. Revolutionary non-aid for revolutions.

There was no cheering, no spontaneous shouting of "Fidel, hit the Yankees hard!" or *"viva la revolución!"* As the camera scanned the multitudes, it paused for a moment, with unpremeditated irony, on a large banner off to one side, held aloft, presumably by a contingent of Venezuelan revolutionaries. The banner read: LAS FUERZAS ARMADAS DE LIBERACION NACIONAL DE VENEZUELA (The Armed Forces of National Liberation of Venezuela). There was some additional text, probably some form of greeting to the Cuban Revolution, but it was blurred on the television screen.

Familiar Rhetoric

The camera moved back to Fidel, who was now gesticulating vigorously, a sudden anger in his voice amplified manyfold by the loudspeakers. "And if they don't respect Cuba," he shouted, "the countries which meddle in the internal affairs of Cuba and promote counterrevolution have no right to complain that we help revolution in those countries. We believe this to be something clear and elementary!" With this he launched into an attack on the Organization of American States, "that collection of garbage, that Yankee ministry of the colonies, which, as you know, has met to pass judgment and impose sanctions on Cuba, accusing Cuba of having sent a shipment of weapons to the Venezuelan revolutionaries."[2]

One had to admire his skill in quickly converting a disagreeable setback into a tidy asset. He had sent out unmistakable signals to Washington that he was ready to abandon the Latin American revolution in exchange for normal relations. Simultaneously he had to grapple with the awkward task of seasoning the message for home consumption. Now, at the critical moment of uncertainty in the sea of faces in front of him, he became once more the familiar commander-in-chief, scornfully denouncing and challenging the imperialist enemy and its contemptible vassals. The mood of the assembly changed perceptibly as he hammered away at the OAS, reading and commenting on the resolutions passed that morning in Washington, heaping abuse on several of the Latin American governments that had signed them, and singling out the government of Venezuela as the chief culprit. Adroitly restoring his revolutionary image, he sent a message of "fraternal and deep-felt greetings . . . to the heroic revolutionaries of Venezuela. . . . We say to them: do not forget the example of Cuba! . . . The imperialists will not be able to crush the revolutionary movement of Venezuela. . . ."

2. Castro sidestepped the question of whether or not the accusation was true.

For President Johnson and Peace

For a while, Fidel digressed to the political situation in the United States, which he characterized as a contest between "the bad and the worse." Johnson, he said, "is no saint," but "Goldwater would be . . . the most dangerous president for the United States and for the world. This is not only our opinion, but it has been expressed by the immense majority of thinking men and women in the world." (Of this he had mainly been persuaded by the Kremlin, which he understandably failed to mention.) We are for peace, he continued, hence our restraint in the face of provocations at Guantánamo instigated by the ultrareactionary base commandant. Because if "we returned the fire and killed a couple of Yankee marines," the Goldwater camp "would use it in the electoral campaign . . . against Johnson." Then, once again, Fidel summed up his basic proposition of the day: "Our position is that we are disposed to live in peace with all the countries, all the states, of this continent, irrespective of social systems. We are disposed to live under a system of international norms to be complied with on an equal basis by all countries."

The Declaration of Santiago

Finally, to end on a note of customary patriotic and revolutionary fervor, Fidel pulled out a few sheets of paper and began to read a "Declaration of Santiago, Cuba" as a reply to the "Declaration of the OAS," and "in the name of the Cuban people." It contained twelve articles bristling with indignation and defiance, of which the next to the last touched off a round of cheers: "The people of Cuba warn that if the pirate attacks proceeding from North American territory and other countries of the Caribbean basin do not cease, . . . as well as the dispatch of agents, arms, and explosives to Cuban territory, the people of Cuba will consider that they have an equal right to aid with all the resources at their command the revolutionary movements in all those countries which engage in similar intervention in the internal affairs of our Fatherland."

Declaring that he was submitting the document for the vote of the Cuban people, and satisfied by the great shouting and a forest of right arms raised in approval, he declared the document to be officially adopted, and signed off with the invariable benediction, *"Patria o Muerte, Venceremos!"* (Fatherland or Death, We Shall Overcome), but this time preceded by two *vivas*: *"Que viva la Revolución Socialista!"* and *"Que viva el Marxismo-Leninismo!"*

Epilogue

Among those seated on the platform behind Fidel were fifty foreign journalists, including a score representing leading American newspapers and
wire services. In a totally unprecedented gesture of conciliation—and
breach of security—Castro had invited them to be present at the meeting
and also to tour the island. The next day, he gave them a three-hour interview in the local party auditorium. It was a lively affair, with Fidel fielding
questions with his customary skill.[3] The substance of the lengthy exchange
need not detain us, since fundamentally Castro confirmed the basic points
of his offer to resume normal relations with the United States. If any doubt
possibly remained as to the significance of his extraordinary discourse on
the 26th of July, it was eliminated by the no less extraordinary epilogue of
the following day.

3. The complete stenographic report filled half of the July 29 issue of
Revolución.

13

■

Castro's Peace Offensive (III): Rationale and Response

Miscalculation in Washington

IT WAS ANOTHER MOMENT when history might have taken a sharp turn—for the mutual benefit of both the United States and Cuba—were it not for the gross miscalculations of the decision-makers in Washington. These may have been partly based on faulty information concerning the underlying stability of Castro's power. However, a significant role in the flawed analysis can be attributed to other considerations, such as public opinion in the United States and the manipulation of that opinion in connection with the forthcoming elections. On a purely subjective level, there was also the sheer animosity in Washington generated by the long-standing frustration at previous failures to bring down an exceedingly troublesome and thoroughly detested enemy.

However that may be, Castro's elaborately staged appeal for an end to hostility seemed to confirm the estimate in Washington that he was in deep trouble and that maintaining and increasing the pressure would soon topple him. In the disorganization of the Cuban economy, coupled with the steep decline in the price of sugar on the world market, the Americans mistakenly saw impending disaster. They overestimated the effectiveness of the trade embargo, despite the refusal of Britain, France, Spain, Japan, and Canada to cooperate. They underestimated the capacity of the Soviet Union to provide the basic necessities for survival. And they erroneously counted on American-supported subversion to trigger the uprising that would sweep Castro from power. Thus, after the failure of the Bay of Pigs intervention in 1961 and President Kennedy's crippling promise to the Russians in 1962 not to invade Cuba in return for the removal of their nuclear missiles, the conditions once more appeared to be ripe for the fulfillment of a long delayed and deplorably thwarted objective: the elimination of the Castro regime. The mood in Washington was accurately reflected by Secretary of State Dean Rusk, who hailed the OAS conference on the day of its successful conclusion as "the most important ever held in the hemisphere." Carried away by his own euphoria, he added that "Castro has no future in Cuba or in this hemisphere."[1]

Only Senator J. William Fulbright, among important politicians in and out of Washington, made a realistic appraisal of the situation. Earlier, in a speech on March 25, 1964, according to the *New York Times* of the following day, he urged the United States to abandon "old myths," including the "master myth . . . that the Communist bloc is a monolith," and to base Cuban policy on "objective facts," singling out the boycott policy as a failure. Castro, he said, was a "distasteful nuisance" but not an "intolerable danger" to the United States. Consequently, the best alternative was to accept "the continued existence of the Castro regime."

Fulbright was quickly called to order by, among others, Adlai Stevenson, Robert Kennedy, Richard Nixon, Barry Goldwater, and the top brass of the State Department.[2] This pressure, and apparently feedback from the grass roots, forced Fulbright to retract in an awkward article in the *Saturday Evening Post* of May 16, 1964. It would take a decade, at which time Castro's Cuba would be thoroughly, and perhaps irrevocably, integrated into the Soviet bloc, before Washington would contemplate moving in the direction originally proposed by Senator Fulbright.

A Neglected Aspect of Cuban Policy

The failure of Castro's bid for a Cuban-American accommodation, and with it the initiation of his ultrarevolutionary drive in both domestic and foreign affairs—a phase that was to last some five years—probably accounts for the fact that it was quickly forgotten and that his undeserved reputation as an uncompromising foe of American imperialism remained untarnished. It was, moreover, not the first time since the break in Cuban-American relations, in January 1961, that the Castro government publicly took a pragmatic and conciliatory approach toward patching up the quarrel

1. *Facts on File*, 24:1239 (July 23–29, 1964), 241.
2. *Hispanic American Report* (Stanford University), 27 (1964), 225 and 317.

with the United States. And on each occasion, Castro revealed a realistic perception of national interests that transcended his commitment to promote armed struggle for the emancipation of Latin America. It is an aspect of Fidel's political behavior that has been completely obscured in Cuban writing and among apologists for the Cuban Revolution abroad.

The first recorded Cuban proposal for a settlement with the United States was made at an inter-American economic conference held near Montevideo, Uruguay, in mid-August 1961, four months after the defeat of the American-sponsored invasion at the Bay of Pigs. At that time, ironically enough, it was Ché Guevara, leader of the Cuban delegation, who made the explicit offer of halting Cuba's export of revolution as part of a settlement between the two countries. As in 1964, Soviet influence appeared to have played a significant role in shaping Cuban policy. The proposal was instantly rejected by the United States.[3]

The offer to normalize relations in mid-1964 was far more conspicuous, but it was also the result of a much longer period of gestation. In a sense, Castro's speech on the 26th of July had been a year in the making. In June 1963, he had returned from his first visit to Moscow as a convert to Khrushchev's thesis that an era of peaceful coexistence between the Soviet Union and the United States was about to dawn. Logically it could involve an early and firm settlement of the Cuban issue between the two superpowers, thus facilitating the normalization of Cuban-American relations. For Fidel, this opened up a new perspective; and in his lengthy televised report to the Cuban people on his return from his first visit to Moscow, he notably reduced his anti-American invective. At the same time, mindful of the passive role to which he was reduced in the settlement of the missile crisis, he decided to initiate contact with Washington in order to forestall another Soviet-American deal on Cuba behind his back, and to bring into full play whatever bargaining power he had. This would be a plausible explanation for what took place a few months later.

The Quest for Accommodation in 1963

In September 1963, the Cuban mission at the United Nations secretly contacted the American mission in order to probe the possibility of negotiating the normalization of relations between the two countries. The Cuban overture was reported to President Kennedy, who considered it worth ex-

3. For details on this episode, see my *The Rise and Decline of Fidel Castro* (Berkeley and Los Angeles: University of California Press, 1972), pp. 116 ff.

ploring. As a result, a discreet exchange of messages took place. The United States requested Cuba to indicate what it proposed to include in an agenda for a hypothetical meeting between the two sides. Castro made it known that he agreed to comply with the request. In late October, while contacts on the diplomatic level moved cautiously ahead, Kennedy invited Jean Daniel, a well-known French journalist about to depart from the United States for Cuba, to come to the White House. The gist of the message was clear: Kennedy was prepared to explore the basis for negotiations between the two countries. In addition, he asked Daniel to visit him at the White House on his return from Havana.

Castro's reaction to Daniel's report on his conversation with Kennedy was euphoric. In his reply to Kennedy via Daniel, he expressed enthusiasm over the prospect of an accommodation for which he was prepared to make important concessions. President Kennedy was assassinated on November 22, 1963, on the very eve of Daniel's departure from Havana. With Kennedy's death, the new administration broke off communications with Castro on both the diplomatic and White House levels.[4]

Perspective on the Initiative of 1964

During his second visit to Moscow, in January 1964, as has been noted, Castro confirmed his commitment to Khrushchev's policy of peaceful coexistence, with its now clearly implied corollary envisaging a normalization of Cuban-American relations. In Moscow there was optimism concerning President Johnson, and Castro no doubt accepted the Soviet thesis that the new president, once elected to office in his own right in November, and thereby relieved of campaign pressures exerted by his Republican opponents, would resume the "dialogue" between the White House and Havana cut short by Kennedy's death.

With Castro's uncertainty allayed concerning the new administration in Washington, he could once more look forward to the prospects of coming to terms with Yankee imperialism. What he hoped to achieve was not difficult to surmise. For the first time since the traumatic experience of the missile crisis in October 1962, he could foresee an arrangement that would guarantee the security of his regime against external military, political, and economic aggression. In addition, the prospect of adding to Soviet economic support the resources made available by the lifting of the American

4. For details on the negotiations initiated at the United Nations and on the Daniel mission, see ibid., pp. 287–297.

trade embargo and, at the same time, by the reduction of the costly investment in nonproductive manpower and its upkeep represented by his military establishment, would provide optimum conditions for developing Cuba's faltering socialist economy, his most urgent task.

So far, what Castro hoped to accomplish was also what the Russians expected would result from the course it had advised him to follow. However, in all likelihood Castro had another goal not entirely shared by the Kremlin: the eventual prospect of some freedom to maneuver between the Russians and the Americans, and thus to modify his total dependence on the Soviet Union and the danger of satellization which it implied. In the end, as we know, after the failure of his "peace offensive" in 1964, and subsequent desperate efforts employing a different strategy, it was a goal that he was unable to achieve.

During the six months that transpired between his second visit to Moscow and his Santiago speech on July 26, in any case, Fidel uncharacteristically managed "to keep his cool" in the face of an avalanche of abuse and provocations directed against Cuba from the United States. Moreover, he was willing to risk pursuing the initiative for an accommodation with Washington to the point of publicly exposing the price he would be willing to pay—politically and ideologically a high price for the undeviating champion of the Latin American struggle against imperialism. Undoubtedly, the normalization of relations with the United States had become for him a matter of overriding importance, to the extent that he was subjectively conditioned to perceive a more sanguine prospect than was objectively warranted.

14

■

The Hard Line Restored: Ché Guevara at the United Nations

Early Symptoms

IF A SIGNAL to Washington—and to Moscow—were needed that Fidel had abandoned his hope for normalizing relations with the United States, the presence of Ché Guevara as leader of the Cuban delegation at the nineteenth meeting of the General Assembly of the United Nations amply would have served the purpose. Even before he uttered a word, the appearance of Cuba's renowned and dedicated exponent of militant and uncompromising struggle against Yankee imperialism could leave little doubt that a sharp turn in Cuban policy had taken place.

Actually, Ché's appearance in New York in early December 1964 was less a signal than a confirmation of earlier indications of Castro's reevaluation of his position put forward in his memorable speech of July 26. Ironically, less than a fortnight after that speech, President Johnson made the fateful decision to escalate American participation in the Vietnam War. On August 5, United States navy planes bombed North Vietnam in retaliation, it was explained, for attacks by North Vietnamese PT-boats on American destroyers in international waters in the Gulf of Tonkin. For Castro, the precedent understandably had ominous implications. Thus, his reaction was swift and harsh. On the same day, his government issued a formal declaration denouncing the American action with all the invective of which the Spanish language was capable.[1] Significantly, the declaration also included a fervent appeal for world solidarity with North Vietnam, with more than a hint about the special obligations of Moscow and Peking. "At this moment, more than ever," the document stated, "the unity of all the forces of the socialist camp is necessary. . . . Let us quickly put an end to Yankee imperialist aggression." Whether or not Castro had a premonition of things to come, here in effect was an early warning that the renewal of his cold war with the United States over the Vietnam issue could complicate Cuban-Russian and Cuban-Chinese relations.

On the night of September 13, the Spanish freighter *Sierra Aránzazu,* en route with cargo from Cuba to Europe, was machine-gunned off the northeast coast of the island by two speedboats, killing the captain and two mates and setting the vessel on fire. It was by far the most serious hit-and-run attack of its kind since the Soviet freighter *Baku* was fired on and damaged while still in Cuban waters in late March 1963. The *Baku* episode, affecting Soviet-American relations, prompted President Kennedy to take quick action, with the result that the United States Navy began to intercept counterrevolutionaries heading for Cuba.

Had the two speedboats which fired on the *Sierra Aránzazu* successfully evaded American surveillance, or was there no longer surveillance? Fidel was in no mood to consider such fine points, even though, looked at from the American point of view, an attack on Spanish shipping by anti-Castro Cubans based somewhere in territory under or adjacent to United States jurisdiction could only be counterproductive.[2] The State Department, in fact, denied any knowledge by the American government concerning the perpetrators of the attack, but this was dismissed by a Cuban statement as "cynical," and full responsibility for "this barbarous and crim-

1. The statement, signed by both President Dorticós and Prime Minister Castro, was entitled "Declaration of the Revolutionary Government of Cuba, of August 5, 1964, Condemning the Unjustified Attack of the Armed Forces of the United States against the Democratic Republic of Vietnam" (*Política Internacional,* 7 [third trimester, 1964], 183–184). On August 7, the U.S. Congress gave overwhelming approval of what came to be known as the Gulf of Tonkin resolution, in effect authorizing the President to continue his military operations against North Vietnam at his own discretion. The resolution could only have reinforced Castro's misgivings about his own security.

2. On September 26, the Spanish government, under strong United States pressure to break off commercial relations with Cuba, informed Washington that it would continue to trade with Cuba (*Política Internacional* 8 [fourth trimester, 1964], 303).

inal act" was attributed to the government of the United States as "part of its policy of aggression and blockade . . . against Cuba."[3]

The Cairo Conference

Three weeks later, at a meeting of nonaligned countries in Cairo, President Dorticós continued the offensive against the United States and, significantly, raised the question of peaceful coexistence. We accept as "useful," he declared, coexistence between capitalist countries and "a nuclear power in the socialist camp. . . . It lessens the immediate dangers of world conflagration." However, he added, "there cannot be peaceful coexistence and simultaneously imperialist aggressions against small countries."[4] No doubt, this not too subtle reference to the Soviet dilemma did not go unnoticed in Moscow. Nevertheless, when Dorticós reached the Soviet capital for an official visit on October 15—by an embarrassing coincidence, the very day that Khrushchev was sacked—on the surface, Cuban-Soviet relations remained serene.

Thus, the momentum of the political campaign against the United States gathered steam. On November 25, another "Declaration," this time signed by both Castro and Dorticós, "condemn[ed] with indignation the criminal aggression in the Congo," singling out Belgium along with the United States as the chief culprits in the civil war under way in the recently decolonized territory. And once more it repeated the familiar warning that American "aggression and intervention" should not be allowed to continue

3. Statement issued by the ministry of the armed forces, September 15, 1964 (*Política Internacional*, 7 [third trimester, 1964], 223).

4. *Política Internacional*, 8 (fourth trimester, 1964), 148. The meeting, from October 5 to 10, 1964, was the "Second Conference of the Heads of State and Government of the Non-Aligned Countries," at which twenty-five voting members, including Cuba, attended. As at the first conference in Belgrade, Yugoslavia, in September 1961, a resolution was passed calling for the withdrawal of the United States from its Guantánamo naval base. Curiously, Cuba was the only indisputably "aligned" member, i.e., Soviet-aligned, of the conference. The explanation given was that Cuba was not a member of a military bloc, such as the Warsaw Pact. At the 1973 summit meeting in Algiers, attended by Castro, and subsequently, Cuba became the faithful and undeviating spokesman of Soviet policy, causing sharp dissension in the conference's considerably enlarged membership, but enhancing Cuba's leadership role of the radical Arab bloc and other left-leaning governments. The scheduling of the sixth summit conference in Havana, in 1979, the first time in the western hemisphere, was a major achievement of Soviet-Cuban strategy.

"with impunity." [5] The occasion was the capture of Stanleyville, the leftist-held capital in the eastern province of Katanga (later renamed Shaba).

Early Warning to Moscow

Shortly before leaving for New York, Ché Guevara delivered an important speech in which he clearly spoke not only for himself but on behalf of his government. [6] It was in part a preview of what he was to say at the United Nations and in part a reflection of the developing discrepancy between Cuba and the Soviet Union, as when he sharply criticized the Communist parties of Latin America (refraining only from directly naming them) for "dragging their feet" in the revolutionary struggle. Notable also was his emphasis on the importance of "hatred" as a "combat reinforcement" in the war against imperialism. It was, whether by coincidence or direct influence, an echo of the bloodcurdling morality of Franz Fanon. [7] By the time of Ché's celebrated message to the Havana-based magazine *Triconti-nental*, released in mid-April 1967 (at the time, it later transpired, Ché was in Bolivia), the "hatred syndrome" had taken full possession of him. It was "an unwavering hatred of the enemy, . . . beyond the natural limitations of a human being, . . . transforming [the revolutionary] into an effective, violent, selective, and cold killing machine." [8]

Ché, it should be noted, had headed the Cuban delegation at the November 7 anniversary of the Bolshevik revolution in Moscow. It can be presumed that, whatever other considerations were involved, he had been chosen by Castro to impress upon the new Brezhnev-Kosygin leadership Fidel's serious reservations concerning Khrushchev's conception of peaceful coexistence, particularly as it affected Cuban-American relations and

5. *Política Internacional*, 8 (fourth trimester, 1964), 237–238.

6. This speech was made in Santiago, Cuba, on November 30, 1964, at a formal commemoration of an unsuccessful uprising in that city on the same day in 1956. The uprising was timed to coincide with the arrival of the *Granma* expedition from Mexico, and was designed to distract Batista's attention from the invasion. As it happened, the uprising, costly in human life, was premature, since the *Granma* was delayed and did not reach Cuba until December 2. Such was the type of miscalculations and disasters which miraculously brought Fidel to power.

7. Fanon's *Les damnés de la terre* (The Damned of the Earth) was first published in 1961. Ché had a good knowledge of French and was able to conduct an interview in French with Fanon's widow in Algiers, as will be related in the next chapter.

8. *Política Internacional*, 18 (second trimester, 1967), 180.

Cuban policy toward Latin America. Apparently, during or shortly after Ché's visit, the Kremlin, caught between Castro's determination to step up export of revolution to Latin America and the Chinese campaign to subvert the Soviet-oriented Communist parties in Latin America, decided to back a conference in Havana of all Moscow-approved Latin American parties.[9]

The Havana Conference

Held "at the end of 1964," according to the communiqué published simultaneously in Moscow and Havana,[10] the meeting worked out a compromise—in due time destined to break down—whereby Castro in effect promised to support the general "evolutionary" political line of Moscow and its Latin American satellite parties against the pro-Chinese and other dissident "revolutionary" Marxist factions. In return, he was promised unremitting solidarity by the muscovite parties, and a free hand, with Russian backing, for clandestine Cuban aid to guerrilla movements in several specified countries with whose governments the Soviet Union at the time saw little prospect of normalizing relations. Finally, the mere fact that the conference, the first of its kind outside Moscow, took place in Havana amounted to "official" recognition that the regional headquarters of Latin American Communism was located in Cuba.

It was more than a decade later before a second publicly announced conference of Latin American Communist parties would meet in Havana, under circumstances that could not be imagined in late 1964. This time there was no question of "compromise." Fidel's heresies, both in domestic and foreign policy, had been laid to rest by "life itself," as the Russian expression goes. However, from the rubble of economic and ideological defeat, Fidel rose Phoenix-like to resume his paramount status among the

9. According to Régis Debray, who was in a position to know, the calling of the conference was partly due to pressure from the Argentine Communist Party, "which protested violently against 'foreign' interference in connection with the [Cuban-sponsored] Masetti guerrilla operation . . ." (*La Guérilla du Ché* [Paris: Editions du Seuil, 1974], p. 34). Masetti, an Argentine journalist, and his band were wiped out in northwestern Argentina in the spring of 1964. Ironically, the operation was masterminded by the ex-Argentine Ché Guevara. See my *The Rise and Decline of Fidel Castro* (Berkeley and Los Angeles: University of California Press, 1972), pp. 332–335.

10. The text is reproduced in *Política Internacional*, 9 (first trimester, 1965), 153–154.

Communist parties of Latin America, only this time as a faithful exponent of Soviet doctrine.[11]

The Stature of Ché Guevara

It would be no exaggeration to say that among the scores of speakers who addressed the nineteenth General Assembly of the United Nations, no one was listened to more intently than Ché Guevara. This was not only because he was the spokesman of the Cuban Revolution, at the time a phenomenon to which the governments of few countries were indifferent, but also because, like Fidel, he had emerged from the revolutionary process as a personality of exceptional stature. It was by sheer accident that the restless young Argentine was recruited in Mexico as physician for the *Granma* expedition and its only non-Cuban member. Then, as one of the most fearless in Fidel's band of guerrillas, he survived two years of combat by mere luck. Such were the early elements of chance in the extraordinary course of events that provided the Cuban Revolution with not one but two figures of world renown.

Ché was intellectually more impressive than Fidel, but physically less so. Ché's mind in part had been disciplined by his medical studies in Buenos Aires, where standards were comparable to those of European universities. Fidel was a law student at the University of Havana, where, by his own account, the faculty of law was a hotbed of political intrigue with extremely low standards of scholarship. Ché's middle-class parents were conversant with the world of books, ideas, and the fine arts. In contrast, Fidel's father was an uneducated immigrant from the Spanish province of Galicia, a self-made prosperous plantation owner, while his mother had been his father's cook before their marriage. Ché was a gifted writer, the author of an internationally acclaimed treatise on guerrilla warfare and a book of reminiscences of genuine literary merit.[12] Fidel, on the other hand, although a genius of the spoken word and a voracious reader with a keen intelligence, lacked the reflective, sensitive temperament of the literary mind

11. See "Conference of Communist Parties of Latin America and the Caribbean, Havana, June 9–13, 1975," in *Granma Weekly Review*, June 22, 1975.

12. *La Guerra de Guerrillas* (Havana: Departamento del MINFAR, 1961), translated as *Guerrilla Warfare* (New York: Monthly Review Press, 1961); and *Pasajes de la Guerra Revolucionaria* (Havana: Ediciones Unión, 1963), translated as *Reminiscences of the Cuban Revolutionary War* (New York: Monthly Review Press, 1968).

and the urge or capacity for systematic thought. The "works" of Fidel are his speeches in print.

Ché could not match Fidel's charisma, projected by the tall upright figure, the head that might have been chiseled by an ancient Greek sculptor, the flashing eyes, the luxuriant black beard, and the skill of a superb actor. Ché's posture, features, and manner were unassuming. The subtle nuances of his expression, his sophistication and charm in intimate conversation, were all lost when he was on the podium. His voice lacked sonority, probably because of his asthma. His beard was scraggly, and, depending on the angle of view, his face bore a striking—and disturbing—resemblance to that of Cantinflas, the classic comic tramp of the Mexican cinema. Standing in front of the great gathering of diplomats at the United Nations, his olive green uniform neatly pressed and his boots freshly polished, he scarcely resembled the idealized poster-image of the revolutionary martyr which circled the globe after his death. But what Ché lacked by way of charisma was compensated for by his already semilegendary reputation as a master of the theory and practice of guerrilla warfare and as a dedicated foe of imperialism. It is a fair assumption that nobody at the United Nations dozed while Ché spoke.

The Cuban Position

Ché Guevara's address, delivered on December 11, lasted well over an hour.[13] Later he returned to the podium to rebut attacks made by a number of hostile Latin American delegates and by Adlai Stevenson, who represented the United States. Looking back at his performance after a lapse of many years, it is still impressive as a philippic of classic proportions. "We should like to wake up this Assembly," he declared at one point. "Imperialism wants to convert this meeting into a useless oratorical tournament instead of solving the serious problems of the world. We must prevent them from doing this." Nevertheless, without much credit either to Ché or to the United Nations, many of the issues stressed by Ché, such as Tshombe's seizure of power in the Congo (Tshombe is long dead and the Congo has become Zaire), the admission of the People's Republic of China to the United Nations, the liberation struggles in Portugal's African colonies, and the American intervention in Vietnam, were eventually solved, to be re-

13. The text of the address is in *Política Internacional*, 8 (fourth trimester, 1964), 259–270.

placed by other issues still in the womb of history and which Ché was not destined to know.

What remains of interest to the student of the Cuban Revolution is Ché's formal reinstatement of Cuba's "hard line," essentially that of the "Declaration of Havana" issued in February 1962,[14] on all matters concerning Cuba's relations with the United States and Latin America. Thus, a large section of his speech was devoted to an appeal for the "liberation of Latin America from the North American colonial yoke," with special references to "the peoples of Venezuela, Colombia, and Guatemala, who are engaged in armed struggle for their freedom." At the very moment he spoke, Cuba was providing significant material support to guerrilla movements in these countries, although Ché would only admit to "moral" support and "solidarity."

Finally, Ché reiterated and formalized the Cuban thesis on peaceful coexistence, which "must apply to all states irrespective of their size." However, he added a stipulation which further complicated the issue. "As Marxists," he declared, "we have maintained that peaceful coexistence does not include coexistence between exploiters and exploited, between oppressors and oppressed." Thus, a holy war rather than peace was Ché's prognostication for the great mass of humanity—and in the first instance, for the exploited peoples of Latin America. In his closing paragraphs, he conjured up an apocalyptic vision of an unremitting life-and-death struggle against Yankee imperialism, "invigorated by [Cuba's] example" and counting on the support of "all the peoples of the world, and especially of the socialist camp led by the Soviet Union." Ché had thus far barely mentioned the "camp" and the USSR. Nevertheless, the Russian delegation must have received Ché's closing tribute (omitting any mention of China) with mixed feelings, if not with alarm. This was not the kind of peaceful coexistence that Moscow was promoting.

14. See my *Rise and Decline of Fidel Castro*, pp. 137–140.

15

■

The Hard Line Implemented: Ché Guevara in Africa

The African Potential

CHÉ AND HIS ENTOURAGE flew from New York to Algiers, where they arrived on December 19, 1964. It was the first stop on an extended tour of the then seven "anti-imperialist" African states: Algeria, Mali, Guinea, Ghana, Egypt, the "Brazzaville" Congo Republic (renamed the People's Republic of the Congo in 1970), and Tanzania. The tour was interrupted by a visit to Peking and apparently included a secret excursion into leftist-held territory in the "Kinshasa" Congo (renamed the Democratic Republic of Zaire in 1971). On February 24, Ché addressed the Second Economic Seminar of Afro-Asian Solidarity, which met in Algiers, after which he and his party returned to Havana on March 14.[1] Shortly thereafter, Ché disappeared from public sight, and a veil of secrecy covered his whereabouts until his corpse surfaced in the Bolivian wilderness on October 8, 1967.

From Ché's public statements during his trip, and from events that later transpired, it is clear that Ché's tour was directly related to the turn in Cuban

1. Ché's itinerary was not fully reported, but available information indicates that he left Algiers for Mali on December 26, flew to Guinea on January 1, 1965, and was in Ghana for an undisclosed period before January 18, the day when a joint Cuba-Ghana communiqué was released. His next public appearance was in Peking on February 3. He reached Cairo on February 11, spent some time in Brazzaville before February 18, when he gave an interview in Dar-Es Salam, and returned to Cairo on approximately February 21. On February 24, he was again in Algiers, and then there was no further word concerning him until his return to Havana on March 14.

foreign policy which his speech at the United Nations had signaled. In Havana, there was increasing skepticism concerning Moscow's peaceful co-existence orientation toward the United States, along with growing apprehension about American intentions toward Cuba. The steady deterioration of Sino-Soviet relations cast a deepening shadow over the "unity of the socialist camp," which was deemed important for Cuban security. Finally, the bombing of North Vietnam and the failure of both Russia and China to challenge the American aggression against a "fraternal republic" provided concrete evidence that neither the Soviet commitment to defend Cuba nor the rhetoric of Marxist-Leninist international solidarity was a sufficient guarantee of immunity against military attack.

At the same time, Castro had reason to be discouraged by developments in Latin America. Cuban-supported guerrilla operations had thus far been largely ineffective. In April 1964, the left-leaning Goulart government in Brazil was overthrown by a military coup d'état. The following August, Castro's socialist friend Salvador Allende failed to win the presidential election in Chile.[2] Thus, Castro turned to Africa as an area in which to launch a bold political and military counteroffensive. Moreover, as later explained by Guevara, from a military point of view Africa enjoyed an advantage over Latin America "because of its greater distance from the United States and its greater possibilities for logistical support" (from the USSR, China, Egypt, and Algeria).[3] In short, if the counteroffensive were successful, Castro reckoned that it could provide him simultaneously with enhanced international prestige and with much needed bargaining power vis-à-vis both the Americans and the Russians.

Africa was not *terra incognita* for the Castro regime. Shortly after Castro's seizure of power, emissaries of the new government began to circle the globe, propelled by an upsurge of national pride and a compulsion to emerge from under the shadow of the United States and from Caribbean isolation. Then, as confrontation with the United States intensified, political relations with the Third World took on more practical importance. Thus, Africa became an early target of Cuban diplomacy. This began with Ché's visit to Cairo in June 1959. In September 1960, Castro and Nasser embraced at the meeting of the United Nations General Assembly in New

2. The winner was Christian Democrat Eduardo Frei. Allende won the next election in 1970, and in 1973 was overthrown by a military uprising which also cost him his life.

3. Cited by Daniel James, *Ché Guevara: A Biography* (New York: Stein and Day, 1969), p. 159.

York. When Patrice Lumumba, the radical Congolese prime minister, was assassinated in February 1961, he was hailed in Cuba as one of the great martyr-heroes of modern times.

In October 1962, on the very eve of the missile crisis, the spectacular visit of Ahmed Ben Bella to Havana signaled the beginning of especially close relations between Cuba and newly independent Algeria. Exactly one year later, Castro rushed a boatload of men and arms to Ben Bella, briefly threatened by a border conflict with Morocco.[4] At the same time, "students" from the strife-ridden former Belgian Congo could be seen in the streets of Havana. It was a fair guess that they were members of rotating contingents of guerrilla fighters receiving special military training in Cuba. As time went on, the Cuban press began to give increasing attention to the war in the Congo; and for several months preceding Ché's departure from New York, scarcely a day passed without a feature story about the unflinching struggle against American and Belgian imperialism in the former colony.

Neglected Clues

In retrospect, it is astonishing that when Ché disappeared from view after returning from Africa in the middle of March 1964, the vast amount of public speculation in the western world as to his whereabouts failed to include even a suspicion that he had gone to fight in the Congo, a fact that came to light after he had abandoned the Congo and was bogged down in the eastern Bolivian jungles. In several published interviews, he gave more than a hint of what he might have been up to. A few days after reaching Algiers,[5] he told Josephine Fanon that "*Africa is one, if not the most important*, field of battle against imperialism . . ." (*Revolución*, December 23, 1964, emphasis added). Again in Algiers, in an interview in *Alger Ce Soir*, he spoke of "combining our resources" to resist "imperialist aggression, *for example in the Congo*" (January 30, 1965, emphasis added). In the same interview, he was quoted as saying that in Cuba "we were always conscious of our popular culture. . . . Cuba and Africa are relatives." And then, significantly, "*This bond is more visible in the Congo*: it is possible to observe ethnic—and even physical—similarities. . . ." (emphasis added). In Dar

---

4. See my *The Rise and Decline of Fidel Castro* (Berkeley and Los Angeles: University of California Press, 1972), pp. 276–278.

5. Ché was no stranger in Algiers. He had been there in early July 1963, heading the Cuban delegation to the celebration of the first anniversary of Algerian independence; and again in April 1964, coming from Geneva, where he led the Cuban delegation to the first United Nations Conference on Trade and Development (UNCTAD).

Es Salaam, capital of Tanzania, Major Guevara, according to a *Prensa Latina* dispatch dated February 16, "spoke with representatives of [African] movements of National Liberation. . . to whom he expressed full moral support by Cuba." [6] One of the movements that maintained an office in Dar Es Salaam was the Congolese rebel organization. Tanzania, which borders the eastern Congo, provided direct access to the zone of military operations. Did Ché himself cross the border? And was it only "moral" support that he offered? Apparently these matters were overlooked at the time by the western press and perhaps also by the western intelligence agencies.

Among those who knew the facts and kept the secret were President Nasser and his closest collaborator, Mohammed Hassanein Heikal, editor of the semiofficial daily *Al Ahram*. In his book of reminiscences, *The Cairo Documents*, Heikal relates that on February 12, the day after the Cuban delegation arrived in Cairo, Ché met with Nasser and told him that he was going to Tanzania. "Guevara returned after ten days," Heikal continues, "during which time he had been in the Congo. . . . He had been visiting the force of two battalions of black Cubans . . . sent from Cuba to fight for Antoine Gizenga, the man who had tried to inherit Premier Lumumba's mantle." Ché told Nasser that he was planning to take command of the black Cubans. "I shall go to the Congo," he said, "because it is the hottest spot in the world now. . . . I think we can hurt the imperialists at the core of their interest in Katanga." Heikal adds that Nasser was astonished. He told Ché: "If you want to become another Tarzan, a white man coming among black men, leading them and protecting them, . . . it can't be done." [7]

A Dual Mission

There has been no confirmation from any other source that Cuban troops were already in the Congo at the beginning of 1965. In any event, Ché's mission was to determine the feasibility of either initiating or escalating Cuban military intervention in the region, under his personal leadership. A factor to be considered would be the collaboration of radical African governments. Apparently, Ché received no encouragement from Nasser, but it is more than likely that Ben Bella, already involved in a number of African guerrilla enterprises, had taken a different attitude. In the end, Fidel decided to take the risk of sending Ché to step up the struggle in the Congo.

6. *Política Internacional*, 9 (first trimester, 1965), 215.
7. *The Cairo Documents* (New York: Doubleday, 1973), pp. 348–349.

Ché's African mission was double-pronged. In public statements made during his tour, he spoke of the need of broadening intercontinental cooperation in the conflict against imperialism, colonialism, and neo-colonialism. What he was driving at he finally spelled out in Dar Es Salaam on February 16. "After completing my trip through seven African countries," he was quoted as saying by the Cuban press agency *Prensa Latina*, "I am convinced that it is possible to create a common front in the struggle. . . ." *Prensa Latina* then explained that he was referring to "a common front uniting the countries of Latin America, Africa, and Asia in the struggle against imperialism."[8] It was an ambitious proposal to supplant the existing and none-too-effective Afro-Asian People's Solidarity Organization with a new Third World coalition in which Cuba would play a leading role. As it turned out, in contrast to the disaster that befell the military adventure in the Congo, this project was a brilliant *tour de force*. Taking advantage of Soviet-Chinese rivalry for predominance in the Afro-Asian grouping, Fidel managed to pull off one of his major political exploits by hosting—and dominating—the founding conference of the new Organization of Solidarity of the Peoples of Africa, Asia, and Latin America (OSPAAAL), held in Havana in early January 1966. (This event will be the subject of a later chapter.)

Peking Interlude

Ché Guevara, it will be recalled, interrupted his African rounds for a brief visit to Peking. It was not a sentimental journey, although at the time it used to be said that while Fidel's stomach was in Moscow his heart was in Peking. Even more was it said that Ché vastly favored the Chinese over the Russian views on revolution and communism. The Chinese, on the other hand, did not reciprocate in their opinion of Ché, whom the Chinese press, except on the occasion of his first visit in November 1960, generally ignored. Months after his death (not even reported in China when it occurred), an editor of the *People's Daily* (*Jenmin Jih Pao*) stated that Ché had pursued "an adventurist policy" in Bolivia.[9]

8. *Política Internacional*, 9 (first trimester, 1965), 215.
9. Feng Pao, in a speech on April 9, 1968, cited by Daniel James, *Ché Guevara*, p. 305. K. S. Karol, in his *La Deuxième Révolution Chinoise* (Paris: Robert Laffont, 1973, p. 428), relates that in his 1971 visit to China he was privately reproached for having been, in an earlier book on Cuba, "too lenient toward 'Guevarism'; for he [Ché] was doomed to failure from the beginning and created a diversion [in Bolivia], deflecting peoples from mass struggle."

However, neither Fidel's "heart" nor Ché's "Maoism" mattered when it came to doing business with the Chinese—and vice versa. Accordingly, Ché arrived in Peking on February 3, 1965, accompanied by several members of his staff. A photograph released at the time showed him shaking hands with a smiling Mao Tse-tung,[10] but nothing else was publicly revealed concerning his stay in Peking. At the moment, Chinese-Cuban relations were ambivalent and mainly reflected their respective needs vis-à-vis the Soviet Union. Sensing Fidel's growing doubts concerning Cuban security in the context of the Kremlin's policy of peaceful coexistence, and probably noting the delay in the conclusion of the annual Soviet-Cuban trade and aid agreement,[11] the Chinese, a month or so before Ché's visit, had accepted Fidel's eagerly sought agreement for a five-year exchange of sugar and rice between the two countries (more about this later). With relations thus improving, presumably Ché was now in Peking to inform the Chinese about his African plans and to enlist support for convening an Asia–Africa–Latin America solidarity conference in Havana.

Ché's presence in Peking undoubtedly annoyed the Russians, who were further annoyed by the attention he received. As the French journalist Léo Sauvage noted, when Ché arrived in Peking, the Chinese already knew that Soviet Premier Alexei Kosygin, on his way to Hanoi, was scheduled to stop in Peking two days later. Thus, Ché "was warmly received by Mao Tse-tung himself," while Kosygin "was received politely by Chou En-lai. Such things do not pass unnoticed in the 'socialist camp.'"[12]

A Provocative Speech

The last public address which Ché Guevara was ever to make took place in Algiers, on February 24, 1965, at the Second Economic Seminar of Afro-Asian Solidarity.[13] It was a speech "from the heart," ingenuous and bold, and altogether a fitting "swan song" for one of the most articulate expo-

10. The picture is reproduced in Daniel James, *Ché Guevara*, following p. 94.

11. The agreement was finally signed on February 17 with generous terms for Cuba, possibly reflecting Soviet concessions stimulated by Ché's reception in Peking.

12. Léo Sauvage, *Ché Guevara: The Failure of a Revolutionary* (Englewood Cliffs, N.J.: Prentice-Hall, 1973), p. 87; originally published as *Le Cas Guevara* (Paris: Editions de la Table Ronde, 1971).

13. Some forty delegations attended, representing member governments, "liberation movements," and observers. Cuba, the USSR, and China were among the latter. (See the *New York Times*, February 28, 1965.)

nents of inflexible revolutionary and socialist idealism of his generation. Much of the speech covered familiar ground and need not detain us here. What was new and unexpected was a frontal attack on the Soviet Union. It came about during Ché's analysis of trade relations between the socialist and developing nations. The former, he insisted, should abandon the practice of buying raw materials from, and selling manufactured goods to, the latter on the basis of "world"—that is to say, capitalist—market prices, which inevitably discriminated against the raw material producers (a debatable thesis accepted as axiomatic in socialist and other anti-imperialist economics and referred to in current Marxist terminology as "unequal trade").

The socialist countries, he went on to explain, have the responsibility, as part of their "international obligation" and "the duty imposed by [their] ideology," to be guided in their trade policy only by the needs of the poor countries. In other words, "the socialist countries must bear the cost of development of the countries which are now beginning to embark on the road to liberation." Having established this principle, he concluded that no argument "eliminates the immoral character" of current trade relations between the two groups of countries. "The socialist countries," he declared, "are in a sense accomplices of imperial [*sic*] exploitation. . . . The socialist countries have the moral duty of liquidating their complicity with the exploiting countries of the West."[14]

The impact of this bombshell in the capitals of eastern Europe, and more particularly, in Moscow, could easily be imagined. Although Ché

14. *Política Internacional*, 9 (first trimester, 1965), 238. Ché admitted in his speech that he did not know "what methods exist for determining equitable prices." This is a matter that has stumped greater experts in Marxist economics than Ché. The fact is that international trade takes place in a world of nation-states, whether socialist or capitalist, each unavoidably giving priority to national interests over other commitments. Moreover, the great bulk of international trade is transacted in capitalist markets. Socialist trade in these markets is marginal and hence is governed by capitalist prices. Even in trade between socialist countries, transactions are invariably calculated with reference to "world"—that is, capitalist—market prices, since the socialist ideologues have not yet invented any other practical criteria for determining "value." A story imported from eastern Europe and making the rounds in Havana in the late 1960s illustrates a hypothetical dilemma that arises when socialism finally triumphs on the planet and only one capitalist country remains. A meeting of socialist leaders takes place to consider what to do about this situation. They decide that capitalism should be preserved in this last holdout in order to provide "world" prices for international trade.

did not single out any of the socialist culprits by name, the Soviet Union was the originator and incomparably the largest and most powerful practitioner of the "immorality" which he denounced. Nor was Ché presumably speaking only for himself. He was the head of an official delegation of the Cuban government. In the Soviet view, his remarks amounted to gratuitous and inadmissible slander.

I recall my astonishment on reading the speech a few days later. When I asked a high official in the ministry of foreign trade what the meaning was of Ché's blast, he answered with a broad grin: "It represents the Cuban point of view." Given the then prevailing drift of Fidel's speeches and the growing annoyances with Soviet trading methods in the ministry—hardly justified in view of Cuban irresponsibility, among other circumstances—this was not beyond belief. Nor, as it turned out, was Ché speaking only for himself in other provocative remarks which he had scattered around during his African travels. Noteworthy was an interview he gave in Accra, Ghana, on January 18. "Our [party] organization will be different from that of other fraternal parties," he declared. "We want the party really to be the vanguard of the people, . . . respected by the masses." Further on, he spoke of what other peoples could learn from the Cuban Revolution: "First, . . . to study, observe, and think with [your] own heads, . . . not copy anybody. . . ."[15] Fidel was soon to be making comparable statements in Havana.

Fidel was at the airport to greet Ché when he returned to Havana on March 14. It was a way of publicly saying to his top-level emissary back from a long and arduous series of missions abroad: *well done!* The "message," of course, was picked up in Moscow, which undoubtedly had earlier sent Fidel a blistering note protesting Ché's outrageous conduct in Algiers. Then, in a matter of days, another "message" reached Moscow: *Ché had vanished!* and with him the issue raised by his speech. Thus, Fidel had extricated himself from the embarrassment of any formal approval or retraction of Ché's offensive remarks. In any case, informed opinion in Havana at the time assumed that this was in part the explanation of the strange sequence of events which followed Ché's return from Algiers.

Diverse Speculation

When Ché's continued absence from the scene, and the complete blackout concerning his whereabouts, began to attract attention abroad, there

15. Interview with the daily *L'Etincel* (Accra, Ghana) and with *Prensa Latina*, reproduced in *Política Internacional*, 9 (first trimester, 1965), 149.

was a rash of speculation by western commentators about a titanic crisis over personal and ideological relations between Ché and Fidel. Some suspected that Ché was under arrest, others that he had suffered a nervous breakdown and was hospitalized, and still others that he had been executed. Even after Ché's death, when the secret of his guerrilla exploits in Africa and Bolivia was revealed, some continued to maintain that he had had a violent dispute with Fidel on his return from Algiers, and they went on to propose that his new assignment had been in large measure decided upon as a solution to the problem of their personal relations. Nevertheless, it is entirely possible, and even reasonable to suppose, that some of the "clues" which led to these conclusions were deliberately fabricated in Havana in order to provide cover for Ché's secret mission.

Possibly, harsh words were exchanged between the two men concerning the Algiers speech. The fact that it was eventually printed in full in the appropriate quarterly issue of the official *Política Internacional* (released in May—that is, two months after Ché's return from Algiers) would clearly indicate that only a matter of tactics and timing, and not the content of the speech, might have disturbed Fidel. That there had been friction from time to time between the two men could be assumed, as could the idea that Ché had felt frustrated as an economic planner and administrator and engineer of the "new socialist man" in the Cuban setting. And, given Ché's temperament, his convictions, his conception of his own identity as a Latin American more than as a Cuban, and his inflated belief that his role in Castro's guerrilla band had prepared him to duplicate his exploits in other parts of the world—all of this may well have figured in Ché's willingness to embark on his new and fatal career.

However, in the last analysis, a decision of this importance could only have been taken with compelling political objectives in view. As previously argued, it was part of Fidel's strategy to strengthen his hand in his confrontation with the United States and in his increasingly irritable relations with the USSR. The strategy had undoubtedly been conceived before Ché's departure for New York, probably with a prior exchange of views with Ben Bella, and from the beginning must have involved Ché's leadership of the Congo operation. The final decision could only take place after Ché's reconnaissance in Africa. Whatever else may have transpired when Ché returned from Algiers, Fidel must have been primarily concerned with the implementation of the Africa strategy.

Most improbable of all the speculations at the time was that an ideological confrontation between Fidel and Ché had taken place. They were, to be sure, men of different intellectual temperaments. While Ché had fairly well defined his heretical views on questions of Marxist-Leninist doctrine by 1961, and thereafter steadfastly kept to them, Fidel was a less systematic thinker and a more pragmatic political operator. Nevertheless, they were ideological mavericks of the same species. Neither had come to accept Marxism-Leninism via the classical Communist Party route.[16] Castroism and Guevarism were not antithetical; they were complementary. When the two men disagreed over issues of policy, it is very unlikely that Fidel's position was ever based on other than practical grounds. Until Cuba's economic crisis of 1970 finally proved the bankruptcy of Ché's utopian vision, Fidel had not irrevocably rejected the fundamentals of that vision. He kept them in reserve, as options to be adopted at the appropriate moment. And precisely when Ché returned from Algeria, Fidel was in the process of implementing such an option. In a little over six months, he would unveil his new and unconventional Communist Party of Cuba, first hinted at by Ché in his Accra interview. Fidel would announce the physical separation of Ché from his functions in Cuba and from his juridical identity as a Cuban while simultaneously exalting his spirit. In a short time, it would become crystal clear that although Guevara was gone, Guevarism remained—stronger than ever.

The Congo Disaster

Very little has been revealed concerning Ché's campaign in the Congo. It appears that he left Cuba in late April 1965, that in July he took command of some two hundred well-armed Cuban combat veterans, that despite their assistance the native rebel forces disintegrated, that Ché withdrew in disgust, and that he was back in Cuba with an unknown number of his

16. It is interesting to recall that Ché did not consider Fidel to be a Marxist at the time Fidel was leading the guerrilla war against Batista. In a letter from the Sierra Maestre dated December 14, 1957, addressed to a guerrilla leader later killed in action, Ché wrote: "On account of my ideological preparation, I am one of those who believes that the solution of the world's problems lies behind the so-called iron curtain, and I consider [Fidel's] movement as one of the many which are motivated by the eagerness of the bourgeoisie to free itself from the economic chains of imperialism. I always considered Fidel to be an authentic leader of the leftist bourgeoisie, although his stature is enhanced by personal qualities of extraordinary brilliance which place him high above his class" (Carlos Franqui, *Diario de la revolución cubana* (Barcelona: Ediciones R. Torres, 1976), p. 362).

troops toward the end of the year.[17] Something of what transpired could later be gleaned from remarks by Ché in the spring of 1967 to a visitor at his guerrilla base in Bolivia. "The human element [in the Congo] failed," Ché was reported to have said. "There was no will to fight. The leaders are corrupt. In a word, nothing could be done."[18]

Some additional details were supplied by a defector who had worked in the intelligence department of the Cuban embassy in Paris, where he had talked with a survivor of Ché's Congo operation. According to the latter, the "Cubans had endured severe privations, . . . they were busy trying to keep the tribes from fighting among themselves. . . . There were angry arguments. . . . Guevara and his Cubans had to flee through the jungles, pursued by enemy troops and their former allies. It took them a month to get to safety. . . ." The intelligence official also learned that the "Russians had been against Guevara's African adventure. . . . Fidel Castro had not agreed, and there had been friction between him and the Russians over the matter."[19]

The disaster did not enhance Ché's revolutionary stature or Fidel's political judgment, which may explain why, for more than a decade, the presence of Ché and his Cuban detachment in the Congo remained a "non-event" in the voluminous accounts of Ché's exploits and virtues which emanated from Havana after his death. It was only in January 1977 that a Castro-approved account of Cuba's massive armed intervention in the Angolan civil war (1975–1976) finally mentioned Ché's campaign in the Congo. It was a brief, thoroughly sanitized version designed to associate the image of the incorruptible Ché with a military incursion of an entirely different order and thus bolster Castro's claim that Cuban involve-

17. Gaston Soumaliot, the top political leader of the rebellion in the eastern Congo after April 1965, spent the first two weeks of September 1965 in Havana. Castro personally showered him with attention, while *Revolución* (September 4, 11, and 13) gave him front-page publicity. Ché was still in the Congo at the time. After Soumaliot's departure, the Cuban press, which for months had featured events in the Congo, abruptly ceased to report on the Congo struggle. Presumably, news of Ché's difficulties had begun to reach Havana.

18. The visitor was the Argentine journalist Ciro Roberto Bustos, who along with the French writer Régis Debray was apprehended by the Bolivian military. Bustos gave the authorities a long written statement about his experience in Ché's encampment (quoted here from Daniel James, *Ché Guevara*, p. 159).

19. Orlando Castro Hidalgo, *Spy for Cuba* (Miami, Florida: Seemann, 1971), pp. 54–55.

ment in Africa had always been motivated by high moral purpose. Ché
Guevara's presence in Africa, the writer piously declared, "planted a seed
that no one could uproot."[20]

20. The account was written by Gabriel García Márquez, noted Colombian
novelist and staunch supporter of Castro's regime. It was said to be based on numerous interviews in Cuba. *Prensa Latina*, the official Cuban news agency, gave it
wide distribution. The *Washington Post* published three substantial extracts from
January 10 to 12, 1977. In the third (January 12, p. A-12), the writer stated that Ché
left Cuba on April 25, and "three months later, in the Congo, he joined 200
Cuban troops who had traveled from Havana" by ship. He stayed until "December
1965, not only training guerrillas, but also directing them in battle and fighting
alongside them." After the "defeat" of the enemy, "Ché Guevara left as he had
come, without fanfare."García Márquez carefully avoided commenting on the actual fighting and left the impression that Ché's departure "without fanfare" was due
to modesty. He did not inform the reader that, prior to his story, the Cuban government had treated Ché's Congo operation as a dead secret.

16
■

Agriculture and the Cult of Grass

Fidel's Fantasies

IT WAS LONG ANTICIPATED that 1965, the new year coming up, would be dubbed "*El Año de la Agricultura*" (The Year of Agriculture) in the revolutionary calendar.[1] For months, Fidel had been exhorting, scolding, and cajoling his fellow countrymen with the vision of bountiful crops. Patriotic and intelligent dedication, he reiterated, could not fail to produce great quantities of food, given Cuba's fertile soil, ample moisture, and abundance of tropical sunshine. Thus, with exuberant optimism he had foreseen the end of the rationing of *viandas* in no later than twelve months.[2] These were the tubers, such as *malanga* and *boniato*, the low-cost vegetable staples in the Cuban diet that were always in plentiful supply before the Revolution. Then again, looking ahead to 1970, he had announced that the mighty, never-before-achieved ten-million-ton sugar harvest (destined to be a great calamity) was not only assured but "already sold." At that time, he confidently predicted, "we'll be figuring on how to produce another two or three million tons."[3]

1. The practice of selecting an annual slogan highlighting the overriding goal or significance of the year still continues. The slogan is displayed on all official documents and correspondence. The slogans of 1962, 1963, and 1964 featured, under different rubrics, the improvement of the economy—with no measurable impact on performance.
2. Speech on September 28, 1964; reported in *Revolución* the following day.
3. Speech on November 14, 1964; reported in *Revolución* the following day.

And so it went, with Fidel almost daily reaching new levels of fantasy. "By 1970," he declared early in the Year of Agriculture, "we shall possibly be one of the best nourished peoples in the whole world." With vast quantities of milk, "an unlimited source of protein for the people, . . . we'll really have more than enough for three times the present size of our population in just a few years, . . . and also great quantities of meat and fish."[4] A week before this absurdly optimistic prediction (in 1970, supplies of food were to reach their lowest point), he had dramatized the anticipated achievement of the new goals by taking over the presidency of INRA (the National Institute of Agrarian Reform—in effect, the ministry of agriculture) "in order to activate all available resources."[5] Fidel had appointed himself the first president of INRA when it was created, but he relinquished the post to Carlos Rafael Rodríguez on February 6, 1962. When Fidel resumed the presidency, Rodríguez was given the title of minister, with undefined duties related to the economy. Apparently, Rodríguez was dismissed not for lack of competence but for lack of the kind of leadership authority required to push through the new program.

If there was any doubt about Fidel's predictions, it was dispelled by a "unanimously" approved report at a national convention of the government's agricultural leadership and several hundred state farm managers on January 29, 1965. Issued in the form of a long and (according to established custom) obsequious letter addressed to the Prime Minister, the convention confessed the many errors of the past in agricultural planning and management, paid tribute to the Prime Minister's scorching criticism of past deficiencies, and praised the wisdom of the goals he had set forth for the future, including the ten-million-ton sugar harvest in 1970 and the end of the rationing of *viandas* before the close of the year. "We assure you," the assembly pledged, "that with respect to work discipline, financial [responsibility], and agricultural and livestock technology, [we] will make every effort to move forward this year, according to the line which you have given to the Party and the People. . . ."[6]

A skeptic might have wondered about the precise schedule for derationing *viandas*. As for the great sugar harvest and beyond, it was still too far off for speculation. There was, to be sure, a respectable increase in

4. Speech on January 21, 1965; text from *Política Internacional*, 9 (first trimester, 1965), 173.
5. January 14, 1965; reported in *Revolución* the following day.
6. *Cuba Socialista*, March 1965, p. 132.

sugar production in 1965: over six million tons compared to some 4.5 million the year before. Although this provided a boost in morale, paradoxically it resulted in less income of always-too-scarce convertible currency because of the drop in the price of sugar sold on the world market.[7] Nor would six million tons be the start of the planned climb to ten million tons. In 1966, production would again fall to 1964 levels. As for the *viandas*, they would continue to be rationed for many years to come. More serious was the spectacular decline in the production of rice, the staple cereal in the Cuban diet. In January 1966, a deep cut would take place in the monthly rations.[8] For the rest of the edibles, there were gains and losses in a wide variety of products. Buttressed by increasing imports and controlled by rationing, the Cuban economy still had enough food—of limited variety—to go around. The worst was yet to come.

The Arrival of André Voisin

No account of Castro's impetuous leap into the "Year of Agriculture"—nor indeed of the extraordinary character of Cuba's Maximum Leader, and hence of the Cuban Revolution—would be complete without the story of André Voisin's brief and tragic visit to Cuba in December 1964. Voisin, at the time in his early sixties, was a successful French farmer, teacher, and agronomist, unknown outside his narrow field of specialization, and with no strong political views of any kind. He had published several books dealing with soil chemistry, the care and management of pasture lands, and, for more popular consumption, the relation of soil to human health.[9] It is not clear how Castro discovered him, but once he did he was convinced that Voisin provided the solution to a fundamental problem of Cuba's ailing animal husbandry: how to nourish cattle, especially dairy herds, on

---

7. According to Castro's figures, the average price in 1964 was 5.88 cents per pound; in 1965, 2.18 cents (*Política Internacional*, 13 [first trimester, 1966], 219). Hard-currency income declined from approximately $134 million in 1964 to $92 million in 1965, a drop of thirty percent. (*El Comercio Exterior de Cuba y Sus Tendencias* [Havana: Ministerio de Comercio Exterior, 1967], p. 75).

8. Production in 1965 declined by sixty percent compared with 1964 (calculated from data in *Anuario Estadístico de Cuba 1973* [Havana: Junta Central de Planificación, 1975], p. 91). The per capita ration of six pounds per month established in March 1962 was reduced by one-half. By the mid-1970s it was restored to six pounds, and in the late 1970s it was reduced to five pounds.

9. A brief encomium containing biographical data appeared on the anniversary of Voisin's death in the weekly Havana *Bohemia*, December 20, 1968.

pasture grass rather than on imported feed, which the Soviet Union could not provide (indeed, could not produce enough for its own needs), and which therefore meant a constant and considerable drain on Cuba's limited convertible currency.

For anyone except Fidel, the discovery of Voisin might have led to a deliberate and painstaking consideration of his pasturage system by local and perhaps other foreign experts. This might then have been followed by some discreet experiments. The process could consume a year or more. But this was not in keeping with a man of Fidel's temperament—and the unlimited power to pamper his temperament. As if inspired by a providential revelation, Fidel decided to adopt the Voisin system and to mount a massive campaign of "grass indoctrination" of the entire Cuban population. As the first step in the campaign, Professor Voisin was invited to give a series of lectures in Havana. Accepting with some hesitation, as he later explained, he worked day and night for two months, and at the end of September sent the text of his lectures to Havana for translation. At two o'clock in the morning of December 3, Voisin, accompanied by his wife, stepped off the plane at the José Martí International Airport—into the waiting arms of Fidel Castro.

The Inauguration of Professor Voisin

A few days later, an elaborate inaugural ceremony took place. Voisin, in the presence of Castro, was introduced by the French ambassador to an overflow audience of students and assorted university and government notables and to television viewers throughout the island. The ambassador was no doubt astonished by the homage being paid to a fellow countryman of whose existence he must have been unaware before Fidel discovered him. When the professor's turn to speak came, he expressed his own astonishment. The "first revolution" he encountered, as he put it, was to find a "head of government" waiting at the airport "to greet a modest French scientist at two o'clock in the morning." There were more surprises, he continued, addressing the "head of government" seated on the platform behind him: "you accompanied us to our residence [a witness claimed that Fidel carried some of their luggage]. Then you said with the utmost consideration that we must be very tired and that you would stay for only five minutes. Very soon I forgot how tired I was. I listened to you talk with greater and greater astonishment. . . . It was 6 A.M. when you left."[10]

10. *Revolución*, December 9, 1964.

The professor was not exaggerating. As others have reported, Castro in a tête-à-tête conversation casts an hypnotic spell on his interlocutor, sitting close to him, transfixing him with his piercing black eyes, gesticulating freely, occasionally patting his victim on the knee, with an incessant stream of flawless rhetoric flowing from his mouth, and all the while totally oblivious to the passing of time or the lateness of the hour.

Voisin also told how Fidel had presented him with a "beautiful book containing a complete translation of all my lectures." He had never expected the translation to be finished in so short a time, much less as a printed bound volume. When he asked how this was possible, the Prime Minister explained to him that "it was teamwork, . . . many translators, designers, typographers, workers. . . ." Almost certainly, nobody in the audience shared the professor's amazement. This was one of the distinguishing characteristics of the Cuban Revolution. The commander-in-chief would have a brainstorm, for better or worse. This would trigger a crash program, with total mobilization of all available resources. If it came to nothing, the failure was never acknowledged. If it succeeded, as it sometimes did, it was hailed as an example of the superiority of socialism over capitalism. In neither case were the costs taken into account.

The Science of Grass Expounded

The Prime Minister was the last to speak. He told about reading three books by the professor and how one of them, The Productivity of Grass (in Spanish, La Productividad de la Hierba, as translated from the French), expounded a "system of rotating pasturage, . . . from the practical point of view an inestimable contribution. . . . It can add hundreds of millions of pesos to our economy. . . . With this system plus fertilization, present yields of our pastures can be increased sevenfold. . . ." This was, of course, what first drew Fidel to Professor Voisin. Grass was the quick, easy, "scientific" solution to the intractable problem of producing fodder for Cuban cattle. As sometimes happens with nonscientists who worship science, Castro tended to confuse science with magic.

Fidel spoke for nearly two hours. Part of the time he delved into the intricacies of soil chemistry, branching out into the "scientific laws of fertilizer application" and the "dialectical laws" of pasturage, all the while revealing his amazing capacity for rapidly assimilating and expertly expounding great quantities of newly acquired technical knowledge. It was one of his frequent demonstrations of sheer brain power. It dazzled even his most sophisticated listeners and gave a special quality to his charisma. Towering as he did over his subordinates, his awareness of his unique gift was in large part the source of his unwavering self-confidence. Even Voisin was enthralled, exclaiming that Fidel was his best student and that he could not understand how a Prime Minister, with the heavy burdens of his office, could manage to master such a complex technical subject in so short a time.

What Voisin never discovered—he did not live to see his system in operation (see below)—was that Fidel's mastery of a subject could be very costly. As another French agronomist explained, after observing Cuban management of rotating pasturage, Castro applied the Voisin method "as if it were something like the Gospel. . . . Organizing pastures of identical size with identical fertilizer, . . . everybody doing the same thing at the same time," without any consideration for differences of soil, moisture, and the varying capacities of unit heads to respond intelligently to local conditions. "Something is always missing," the agronomist added, "for prefabricated schemes to work out as expected." [11]

If a cost-benefit accounting of the grass blitz was ever made, which is unlikely, it was never revealed. A painful and prolonged period of trial and error eventually produced a modest contribution to Cuban animal husbandry. Grass, however, could not be the panacea that Fidel proclaimed it to be. After the Voisin euphoria wore off, Fidel turned his attention to developing conventional feed crops and to utilizing molasses, a by-product of sugar production, as a feed supplement. This time he imported British and Israeli experts, and still others later, but again without any resounding success. [12]

To return to Castro's speech: at one point he introduced his audience to another book by Voisin, *Soil, Grass, and Cancer* (giving the title in

11. René Dumont, *Cuba est-il socialiste?* (Paris: Seuil, 1970), p. 153.

12. In 1965, along with two colleagues, Dr. Thomas Preston, who had gained a reputation in England by using barley to fatten cattle, set up an experimental station on the outskirts of Havana. Fidel promptly gave it the inflated name of Institute of Animal Science. In 1969, Preston and his English staff publicly and severely criticized the incompetence of their Cuban collaborators. This led to a crisis in their relations with Fidel and their eventual departure from Cuba. In 1967, I accidentally ran into two Israeli agronomists in Havana. They were experimenting with the cultivation of sorghum, a source of fodder in many countries. Apparently nothing came of the experiment. The presence of the Israelis in Cuba was never publicly acknowledged. It would have complicated relations with the Arab brethren.

Spanish). This, he explained, is "a book for farmers, but even more so for doctors." As he went on, his enthusiasm mounted. "There are things in this book," he exclaimed, "really new, really unbelievable, and at times breathtaking. This book analyzes the influence of soil on man as transmitted by animals and plants. It permits us to see the extraordinary relationship between human health and soil. . . . Professor Voisin . . . is an apostle of humanity, of human health, and especially of preventive medicine." Then followed another dazzling display of newly acquired erudition on the role of fertilizers, minerals, and vitamins in the metabolic processes of the human organism, interspersed with exchanges of questions and answers from medical students among his listeners.

Voisin the Humanist

Here, then, was a second and most convenient virtue that Fidel had discovered in the works of Voisin: the professor's "humanity" dovetailed perfectly with the incessantly proclaimed socialist ethics of the Cuban Revolution. Hence, it further justified Fidel's inordinate praise for the scientist whose championship of grass would provide the Cuban economy "with hundreds of millions of pesos" of new wealth. Meanwhile, as was its invariable custom, the press dutifully projected and amplified the leader's vision. One writer, for example, declared the professor to be a "genuine revolutionary" and hailed his visit as proof that "the Technical Revolution is beginning to become a reality in Cuba." [13]

Voisin had still a third virtue which reinforced the others, although Castro did not make it explicit. The professor was a Frenchman and not a Russian. Animal husbandry in the Soviet Union was notoriously backward. Voisin's presence in Cuba inevitably drew attention to this fact and must have irritated the Russians, which could not have displeased Fidel. It was a time in which he was becoming increasingly suspicious that he had been entrapped by the Kremlin's policy of peaceful coexistence with the United States and hostility toward China. (This was several years before his unconditional surrender to Soviet hegemony.) Thus, the "French connection" was something of a demonstration of independence in Cuba's foreign relations, and also of success in circumventing American pressures to.cut off Cuba's access to western technology. In his closing remarks, Castro pointedly expressed his gratitude to the French ambassador for his presence and for introducing Voisin to the assembly.

13. *Revolución*, December 14, 1964.

The Publication of the Lectures

Voisin opened the first of what was scheduled to be a series of ten lectures on December 9. There was full radio and television coverage. The next day, *Revolución* displayed a large photo showing Fidel seated in the audience, listening intently to the professor. On December 14, readers of the daily press discovered a special treat: facsimile reproductions of the first twelve pages of the book containing the professor's lectures.[14] These were accompanied by the news that the reproductions were the start of the serial publication of the entire work. Nothing like this publishing stunt had ever occurred in Cuba before (nor was it likely to ever recur after grass failed to live up to its promise), not even with the hallowed works of Marx, Engels, or Lenin. The science of grass was like a new religion; Voisin was its prophet and Fidel its high priest. It did not matter that the sacred text, replete with tables, graphs, equations, chemical formulae, and footnotes, would be incomprehensible to ninety-nine percent of Cuban newspaper readers.

Like the entire staging of Voisin's visit, this was part of Fidel's instinctive—and frequently expensive—showmanship, undoubtedly effective with his constituency because it projected an element of sincerity. But it was also eminently self-serving showmanship. Here was the commander-in-chief seeking the practical benefits of science for his people; discovering the life-giving science of grass; modest in the presence of an unheralded scientist; an eager student of science; and now incorporating the masses into the process of scientific learning. Foreign admirers of Castro who were impressed by the brilliant display of his talents failed to see the vanity and folly which they often concealed.

Hero and Martyr of the Revolution

On Monday evening, December 21, there was no lecture. Castro appeared in the auditorium to announce that Professor Voisin had died of a heart attack a few hours earlier. The next morning, the news was headlined on the front page of *Revolución*. That afternoon, Voisin was given a state funeral, with Castro delivering the oration. The professor was buried as a hero and martyr of the Revolution. The final installment of his 263-page book appeared in *Revolución* on January 26, 1965. Later an institute was named for him. In the years that followed, Madame Voisin would appear from

14. *Influencia del Suelo Sobre el Animal a Través de la Planta* (Influence of Soil, Transmitted by Plants, on Animals), the underpinnings of the science of grass.

time to time among the notable guests invited to celebrate the July 26th national holiday.

Whether or not André Voisin had a history of cardiac disease before coming to Cuba was not revealed. However, it is likely that his martyrdom was not entirely due to the previous state of his health. He had been under great pressure to complete his lectures before leaving France. His trip was a perilous and exhausting one, lasting three days. His plane was caught in a storm off the coast of Newfoundland and had to double back to Ireland before crossing the Atlantic a second time. His first meeting with Fidel was physically and emotionally wearing. What remained of his health was drained by the excitement of his unexpected fame and the strain of lecturing and attending many meetings with party, government, and university leaders. He was not the first or the last victim of Fidel's ruinous embrace.

17
■

A Digression: The Case of Oscar Lewis

The Unfinished Project

OF THE SEVERAL WESTERN scholars and journalists who at one time or another had a personal relationship with Fidel Castro, none paid a greater penalty than Oscar Lewis. Hence, it might be appropriate at this point to digress from the chronology of our narrative in order to examine his encounter with the Cuban Revolution.

The late Oscar Lewis, for many years a professor of anthropology at the University of Illinois, earned fame and fortune with his widely read studies of life in the slums of Mexico and Puerto Rico.[1] Subsequently he turned his attention to socialist Cuba. Oscar and Ruth, his wife and collaborator in nearly all his previous publications, arrived in Havana early in 1969 for what they had planned to be a three-year stay. Using the technique of tape-recorded autobiographies that they had developed in their earlier work, and assisted by a sizable staff of Cubans and non-Cubans, they managed to accumulate many thousands of pages transcribed from tape, when suddenly their work was halted. At the end of June 1970, with less than half of the planned research completed, the Cuban authorities

---

1. Among his books: *The Children of Sánchez* (New York: Random House, 1961); *Pedro Martínez* (New York: Random House, 1964); and *La Vida* (New York: Random House, 1966).

abruptly forced the project to close down and confiscated its files. At the time, the files contained about half of the materials which had thus far been collected, the other half having been removed from Cuba earlier.

When the Lewises returned to the United States, the question of what to do with the 20,000-odd pages of transcripts which remained in their possession was further complicated by Oscar's unexpected death, six months after leaving Cuba. Nevertheless, with the help of Susan Rigdon as co-editor, Ruth decided to go ahead with the tasks of organizing, translating, and editing, with the result that three large volumes, described as "an oral history of contemporary Cuba," were eventually published.[2] Like Oscar Lewis's previous work, and despite the loss of half the material collected and the unfinished research which remained to be done, the volumes turned out to have considerable documentary value. At the same time, of at least equal interest were the circumstances under which the original project was undertaken, and arbitrarily terminated, since these shed light on the personality of Fidel Castro and, in a broader sense, on what might be called the comparative sociology of knowledge in Marxist-Leninist, as contrasted with "bourgeois" democratic, environments. Ruth Lewis dealt with this topic in an extensive foreword to which I can add a few details and suggest a perspective in some respects different from hers.

Origin of the Project

I had known Oscar for a number of years when, after a long lapse, we met in Montreal in the summer of 1967. I had come from Cuba for a brief holiday, including a visit to "Expo 1967." Whatever else brought Oscar to Montreal, he was anxious to get my opinion about the feasibility of doing one of his now classic types of studies on family and community life in socialist Cuba. His interest in Cuba was not new, since he had spent a few months as a visiting professor at the University of Havana in 1946. Nor was his interest in the Cuban Revolution and socialism new. He had managed to spend a few days in Havana in 1961 and had noted promising changes in the slums that he had visited previously. Now that socialism was firmly established, he could reveal in intimate detail how life had changed, and it would be another, and bigger, feather in his cap. No western anthropolo-

---

2. Oscar Lewis, Ruth M. Lewis, and Susan M. Rigdon, *Four Men* (Urbana: University of Illinois Press, 1977); *Four Women* (Urbana: University of Illinois Press, 1977); and *Neighbors* (Urbana: University of Illinois Press, 1978). The three volumes are subtitled: *Living the Revolution: An Oral History of Contemporary Cuba*.

gist had thus far been able to penetrate a socialist country and describe the impact of the new values on the "culture of poverty." The question he wanted me to answer was: could he persuade the Cubans to allow him to undertake such a project?

I told him that it was unlikely. The kind of freedom he would require to conduct his research and then publish its results was incompatible with the rigid controls maintained by any Marxist-Leninist state, including Cuba. In any event, he would have to take it up directly with Fidel Castro, since only he could authorize such a project. Castro was erratic, and might conceivably be persuaded. Even then, Oscar would have to assume that the project would be subject to surveillance by the security police.

The following February (1968), Oscar showed up in Havana. When he came to see me, he was bubbling over with enthusiasm. On his way to Cuba, he had stopped off in Mexico City, where he interviewed one of the slum dwellers featured in *The Children of Sánchez*. The topic was Fidel Castro, and the result was a tribute to the great Cuban champion of the poor and oppressed. Oscar played the tape for Fidel, who was deeply moved. Moreover, he had accepted Oscar's proposition. I did not see Oscar again. I left Cuba in April, nearly a year before Oscar returned to set up his project.

The Terms of the Project

As Ruth Lewis tells the story,[3] Oscar explained in his meeting with Castro that he would undertake the project only if certain basic conditions were met, including "freedom of investigation, that is, the right to decide what and whom to study, without censorship or intervention by the government, including the right to take taped interviews, manuscripts and other material out of Cuba without having them read or inspected," and "assurance that the government would not harm or punish any of the subjects for cooperating with the study." Castro accepted the conditions.

As the project got under way, and for some time thereafter, it appeared that Oscar's stipulations were respected, although Ruth notes that "field work in socialist Cuba was a profoundly unique experience. . . . Not a single important aspect was not affected in some degree by the great societal changes in Cuba, above all the ubiquitous presence of the state." From the moment that Oscar and Ruth arrived at the airport, "the government had assigned a trusted militant [euphemism for Communist Party member] . . . to administer to the needs of the project and its staff and act as in-

3. Foreword to *Four Men*, pp. vii–xxv.

termediary with the government and its agencies." Among the multitude of services he performed was to introduce "Oscar to the local authorities in places where community studies were to be conducted." Given the total bureaucratization of life under socialism, it is understandable that Ruth found this man's role in the project to be "indispensable."

The Project Terminated

The full impact of the "ubiquitous presence of the state" struck Oscar on June 25, 1970. Summoned to appear before the Foreign Minister, "he was shocked to be formally notified by Dr. Roa that Project Cuba, as they called it, had been suspended by the government. Reasons were given in the form of alleged breaches of the original agreement. . . ." That Oscar was shocked is to put it mildly. At the moment when Roa finished reading the indictment, Oscar suffered a heart attack and collapsed, although Ruth unaccountably fails to mention this. The charges were groundless, with ugly connotations of intentional deceit and even espionage. These were later spelled out in lurid detail in 1972 in a speech by Raúl Castro, Minister of the Armed Forces and Fidel's brother and designated successor.[4]

The real reason, as the Lewises at once suspected and then confirmed, was that three months earlier Oscar had begun to interview an individual who was sharply critical of the regime and its leadership. Data considered highly objectionable by the regime had also begun to emerge in another study. All this material formed part of the files seized by security agents, and was therefore lost to the project. Before his departure, Oscar tried desperately to contact Fidel, but without success.

The final blow came soon after the Lewises left Cuba, when they learned that their dissident informant was in prison. He had accepted Oscar's assurance that, under the agreement with Castro, no harm could befall him for cooperating with the project. Hence, as Ruth laments: "The news of his arrest affected us deeply. We felt personally responsible. . . ."

The plain and simple fact of the matter is that Castro personally double-crossed Oscar, although Ruth is reluctant to say so bluntly. At one point, she states that "we did not question the right of the Cuban government to reverse its position and close down Project Cuba, but were dismayed at the reasons given for doing so." Yet, it was not the "Cuban government" that had accepted Oscar's project and conditions, but the Maximum Leader himself, in Oscar's presence and without consulting the "Cuban govern-

4. The text is on p. xxiv of the Foreword to *Four Men*.

ment." Likewise, only the Maximum Leader could have the authority to "reverse" a decision which he had made. The matter of "right" is also puzzling. Did it include the "right" to send a man to jail after he had been promised immunity? Ruth does not explain. At first their reaction was the classic one reminiscent of Stalin's victims who were convinced that "if only Stalin knew. . . ." In the end they concluded that "Castro had full knowledge of what had taken place and that it had been his *political* decision to scrap the project" (emphasis added). Presumably, this had included the decision to imprison their unfortunate collaborator, but she does not say so.

Illusion and Betrayal

Ruth's efforts to account for their misfortune are less than satisfactory—in part, it would appear, because of an unwillingness to shed some of the naivete about socialism in general, and Castro in particular, that had led Oscar into the fatal trap. While Oscar to some extent realized that his research could run into political obstacles (hence the "deal" with Castro), he really did not anticipate that such problems would arise. His sympathetic view of the Cuban Revolution led him to believe that his study could only enhance the image of the Revolution. This is the impression I got when I spoke with him in Montreal, and again in Havana. Thus, there would be no reason for censorship, and Castro's guarantees must have reinforced his conviction. When Oscar discovered that independent research was more difficult than he had expected, and when unflattering and then very critical data began to accumulate, his integrity as a scholar prevailed over any other consideration. Instead of self-censorship, which a firm commitment to Castro's Cuba would require, he continued to do whatever was possible to meet his commitment to professional probity, never suspecting that Castro himself would betray him. It was another demonstration of his naivete, for which he paid dearly.

The encounter between Oscar Lewis and Fidel Castro, while not pleasant to contemplate, was instructive. What quixotic impulse moved the Commander-in-Chief to accept Oscar's proposition? Ruth supplies the key to the answer when she quotes what Fidel told Oscar at the time of their meeting: "We are probably the only socialist country in the world that would allow you to do your kind of studies with the complete freedom you need." The Lewises, however, did not realize that the boast was typical of Fidel's congenital urge to demonstrate his originality and courage, to defy precedent, to advance where lesser mortals feared to tread—and at the time of Oscar's visit early in 1968, to prove that he was not a mere imitator of the Russian model—while enhancing his prestige among western leftist intellectuals, whom he was currently courting. (Later he accepted the Russian model without reservations.) But Fidel was also shrewd. Oscar, he knew from his writings, had been consistent in exposing the appalling deprivations and injustice to which the poor were exposed in capitalist Mexico and American-dominated Puerto Rico. Oscar was a friend of the Cuban Revolution. Oscar flattered him with the tape recording he brought from Mexico. Oscar, in short, could be trusted. If Fidel perceived a slight risk that Oscar might not perform as he expected, he had the means to control the situation. All of this is not to say that Fidel cold-bloodedly calculated the odds in his gamble, or that he consciously perceived it to be a gamble. For Fidel, the decision-making process was often intuitive and spontaneous.

In the fall of 1970, Oscar called me on the telephone from his home in Urbana, Illinois. He was obviously distraught. Could I suggest how he might retrieve his files? Did I know somebody in Havana with influence? He couldn't get through to Fidel. He did not want to tell me the full story, he said, "over the telephone," but he was in deep trouble. He threw out hints which I could not completely fathom, but it was clear that his project had collapsed. No, I could not help him. After the conversation, I wondered about his fear of the telephone. Was it a touch of paranoia which he had picked up in Havana? Three months later, I learned that he had died of a heart attack. It was hard to dismiss the thought that Castro, in part at least, was responsible for his untimely death. He was fifty-six years old.

Perspective on the Revolution

It is ironic that Fidel's claim that Cuba was the "only socialist country in the world" that would allow Oscar Lewis the "complete freedom you need" turned out to be sufficiently true, despite his belated change of mind, to provide the foreign reader with the kind of intimate and authentic perspective on everyday life not available in any other socialist country, nor likely to be in the foreseeable future. Oscar's unfinished Cuban project can thus take its place as another one of his pioneering investigations. Turning now to the work itself, the great bulk of the scores of individuals who appear in it came from the urban poor or near-poor, although, as they tell their stories, none could be described as having been completely destitute under the old regime. Thus, they might represent perhaps the fifteen or twenty percent (my estimate) of the urban population (which in turn was close to sixty percent of the total population)[5] whose welfare was of particular concern to the Castro regime. Although it is a small sample—and selected with some official guidance, as I have explained—it is probably a fair one.

The reader with the patience to plow through this material comes away with a number of general impressions. Sexual activity, for example, is as intense and varied under the Revolution as before, possibly more so with the greater housing congestion, the absence of men from their wives during long periods of "voluntary" labor in the country, and the incorporation of more women in the work force. Marital instability, whether in unions of the legal or the consensual variety, appears to be endemic. And in this connection, male dominance is all-pervasive and fully accepted by women.

The Role of Women

The question of women's liberation, or rather the lack of it, in socialist Cuba is a matter of more than passing interest to Ruth Lewis and her coeditor. In a long introduction to *Four Women*, as the second of their three volumes is entitled, they note that "the primary impetus for liberating Cuban women from the traditional sex role was to free them to serve . . . in the labor force." As for the Federation of Cuban Women, a mass organization comprising three-quarters of the adult female population, the role of its women leaders "has been confined largely to the process of implementing programs and achieving objectives set for them by men at the top of the Party hierarchy. Raúl Castro has said that of all Party and government leaders, Fidel Castro 'most clearly understands . . . the problems of women in society and their decisive role in the Revolution.'" To put Raúl's statement in proper perspective, the editors should have explained that it is something akin to Holy Writ in Cuba that Fidel Castro "most clearly understands" *all* problems. Nevertheless, this would not exculpate Castro, whom they find to be woefully retarded by North American feminist standards. Thus, for example, they quote from a speech of his in 1974 in which he said that women were entitled to "certain small privileges" and to "special considerations" and "proletarian courtesies" because nature made them "physically weaker than men." However, they continue:

5. According to the Cuban census of 1953, the urban population was fifty-seven percent of the total (Leví Marrero, *Geografía de Cuba* [Havana: Editorial Selecta, 1957], p. 156). The estimate for 1976 was sixty-four percent (*World Population 1977* [Washington, D.C.: U.S. Department of Commerce, Bureau of the Census, 1978], p. 256).

What is important is not Castro's gratuitous remarks about courtesy, but
the fact that the belief in women's physical inferiority may have found
expression in the new Constitution. In article 41 of Chapter V, sexual
discrimination is prohibited, but article 43 states: "In order to assure the
exercise" of women's right to work, "the state sees to it that they are
given jobs in keeping with their physical makeup. . . ." [The system
freezes] certain job categories (e.g., light work in textile factories or in
sugar mills) for women, while closing other jobs to them. . . . If low
skill jobs continue to be reserved for women, their over-all earning
power will be less than that of men.[6]

One of the virtues of the study is the abundant explanatory material
that the editors provide in their introductory essays and footnotes, although
with a few notable exceptions, as in the example above, the bias generally
favors the Revolution, and errors of fact occasionally crop up. Referring to
the drastic anti-loafing law of 1971, in practice not applied to women, they
state that the law was "adopted to combat the serious absentee and vagran-
cy problem presented by Cubans unaccustomed to year-round employment." Actually, the problem arose for an entirely different reason: lack of
"material" incentives combined with an indifference to the "moral" incentives promoted by the regime. The rationing of food and clothing at low
prices, the near-elimination of house rent, and the many free public services (health, education, funerals, entertainment, etc.)—as well as the
lack of goods to buy with surplus cash—meant that any number of individuals so disposed could earn enough in six or eight months to get by for a
year or more. Rationing, initiated in 1962, still continues in Cuba (as of
1980), but in recent years coercion as a work incentive has been supple-
mented by the availability of nonrationed but high-priced "luxury" goods
(cigarettes, for example) and by widening wage differentials.

"Living the Revolution"

Coping with the rationing system is one of the features of "Living the Revolution," as the books are subtitled, about which the people interviewed
spoke freely and abundantly. Picking some examples almost at random:
    Amalia, wife of a former slum dweller, in *Four Men*:

I won't say that I ate any better before the Revolution, but I didn't eat
badly in those days. . . . You could vary your meals. . . . Now I buy

6. Foreword to *Four Women*, pp. xxv–xxvi.

whatever food we have in the ration book. If we don't like it, we eat it anyway. . . . The clothes shortage is as much of a problem as the food shortage. . . . [Clothes] wear out because its wash, wash, wash, scrub, scrub, scrub, until the cloth tears and you're naked. I manage because I'm short and skinny and I can get two dresses out of the 3½ meters' ration of cloth. . . . Fatties aren't as lucky because they have to use the full ration for just one dress (pp. 136–139).

Alfredo, former slum-dweller, in *Four Men*:

Today the worst problem our country faces is the food shortage. . . . At least now people can get their fair share of whatever there is. . . . Still we don't eat as well now as we did before the Revolution. . . . Why aren't there any vegetables today? . . . They imported Russian farm machinery to sow the land with sweet potatoes, but it seems wherever Russian iron touches a piece of land, no more sweet potatoes grow on it (pp. 243–245).

Gracia, ex-nun, in *Four Women*:

As far as food goes, we were better off before the Revolution. During the times when *papá* was unemployed, . . . it was always possible to get something to eat. We'd borrow one day, sell something the next, anything to survive. Nowadays we are given a fixed quota of food that is simply too little (p. 313).

Eulalia, wife of a Party member, in *Neighbors*:

The problems start when you have to stand in different lines for different products. I stand in one line and wait until someone else comes to stand in the back of me, then I tell her, "wait, I'm going to another line." So I go to the end of another line and wait until someone stands behind me there and do the same thing so I can go save a place in a third line. I mark my place in the three lines at once and keep switching so that I spend a few minutes in each. Of course you lose your turn if the person you asked forgets and leaves before you get back. . . . One day, . . . a little old man lost his turn and everybody started arguing. Fina and I managed to slip ahead in the line because they were too busy arguing to notice. We got our things and left everybody. That's illegal and I don't like to do it—or to get into an argument in line, either (p. 391).

Lest the reader suspect that Oscar Lewis and his team stumbled into some subversives, particularly those of humble origin who claimed that they ate better before the Revolution, it should be mentioned that all of the above characters at one or more points in their stories proclaim their loyalty to the Revolution. This could lead a skeptic to wonder whether some of the protestations were a matter of ritual, or perhaps prudence. The editors, however, appear to take them at face value. Practically every autobiography, no matter how contradictory and unflattering a picture of Castro's Cuba emerges, is made to end on a note of cheerful support for the Revolution.

Housing is another major subject of complaint. Even those relocated from a shantytown to a newly constructed apartment project look back with nostalgia to their dilapidated shacks. What they miss, ironically enough under socialism, is the feeling of community and the informality of personal relations which they enjoyed in the old villagelike slum. As the editors note, this is not unlike one of the problems encountered in the United States when rundown urban neighborhoods are demolished and their inhabitants resettled in high-rise apartment projects. One suspects that although the Revolution aimed to improve the lot of Cubans living in the shantytowns, it is not the kind of improvement that they would have voted for had they been consulted.

In *Neighbors*, concerned with a formerly middle-class apartment house now shared by five heterogeneous families, differences of class background, racial antipathies, uneven allocation of space, utility failures, water shortages, access to toilet facilities (reading these details requires a strong stomach), the incompetence of housing bureaucrats, and their indifference to requests for relief—all of this generates the pressures which make the families a very quarrelsome lot. In addition, they have to contend with thieves and the surveillance of the local block unit of the nationwide Committees for the Defense of the Revolution.

And what of the social achievements of Cuban socialism thus far? All of the characters acknowledge that some things are better than before, such as job security, medical care, schooling, and the absence of the kind of corruption and venality that characterized the Batista regime. Only a few, however, such as an ex-prostitute and members of the Communist Party, stress the positive changes that have taken place. The rest appear to be much more directly concerned with the negative aspects of the new order. They have little real interest in politics and none in ideology. What they speak about with the most conviction are the frustrations of daily living.

Paradoxically, they admire Fidel Castro, still the charismatic father figure, while they are not enthusiastic about his government. They tolerate it, partly because it is not completely intolerable, and partly because they have no choice.

Clearly, "living the revolution," at least for the sample of the Cuban people we meet here, is not life in a bed of roses. Castro will occasionally admit this in his speeches, and foreign scholars wrestling with available Cuban statistics provide some confirmation. However, for an intimate recording of the trials and tribulations of what may well be a large majority of Cubans, there is currently no substitute for this study. Although some improvements in everyday life have been noted (and disputed) since the study was completed, it is safe to say that the changes have been marginal. What is most to be regretted about this valuable compilation is that it could not be completed, since half of the materials collected were confiscated and access to others was cut off. The absence of Oscar Lewis during the preparation of the three volumes adds to the adversity which befell his project. On the other hand, it is fortunate that Cuban security surveillance was lax, for in a sense the police locked the stable after some of the horses were stolen.

18
■

The New Strategy

Motives and Circumstances

To return to our narrative, it will be recalled that 1965 was to be officially designated as the "Year of Agriculture." However, for the historian looking back on this period, politics rather than economics was the realm in which the Castro regime made its most significant decisions. From that perspective, 1965 might well be described as the Year of the New Strategy.

In earlier chapters and other contexts, I have already touched on motives and circumstances which shaped the emergence of this eventful shift in Cuban policy. At this point it would be useful to recapitulate before examining the process in greater detail. Briefly stated, the new strategy was motivated by fear of a new and, this time, massive aggression by the United States, combined with a deep distrust of the capacity or willingness of the Soviet Union to prevent the aggression or defend Cuba once it was attacked. The main thrust of the strategy was to mobilize and take the leadership of a broad spectrum of Third World "anti-imperialist" governments and movements, thereby confronting both the United States and the Soviet Union with the kind of political backing which neither could ignore. This objective led to the establishment in Havana, in early January 1966, of the Organization of Solidarity of the Peoples of Africa, Asia, and Latin America, an event that will later be examined in some detail.

Other policy decisions implemented during the year were partly or wholly related to the task of establishing Cuban leadership of the "Tricontinental," as the new organization came to be called. Thus, Cuban military intervention in "liberation" struggles was extended from Latin America to Africa, and at the same time accelerated in Latin America. Similarly, it will be recalled, at the February economic conference in Algiers, Ché Guevara defended the Third World against what he defined as Soviet exploitation. In matters of Marxist ideology, Castro asserted Cuba's independence from both the Soviet Union and China and condemned their quarrel as playing into the hands of imperialism. A Cuban model of a Communist Party was timed to be unveiled shortly before the opening of the Tricontinental conference. Thus, in October 1965, Cuba's "vanguard" political party, the United Party of the Socialist Revolution (PURS), was transformed into the new Communist Party of Cuba, a streamlined "fighting" organization, uncontaminated by Russian revisionism or Chinese dogmatism, and firmly dedicated to achieving genuine communism at home and to upholding the principle of self-sacrificing internationalism in the struggle against imperialism.

The new strategy in no sense represented a complete break with previous policies of the regime but rather a resurrection and crystallization of dormant and semidormant trends and attitudes. Its roots were imbedded in such experiences as the Bay of Pigs invasion in 1961, the humiliation of the missile crisis in 1962, and more generally in Fidel Castro's personality: aggressive, innovative, prone to heresy in Marxist ideology, thirsty for leadership on a global scale, and messianic. However, what determined the direction of policy in 1965 were more recent events. Of decisive importance was the fact that Castro's dramatic proposal in mid-1964 for the normalization of relations with the United States had been flatly rejected by Washington. For having exposed himself to this rebuff he could blame Khrushchev, since in taking the initiative for a settlement he had accepted the chairman's optimistic evaluation of President Johnson's intentions. In addition, the Kremlin's promotion of peaceful coexistence between the superpowers, he now strongly suspected, was no guarantee of security for Cuba, and might even jeopardize it, since Cuba could be sacrificed for the larger interests of Russo-American détente.

Resentment and Setback

Earlier, Castro had also come to the conclusion that in signing the joint Cuban-Soviet communiqué in Moscow in January 1964, he had been tricked into endorsing the integrity of Moscow's intentions toward China by Khrushchev's assurances that a solution to the Sino-Soviet controversy was imminent. Instead, relations between Peking and Moscow deteriorated. Unable or unwilling to see that this was the result of irreconcilable national interests, Castro placed the major part of the blame on Khrushchev's personal stubbornness and arrogance. As he told Cyrus Sulzberger, who interviewed him on October 30, 1964: "I feel that existing differences between Russia and China are transitory and they can find common points to overcome their divergencies. . . . In my opinion the political change in the Soviet Union [Khrushchev's removal] creates the opportunity to make a serious effort to overcome the difficulties between Russia and China."[1] However, by the end of the year that hope had all but vanished.

Here, then, was another setback for Castro, and in a double sense. The widening breach in the Sino-Soviet bloc was a demonstration to his people that the universal Marxism-Leninism, and its corollary of proletarian internationalism which he had sold them, was not in practice what it purported to be in theory. At the same time, he saw the split in the socialist camp as a threat to Cuban security. As he had told Sulzberger, Sino-Soviet unity would "strengthen the socialist camp. That would increase the security of smaller socialist countries like our own."[2] Thus, the Sino-Soviet conflict, by threatening to undermine both an ideological pillar of the Revolution and also the Revolution's security from foreign aggression, provided another powerful incentive for the new strategy.

As Castro moved toward his objectives, there were turns and twists in his tactics: at one moment he was flirting with the Chinese, at another he was supporting Soviet policy, and always he was striving to keep his options open to meet developing contingencies, at all times maneuvering within the restraints imposed by dependence on the Soviet Union for economic and military sustenance while testing the limits of his political bargaining power with the Kremlin. In his incessant public pronouncements, however, there was continuity in his main themes: he was always lambasting Yankee imperialism, praising the heroic resistance of the Vietnamese and the armed struggle of insurgent movements in Latin America and Africa, bewailing the Sino-Soviet conflict, and pointedly asserting Cuban ideological and decision-making independence. Without mentioning independence from whom, the inference was clear: the Soviet Union. Nevertheless, the Chinese were by no means immune from criticism. Toward the end of 1965, a great storm in Cuban-Chinese relations would be shaping up.

The Sixth Anniversary

On January 2, 1965, Fidel delivered his now traditional discourse commemorating his seizure of power, this time for the sixth anniversary. There

---

1. Cyrus L. Sulzberger, *An Age of Mediocrity: Memoirs and Diaries* (New York: Macmillan, 1973), p. 125. In a later interview with another journalist, Castro is quoted as saying that at the time of Khrushchev's fall, "our relations had reached their lowest point, with him personally and his government" (Lee Lockwood, *Castro's Cuba, Cuba's Fidel* [New York: Macmillan, 1967], p. 226).

2. Sulzberger, *Age of Mediocrity*, p. 125.

were never less than half a million spectators gathered in the Plaza de la Revolución on these occasions, the speech never lasted less than three hours, and Fidel never failed to make it worthwhile for the student of the Cuban Revolution to pay close attention to what he said. Fidel alone made policy in Cuba, policy about everything; and only Fidel could spell out facts, goals, hopes, illusions, and mystifications without prior consultation with anybody. In those days, Fidel always spoke without a prepared text. Although he occasionally glanced briefly at a single sheet of paper containing a list of his major topics, his largely spontaneous delivery could provide intriguing and illuminating formulations and digressions.

Dark Omens

Thus, what at the beginning promised to be a speech mainly devoted to problems and perspectives in the "Year of Agriculture" that lay ahead unexpectedly turned into a series of astonishing political pronouncements. The imperialists, Fidel explained at one point, have rejected our offer to discuss our relations, to seek a peaceful solution to our differences. What does this mean? "We are a small country," he went on to say, "we have an imperialist enemy facing us, we have the socialist camp on our side, but in the socialist camp various kinds of problems have come up. What is our situation?"[3] Bringing up the threat from imperialist aggression was no surprise. It was standard fare in Fidel's speeches. But that there were "problems" in the socialist camp was unsuspected by the great mass of Cubans. What problems? The time was not ripe for tackling the Russians head on. Instead, Fidel uncorked a riddle.

The situation, he went on to explain, is that we have come to take socialist aid against imperialist aggression too much for granted. It created "a kind of obsequious [*acomodaticio*] attitude on the part of our people" toward our benefactors. Hence, "something is lacking in our revolutionary spirit"; and even more important, there was the danger of "lowering our revolutionary dignity." If his listeners were not yet sure of what he was driving at, they must have been startled by the pronouncement which followed. "When would we become a completely revolutionary people?" he asked. "The day we decided—now listen carefully—that even if absolutely no aid whatsoever could reach Cuba from abroad, our people would stand firm [*resistir*]." Let us imagine, he continued, "a total blockade, cut off from fuel, from everything; let us examine the worst circumstances. . . . If

3. The text of the speech was published in *Política Internacional*, 9 (first trimester, 1965). Citations used are on pp. 116–120.

one day we should be faced with this situation, fuel will be reserved for
. . . the armed forces. And what about the urban population? We would
move en masse and join our rural population, we would work with oxen,
with hoes, with pick and shovel, and we would stand firm."

Coming after the rosy picture of the future which he had painted earlier in his speech, the vivid scenario of a survival crisis could create confusion. Hence, it was important that he provide a reassurance that there
was no likelihood that the crisis would occur: "We can develop, we can
grow, we can make progress in our economy, I am absolutely sure of this.
We don't have a dark period ahead of us, a terrible outlook. No! When we
speak of this, we mean only the state of mind we must have, the conviction
we must have [that we can overcome even unthinkable obstacles]."

A Double Target

When he wanted to, Fidel could spin out a complicated web of innuendo
simultaneously aimed at more than one target. This time there were two
targets. For his unsophisticated compatriots, the message was blurred but
effective in creating a "state of mind," as he put it, the first awareness that
there were problems in Cuba's relations with the socialist camp, that socialist aid—and when he mentioned fuel it could only be Soviet oil—
could not be relied upon, that Cubans should be less deferential toward
their socialist suppliers, that they should become more self-sufficient and
prepared to pay the price. For the Russians, his second target, the message
was easy to decipher. It was at best a threat, at worst a firm decision, by
Castro to assert his independence from Moscow's political directives and
thereby test the limits of Soviet tolerance.

There were more admonitions, less dramatic, but whose cumulative
effect was to reinforce both the domestic and foreign impact of the message. "We are a people," Fidel declared, "with the right to speak with our
own voice, on the basis of our [own] judgment and thinking. . . . We
must interpret the ideas of Marx, Engels, and Lenin, . . . reaching our
own conclusions in the light of new circumstances, new conditions." This
also applies to our party, he added. Our party is in power and is legal;
hence, we have a different background than a party created "in the struggle
for power and under conditions of secrecy and illegality."

The upshot of this comparison was that the Cuban party, "the vanguard . . . and representative of the workers, . . . cannot be organized
without the participation of the masses." For the Kremlin, at least, the implications were clear and ominous. The Soviet Communist Party, Fidel

was saying, rules *over* the masses but not *with* the masses. The recent convert to Marxism was challenging the legitimacy of the Soviet model of a Communist Party. Castro, whom the Kremlin had with such difficulty roped into its ideological corral, was breaking loose and once more promoting heresy.

The Dictatorship of the Proletariat

But Fidel had still more to say on the subject. "Marxism-Leninism," he added, "includes the concept of the dictatorship of the proletariat." For most Cubans it was a new concept, certainly absent from the Maximum Leader's public pronouncements on ideological matters. The reason for this was the aversion of the Cuban people to the term "dictatorship," which was associated with the rule of Batista and the Latin American military regimes constantly denounced by the Cuban press. The time had come, however, to initiate the people into the mysteries of this fundamental doctrine. Fidel then continued at great length with the standard "class" explanation of dictatorship, in which it turned out that the dictatorship of the proletariat was a form of democracy. It simply meant the rule of the great majority over a minority of former bourgeois exploiters who, during the transitional period from socialism to communism, "no longer have political rights, nor the right to govern." Thus, for example, "the bourgeoisie has no right to publish anything. . . . The newspapers belong to the workers, who can publish anything they want against the exploiters and the imperialists."

Thus far, so good. It was as if Fidel anticipated the charge of heresy and was refuting it with a declaration of faith in bedrock Marxism-Leninism. This had the added benefit of disposing of the issue of freedom of the press, which lurked in the memories of great numbers of educated Cubans. At this point, however, Fidel revealed what he was mainly driving at. "We must establish institutions," he declared, "in which there is full implementation of the concept of proletarian democracy, within the concept of the dictatorship of the proletariat. . . . For the socialist regime must be a dictatorship as far as the exploiters are concerned, and at the same time a proletarian democracy." On the surface, Fidel's proposition was standard, impeccable, textbook Marxism-Leninism. At the same time, it carried an encoded message addressed to the Kremlin which the Kremlin would have to swallow in silence. Fidel's insistence on "proletarian democracy" was a barely concealed charge that it was absent in the Soviet Union.

Fidel concluded his critique-by-implication of the Soviet political model by rejecting what he called "formal institutions," such as constitutions "with an exclusively formal or formalistic character." That is why, he explained, "we have not been in a hurry to create formal institutions." Nevertheless, the time had come, he added, to begin to give serious considerations to solving the problems of our "state institutions, local institutions, constitutional law. . . . Our country has a responsibility, a very great duty in this respect." Here Fidel struck hard at the Soviet Union—and indeed at the entire socialist camp—as he assumed the role of leadership in the purification of Marxist political institutions. "Our people," he declared, "must find solutions which bring about the unity of form and substance, and not the divorce between form and substance. And there is still a long way to go in this direction."

An Egalitarian Dream Refurbished

While the timing of Fidel's strictures on politics and ideology was primarily determined by foreign policy objectives, it is likely that what he had to say was nonetheless sincere. His words reflected a residue of the "humanism" with which he had launched his insurrection against a corrupt and autocratic regime. But they also reflected a measure of self-deception and naivete. He was unable to grasp the paradox that existed between his instinctively charismatic exercise of power and his rational and ethical perception of the need to institutionalize power. Time and again in the past he had referred to this need, but nothing had come of it. Proletarian democracy, on the other hand, was a new promise, happily consistent with his latter-day conversion to Marxism-Leninism but also a projection of his earliest egalitarian dreams. However, he did not understand until very much later that the absence of democracy, proletarian or otherwise, in the Soviet Union and the "fraternal" republics was not the result of a willful distortion of Marxist principle, but was part of the very nature of the Communist Party state invented by Lenin and perfected by Stalin.

It would be another decade before the process of institutionalization would take place in Cuba, following the defeat of the new strategy and the bankruptcy of the economy—convincing demonstrations of the perilous shortcomings of idealistic goals imposed by charismatic authority. While Fidel spoke on this sixth anniversary of the Revolution, neither he nor anyone else could have imagined that Cuba's transformed political structure inaugurated a decade later would be a faithful copy of the very Soviet model that he was belaboring for its lack of integrity.

19

■

Growing Tensions

The Soviet Union and China Rebuked

IT WAS AN EVENTFUL YEAR that followed Castro's provocative speech on January 2, 1965, and most of what happened reinforced his decision to adopt the policies which we have defined as the new strategy. When the Americans began their systematic bombardment of North Vietnam on February 7, at the very moment when Soviet Prime Minister Alexei Kosygin was in Hanoi, there was understandable alarm in Havana. Was Cuba next? The answer could easily be "yes" as the weeks rolled by with no effective reply from Moscow—or, for that matter, from China, which meekly accepted the humiliation of being unable or unwilling to protect a fraternal socialist state on its border.

In a speech on March 13 before a large gathering of University of Havana students, Fidel delivered a stinging rebuke to the two Communist giants for permitting Yankee imperialism to rain death and destruction with impunity on the Vietnamese people.[1] Neither of the countries was named, but their identity was obvious even to the less sophisticated members of Fidel's audience who were listening to the radio broadcast. A major factor in encouraging the aggression, he declared, was the unwillingness of these countries to maintain a united front against the imperialist enemy. Admitting that it was "embarrassing to wash our dirty linen" in full view of the enemy, Fidel nevertheless went on to heap scorn on the "Byzantine" ideological quarrels between the Communist giants and to condemn their rivalry for domination of the world revolutionary movement. He even

1. *Política Internacional*, 9 (first trimester, 1965). Citations used are on pp. 260–263.

went so far as to question the sincerity of their support for the peoples struggling for national liberation. "For us," he said, "the liberation is not a matter of demagogy, but something we have always truly believed in."

Charges not only of bad faith and opportunism but also of cowardice were strongly implied when he reached a climax in his diatribe. "Faced with the concrete situation of a country like Vietnam," he exclaimed, "we take an invariable position. . . . We propose that Vietnam be given all the aid which may be necessary! Aid in weapons and men! Our position is that the socialist camp run whatever risks may be necessary!" At this point, massive and prolonged cheering broke out among the several thousand students who comprised the bulk of his visible audience. It was not only patriotism that moved them—they saw the Yankees as a real and constant enemy—but the excitement of combat and danger to which Cubans in general, and Cuban youth in particular, have traditionally responded with enthusiasm. There was perfect rapport between the charismatic leader and his followers.

There was undoubtedly less enthusiasm in Peking, and least of all in Moscow. Fidel's reference at one point to the "strength of an atomic power" would seem to have singled out the Soviet Union as his principal target, since the Chinese at the time lacked atomic weapons. At another point, boasting about Cuba's uncompromising revolutionary principles and fearless resistance to imperialism, he recalled that Cuba "did not vacillate . . . in order to strengthen the socialist camp . . . and defend the Revolution . . . in risking the dangers of thermonuclear war . . . on our soil when we agreed to the installations of strategic thermonuclear missiles on our territory." He might have stopped there, since the reproach to Moscow was clear enough, but he was carried away by indignation. "And in addition," he continued, "not only did we agree to their installation, but we did not agree to their removal! And I believe this is absolutely no secret to anyone!"

It was the first time that Castro publicly contradicted the Soviet explanation that the only reason for the emplacement of the missiles was the defense of Cuba. The revealing words were *in order to strengthen the socialist camp* with *strategic* missiles—that is to say, the intent was also to strengthen the offensive capability of the Soviet Union. As for the removal of the weapons, Fidel's objection, as he stated, was no secret, but he had never before flatly said so in public. In any event, pulling this "dirty linen" out of the archives must have appalled the Russians and delighted the Chinese, who had severely condemned the Kremlin's behavior at the time of the missile crisis.[2]

The Propaganda War in Havana

There was another matter which Fidel decided to air at this time. It provided further opportunity to flex his muscles and underscore Cuba's political and ideological autonomy. Havana had become a propaganda battleground between China and the Soviet Union, with each embassy circulating a steady flow of polemical bulletins and pamphlets in the various ministries, including that of the armed forces. (From what I was able to observe at the time, few converts were made by either side, but some readers became ideological agnostics.) At first, Castro imposed quotas strictly limiting the amount of materials and their areas of distribution, and then he imposed an outright ban. Now, in his speech, he thundered against those who would introduce "the apple of discord . . . in our midst," and proclaimed that "we have the full and absolute right to proscribe" unauthorized propaganda. "Let it be known," he exclaimed, "that here it is our Party which produces propaganda! Here only our Party can provide guidance [to our people]." And he warned against any attempt to smuggle in foreign propaganda. This time the culprit, which he did not identify, was the Chinese embassy in Havana. Unlike the more prudent Soviet embassy, it had actually engaged in a bit of "smuggling." Early in 1966, Fidel would make this explicit during his denunciation of the Chinese on another score.

Finally, in anticipation of the Havana tricontinental conference, which he was zealously promoting behind the scenes, Fidel skillfully worked in a reference to Cuba's affinity with the national liberation movements of the Third World. The struggle against Yankee imperialism, he declared, "became the great historic task of our people, . . . coinciding with the similar tasks of other peoples in this same continent, and in Africa and in Asia . . . and wherever peoples are struggling, ever more firmly, against colonialism and imperialism."

2. In his memoirs, Khrushchev noted that when "Castro and I talked about the problem [whether or not to install nuclear missiles in Cuba], we argued and argued. Our argument was very heated. But in the end, Fidel agreed with me" (*Khrushchev Remembers: The Last Testament* [Boston: Little, Brown, 1974], p. 511). If the chairman is to be believed (his memoirs are generally considered credible), Castro was not so eager as he claimed to "strengthen the socialist camp" and "risk the dangers of thermonuclear war on our territory."

The American Intervention in the Dominican Republic

If more than the attack on North Vietnam were needed to convince Castro that his new strategy was grounded in reality, it was the intervention of the United States in an armed struggle between two contending factions that had erupted in the Dominican Republic. Apparently convinced that a "second Cuba" could be in the making, President Johnson ordered the landing of 4,500 American troops on Dominican soil on April 28, 1965.[3] By coincidence, this took place three days before the May Day mass meeting in Havana that was customarily addressed by Fidel. Apparently he was caught by surprise. He had intended to deal primarily with domestic matters, as he explained, but it was only in the closing minutes of his four-hour speech that he spoke of the success of the sugar harvest which was nearing completion.[4]

One had to marvel at his ability on such short notice to whip up a devastating attack against the American involvement in the Dominican crisis. True, the landing of American troops was made to order for Fidel's thesis on the incorrigibility of Yankee imperialism and its consequences for the rest of the world. Nevertheless, his enormous skill in marshaling the political and military details of the crisis, the facility with which he incorporated the crisis into his perception of the larger issues at stake, and the power of his invective demonstrated an extraordinary virtuosity.

Significantly, there was no mention of the division in the socialist camp as having encouraged the new American aggression. For one thing, the obligation of the socialist camp was not so clearly defined as in the case of Vietnam. At the same time, geography did not suggest that either the Soviet Union or China was in a position, jointly or separately, to intervene in the Dominican conflict. The only socialist country close by was Cuba, which was morally obligated on three counts to come to the aid of a country resisting an American invasion, for Cuba was (1) socialist, (2) anti-imperialist, and (3) Latin American. Castro, however, covered himself from any reproach for not taking on the Americans—a suicidal undertaking, to be sure—by stating that "we are really a small part of the world, our resources are limited." Thus, Fidel's exhortation that "it is necessary to de-

3. This was the first contingent of what was to be an "inter-American" army of 22,000 Americans and 1,700 Latin Americans, mainly Brazilians with token representation by Hondurans, Nicaraguans, and Costa Ricans.

4. *Política Internacional*, 10 (second trimester, 1965). Citations used are on pp. 199–201.

mand the withdrawal of the imperialist troops from the *sovereign and independent state* of Santo Domingo" (emphasis added) was rhetoric addressed to world opinion rather than the socialist camp, and more specifically to "all the nonaligned countries" and the nations of "Asia, . . . Africa, . . . Latin America," where the imperialists were striving to "halt the march of history." Not that Fidel expected the demand to be effective. He was taking advantage of an opportunity to prepare the political groundwork for the Third World alliance which he hoped to forge and lead at the forthcoming Havana tricontinental meeting.

The Risk Imposed by History

The moment was also propitious for issuing another challenge to Moscow. Without mentioning his target by name—a small concession to the sensibilities of his increasingly more irritated benefactors—Fidel derided the Kremlin's policy of peaceful coexistence as "this strange concept of peace for some and war for others." The Yankees, he declared, believe that "nuclear equilibrium" gives them immunity from nuclear war, and thus they count on having "a wide field for perpetrating their crimes in the form of limited war, . . . aggressions, aerial attacks," and so on. It was necessary, he went on, "to change the attitude of the imperialists. . . . As long as they believe that they don't risk their own hides, they will do whatever they please; as soon as they understand that they really risk being incinerated, they will begin to think differently." We must call the bluff of Yankee nuclear blackmail, he concluded: "We must face up to this reality and take this risk which history imposes on us at this time. Somewhere or other we must cut off the hands of the imperialists, in Vietnam or wherever it may be!"

There was logic and madness in Fidel's appeal, a potent combination for arousing the emotions of his own people, the frustrated revolutionaries of the Third World, and their fellow travelers in other parts of the world. It was also a welcome contribution to the propaganda war being waged by the Chinese against the Russians.[5] However, it had no discernible effect on the

---

5. Early in March, Chinese hopes for Cuban support suffered a severe setback. A Cuban delegation headed by Fidel's brother Raúl had attended a meeting of Communist parties (boycotted by the Chinese, Albanians, North Koreans, North Vietnamese, and "neutralist" Rumanians, among others) in Moscow and had signed the joint communiqué released on March 10, 1965. Referring to the nineteen parties present at the meeting, Peking commented that "Some of them

course of events in the Dominican Republic. When the Americans finally withdrew in the fall of 1966, they left behind a new stable government acceptable to Washington. Whether or not a "new Cuba" had been in the making, nothing resembling Cuba emerged.

Epilogue to the Dominican Episode

Almost a decade after the American intervention, and with the storm it raised all but forgotten, new information surfaced which in a sense provided an epilogue to Fidel's speech. Writing in *Esquire*, Tad Szulc revealed that the CIA, presumably acting with President Lyndon Johnson's consent, "set in motion in late 1964 . . . a new secret plan to combine Castro's assassination with a second invasion of the island by Cuban exiles, from bases this time located in Costa Rica and Nicaragua." According to Szulc, "the whole assassination-invasion plan had to be cancelled when a rebellion unexpectedly erupted in the Dominican Republic in April, 1965."[6] It was at least a minor bit of irony that the Dominican invasion against which Fidel fulminated in his May Day speech had prevented what he feared most in his assessment of that invasion.

By a strange coincidence, in February 1974, the same month that the *Esquire* article appeared, the Cuban minister of education delivered a long eulogy to commemorate the first anniversary of the death of Francisco Caamaño Deñó. Colonel Caamaño had led the Dominican forces that resisted the American invasion. In an agreement which ended the conflict, he accepted the post of military attaché in the Dominican embassy in London, arriving there in January 1966. Late in the following year, he left the embassy and more or less disappeared from view. From time to time there were unconfirmed rumors that he was in Cuba. In any event, it was not until February 16, 1973, that his whereabouts were definitely established. On that day, in a mountainous region of the Dominican Republic, his body was recovered among a band of nine guerrillas killed in a brief encounter with an army patrol.

---

wholeheartedly supported . . . revisionism and splitism; some did so half-heartedly; others, for reasons they might find it awkward to divulge, had to attend under orders; and still others may have temporarily fallen into the trap from naiveté" (*Peking Review*, March 26, 1965; cited here from William E. Griffith, *Sino-Soviet Relations, 1964–1965* [Cambridge, Mass.: MIT Press, 1967], p. 407). The Chinese left it up to Castro to decide to which unflattering category he belonged. No public comment came from Havana.

6. "Cuba on Our Mind," *Esquire*, February 1974, p. 90.

The eulogy revealed some of Colonel Caamaño's virtues that had hitherto not been publicly revealed. He was an "immortal Dominican revolutionary" and an "internationalist fighter" like "Ché, Salvador Allende," and other fallen heroes. It was in Europe, we are informed, that he began "a stage of ideological maturation," finding his "inspiration chiefly in the Cuban Revolution," and identifying "with the figure of Ché to such an extent that he wanted to follow in Ché's footsteps. . . . Therefore, by the time he returned to his homeland on February 2, 1973, at the head of a small—and immortal—group of men, he had completed a magnificent stage of revolutionary development."[7] Where the group had been outfitted and trained, and from what place it had set out for the "homeland," the eulogist failed to mention.

It would seem that if the Colonel were not already an admirer of the Cuban Revolution in April 1965, he was not immune to its attractions. According to the eulogist, it was Caamaño's experience in the rebellion that led to his "ideological maturation." However, what is more easily verified is that the experience led to his martyrdom and incorporation in the Hagiographa of the Cuban Revolution.

7. *Granma Weekly Review*, February 24, 1974. The speech was delivered at a junior high school named in Caamaño's honor.

20

■

Gestation and Innovation

Toward the New Romanticism

"THE ROMANTIC PHASE of the Revolution is over." This was the conclusion reached by an eminent British political economist following a visit to Cuba in mid-1965.[1] In a sense it was so. The dreams that a society without capitalists would produce instant abundance, that an economy dependent on sugar would rapidly be diversified and industrialized, and that the "unbreakable bonds of proletarian internationalism" were a safeguard against imperialist aggression—these dreams had vanished.

However, the fact of the matter was that the Revolution in 1965 was entering a new and more extravagant romantic phase. Thus, there were new dreams, as well as new versions of old dreams: of great sugar harvests providing the wherewithal for an economy of abundance; of an egalitarian Cuba, free from the evils of bureaucracy and selfish material incentives; of Cuba confounding the textbook Marxists by creating socialism and communism simultaneously; of Cuban ideological and political independence within the socialist camp; of Cuba defeating imperialism in Latin America by multiple guerrilla incursions; of Cuban leadership among the revolutionary movements of the Third World; and of other glorious achievements to come. Most of the dreams were already guiding policy in 1965. Others were incubating and would hatch soon thereafter. And nearly all were destined to be shattered within five years.

Nor was Fidel's romantic style of leadership any less flamboyant in the

---

1. Joan Robinson, "Cuba—1965," *Monthly Review*, February 1966, p. 10.

year 1965. In mid-April, he moved his government to a sugarcane field in Camaguey, some three hundred miles southeast of Havana, where he and his ministers put in a week of "voluntary" labor cutting cane.[2] Massive press coverage provided a flow of photos showing the Maximum Leader in a typical field worker's costume swinging his machete among the cane stalks. Fidel's "score," measuring the weight of cane that he cut, was daily front-page news. What was not shown was the far from typically spartan cane cutter's quarters set up for Fidel and his entourage. Also unreported was the cost of the stunt: the elaborate campsite prepared for Fidel's large retinue, the transport and communications network linking the camp with Havana, and the security arrangements protecting the camp.

The Fall of Ben Bella and the Rise of Kim Il Sung

As bombastic, abusive, and reckless a pronouncement as Fidel had ever made greeted the news of the coup d'état which overthrew Ben Bella in Algiers on June 19.[3] The brunt of Fidel's vituperation fell on Abdelaziz Bouteflika, Ben Bella's foreign minister, who helped engineer the coup and kept his job in the new regime. Indulging in an obnoxious form of humor suggesting a slur on the culprit's manhood, Fidel referred to Bouteflika as this "Butterfly or Butterflika" (which he pronounced "Booter-fly" and "Booter-flika"). The ease with which Ben Bella, a charismatic Maximum Leader with whom Fidel had established very close relations, had been unseated must have appeared to Fidel as an ominous precedent. In addition, Ben Bella undoubtedly figured in the plans for supplying logistical support for Ché, who was already operating in the Congo. As for Colonel Hourari Boumediène, who seized the government and was no less a radical than Ben Bella, Fidel predicted that it would be "almost a miracle" if he did not come to terms with imperialism.[4]

2. The traditional Easter week holiday was declared to be a week of patriotic labor in the sugarcane harvest to commemorate the Bay of Pigs victory in 1961 (known to the Cubans as the Girón Beach victory). What started out as "Girón Week" was later stretched out to "Girón Month."

3. Arrested on June 19, 1965, by Colonel Boumediène, perpetrator of the coup, Ben Bella remained in confinement until his release in July 1979 by Chadli Benjedid, who became president of Algeria after the death of Boumediène (Reuter dispatch from Algiers, *Vancouver Sun*, July 5, 1979). Ben Bella was never charged with any crime, let alone tried.

4. *Revolución*, June 28, 1965. The speech took place two days earlier. For a fuller account of this episode, see my *The Rise and Decline of Fidel Castro* (Berkeley and Los Angeles: University of California Press, 1972), pp. 277–279. The reper-

However, the "miracle" took place. The "Butterfly" was an honored guest in Havana in November 1968; and a few years later, Fidel himself showed up in Algiers. The record does not reveal whether Fidel asked Boumediène about the health of Ben Bella, who was still under detention a fair distance from Algiers.

Fidel's loss of a friend in North Africa was quickly followed by the gain of a new friend in North Korea. On July 6, *Revolución* carried a front-page banner headline announcing another triumph of Cuban diplomacy: KOREA BACKS CUBAN LINE FOR CONSOLIDATION OF REVOLUTIONARY CONQUESTS AND ACCELERATED SOCIALIST CONSTRUCTION. Below was a large photo revealing the inscrutable features of Kim Il Sung, the firmly entrenched ruler of the Democratic People's Republic of Korea. The occasion was a press interview, claimed to be the first ever granted by Kim. The gist of the interview was that Kim backed the Cuban "line" of militant struggle against imperialism everywhere, with special emphasis on Latin America, and of "active" support of the Vietnamese people. It was, in effect, an announcement that Fidel had persuaded Kim to join him in setting up a common front, along with North Vietnam, of the three small Communist countries directly confronting the armed might of the United States, while the two Communist giants remained unwilling "to take all the necessary risks," that is, to commit their armies to repel the imperialists.

It was, of course, a romantic notion that the miniature "axis" could exert any serious leverage on the Soviet Union and China, each of which was moved not by rhetoric or ideology but by its own perceptions of national interest. For Kim, who had learned his lesson the hard way in the Korean War, embracing Fidel could have been no more than one of his recurring gestures of "independence" from his quarreling fraternal neighbors. As for Fidel, he apparently regarded the alliance with Kim as an important achievement, for relations with North Korea henceforth were prominently featured in Cuban propaganda. It was probably more than a coincidence

---

cussions of the coup involved more than Cuban-Algerian relations. The Russians, like Fidel, were dismayed, though for other reasons. They had invested heavily in supporting Ben Bella's leadership ambitions in African affairs. The Chinese, on the other hand, were delighted and immediately endorsed Boumediène (see William E. Griffith, *Sino-Soviet Relations, 1964–1965* [Cambridge, MIT Press, 1967], p. 104). At the same time, the Cuban-Russian alignment was another demonstration to the Chinese that they could expect little benefit from Castro' posture of ideological independence from Moscow.

that Kim's endorsement of the Cuban "line" was obtained during the preparations for the tricontinental meeting in Havana, due to take place six months later.

Emigration Policy Revised

It was, indeed, a year of novel and imaginative undertakings by Castro. At the end of September, he made a surprising announcement. Speaking at a monster rally in the Plaza de la Revolución, he declared that anybody in Cuba who wished to emigrate to the United States was free to do so. It was a dramatic shift in policy, but he went even further. He offered a plan for an organized exodus and would contribute part of the costs. He proposed to designate a small port at Camarioca, easily reached from Key West, where Cubans wishing to leave could be picked up by relatives and friends living in the United States. "We can already set a date," he said. "By October 10 we can have everything ready, including a place to spend the night." Those arriving from Florida could stay forty-eight hours, and accommodations "will be free, including meals." More than that, he added, "we'll even lend small boats to those who want to leave, . . . so they can travel without any danger or risk."[5]

Fidel presented this proposition as a challenge to the United States and, as he explained, to put an end to the propaganda that Cuba was responsible for the drownings of people leaving the country surreptitiously in unseaworthy craft or on rafts. It was not Cuba, he declared, but the United States which cut off normal means of transport between the two countries following the missile crisis in October 1962. About this he was correct, although Cuba had reciprocated by sealing its borders. After a mad scramble by Cubans to get out under Fidel's original plan, a bilateral agreement between the two countries set up an airlift, operated and financed by the United States, which went into effect on December 1, 1965. It was an extraordinary undertaking, with no precedent since the invention of the airplane. Until Castro quietly put a stop to the exodus six years later, an estimated 250,000 Cubans were flown to the United States, adding to the 200,000 refugees who had arrived prior to the missile crisis.[6]

5. *Política Internacional*, 11–12 (third and fourth trimesters, 1965), 237–238. The speech was delivered on September 28.
6. *New York Times*, September 15, 1971.

The Airlift Appraised

There was much speculation concerning Castro's motives for what was, while it lasted, an unheard-of emigration policy in the Communist world (if Yugoslavia is excepted). Was it a desire to create a safety valve for internal disaffection? Or to relieve the housing shortage? Or to embarrass the United States, not expecting President Johnson to accept his challenge? Castro may have given some thought to any one of these considerations, although none would appear to be sufficient to justify so bold a move. All evidence indicated that internally the regime was reasonably secure. The housing made available and the household and personal effects that emigrants were required to leave behind could make some impact on the needs of the population. Nevertheless, against these inconclusive gains were the losses in manpower. As the *New York Times* reported on September 15, 1971, when the airlift ended: "According to United States Government statistics, more than 33 percent of the airlift refugees were employable professionals, skilled and semi-skilled workers and farmers. Almost 44 percent were between the ages of nineteen and forty-four."

What was generally overlooked, however, was that Castro, after the few weeks of the Camarioca embarkations, far from encouraging emigration, in fact imposed penalties on those applying for permission to leave, apart from allowing them to take with them only the clothes on their backs. Applicants were at once dismissed from their jobs, and the men were assigned hard agricultural labor, frequently involving long absences from their families. These hardships could last for years while they waited their turn for seats on the airlift. Labeled traitors by the official propaganda, they suffered humiliation and social discrimination as well as material deprivation.

This was the other side of the coin, which the world did not see. What the world was permitted to see was that Cuban communism was humane and magnanimous—not a slavish imitator of the other Marxist-Leninist regimes, but "creative" and of course "independent." More than likely, the reinforcement of this kind of image was a significant, if not decisive, motive in Fidel's decision to adopt his new emigration policy. Nor, in all probability, was the timing entirely accidental. It was at the end of September that Fidel delivered the speech in which he revealed his plan. Seated behind him on the platform was El Mahdi Ben Barka, president of the tricontinental preparatory committee.[7] Final arrangements were at that

7. Ben Barka was a prominent exiled Moroccan revolutionary who was later assassinated by the Moroccan secret police in Paris at the end of October 1965.

moment under way for the great conference shortly to take place in Havana. It was an appropriate occasion to impress Ben Barka and the committee with some of the unique qualities that would justify Cuba's bid for the leadership of the tricontinental organization.[8]

8. Another major exodus to the United States was set in motion in April 1980, when Castro again lifted emigration barriers, this time as the aftermath of a miscalculation on his part. In a quarrel with the Peruvian embassy in Havana over several Cubans who had crashed through the police barriers, seeking political asylum and safe conduct out of the country, Castro temporarily removed the police "protection," expecting to punish the embassy by taxing its facilities with an influx of perhaps several score disaffected Cubans. Instead, more than ten thousand rushed into the embassy grounds, prepared to stay until granted safe conduct to Peru or any other country willing to receive them. To relieve the dangerous and intolerable congestion—the stench of human excrement extended beyond the embassy grounds—Castro himself offered safe conduct as an inducement to vacate the embassy. To make the offer more credible, he extended it to anybody wanting to leave the country. As of the beginning of May, twelve thousand Cubans (thousands more were to follow) had arrived in Key West, transported in a "sea-lift armada" of hundreds of small boats owned or chartered by Cubans residing in the United States and hoping to remove their relatives before Castro changed his mind (*Province* [Vancouver, British Columbia], May 5, 1980). According to the *New York Times* (April 27, 1980), "western diplomats [in Havana], besieged for visas, estimate the number [of Cubans wanting to leave] at 200,000." One Cuban arrival in Florida was quoted as saying: "If the people of Cuba have the opportunity, Castro will be the only one left there" (*Vancouver Sun* [British Columbia], May 2, 1980). For more on the context and meaning of the episode, see the Epilogue, note 16, below.

21

■

The New Communist Party

The Party in Power

THE RESTRUCTURING OF the United Party of the Socialist Revolution (PURS), alluded to by Fidel on various occasions since the beginning of the year (and by Ché Guevara before his disappearance), took place in a series of meetings beginning on September 30 and ending on October 3, 1965. On the latter day, in what was then the Chaplin Theatre (later the Karl Marx Theatre), Havana's largest auditorium, Castro presented the new Central Committee to an assembly of what must have been close to two thousand party functionaries and other selected members and guests. The formality of the three-day deliberations and the solemnity of the final event were in sharp contrast to the casual manner in which the birth of the PURS was announced two years earlier and the birth of its predecessor, the ORI (Integrated Revolutionary Organizations), was announced in mid-1961. The party, so to speak, had now come of age.

Predictably, the new party was not to be a dull copy of any of the ruling fraternal parties. Earlier, Fidel had already said that "political power is exercised by the Party of the workers. . . . We shall suppress this business of duality of government and party [as for example, in the Soviet Union] because the party governs."[1] There was a strong implication in Fidel's statement that this "duality" was not only a negation of Marxist principle but also a cosmetic device to conceal the party's real monopoly of power. Thus, at one of the organizational sessions preceding the Chaplin Theatre meeting, Fidel did not exempt any level of government from direct party management. "If we start with the concept that the Party represents the

1. Fidel said this in a speech on July 26, 1965, in Santa Clara. It is quoted here from *Política Internacional*, 11–12 (third and fourth trimesters, 1965), 194.

working masses," he declared, then we "reach the conclusion that . . . the Party could and should elect the municipal administrations."[2] It was a matter of elementary logic.

Later in his discussion, Fidel generalized on the "thousand times more revolutionary, . . . thousand times more democratic" system he envisaged. "We shall never cut that umbilical cord which unites the masses with the Party," he maintained, "and therefore we can say that the Party is the legitimate representative of the working masses, that revolutionary power is the power of the workers exercised through their legitimate representatives who are the cadres of the Party, functioning within the Party. . . . And we shall be ready when the time comes to discuss these matters [with the fraternal parties], to defend the institutions of our Revolution, to debate in any group, in any University, in any intellectual center of the world, and demonstrate that it is a very superior form of government, and a much more democratic system of government—the government, of course, of a class, the government of the workers. When all the citizens will be workers, then we shall have a government of the whole people."

The True Road to Communism

There was already enough innovation and provocation for lively disputation forthwith in the international Marxist community, but Fidel went further. "We must struggle tirelessly to establish . . . a communist society," he insisted, "and I believe we have to begin to construct it at the same time as we develop our Socialist Revolution. Otherwise we may reach a point where these two paths diverge: the path of socialist development [to each according to his work] and the path of communist development [to each according to his needs]. We must see to it that they move ahead side by side, and then the day will come when communist institutions will predominate."[3] This was the crowning heresy. Whatever moved Fidel to challenge the firmly established theory and practice of Marxism-Leninism, not the least objective was the leadership image of an ideologically exemplary and independent Cuba on the eve of the tricontinental conference.

Alas, it was an ideological illumination that was destined to be extinguished. In 1975, when the party was finally reorganized as a faithful copy of the Soviet model, Fidel confessed that his version of the truly "revolutionary" and "democratic" Communist Party state had been a failure.

2. *Cuba Socialista*, November 1965, pp. 20–21.
3. Ibid., p. 37.

Fidel offered explanations for the false start, such as "lack of experience" and "subjectivism," as well as "chauvinism and petty bourgeois spirit, . . . arrogance and an overdose of self-esteem, . . . errors of idealism," and ignoring the "existence of objective economic laws. . . ."[4] It would be an astonishing admission of error, unparalleled by any ruler of a Marxist-Leninist state. But the circumstances and the character of the ruler were also without precedent.

The Role of Fidel

Fidel was predictably elected First Secretary of the new party, but how would he adjust to "collective" leadership now that the party had a Central Committee, Politburo, Secretariat, and the rest of the machinery of a governing body? It was left to President Dorticós, a member of the new Politburo, to deal with this question. At the first meeting of the Central Committee, a day before the full assembly at the Chaplin Theatre, he extolled the virtues of the Commander-in-Chief in a brief but moving panegyric. "The creation of the new instruments of leadership," he said, "is the result of an idea elaborated by Fidel and represents his political philosophy. . . . Far from reducing his personal role in the Revolution, it will increase the importance of his role day by day. . . . Today without a doubt, more than ever—I know that I express the sentiments of all of you—Fidel is and will be our guide, our leader. . . ."[5]

It was clear from the context in which Dorticós spoke that all of this was not meant to be taken literally but to flatter and soothe Fidel, who was expected to share power with the "new instruments of leadership." But Fidel, like the proverbial leopard, was not about to change his spots—at least not for another decade, when the party was once more overhauled. Thus, Dorticós's encomium turned out to be prophetic rather than symbolic. The new party was to be as subservient to Castro's wisdom and whim as the old.

The Choice of Names

Fidel's speech on October 3 was broadcast to the nation in the form of a report to the people concerning the decisions taken during the closed meetings of the three previous days. One decision was to convert the two

4. *First Congress of the Cuban Communist Party: Information Roundup* (Havana: Prensa Latina, n.d.), p. 22. The Congress took place in late December 1975.

5. *Cuba Socialista*, November 1965, pp. 57–58.

daily "political" newspapers, *Revolución*, originally the spokesman for Castro's Movement of July 26, and *Hoy*, the venerable mouthpiece of the "old" Communist PSP, into a single official organ of the Central Committee, to be known as *Granma*. It will be recalled that this was the name of the yacht which transported Fidel's expedition from Mexico to Cuba at the end of November 1956. Most Cubans were unaware of the fact that the hallowed name was the diminutive for the English word *grandmother*, but everybody knew that the *Granma* was Fidel's boat. For the Cubans, it was almost as if the consolidated newspaper were named *Fidel*. Among the invariably sober names of the fraternal party organs, "Granma" was unquestionably and conspicuously original.

Another matter brought before the assembly was the name of the new party. "What do you think should be the name of our Party?" Fidel asked, addressing the question to the assembly. Confident of obtaining the answer he wanted, this was a favorite device of his for getting "the people" to initiate and approve a decision already taken. From various parts of the auditorium, those in the know began to shout "Communist." Pointing in the direction from which the shouts came, Fidel asked: "What was that, comrades?" More shouts of "Communist." "Communist Party of Cuba!" he announced. According to the published transcript of the speech, this was followed by an ovation and more shouting: "Communist, Communist, Communist."[6] It is safe to say that no ruling Marxist-Leninist party had ever before chosen its name in this manner.

Despite the great enthusiasm, Fidel thought it necessary to go into a long explanation of why this was the most appropriate name for the new party. Citing the *Communist Manifesto* of Marx and Engels, and recalling the fear and hatred of the word *Communist* by the capitalists, he predicted that "within one hundred years there will be no greater honor, nor will anything be more natural and logical, than to be called a Communist." Meanwhile, he declared, we are proud to be called Communist, because "we are moving toward a Communist society." And, by implication, here was something to distinguish Cuba's party from those fraternal parties in eastern Europe which, after years in power, still clung to the transparent disguise of euphemisms instead of honestly and boldly declaring themselves to be Communist parties.[7]

6. *Política Internacional*, 11–12 (third and fourth trimesters, 1965). Citations from the speech are from pp. 246–253.

7. Note, for example, the Polish United Workers' Party, the Hungarian Socialist Workers' Party, and the Socialist Unity Party in the German Democratic Republic.

Earlier, there had been some preparation for the new name. On August 16, in the same Chaplin Theatre, there had been a solemn convocation to commemorate the fortieth anniversary of the founding of the original Communist Party of Cuba.[8] It was the first time since the Revolution that the "old" party had been given this kind of recognition. The Popular Socialist Party (PSP), as it was known after 1943, had lost its identity in Fidel's amalgamation of revolutionary organizations in 1961. It had been in popular disgrace since March 1962, when Fidel denounced it for "sectarianism" and Soviet-style dogmatism and bureaucracy, and expelled its most prominent leader from Cuba. Now its memory was rehabilitated, its early militant virtues were extolled, and its later sins went unmentioned, to provide historic continuity with its *Fidelista* reincarnation when the moment came to announce the event. Nevertheless, it came as no surprise on October 3 that the "old" Communists had only a token representation in the 100-member Central Committee, none at all in the key eight-member Politburo, and two places out of six in the lesser Secretariat.[9]

Ché's Farewell Letter

Halfway through his speech, Fidel revealed what was already generally suspected by sophisticated Cubans but about which there had been lively speculation abroad: that Ché Guevara had left Cuba to engage in active guerrilla warfare in a country which could not be revealed for security reasons. Fidel read the text of a short letter that Ché had addressed to him. It was undated, Fidel explained, so that it could be made public at an appropriate time. With Ché not listed among the members of the new party hierarchy (and his whereabouts still a carefully guarded secret), the time

8. See the report in *Política Internacional*, 11–12 (third and fourth trimesters, 1965), 203–209.

9. A novel feature of the Central Committee was the fact that over half of its membership was in active military service. As for the Politburo, its members were listed as follows (*Cuba Socialista*, November 1965, p. 9): Fidel Castro, Raúl Castro (also Second Secretary of the party), and, in the order of presumed rank, Osvaldo Dorticós (also President of the Republic), Juan Almeida, Ramiro Valdés, Armando Hart, Guillermo García, and Sergio del Valle—all originally members of Fidel's Movement of July 26 and, with two exceptions, "comandantes" in Fidel's guerrilla army. When the party was reorganized in late December 1975, the new Politburo had thirteen members, including all of the original eight and with the significant addition of the two stalwarts of the pre-1961 PSP–Communist Party: Carlos Rafael Rodríguez and Blas Roca (*First Congress of the Cuban Communist Party: Information Roundup* [Havana: Prensa Latina, n.d.], p. 52).

had come. The letter had actually been delivered to him, Fidel explained, on April 1, "exactly six months and two days ago." [10]

It was a moving letter, composed with Ché's customary literary skill. "Other lands in this world are asking for the cooperation which my modest efforts can provide," he wrote. "I can do what you are prevented from doing because of the responsibility you bear for Cuba. The time for us to separate has arrived. . . . In the new battlefields, I shall bear the faith which you implanted in me, . . . the feeling of fulfilling the most sacred of all duties: to struggle against imperialism wherever it may be. . . ." At the same time, Ché announced his resignation from his various posts in the party, government, and army, and the relinquishing of his Cuban citizenship. This divestiture was obviously designed to relieve Cuba of any legal responsibility for his new adventures, although he was equipped and financed by Fidel, had high-ranking Cuban military personnel on his staff, and maintained constant communication with Havana. It is more than likely that Ché's letter was written in close consultation with Fidel.

After Fidel read the letter, there was even more speculation abroad about Ché than before. Was the letter genuine? Where was Ché? What exactly was he doing? And so on. Not until Ché surfaced in Bolivia two years later did the speculations end. Yet, Ché's letter carried the full imprint of his style and character, and its message was wholly credible within the context of Castro's foreign policy at the time. Perhaps what was most significant about Fidel's revelation concerning Ché could not easily be discerned at the time it occurred. A double-page spread completely dedicated to Ché appeared in the first issue of *Granma* on October 4. It contained a photo of Ché's handwritten letter to Fidel and numerous pictures of the departed leader. This was the beginning of the cult of Ché. Constantly promoted by Cuban propaganda and reinforced by Ché's sacrifice in Bolivia, it spread far and wide, excepting eastern Europe and China, where Ché's heresies had always been unwelcome. In Cuba, the cult of Ché was intensified for several years, and only slightly diminished in the 1970s after Castro's surrender to Soviet-style Marxism-Leninism. Ché's rejected theories were discreetly removed from the cult, but his image as the dedicated revolution-

10. In the García Márquez account, authorized by Castro, the author wrote of the Cuban military intervention in Angola in late 1975: "On April 25, 1965, he [Ché] gave Fidel Castro a farewell letter . . ." (*Washington Post*, January 12, 1977, p. A 12). It was the same letter that Fidel claimed to have received on April 1. Presumably, Fidel had some reason at the time to advance the date, and whoever supplied García Márques with his data forgot to make the adjustment.

ary and noble martyr could still play a role in nourishing allegiance to authority in Cuba and promoting support for Fidel's regime abroad.

Peking Chastized

To return to Fidel's speech, the rest of it was mainly a ringing declaration of self-reliance and independence, largely a recapitulation of themes which he had developed in a number of earlier speeches. By clear implication, he was addressing himself both to Moscow and Peking, but with Peking this time taking the brunt of his warnings against attempts to influence Cuban policy. "Our Party will educate the masses, our Party will educate its members," he exclaimed. "Let this be clearly understood: our Party! No other Party but our Party and its Central Committee!" This was an unmistakable reference to an ultimatum that he had recently sent to the Chinese embassy to stop distributing their anti-Soviet propaganda in Havana. "We shall never say," he added, denouncing a now standard Chinese accusation of Soviet complicity with imperialism, "that those who have helped us defeat the imperialists are the accomplices of the imperialists."

Moscow Admonished

While Moscow could derive considerable satisfaction from these statements, it could scarcely be pleased by an obvious reference to the Kremlin: "We can differ on any point with any Party," Fidel declared. "It is impossible . . . to conceive of Marxism as if it were a church, a religious doctrine, with its Rome, its Pope, and Ecumenical Council." There would be more of this analogy, and even less inhibited attacks directed against the Kremlin, when relations reached a critical point two years later. For the moment, however, whatever their misgivings, the Russians preferred to ignore the rhetoric of their wayward client. A few weeks earlier, they had agreed to provide Cuba with additional economic aid and technical assistance.[11] A month later (November 7), Raúl Castro was perched on Lenin's tomb, with Brezhnev and Kosygin on either side, reviewing the parade marking the anniversary of the Bolshevik Revolution.[12]

In a final salvo, projecting bravado and admonition, Fidel proclaimed the autonomy of the Cuban Revolution as the natural result of its indigenous origins—with ugly implications for the Soviet-dominated brethren of

11. The agreement was signed in Moscow on September 6, 1965. See *Política Internacional*, 11–12 (third and fourth trimesters, 1965), 223.

12. The photo appeared in *Granma* on November 8, 1965.

eastern Europe. "This Revolution was not imported from anywhere," he boasted, "it is a genuine product of this country! Nobody told us how we had to make it, and we made it! Nobody will have to tell us how to continue making it, and we shall continue to make it! We have learned how to write history, and we shall continue writing it! And let nobody have any doubt about this!"

22

■

Two Revolutionary Spectaculars

The Great Ascent

As 1965 WAS DRAWING to an end, the mood was that of revolutionary revival, Cuban style—that is to say, it consisted of a unique combination of the spirit of derring-do and the carnival. The prime mover was, of course, Fidel himself, who concocted two spectacular demonstrations of the mounting tempo of patriotic and revolutionary zeal. On November 9, the front page of *Granma* headlined the news that the graduation ceremonies of four hundred medical students (and twenty-six dental students, as it later transpired) were to take place on the Pico de Turquino. The place was doubly symbolic. It was the top of a 6,500-foot steep and densely wooded mountain in the Sierra Maestra, the scene of Fidel's guerrilla exploits in 1957–1958. It was also the tallest mountain in Cuba, a mighty beacon, so to speak, visually projecting the indestructible power of the Cuban Revolution. Radio and television equipment was to be airlifted by helicopter so that the proceedings could be broadcast to the whole nation. There was a large picture of Fidel in combat outfit, with a rifle slung over his shoulder, making his way through thick vegetation. The text said that Fidel would once more "traverse the historic route up the mountain, . . . guiding the . . . new doctors forged in and by the Revolution." The broadcast of graduation ceremonies was scheduled to begin at 8 A.M. on November 14, with Fidel as the main speaker.

Accompanying Castro and the graduating students were their professors and several hundred notables, party functionaries, government bureaucrats, and a mass of assorted activists. Fidel had urged the participants to make the climb in less than four days, but it was five days before the last of the exhausted stragglers reached the top. Many of those who started dropped out along the way. During the entire period, and for some time after, the press was saturated with news and views of the "ascent."[1] There were accounts of hardy and surefooted peasants bringing up food and other supplies, and of first-aid stations located at convenient intervals. At the 3,000-foot level, a camp for fifteen hundred climbers had been set up. Miraculously, ice cream was provided for those who reached the top. There was a photo of weary climbers reclining in hammocks slung among the trees, with an explanation that they were "tending to their lacerated feet. . . . Many comrades are not accustomed to such long days of marching over mountain trails."[2] Not unexpectedly, pictures of Fidel dominated the news coverage. "At 8:21 yesterday morning, Friday the 12th, Fidel reached the summit of Turquino" was the wording of a solemn communiqué under a large front-page photo of the Commander-in-Chief in guerrilla costume.[3] Fidel, as always, was physically fit. He had made the climb in a little under four days.

The Sermon from the Mount

Sunday morning, as scheduled, Fidel addressed the graduating class and the nation. It was difficult for him to speak, he said, because "these mountains are deeply cherished [and] . . . very sacred." Emotion ran high as he recalled the hardships and sacrifices endured during the war and how "men with faith can do great things." Equally moving was his tribute to those who now faced him on the mountain top. "I know very well what all of you have done," he said. "I am fully aware of the long hours . . . of fatigue, thirst, pain, and at times desperation which you suffered, of heroic willpower which you demonstrated to reach this place." And so it went. Not a word of Marxism-Leninism, but back to the roots of Fidel's revolution, the suffering, heroism, and glory of the struggle in the Sierra Maestra, symbol and example of invincible fortitude and faith.

Fidel also spoke of the "irresistible creative torrent of our Revolution, . . . the advance in all aspects of our organization, not only in our teach-

---

1. The last photos and commentary appeared in *Granma* on December 22. The graduation stunt inaugurated a rash of other "ascents" and simulated "guerrilla" campaign marches in the lowlands, but without the elaborate staging of Fidel's climb.

2. *Granma*, November 12, 1965.

3. *Granma*, November 13, 1965.

ing institutions, in our Ministry of Public Health, [but also] in our Television, . . . which for the first time in our country has been able to perform the unimaginable feat of transmitting by television a graduation exercise from the top of Turquino. . . ." He was right. It was "unimaginable" and, one might add, incomprehensible, except for Fidel. It was not only "the first time" but also the last. With the price of sugar on the world market approaching a record low, and with the country on short rations, the stunt was "unimaginably" costly.

In closing, Fidel repeated his now customary challenge to the United States. Coming from the mountaintop, it was like Jove hurling thunderbolts from Olympus. "With imperialism we want no peace of any kind," he exclaimed. "While imperialism exists and while there are peoples who are victims of imperialist aggression and while there are peoples who struggle against imperialism, their cause will be our cause, anywhere in the world." It was a message addressed as much to the Russians and the Chinese as to the Americans. It was also a pledge to the forthcoming tricontinental conference. To the "heroic" amateur mountain climbers facing him, now impregnated with the spirit of the Sierra Maestra, Fidel promised more heroism. "We shall continue arming to the teeth," he added. "We shall continue preparing the people. We shall continue organizing battalions to fight in the mountains, on the plains, and in the cities, everywhere . . . to fight and struggle to the last drop of our blood!"[4]

The scene was now almost set for the great conference in January. The foreign delegates would find a new militant Communist Party in place, led by a warrior Central Committee and guided by an extraordinary Commander-in-Chief. They would be welcomed by a hardened self-sacrificing people ready to take up arms "against imperialist aggression anywhere in the world." So much for the spirit of derring-do. There remained the carnival.

The Great Supper

New Year's Eve is traditionally celebrated in Cuba with feasting and revelry. For the great majority of the people, the main event is the family *cena* (late supper), featuring *lechón* (roast pig), *congrí* (a seasoned mixture of rice and beans), stimulating beverages, and assorted goodies. However, nothing like the gigantic public *cena* which began in the closing hours of

4. Citations from Castro's speech are from *Política Internacional*, 11–12 (third and fourth trimesters, 1965), 283–288.

1965 had ever occurred in Cuba before. In fact, one would have to go back to the heyday of the Roman Empire to find anything remotely comparable. Assembled in Havana's vast Plaza de la Revolución were more than fifty thousand celebrants wielding knife and fork under a star-studded tropical sky.

Planning had begun many weeks before.[5] Enormous quantities of food had to be assembled, stored, and then transported to the Plaza. Fifty canteens were set up, each provided with eight ovens. Three thousand workers were assigned to service the canteens, operating in cafeteria style. On December 31, at 9 P.M., the customers began to line up at the counters. As they moved along, they picked up their plates, cutlery, a choice of roast pig or chicken along with the fixings, a paper cup of wine or cold beer, dessert, and finally a paper hat, a toy trumpet, and a rattle. All of this went for three pesos, considerably below cost price.

Overlooking the multitude, on the huge elevated platform that forms the base of the monument to José Martí, Fidel, his top party and government leaders, and five hundred invited guests were served something more than the standard *cena* by uniformed waiters. Most of the guests were delegates to the Tricontinental, and, as the press later reported, "they were enormously impressed."[6] A guerrilla *comandante* from Venezuela was quoted as saying: "No adjective can really describe it. You can say grandiose, extraordinary, fabulous, unbelievable. But they don't really say enough. I would say that this is the Cuban Revolution. Only a Revolution can change traditions this way. This is the Revolution." I overheard one guest say, possibly in jest, that the *cena* represented a great leap forward from the individualistic capitalist to the collectivist communist mode of celebration.

At midnight, fireworks lit up the sky and a great roar of acclamation rose from the Plaza. Then, fourteen strategically located orchestras went into action, and thousands of people began to dance. Fidel, it was reported, was bubbling over with joy and enthusiasm. According to *Granma*, as he watched the people full of happiness dancing the "mozambique," Fidel told a group of delegates that in "Cuba at times we have ideas which at first seem impossible. But then they turn out very well." If there were Russians in the group, they must have made a mental note that Fidel's "impossible ideas" seemed to work only when the production of material goods was not

5. Some of the details were explained in *Granma* on December 29, 1965.

6. *Granma*, January 2, 1966. All subsequent citations concerning the *cena* are from the same issue of *Granma*.

invólved. As for the *cena*, they must have had mixed feelings about its resounding success. In the last analysis, its whopping cost was subsidized by Soviet credits granted for other purposes.

In any event, for those of us present at the *cena*, there was no question about the "explosive gaity" among the people, as *Granma* put it (there was some rowdyism, too), although one could not be sure that it was mainly a demonstration of "joy in having supper with Fidel and the other leaders. . . ." Undoubtedly, however, we had been present at an historic occasion, aptly summed up by *Granma*: "After all is said and done, this has been a tricontinental New Year's Eve supper with Fidel, massive in its dimensions and incomparable."[7]

7. Additional grandiose entertainment was provided for those attending the tricontinental conference. On January 9, eight thousand students put on a "monumental" pageant depicting the glories of "solidarity." On the 12th, an elaborate candlelight supper was served to more than one thousand guests in the picturesque square facing Havana's colonial cathedral. On the 17th, scores of buses loaded with delegates left Havana for a tour of the island.

23

■

The Tricontinental Conference

The Components of the Assembly

THE EAGERLY AWAITED tricontinental meeting, or "The First Conference of Solidarity of the Peoples of Africa, Asia, and Latin America" (OSPAAAL), as it was officially designated, took place in Havana from January 3 to 15, 1966. According to the record, five hundred and twelve delegates were present.[1] They came from eighty-two countries and colonial territories, quite evenly divided among the three continents. Only a small number of delegations came as official or semiofficial representatives of governments. These were from Africa, as for example, Algeria, Egypt, Ghana, and Tanzania, and from Asia, notably China, North Korea, North Vietnam, and the Soviet Union (Chinese objections that the Soviet Union was a European country notwithstanding). The other delegations, including all from Latin America except Cuba, represented a vast array of anti-imperialist "movements," "associations," "fronts," "parties," and "committees" of various leftist and Marxist persuasions, including the Soviet, Chinese, Castroite, and assorted esoteric varieties.

Some were from serious organizations, such as the South Vietnamese contingent, the Popular Liberation Movement of Angola (MPLA), and the

1. See *Política Internacional*, 13 (first trimester, 1966), 7–16 and 75–79. Many of the Africans and Asians were affiliated with the Afro-Asian Peoples Solidarity Organization, with headquarters in Cairo. Cuba had observer status at its meetings beginning in 1961, at which time Castro's representative first suggested a tricontinental meeting. The proposal was officially accepted by the Afro-Asian body at a conference in Ghana in May 1965.

Liberation Front of Mozambique (FRELIMO). A few others later developed serious potentials, such as the Palestine Liberation Organization (PLO) and the Zimbabwe group from what was then called Southern Rhodesia. But most were ephemeral "ad hoc" clusters. This was particularly true of the numerous Latin American "national committees," formed with Cuban subsidies and guidance expressly for the Havana meeting but eventually dissolved, and the handful of guerrilla bands destined to expire shortly. An exception was the solidly based Chilean Popular Action Front (FRAP) delegation, headed by Salvador Allende, who was to be elected president of Chile in 1970. Later, the FRAP, too, was to be destroyed, and Allende was to lose his life in the military insurrection of 1973.

If to the eighty-two voting delegations are added the hundred or so members of the twenty-one officially designated "observer" participants, seven of them from eastern Europe, including Albania but not "revisionist" Yugoslavia (expressly denied admission), then it was not only the first tricontinental "people's solidarity" gathering, but by far the largest assembly of Third World militants and supporters that the world had ever known. Housed in the capitalist splendor of the expropriated Habana Libre Hotel (formerly the Havana Hilton), attended by scores of foreign journalists, serviced by hundreds of clerks, translators, waiters, cooks, chambermaids, and chauffeurs, and consuming tons of choice food and beverages,[2] the conference's physical and geographic dimensions alone gave the impression that it could change the course of history. Alas, this was not to be. One of the problems was "solidarity."

A Preliminary Note of Discord

Not unexpectedly, Fidel, in his speech on January 2 in the Plaza de la Revolución, this time marking the seventh anniversary of his regime and in the presence of most of the tricontinental guests, had proclaimed 1966 as the "Year of Solidarity" in the revolutionary calendar. Quite unexpectedly, however, he revealed that something less than complete solidarity was in the offing. First, he indignantly rejected the charge made by "those [speaking] from supposedly revolutionary positions" that his recent arrangement with the United States for airlifting thousands of disaffected Cubans to

2. In his closing address to the conference, Fidel boasted that "thousands of Cubans, unceasing in their efforts, giving up their day of rest and vacation time, have worked for the success of the Conference, taking care of the needs of the brotherly peoples" (ibid., p. 195). He might have mentioned other thousands who were unable to obtain their normal food rations while the meetings were in session.

Miami was a "kind of conciliation with the imperialists." Who were the "supposedly revolutionary" culprits? He did not say. Were they lurking among the delegates? This was the implication, and they had to be put in their place. "The last country that will make peace with imperialism," he thundered, "will be this country!"

Second, Fidel dedicated a large portion of his speech to an explanation of a "misunderstanding" between Cuba and China concerning the terms of an exchange of sugar and rice between the two countries. The upshot was that China, unexpectedly for Fidel, had decided to reduce its shipments of rice, with the result that the "Year of Solidarity" would be one of a serious shortage of the most important staple in the Cuban diet (on January 7, the rice rations were cut in half). In his lengthy summary of the negotiations between the two countries, Fidel refrained for tactical reasons from any explicit accusation of bad faith on the part of the Chinese, and he "accepted" their assertion that part of the rice was needed at home and part would be diverted to North Vietnam. "We could never object," he declared with scarcely concealed irony, "especially if they invoke the name of Vietnam. Because we are ready to give the Vietnamese people not only our sugar but our blood, which is worth much more than sugar." [3] There was more than a hint that Chinese "blood"—that is, soldiers who had only to cross the border—would be worth more to the Vietnamese than rice. After the tricontinental conference, a bitter "sugar and rice" polemic between the two countries would erupt, as we shall see.

Emerging Quarrels

Once the conference got under way, the chill in Cuban-Chinese relations was noticeable but not conspicuous as other quarrels came to the surface. Some occurred within delegations, which split in two and sometimes three rival factions. These factions were mainly from the smaller countries or colonies, but they were none the less noisy and disruptive, since each faction usually had ties with one of the "majors." [4] These were the Russians,

3. Citations from the speech are taken from ibid., pp. 61–62 and 70.
4. A case in which a tiny speck in the Caribbean provoked a political hurricane was the resolution on Guadeloupe, technically an overseas department of France but included in the conference agenda as a colony. The burning issue was whether to support the position of the French Communist Party favoring autonomy or to take a more militant stance for independence. In the prolonged verbal battle, the Communist Party members of the Latin American delegation, backed by the Soviets and other moderates, lined up against their "leftist" colleagues, sup-

the Chinese, and, of course, the Cubans, who as hosts had played a leading role in structuring the conference and, particularly, in determining the
composition of the Latin American delegations. Once the conference was
in session, the Cubans had a decided advantage in manipulating its machinery. The delegations with the highest prestige were understandably
those representing the embattled Vietnamese, of both the north and south.
Their speakers were given unlimited time and were frequently rewarded
with an ovation. However, they mainly stuck to their "business"—the war
in Vietnam—and prudently maintained a low profile on serious issues that
could embroil them with their Russian and Chinese benefactors.

One of these issues, which went to the heart of the Sino-Soviet po-
litico-ideological conflict, was the question of "peaceful coexistence." In
the debate, the Chinese launched a bitter and prolonged attack against the
Russians, advancing their familiar charge that the Soviet formula was the
equivalent of "joint action with American imperialism." The Soviet Union
was thus portrayed as "an ally of American imperialism," fearful of a "paper tiger" whose nuclear weapons were "really nothing exceptional." [5] The
Chinese, however, overplayed their hand, with most delegations recognizing that their diatribe, if accepted, would break up the conference. Thus, a
resolution was finally approved which accepted the doctrine of peaceful
coexistence, with an ambiguous definition similar to the standard Soviet
interpretation that the doctrine did not inhibit wars of national liberation.
In this confrontation, Cuba, although for a long time a critic of Soviet-
style peaceful coexistence, backed the Soviet Union.

The "Armed Struggle" Thesis Upheld

For the occasional support which the Russians received from Cuba, the
price they paid was high. One of Castro's principal objectives at the conference was to get endorsement of his Latin American policy of "armed
struggle" as the predominant, if not exclusive, means of defeating Yankee
imperialism and its puppet governments in the western hemisphere. A first

---

ported by the Chinese, Vietnamese, and Cubans, among others. The "autono-
mists" lost. Thus, the conference went on record to "condemn . . . the colonial
policy of the French government," to "affirm . . . the right of Guadeloupe to national independence," and to "recommend . . . all necessary aid for the Guade-
loupan revolutionaries" (ibid., p. 154). Beyond the confines of the conference, the
impact of the debate on the destiny of Guadeloupe was imperceptible.

5. Ibid., pp. 35 and 36.

corollary of this policy was the legitimation of existing and future Cuban military involvement in Latin American guerrilla operations. A second corollary was recognition of undisputed Cuban political leadership and direction of Latin American revolutionary movements. Unspoken but implied was Soviet financing of the Cuban strategy—willy-nilly, so to speak, for the costs would inevitably divert funds from the massive Soviet subsidy that was responsible for the survival of the Castro regime. This whole package had been a bone of contention for some time between Havana and Moscow and had led to the uneasy "compromise" reached at the meeting of Latin American Communist parties in Havana at the end of 1964.

Whatever remained from this arrangement became a dead letter in January 1966. Castro, as has been noted, had taken charge of selecting the membership of the Latin American delegations. Excluding Trotskyists and Maoists—a concession he willingly made to the Russians, since these elements were unmanageable in any event—he assured the predominance of pro-Cuban militants over pro-Soviet Communists. Thus, the Cubans and their allies pushed through a series of "armed struggle" resolutions affecting Latin America, notably Colombia, Peru, Guatemala, and, of particular importance, Venezuela. Ironically, at the very moment of debate, a "common front" between the Venezuelan Communist Party and a Cuban-backed guerrilla band was in the final stage of disintegration.

The dismay and discomfort of the Soviet delegation, matched by the satisfaction of the Chinese, were unconcealed. At one point, the chief Soviet spokesman, Sharaf Rashidov, a candidate member of the Soviet party's politburo and first secretary of the Uzbek central committee, sensing the growing mood of skepticism concerning the revolutionary pretensions of his delegation, felt impelled to rescue the Soviet image with an unequivocal—and imprudent—affirmation of revolutionary zeal. "Dear friends," he pleaded, "the Soviet people always supports peoples' liberation wars, the armed struggle of oppressed peoples, and provides them . . . with all possible help."[6] Shortly after the conference, the Rashidov statement and Soviet participation at the conference came under attack at the Security Council of the United Nations, where there was a sharp protest by the Latin American governments (with the exception of Mexico) against Soviet support of resolutions advocating external support for armed intervention in their countries. This forced the Soviet Union into circulating an indignant

6. Cited by Marcel Niedergang in *Le Monde*, January 8, 1966.

statement claiming that the "representatives of Soviet social organizations . . . had taken part in the conference," not "those of the Soviet government,"[7] a transparent fiction which added nothing to Russian prestige.

A Savage Conflict

The final and most savage conflict in the "solidarity" process was a triangular struggle between the Russians, the Chinese, and the Cubans concerning the location of the next meeting and the location of the permanent headquarters of the now duly constituted OSPAAAL. The interest of the Russians in the founding conference of the organization, it would appear (and their willingness to underwrite a large share of its expenses), was to a considerable extent motivated by the expectation that in Havana they could engineer the liquidation of the Afro-Asian solidarity organization by having it incorporated into an enlarged tricontinental body. This would considerably dilute Chinese influence. Equally important, it would justify the cancellation of the next (fifth) Afro-Asian assembly, scheduled to be held in 1967 in Peking, where the Russians would find themselves at a decided disadvantage.

Resistance to this maneuver, led by the Chinese and abetted by Cuban "neutrality," was successful. Thereupon the Russians shifted their efforts to promoting Cairo (then friendly to them) as the permanent headquarters of the new organization, and this time they ran into Castro's determination to have the headquarters located in Havana. A mighty tug-of-war ensued, which ended in a "compromise." Havana was declared to be the temporary headquarters. The choice of a permanent seat was postponed to the next meeting, to be held in Cairo in 1968. In effect, this amounted to a victory for the Cubans and a defeat for the Russians. The Chinese were consoled by the Russian defeat. Thus, Castro, who had already trounced the Russians on the issue of "armed struggle" in Latin America, achieved two of his objectives. Losing no time to achieve a third objective, he rounded up the Latin American delegations on January 16, the day after the conference adjourned, and formally set up a brand-new Latin American Solidarity Organization (OLAS) with headquarters in Havana, where the first conference was set to take place in mid-1967. For Fidel and his fol-

7. Council of the OAS Report on the *First Afro–Asian–Latin American Solidarity Conference and its Projections* (Washington, D.C., November 28, 1966), Vol. II, pp. 285–288; cited by D. Bruce Jackson, *Castro, the Kremlin and Communism in Latin America* (Baltimore: Johns Hopkins University Press, 1967), p. 93.

lowing, this appeared to be the hour of his greatest triumph since the victory at the Bay of Pigs in 1961.

A Final Polemic

At the closing session of the conference, held in the Chaplin Theatre, Fidel was the only speaker. It was expected that he would "accentuate the positive" and, if not "eliminate the negative," according to the old refrain, give it gentle treatment. He did celebrate the "victory of the unity of the peoples," but this was overshadowed by a violent polemic against the Trotskyists in general and a Guatemala guerrilla movement in particular, which he claimed was infiltrated by the Trotskyists. He had been instrumental in selecting a rival guerrilla movement, at the time supported by the Guatemalan Communist Party, as the sole representative of the Guatemalan "people" at the conference.

What also had aroused Fidel's anger was the widespread speculation in the corridors of the Habana Libre concerning the great "absent one," Ché Guevara. Was he dead or alive? Not a single Cuban speaker had mentioned his name at any of the countless sessions. When the leader of the Venezuelan delegation broke the silence and paid homage to Ché, there was a standing ovation. More than anything else, what undermined the credibility of Fidel's earlier explanation of Ché's departure was the fact that Ché had sent no message to the conference. Assuming that he was indeed carrying out a revolutionary mission in "other lands" which could not be revealed, there had been plenty of time—four months, in fact—since the start of the active preparations for the meeting for Ché to write and transmit an appropriate statement to Havana. How could Fidel have overlooked the importance of a message from Ché?

Prior to the conference, Trotskyist publications in Latin America and elsewhere had already accused Castro of doing away with Ché in order to eliminate the apostle of genuine revolution and curry favor with the Russians. Hence, Fidel vented his rage on the Trotskyists in his Chaplin Theatre performance, citing chapter and verse of their infamous printed slanders, which he correlated with similar views in the capitalist press. His conclusion was a slight modification of the familiar Kremlin charge, since the days of Stalin, that "if at one time Trotskyism represented an erroneous position . . . among political ideas, later [it] was converted into a vulgar instrument of imperialism and reaction."[8]

8. *Política Internacional*, 13 (first trimester, 1966), 192.

This was an unexpected bonus for the Russians, but a disturbing climax, to say the least, for a "solidarity" conference and for many participants for whom the absence of a message from Ché remained a puzzle.[9] Actually, Castro could not explain Ché's silence, and for good reason. Very likely, Ché had already secretly returned to Cuba, licking his wounds, so to speak, after his disastrous campaign in the Congo, and hence in no condition to prepare a suitable statement. Whatever the reason for the omission, the error was belatedly corrected more than a year later by Ché's celebrated "Message to the Tricontinental," issued in a glossy illustrated pamphlet of twenty-four pages.[10]

Reality and Fantasy

The First Tricontinental Conference produced close to seventy resolutions, declarations, reports, and messages, filling as many densely printed pages.[11] They voiced the familiar and not so familiar indictments of imperialism and colonialism, from American aggression against Vietnam to the French occupation of Djibouti, from "racist and fascist Zionism" to the "fascist axis" in southern Africa, from the plight of the Dominican Republic to the British intervention in South Yemen. They denounced the "cultural and ideological penetration of imperialism" and included a series of demands for what later came to be known as a "new world economic order." The arch-villain and implacable enemy of the "peoples" of the three continents was repeatedly identified as the United States, and their virtuous and dependable ally was the socialist camp.

How much did this enormous outpouring of grievance and fantasy add to the achievement of the aims set forth at the conference? The resolutions gave the appearance of "solidarity" although behind them lurked serious

9. It also provoked disputes among nonparticipant "tricontinental" enthusiasts, as for example in New York's "independent socialist magazine," *Monthly Review* (see issue of April 1966, passim). Although a stalwart champion of the Cuban Revolution, *Monthly Review* had earlier opened its pages to a Latin American radical journalist who was critical of Castro. In his closing speech to the conference, Fidel unmercifully lumped the *Monthly Review* with the Trotskyists.

10. Ché wrote, in part: "How bright and near the future could be if two, three, many Vietnams would blossom on the surface of the earth, with their quota of death . . . with their daily heroism . . . obliging [imperialism] to disperse its forces, pounded by the waves of the increasing hatred of the peoples of the world" (*Tricontinental*, special supplement, Organization of Solidarity of the Peoples of Africa, Asia, and Latin America [OSPAAAL], Havana, April 16, 1967, p. 22).

11. See *Política Internacional*, 13 (first trimester, 1966), 106–180.

conflict, and after they were approved there was noncompliance. Cuba, for example, did not break relations with Israel until 1973. With a few notable exceptions, the overwhelming majority of the "peoples" in whose name the resolutions were issued had no knowledge of the meeting in Havana, or of the self-appointed delegations that attended it, let alone their declarations. Possibly, the intermingling for the first time of militants from the three continents, the making of new contacts, and the trading of experiences and ideas may have had some influence in some rare instances on the future course of events. The presence of the Soviet-backed Angolan MPLA in Havana, for example, may have been one in a chain of circumstances that led to Cuban military intervention in the Angolan postindependence civil war. By and large, however, the rhetoric of the Havana conference had no discernible impact on the long list of specified goals. Almost certainly it did not contribute to the outcome of the wars in Indochina or to the Portuguese withdrawal from Africa, nor did it weaken the "fascist" Mobutu regime in the Congo (later Zaire), or advance the "territorial integrity" of Cyprus, or prevent the defeat of the guerrilla movements in Latin America. And more than a decade later, issues that were still alive, such as Zimbabwe, Namibia, Palestine, and the "new world economic order," had been moved into other arenas, the United Nations among them.

"The overwhelming majority of mankind gathered in the capital of the Republic of Cuba, the first free territory of the Americas, . . . [and inaugurated] the most grandiose movement of revolutionary peoples, opening a decisive stage in the centuries-old battle against the exploiters of all times and in all latitudes, . . . [justifying] the slogan: 'Guerrillas of the three continents, united.'" Thus wrote an official spokesman of Castro's government in a sixty-page essay summarizing the proceedings and significance of the conference.[12] It was an illusion which bolstered Fidel's reckless optimism and messianic yearning but would end in the decimation of his guerrilla followers in Latin America and Ché Guevara's martyrdom in Bolivia, and finally to Fidel's capitulation to Soviet political and ideological hegemony.[13]

12. Fernando Alvarez Tabío, director of the Institute of International Relations of the Ministry of Foreign Affairs, in ibid., pp. 7 and 8.
13. It also stimulated the imagination of some western radical intellectuals, e.g., the editors of the *Monthly Review.* Undeterred by Castro's insult in his closing address, they wrote: "The Conference aroused and gave dramatic expression to an unprecedented sense of revolutionary militancy and international solidarity among the victims of imperialism . . . sounded the death knell of . . . narcotic illusions of peaceful coexistence . . . [and presented] a profound challenge to the Soviet lead-

A Stillbirth

In May 1966, four months after the end of the conference, a minor shooting incident at the fortified frontier separating the U.S. naval base at Guantánamo from Cuban territory greatly excited Fidel and gave OSPAAAL its first opportunity to call upon the solidarity of its members. The organization issued a shrill appeal on May 28th "to send volunteers to Cuba without delay . . . and to convert each country into a battlefield in defense of Cuba and the struggle against Yankee imperialism."[14] There is no record that the appeal was answered. OSPAAAL, for all practical purposes, was stillborn. From time to time, other "solidarity" exhortations would emanate from its Havana office, which *Granma* prominently displayed on its pages, but which might just as well have originated in *Granma*. Eventually, OSPAAAL became just another Cuban publishing venture, issuing a magazine, *Tricontinental*, first on glossy paper, then on cheap stock, and progressively at irregular intervals. The First Tricontinental Conference turned out to be its last.

---

ership. . . . Is it too much to hope that mounting pressures of this kind will eventually force a change of policy and perhaps even a change of leadership in the Soviet Union?" (April 1966, pp. 3–4).

14. *Política Internacional de la Revolución Cubana* (Havana: Editora Política, 1966), Vol. II, p. 432.

24

■

The Great
Sino-Cuban Quarrel

China Denounced

THE LAST OF THE DELEGATES to the tricontinental conference had scarcely
departed when Fidel exploded a bombshell which shattered all pretense of
normal, let alone brotherly, relations between Cuba and China. It was in
the form of an 8,000-word statement, released to the press on February 6,
1966, and entitled "Reply of Major Fidel Castro, First Secretary of the
Communist Party of Cuba and Prime Minister of the Revolutionary Government to the Declarations of the Chinese Government."[1] It came after
an exchange of communications, initiated by Peking, between the ministries of foreign trade of both countries. The Chinese were provoked by the
implications of bad faith on their part when Fidel, in his speech on January 2, revealed their decision to reduce rice exports to Cuba and the consequences it would have on the Cuban diet. They raised objections to
Fidel's interpretation of the sugar-rice deal to which they had agreed and to
the figures he had used. In turn, the Cuban side refuted the Chinese con-
tentions. The exchange was sharp but polite—and tedious—and the issue
was rice.

It was, of course, suspected by sophisticated observers that a serious
political quarrel lurked behind the rice controversy, and this is what Fidel
confirmed on February 6. Citing facts and figures, he accused the Chinese
of using rice as a weapon in an attempt to impose their political views.

1. References to the document are from the version published in *Política Internacional*, 13 (first trimester, 1966), 213–226.

While he did not say which views, the implication was that they were related to the Sino-Soviet dispute. Surpassing any invective up to that time on record in public discourse between Communist governments, excepting only Stalin's denunciation of Tito, and indeed rivaling his own fulminations against the United States, Fidel charged the Chinese with "perfidy, . . . insolence, . . . extortion, . . . criminal economic aggression," and "violating the sovereignty of our country." The question facing revolutionaries, he stated in the concluding paragraph of the document, was whether "in the world of tomorrow which they are struggling to create, the worst methods of piracy [and] oppression . . . will prevail such as existed under slave-holding regimes, feudalism, absolute monarchy, . . . and in our time, the imperialist states." [2]

It was a spectacular washing of dirty socialist linen in public, all the more so since his bill of particulars against the Chinese was entirely credible. Even so, Fidel did not tell the whole story: the socialist wrecking of Cuban rice production; his own arbitrary and foolhardy decision to eliminate that production altogether; and the context of the Sino-Soviet dispute within which the Sino-Cuban crisis took place. Drawing upon other sources, as well as the data in Fidel's document, it will be possible for us to unravel the complexities which went into the making of this extraordinary episode.

Rice in the Cuban Economy

The Cubans are the only non-Asiatic people for whom rice is the "staff of life," rather than wheat or other cereals such as maize, barley, or rye. The growth of rice consumption was associated with the expansion of the sugar industry in the nineteenth century, when plantation owners began to import large quantities from the Orient to feed their workers, most of whom were black slaves. Rice was nutritious, easy to store and cook, and combined well with other foods produced domestically, particularly beans, the main source of protein in the rural diet. Most important, rice was very cheap and its supply was dependable. Although the Cuban soil and climate were favorable for the cultivation of rice, there was no incentive to produce more than marginal quantities. On the other hand, Cuban conditions were not favorable for growing wheat, in addition to the fact that wheat farming requires extensive acreage which could be put to much more profitable use by planting sugarcane.

With the outbreak of World War II, rice imports from the traditional

2. Ibid., p. 226.

sources of supply were cut off. As a result, the United States, which in the 1930s had accounted for only twenty-five percent of Cuban rice imports, took over practically the entire Cuban market. This was the beginning of the end of cheap rice. After the war, increased domestic consumption in the traditional large Far Eastern exporting countries, among other factors, reduced supplies for the international market. Accordingly, by 1947 Cuba was paying approximately five times more per metric ton of rice than a decade earlier.[3] At that rate, it became profitable for Cuban farmers to expand rice production. In 1949, Cuba produced a little more than ten percent of its domestic consumption and imported the rest from the United States.[4] By 1959, the year Castro came to power, Cuba was rapidly moving toward self-sufficiency in rice. In the course of this process, the latest methods of rice farming employed in Louisiana and Texas had been adopted with notable success. From the point of view of technological development, rice production outstripped that of any other branch of Cuban agriculture; and in terms of money value, rice became one of Cuba's major crops.[5]

As in the case of sugar, the impact of Castro's destructive agrarian reform did not diminish rice output until after 1960. In that year, as a matter of fact, a record harvest of 400,000 metric tons was produced, more than enough to take care of Cuba's domestic needs.[6] By 1962, however, the yield was reduced by nearly one-half.[7] In March of that year, the precipitous decline in Cuba's now fully socialist economy led Castro to introduce a system of general rationing of consumer goods, including nearly all basic foodstuffs, among which was rice. The rice ration was set at six pounds per person per month. In terms of the population as a whole, this reduced per capita consumption to about two-thirds of what it had been at the time Castro seized the government;[8] but for most low-income Cubans, for whom rice formed a more substantial part of their diet, the reduction was

3. As calculated from data in Leví Marrero, *Geografía de Cuba* (Havana: Editorial Selecta, 1957), p. 353.

4. International Bank for Reconstruction and Development, *Report on Cuba* (Baltimore: Johns Hopkins University Press, 1951), p. 849.

5. Marrero, *Geografía de Cuba*, p. 190.

6. *Cuba Internacional* (Havana), 4th year, No. 38 (October 1972), p. 8.

7. The 1962 figure was 207,000 metric tons. See C. Paul Roberts and Mukhtar Hamour, eds., *Cuba 1968: Supplement to the Statistical Abstract of Latin America* (Los Angeles: Latin American Center, University of California, 1970), p. 136.

8. As calculated from data in Boris Goldenberg, *The Cuban Revolution and Latin America* (New York: Praeger, 1965), p. 256.

even greater. In addition to problems which rice shared with a number of other foodstuffs, such as falling production for a growing population, it was difficult to import. The United States trade embargo had cut off the most accessible market, and rice was in short supply in other markets. In addition, the price of rice on the international market was twenty percent higher in 1962 than in 1960,[9] and an upward trend could be expected. Finally, the USSR, which supplied Cuba with one hundred percent of its wheat requirements, produced no rice to speak of.

The Role of Chinese Rice

It was at this point that China was able to provide significant relief for the Cuban economy, as well as bolster the political stability of the Castro regime, since the availability of rice, more than that of any other food, was important for maintaining the morale of the population. In 1962, China exported 120,000 metric tons of rice to Cuba.[10] Without this assistance, the rice ration would have been considerably smaller. Moreover, the increase of Cuba's trade deficit with China resulting from the rice transaction was covered by a $60 million credit, payable in fifteen years at no interest, which China had granted Cuba in 1960.[11] Thus, Castro had his rice, at no cost in hard-to-come-by convertible currency, and in fact at little other cost, except for an unanticipated political obligation that would come due at some future time. Meanwhile, China, in its cold war struggle against the USSR for revolutionary leadership in Latin America, had demonstrated that it could make an important material, as well as ideological, contribution to the cause of proletarian internationalism.

In 1963, as Cuban production of rice continued to decline, China raised its shipments of rice to 135,000 metric tons, a generous increase of 12.5 percent over the preceding year. The same amount was scheduled for export to Cuba in 1964, but as the year wore on, a new crisis in the supply of rice began to shape up. Rice production on the island fell sharply, and by the end of 1964 would total only 123,000 tons, or forty percent less than in 1963.[12] Accordingly, in October 1964, during the preliminary trade ne-

9. U.S. $153 as compared with $125 per metric ton. See Feng-hua Mah, *The Foreign Trade of Mainland China* (Chicago: Aldine-Atherton, 1971), p. 32.
10. *Política Internacional*, 13 (first trimester, 1966), 219.
11. See my *The Rise and Decline of Fidel Castro* (Berkeley and Los Angeles: University of California Press, 1972), p. 142.
12. The figure for 1963 was 204,000 tons. See Roberts and Hamour, *Cuba 1968*, p. 136.

gotiations for the following year, the Chinese agreed to increase their exports of rice from 135,000 to 150,000 tons.[13] It was a gesture of goodwill, although the Cubans had undoubtedly asked for a considerably larger increase. In any event, the additional 15,000 tons would scarcely compensate for the 81,000-ton decline in the Cuban harvest. Cuba was thus faced with the need to buy large quantities of expensive rice on the international market, to be paid for in convertible currency and in cash.

This would not be easy. The market for rice was tight and was further restricted for Cuba in July 1964, when an agreement by the Organization of American States required all members that had not already done so to break diplomatic and economic relations with Cuba. Among other countries, this eliminated Uruguay, which had been selling rice to Cuba. In addition, the price of sugar in the free market had been falling during most of 1964, and the outlook for 1965 was clearly for further sharp decline.[14] Sugar exports at the time provided Cuba with more than ninety percent of its convertible currency. To allocate part of this scarce and dwindling resource for the purchase of rice would compound the hardships which already plagued the other sectors of the economy.

Fidel's Proposition

Such was the situation when Fidel took the unprecedented step of going himself to the Chinese embassy in Havana to bargain for an additional 100,000 tons of rice—and relieve the critical shortage. As he later explained to the Cuban people, "at the end of 1964, . . . I personally made a . . . commercial . . . proposition to the diplomatic representative of the People's Republic of China." Noting that the Chinese consumer paid several times more for sugar than for rice, and that the situation was the reverse in Cuba, "I thought that a larger exchange of sugar for rice would be mutually convenient. Accordingly, I made the proposition that we were willing to deliver two tons of sugar for every ton of rice they would send us."[15] At the prevailing price of the two commodities, this would be something of a bargain for the Chinese.

Concretely, Fidel offered—over and above the October agreement—to exchange an additional 200,000 tons of sugar for an additional 100,000

13. *Política Internacional*, 13 (first trimester, 1966), 217.

14. Ibid., p. 219. As previously noted, the average price of sugar for 1963 was U.S. 8.50¢ per pound; for 1964, 5.88¢; and for 1965, 2.18¢.

15. Speech on January 2, 1966 (*Política Internacional*, 13 [first trimester, 1966], 69).

tons of rice.[16] This would mean that instead of the 150,000 tons of rice earlier agreed to, Cuba would receive a total of 250,000 tons of rice for the year 1965, and as Fidel understood the deal, for an indefinite number of years after that.

Earlier, Fidel had explained that he was motivated by "the principle of the international division of labor, . . . that we are traditionally sugarcane producers . . . capable of obtaining high yields of sugar," but that conditions for producing rice in Cuba were different. Among the reasons for this, he claimed a lack of "technical" knowledge in rice cultivation. Thus, the deal with China was a matter of mutual benefit, because "otherwise I would never have made this type of proposition." Fidel went on to say that the Chinese accepted the proposition and that "their reply was better than I expected,"[17] because they refused to accept the financial profit that would result from the two-for-one exchange.

Very likely, Fidel's explanation to the Cuban people about how he persuaded the Chinese to accept his two-for-one deal was a fairly accurate account of the manner in which he presented his proposition. He could scarcely afford to be candid with the Chinese—or with his own people—about the disastrous impact of the Revolution on Cuba's flourishing rice agriculture, which was in fact technically more advanced than China's.[18] Nor would it have been expedient to admit that he was in an extremely difficult predicament and that he needed help, which the Soviet Union could not give him. Hence his posture of a purely rational deal based on the "international division of labor," of benefit for both countries, and a little more so financially for the Chinese.

Chinese Motivation, Fidel's Naivete

It is unlikely, however, that the Chinese were taken in by Fidel's posture. It was no secret in Havana that domestic rice production was in serious trouble, nor could the Chinese have been unaware of the other factors that went into the making of Cuba's rice problem. Fidel's personal intervention into what had always been a routine commercial negotiation was in itself

16. Ibid., p. 218.   17. Ibid., p. 69.

18. By 1956, cultivation and harvesting of ninety percent of the area planted to rice in Cuba was done mechanically, using tractors and combines. Airplanes seeded and fumigated the fields. Some eighty percent of the area was irrigated. Select varieties of seeds had doubled rice yields per acre between 1940 and 1956. See Marrero, *Geografía de Cuba*, p. 191.

sufficient evidence that Cuba was facing a crisis in the supply of rice. What prompted the Chinese to accept Fidel's deal? From what transpired a year later, it is clear that their motive was purely political.

Almost from the beginning of their relations with the Castro regime in 1960, the Chinese had attempted to utilize Cuba in their cold war against the Russians. This objective was reinforced when the Cuban Revolution began to exert considerable influence in the Third World, and more particularly in Latin America, where Castro was competing with the Russians for leadership of Communist and other leftist movements. The recurring friction between Havana and Moscow—as, for example, following the October 1962 missile crisis—had provided opportunities for strengthening Sino-Cuban friendship, but without lasting advantage for Peking. Thus, as has been noted, in his second visit to Moscow, in January 1964, Castro had in effect endorsed the Soviet position in their quarrel with the Chinese. Despite Castro's increasingly cool relations with most of Latin America's Soviet-oriented Communist parties, he completely ignored the Chinese-sponsored splinter parties that had sprung up in several countries. Furthermore, none of these parties had been invited to attend the conference of Latin American Communist parties that took place in Havana in November 1964. This much the Chinese must have known at the time of Castro's visit to their embassy. The latter took place, according to Castro, "late in the year," but in any event after the initial Cuban-Chinese trade negotiations in October. The Chinese could draw their own inferences, even if they did not know the results of the conference.[19]

For the Chinese, Castro's visit to the embassy must have raised the question of whether his proposition was also a signal that he was prepared to shift Cuban policy closer to their position in their dispute with the Russians, or whether he was naive concerning the proposition's political implications. In either case, the Chinese recognized that the proposition provided them with unexpected leverage, and accordingly they accepted it.

As it turned out, Fidel was extraordinarily naive. To begin with, he

19. In connection with its support for the Soviet-backed line on "Communist unity," the final communiqué of the 1964 Havana Conference of Latin American Communist Parties by clear implication condemned the pro-Chinese parties by stipulating that "all factional activity—whatever its nature and origin—must be categorically repudiated." The text of the communiqué is in William E. Ratliff, *Castroism and Communism in Latin America, 1959–1976* (Stanford, Calif.: Hoover Institution Press, 1976), pp. 198 ff.

immediately set about converting the bulk, including the best, of the rice acreage to sugarcane cultivation. I was in Havana at the time and remember how this came as a shock to some of his technical advisers. Although no one dared openly question the wisdom of the arrangement with the Chinese, privately it was pointed out to Fidel that cane yields in the top-grade rice fields would be uneconomic and that at least these should be spared, but to no avail. Fidel, in fact, was driven by another irrational goal, his promise to produce ten million tons of sugar in 1970. Hence, for him, extending sugarcane acreage was a first priority. The result was that production of rice dropped from 123,000 tons in the previous year to 50,000 tons in 1965.[20] Compared with the banner year of 1960, this was a drop of close to ninety percent. Fidel had indeed assumed that he could rely on the Chinese to supply Cuba's rice needs for an indefinite period. To put it mildly, he had placed himself in a vulnerable position.

The Propaganda War in Havana

At the same time, Fidel became increasingly irritated with the Chinese on another score, and not without reason. Their aggressive propaganda campaign against the Russians in Cuba, perhaps in part stimulated by their belief that they had purchased immunity with their massive shipments of rice, became a source of serious embarrassment for Fidel. He had proposed that both Russians and Chinese refrain from conducting their cold war in Cuba. The Russians complied but the Chinese refused. It became not only a matter of "protecting" the Russians but of asserting Cuban "sovereignty." In his warning speech on March 13, 1965, Fidel did not mention the Chinese by name, perhaps to limit the risk of rice reprisals. However, the Chinese could not fail to recognize that they were the main target when he denounced the distribution of foreign propaganda in Cuba and qualified the Sino-Soviet quarrel as "Byzantine and academic."[21]

Earlier that month, no doubt under considerable pressure, Cuba had participated in the Moscow meeting of nineteen Communist parties, a meeting bitterly denounced by the Chinese. The latter, as previously noted, publicly reproached Cuba but in relatively mild terms. Aware of underlying friction in Cuban-Soviet relations, the Chinese were apparently

20. Roberts and Hamour, *Cuba 1968*, p 136.
21. The Chinese press ignored the speech, while large sections of it were reproduced in *Pravda*. See Jacques Lévesque, *L'URSS et la Révolution Cubaine* (Montreal: Presses de l'Université de Montréal, 1976), p. 130.

not ready to write Fidel off. The flow of rice to Cuba continued on schedule, but there was a significant decline of news about Cuba in the Chinese
press.[22]

Meanwhile, the Chinese paid no attention to the warning in Fidel's
speech on March 13. In Fidel's words, "the Chinese government increased
. . . the massive distribution of propaganda materials in our country" to
the headquarters of the main units of the armed forces, and "in many cases
directly to officers . . . at their home address," as well as "to civilian functionaries, although to a lesser degree." As a result, "President . . . Dorticós
and I, in my capacity as Prime Minister of the government, summoned the
chargé d'affaires of the People's Republic of China [in the absence of the
ambassador] to a meeting on September 14, 1965, at 10 A.M. . . . In the
most energetic terms, we expressed our indignation . . . and our demand
that such activities cease," pointing out "with the utmost clarity that these
methods and procedures were exactly the same as those used by the Embassy of the United States, . . . that our country had freed itself from that
imperialism 90 miles from our shores and was not disposed to permit another powerful state 20,000 kilometers away to impose similar practices on
us, . . . [and] that, whatever the cost, our government was not disposed to
tolerate such acts."[23]

These may well have been the words that Fidel used on the occasion,
since by this time he must have fully realized what the Chinese were up to.
They were, in fact, applying additional, and more blatant, pressure against
him in other parts of the world. As a result, before ending his meeting with
the chargé d'affaires, he denounced what he termed "the campaign of cal-
umny conducted in various parts of the world against the Cuban Revolution by elements closely linked with the Chinese government, which from
our point of view gave added importance to the contempt shown by the
Chinese in connection with the massive distribution of . . . political propaganda." The "elements" he later identified as "satellite" parties in Belgium and Ceylon.[24]

Despite Fidel's indignant protest and warning, the flow of Chinese
propaganda continued unabated. From September 14, the day of his visit
to the embassy, until the end of the year, "58,041" pieces of propaganda

22. Ernst Halperin, "Peking and the Latin American Communists," *China
Quarterly*, 29 (January–March 1967), 148.

23. *Política Internacional*, 13 (first trimester, 1966), 224–225.

24. Ibid., pp. 225 and 229.

reached Cuba from China, and "tens of thousands of other . . . materials of a political character, printed or accumulated by the Chinese representatives in Cuba, were distributed." What rankled Fidel in addition to the Chinese "insolence . . . and absolute contempt for our country" was the fact that, although the chargé d'affaires promised to transmit his complaint to Peking, "the Chinese government offered no explanation of any sort," just as if Fidel had not raised the issue at all. [25]

The Sugar-Rice Agreement Terminated

The "explanation" came three months later. In mid-December, the Cuban delegation that had gone to Peking to negotiate the following year's annual trade protocol reported back to Havana that the Chinese had decided to terminate the sugar-rice agreement as of the end of 1965, i.e., at once. Contrary to Fidel's understanding, the Chinese considered it to have been a one-year deal. Accordingly, they would reduce rice exports in 1966 from 250,000 to 135,000 metric tons, the amount shipped in 1964, and they would also reduce sugar imports to a comparable level. As Fidel put it, this information came "as a complete surprise at the end of 1965, . . . without the slightest previous indication of the Chinese government's new commercial policy toward Cuba." [26] At the same time, the Chinese stipulated that the value of trade between the two countries should be balanced, which would result in a reduction of Chinese exports by forty million pesos and would seriously affect textiles and other consumer goods in short supply that had previously been financed by Chinese credits.

The Chinese explained the reasons on which they based their decisions, but these need not detain us here because they were obviously designed to obscure the real reason. This was made crystal clear by a suggestion added to their list of particulars, namely that if the Cubans considered that they needed more rice, they were free to negotiate "at a higher level, as was done in the past." [27] This was obviously an invitation for Fidel to discuss a trade-off of political concessions for rice with a top figure in the Chinese government.

It would take us too far afield to speculate whether, in late December 1965, the Chinese expected Fidel to be desperate enough to yield to their pressure, or whether they merely wished to add insult to injury. One thing, however, was certain. Their tactics had been singularly heavy-handed, having been predicated on a gross miscalculation concerning the degree to

25. Ibid., p. 226.   26. Ibid., p. 215.   27. Ibid., p. 219.

which Fidel commanded the loyalty of his military and bureaucratic establishments. The Chinese also revealed a surprising ignorance of Fidel's character—unlike the Russians, who, even when severely provoked by their obstreperous client, were always careful not to ruffle his feathers. Finally, the Chinese had undoubtedly concluded that their investment in Cuba had not paid off, and, considering the high price of rice on the world market, that it would not be rational to throw good money after bad. It was probably sound realpolitik but poorly handled. In the last analysis, Fidel had made a convincing case that the mighty People's Republic of China, self-proclaimed standard-bearer of true revolutionary Marxism, had tried to blackmail the revolutionary Marxist government of a small country, hard pressed by the world's most powerful imperialism, and having failed in its blackmail attempt, inflicted drastic punishment on the recalcitrant victim.

On March 13, 1966, at the ninth annual commemoration of the student attack on the presidential palace in Havana, Fidel devoted a major portion of his address to a final settling of accounts with China. One would have to go back to Stalin's excommunication of Tito for a comparable outpouring in the Communist world of political and personal venom.[28] "We must unmask the fascist element which hides under the banner of Marxism," Fidel exclaimed. Along with a liberal sprinkling of epithets such as "imperialist" and "fascist" and copious references to the propaganda of Chinese "satellite" parties as "in the Goebbels style," Fidel directed the brunt of his attack against Mao Tse-tung himself. Without naming him, Mao's identity was unmistakable when Fidel derided the "method and system of absolute monarchies in socialism" and of "turning a man into a god to the point that not even the names of Marx, Engels, and Lenin are mentioned anymore." Particularly brutal was Fidel's insinuation that Mao was senile, "biologically old," as he put it. The Cuban Revolution, he declared, "is fortunately a revolution of young men . . . and we hope that it will always be a revolution of young men, . . . that as we grow biologically old we shall be capable of understanding that we have grown biologically old."[29]

28. See "Cominform resolution on 'the Yugoslav Communist Party in the power of murderers and spies,'" in Stephen Clissold, ed., *Yugoslavia and the Soviet Union: A Documentary Survey, 1939–1973* (London: Oxford University Press, 1975), pp. 225 ff.

29. *Política Internacional*, 13 (first trimester, 1966), 230–231. In 1966, Mao was seventy-three years old and completely lucid.

Fidel's Motivation

In this memorable polemic against the Chinese, beginning with the display of extreme indignation in his February statement and building up to hysterical proportions in his March speech, Fidel's motivation was not as simple as it appeared on the surface. The fact that the Russians would be pleased could have entered into his calculations, for it provided him with political credit at a time when his relations with Moscow were beginning to deteriorate. More important was Fidel's need to distract the attention of the Cuban people from his own political naivete (which he could not completely conceal) and its disastrous economic and social consequences (rice rations were not restored to the 1962 level for a decade). These factors were compounded by his erratic—and never mentioned—decision practically to eliminate the production of rice in Cuba. Thus, Fidel felt compelled to convince the Cuban people that China was sole culprit for new hardships they were forced to endure. The length and intensity of his diatribe were designed to make China a credible scapegoat. In addition, something of Fidel's unseemly wrath can be attributed to his injured self-esteem. The fact that the Chinese had not only tricked him but treated him with contempt was a grievous affront to his colossal ego. Finally, viewed in a broad perspective, the entire episode provided a dramatic example of the contrast, in both Cuba and China, between the theory and practice of Marxist-Leninist virtue.

One might have expected a break in trade and diplomatic relations between the two countries, but neither found it expedient to take the final step. However, intercourse was reduced to a minimum. Meanwhile, both sides were distracted by more pressing problems: Fidel by his growing dispute with the Kremlin, and Mao Tse-tung by the inauguration of his so-called cultural revolution, which the Cuban press initially greeted with ridicule and contempt.[30] Ironically, Fidel later discovered "positive elements" in the Chinese upheaval, as I learned from one of his ministers, who attributed Maoist influence to Fidel's own brief "proletarian offensive" early in 1968. In any event, following his philippic in March 1966, Fidel refrained from any public mention of China, and for a number of years China was rarely mentioned in the Cuban media.

30. *Granma*, August 31, 1966.

The Revival of Tension

China unexpectedly received prominence in the news early in 1972, on the occasion of President Nixon's first visit to Peking.[31] By this time, Cuba's integration as a full and loyal member of the Soviet commonwealth had taken place, and the disparaging treatment of the Chinese reception of Nixon largely reflected Cuba's revised orientation to the Sino-Soviet conflict. Then, in June 1975, at a conference in Havana of Latin American and Caribbean Communist parties, Cuba for the first time unequivocally placed itself on record by ratifying the joint statement supporting the Soviet position on China.[32]

Violent hostility toward China, recalling the bitterness of 1966, flared up again in July 1976, in the wake of the Cuban-Soviet intervention in the Angolan civil war. Enraged by a Chinese news commentary which, among other things, referred to Cuban troops in Angola as "mercenaries," a prominently featured editorial in *Granma* denounced "this barrage of slander, insults, and lies" as "aimed at . . . promoting anti-Sovietism and thus anti-socialism" and "justifying and encouraging the anti-Angolan, anti-African, and anti-Cuban policy of the Yankee imperialists. . . ."[33] It seemed that the bad old days were back again. This was the beginning of a new and prolonged period of intense, blatant hostility, this time mainly a reflection of Sino-Soviet animosity and Cuba's role as a militant partner of the Soviet Union on all international issues.

31. *Granma Weekly Review*, February 27 and March 5, 1972.

32. For a complete text of the statement, see Ratliff, *Castroism and Communism*, Appendix D, pp. 217 ff.

33. *Granma Weekly Review*, July 18, 1976. By the end of the decade, the Chinese government had become "the fascist Peking regime." See for example, an article entitled "Peking's Machinations," in *Granma Weekly Review*, November 25, 1979.

25

■

Concerning Revisionism, Yugoslavia, and Power

Cuba at a Soviet Party Congress

THE MONTH OF MARCH 1966, in the "Year of Solidarity," marked not only Fidel's settling of accounts with China but also a new step in his own campaign against Soviet "revisionism," although he did not use the term or mention the name of the country. The occasion was the twenty-third congress of the Soviet Communist Party. On March 31, Armando Hart, one of Fidel's most intimate collaborators from the earliest days of the struggle against Batista, addressed the assembly in Moscow in the name of the Communist Party of Cuba. The formula for attacking the Russians contained a certain element of prudence, given Cuba's complete dependence on the Kremlin for survival. Nonetheless, it also contained an element of risk, since there was always the uncertainty of how much of a challenge the Kremlin was prepared to overlook.

Hart began his address[1] with brief but fulsome praise for the achievements of the Soviet Union under the leadership of its Communist Party, but then he went on to scold the Soviet and satellite delegates for falling into an ideological rut. "Ideas, tactics, and methods . . . of twenty years ago are obsolete," he declared. The proof was the Havana tricontinental conference, "the most representative international assembly" ever held,

1. "Saludo del CC del PCC al XXIII Congreso del PCUS" [Greeting of the Central Committee of the Communist Party of Cuba to the 23rd Congress of the Communist Party of the Soviet Union], *Política Internacional de la Revolución Cubana* (Havana: Editora Política, 1966), Vol. 1, pp. 279–291. Citations, in the order used, are from pp. 280–282 and 286.

and which "created the broadest and most militant unity thus far achieved. . . . Our Communist parties must analyze the experience of the Conference as an indication of what is occurring in the world."

The Cuban party had already done so, and Hart went on to enlighten the comrades. The lesson boiled down to two propositions. First, there was the primacy of "armed insurrection" for the "peoples struggling for their liberation" and the "duty" of the socialist governments to lend full support to their struggles. Second, the most urgent task of the moment was to "provide decisive aid for the patriotic struggle" of the people of South Vietnam and the "heroic resistance" of the Democratic Republic of Vietnam. Citing the words spoken by Fidel a year earlier, Hart repeated the message destined to fall once again on deaf ears: "We maintain that aid should consist of arms and men! We maintain that whatever risks are necessary should be taken for Vietnam."

For most of those present it must have appeared as the height of impudence for this upstart convert to Marxism-Leninism to face the five thousand veteran Communist delegates assembled in the Kremlin and instruct them on revolutionary theory and practice. At the same time, there could be no doubt that the main target of the speaker was the host party and its following in Latin America. Hence, there was no applause, not even from the Vietnamese, whose own remarks at the congress were sober and discreet.[2] Nor was there any disposition among the delegates to disrupt the congress by directly confronting the Cuban provocation. However, Victorio Codavilla, veteran Argentine Communist leader, without naming the Cubans, made it clear that he had them in mind when he scornfully rejected the "anti-Leninist views of certain petty bourgeois ideologists. . . ."[3] Brezhnev also replied indirectly to the Cuban attack when, in his concluding remarks, he expressed the conviction that "our class brothers around the world realize that the main help to their revolutionary struggle and our main contribution to it lies in the successful construction of Communism in our own country."[4]

The Polemic with Yugoslavia

A few weeks later, *Granma* sharply stepped up the campaign against Soviet "revisionism," again without referring specifically to the USSR or even using the term "revisionism," which was associated with the Chinese cri-

2. See Adam B. Ulam, *Expansion and Coexistence: The History of Soviet Foreign Policy, 1917–1967* (New York: Praeger, 1968), pp. 727 ff.

3. Ibid., p. 727.   4. Ibid., p. 729.

tique of the Russian distortion of Marxism-Leninism. The occasion was
the revival of a polemic with Yugoslavia, which began shortly after the end
of the tricontinental meeting. A Yugoslav delegation had been excluded
from the conference by Castro, who claimed that this was at the request of
the Vietnamese—whose views, moreover, he fully shared. Yugoslavia, a
prime mover of the broadly based self-styled "nonaligned movement," and
hence Cuba's rival for Third World leadership, was understandably irked.
In retaliation, the Belgrade daily *Borba* ran an editorial on January 24
claiming that several resolutions adopted in Havana were in fact not supported by a number of Latin American Communist parties and were counterproductive in the effort to create a united front of progressive forces.
This was an assessment obviously shared by the Kremlin and the Latin
American Communist parties in its orbit, as the Cubans well knew. The
reply came on February 13 in a scorching *Granma* editorial addressed
to the "so-called League of Yugoslav Communists," which it accused of
slander, intrigue, malice, and consorting with the "puppets of the imperialists" in Latin America.

Yugoslavia as a Surrogate Target

However, it was not until May that the issue took on major proportions.
An article in the authoritative Belgrade *Politika* by the newspaper's Latin
American correspondent, which was reproduced in the Mexico City *El
Día*,[5] touched off a 9,000-word response published by *Granma* in four installments (May 5, 6, 7, and 8). What was new in the *Politika* article was
the explicit charge that the main Cuban "line" at the tricontinental meeting was at odds with the Soviet position and that, further, on the basic issues dividing the socialist world, Cuba favored the Chinese position, despite the Sino-Cuban quarrel over the rice-and-sugar deal. In their attack
on Yugoslavia, according to the writer, the Cubans "repeated . . . the
anti-Yugoslav arguments and terminology used by the Chinese." This was
more than a hint that, as the Chinese had done in the early stages of their
quarrel with the Russians, the Cubans were using Yugoslavia as a surrogate
for the Soviet Union.

Why the Yugoslavs chose to reopen the polemic, nearly three months
after the *Granma* editorial of February, was hard to discern. In any event,
the *Politika* article could not have been considered objectionable by the
Kremlin, which from the beginning maintained a discreet silence on the

5. The article was carried by *Granma* on May 3, 1966.

dispute. By coincidence, later in the same month of May, the communiqué issued at a meeting of the Soviet and Yugoslav foreign ministers in Moscow declared that the "review of international questions reaffirmed the closeness or identity of the two countries' views on the chief problems of the present international situation."[6]

The Road to Betrayal

The four-part *Granma* reply[7] to *Politika*, along with the customary bombast and vituperation, was essentially a restatement of the Cuban revolutionary *weltanschauung* at the time, including: the "transcendental" significance of the tricontinental conference; the importance of the Cuban "ideological contribution to the theory and practice of revolution in Latin America"; the duty to "take all the necessary risks" in Vietnam; and the Cuban dedication to "moving forward the revolution in the whole world," even though it was "ninety miles from the [U.S.] empire, threatened by the strongest capitalist country in the world, in the midst of an economic blockade," and so on. The conclusion reached was categorical: "The position of the Yugoslav leaders marks the road toward betrayal. Our position points out the road toward revolution."

The Cubans could properly claim that the blame for provoking the polemic lay with the Yugoslavs. Nevertheless, the great length and burning rhetoric of the Cuban reply gave the impression that the Cubans welcomed the opportunity of doing precisely what their opponents accused them of doing: directing their wrath primarily against the Soviet Union in the guise of an attack on Yugoslavia.

Meanwhile, relations between Cuba and Yugoslavia, which had already cooled off since the early days of the Revolution, were not percepti-

6. Stephen Clissold, ed., *Soviet Relations with Latin America, 1918–1968: A Documentary Survey* (London: Oxford University Press, 1970), p. 293. At the time, Yugoslavia maintained diplomatic and commercial relations with most Latin American countries, while the Soviet Union was actively pursuing a course of normalizing relations in the region—to the great chagrin of Castro. The Soviet press discreetly avoided any mention of the Cuban-Yugoslav polemic. During the entire period of troubled relations between Castro and the Kremlin, the Soviet public response to his provocations was to ignore them and to drastically cut down press coverage on all Cuban news. See Jacques Lévesque, *L'URSS et la Révolution Cubaine* (Montreal: Presses de l'Université de Montréal, 1976), p. 145.

7. This was reproduced, along with the February 13 editorial, in *Política Internacional de la Revolución Cubana*, Vol. 1, pp. 121–166. Citations, in the order used, are from pp. 159, 139, 155, 157, and 166.

bly affected by the controversy. Since, ostensibly, Castro did not personally take part in it, and since there was no direct reference to Tito, it was easier for tempers to subside than in the case of the Sino-Cuban dispute. After 1970, when Fidel finally renounced his ultraleftist heresies, traffic between the two countries increased noticeably. This was highlighted in late February 1974 by the highly publicized (in both countries) visit to Belgrade of Raúl Castro, Fidel's brother and number two in the party and government hierarchy, and now sporting the rank of General of the Army.[8] It was the first visit to Yugoslavia by a top Cuban leader since Ché Guevara's visit in the summer of 1959.

The May Day Speech

Presumably the Russians had no difficulty in decoding *Granma's* "Yugoslav" message of early May. Almost simultaneously they received another message from Havana which required only translation from the Spanish. It was Fidel's speech on May Day, and was manifestly a warning that their erratic client was rapidly moving in the direction of total economic irrationality—for which they would be required to foot the bill. The essence of the message was that Cuba was dedicated to building socialism and communism simultaneously. As Fidel put it: "To say that up to this point we are constructing socialism, and at that point we are constructing communism, can be . . . a great mistake. . . . Among other reasons, in the zeal of achieving socialist goals, we should not give up, or obstruct, the development of communist man."[9] Concerning this matter, he further explained, there had been a certain amount of ideological "stagnation" among Marxist-Leninists, a "rather universal" acceptance of "formulas . . . which depart from the essence of Marxism-Leninism" because the "laws and methods [of socialist and communist construction] in no manner can be the same methods applied in a capitalist society."[10]

The Capitalist Road Rejected

Fidel was referring to the fact that for several years a number of East European countries had been moving toward greater economic decentralization and flexibility, involving profit incentives and increased autonomy for in-

8. Lester A. Sobel, ed., *Castro's Cuba in the 1970s* (New York: Facts on File, 1978), p. 102. Raúl Castro spent a week touring the country.

9. *Política Internacional*, 14 (second trimester, 1966), 200.

10. Ibid., p. 199.

dustrial enterprises, as well as some adaptation of central planning to market factors. Economic and administrative reforms along these lines were first put into effect in East Germany, in 1963. The following year, similar changes, some more modest than others, were announced in Bulgaria, Czechoslovakia, and Hungary. The USSR followed suit in 1965. Hungary instituted more far-reaching reforms in 1968. These were the "capitalist methods" which Cuba rejected. "With the natural resources of this country," Fidel went on to say, "with work and a little technology," we should be able to provide satisfactory levels of all the essential needs of a human being, "health, food, physical and mental education, cultural development, and housing" for the entire population by using the resources and distributing the goods produced by "the whole of society." [11]

What he apparently envisaged was, first, coexistence between the socialist formula, "to each according to his work," that is, inequality of access to a limited range of nonessential goods, and the communist formula, "to each according to his needs," that is, equal access to a broad range of essential goods. Second, the coexistence stage would be a period of fairly rapid transition during which the socialist formula would be phased out entirely. Obviously, so would material work incentives.

The Principle of Internationalism

Fidel then went on to make an even more radical departure from "stagnant" Marxist-Leninist theory. To aim for the "highest levels of communism" while millions in other countries are desperately poor would be immoral. Hence, he declared, "in the future we shall not be able to think of . . . great wealth while there are other peoples that need our help. . . . We must not consider it a duty to provide each one of us with an automobile [a pointed reference to the Soviet Union] before every family in countries far behind us has at least a plough. . . . We must educate our people to have a deep feeling of internationalism, . . . without which nobody can call himself a Marxist-Leninist and without which this First of May, International Labor Day, would have no meaning." [12] Internationalism, to be sure, had additional but unvoiced meanings in Fidel's lexicon: converting the scarcity of consumer goods in Cuba from a harsh consequence of the Revolution to a noble virtue; striving for Third World leadership to create political leverage against both the U.S.A. and the USSR; and gratifying the Maximum Leader's inflated ego.

11. Ibid., pp. 202 and 203.   12. Ibid., p. 202.

The Source of Error

This was the first of three major pronouncements that would bring Castro fully into Ché Guevara's ideological camp and close the debate which Ché lost in 1964. The second pronouncement took place on August 29, 1966, when Fidel addressed a national congress of the Cuban Revolutionary Confederation of Labor (CTC-R).[13] "Revolution is the abolition of the exploitation of human labor," he declared at one point. At the same time, to "free the worker from his [capitalist] exploiters," he added, "does not mean to free the worker from labor." He was referring to the lack of labor discipline and incentive to produce that still plagued the Cuban Revolution. As Fidel saw it, in a true socialist society there was only one solution to this problem. "The methods [successfully] used by the capitalists to make the workers produce," he explained, "could only be replaced by a socialist consciousness. . . . We still do not have a fully socialist consciousness." This was already a theme made familiar by Ché Guevara, and would be further amplified during the next three years. What came as something of a shock was Fidel's explanation for this deplorable lag. Without his mentioning the Soviet Union, it was at once transparent that he identified the root of the evil in the Soviet system that was erroneously adopted by the Cuban Revolution, entrenched in the Cuban bureaucracy, and propagated by the "clichés" and "pontifical infallibility" in the "manuals" [Soviet textbooks] imposed on the students at the university. "It may well happen," he continued, "that a country believes it is building communism and is really building capitalism. . . . Since nobody has yet reached [the communist goal], we have the right to do so with our own methods."

The Abuse of Power Denied

A notable aspect of this speech was Fidel's fascinating digression concerning the decision-making process of his regime and his own role in the process. It was apparent that he detected something less than enthusiasm for the "new order" he was proposing—not among most of the workers who faced him, who would have little understanding of the economic and philosophical complexities of the issue, and from whom his charismatic appeal, as always, could easily extract a vote of confidence, but among the considerable number of middle- and upper-ranking functionaries and aca-

13. All citations from the speech are from the version published in *Granma*, August 30, 1966.

demic experts who had opposed Ché Guevara's views in the 1964 debate. These people had remained hopeful that the Soviet system, imperfect as it was, would eventually take hold and reduce the anarchy and modify the utopian outlook which still afflicted the Cuban economy. Particularly suspect of a pro-Soviet bias would be some of the "old" Communists who had weathered the purge at the time of the Escalante affair in 1962. (At a critical moment early in 1968, as we shall see, a score of them would be sentenced to long prison terms.) The need to soothe some of the more sober cadres, it would seem, is what led Fidel to give assurances that he would not impose his will on anybody and that nobody would be penalized for disagreeing with him.

In fact, at one point he proposed that at the first congress of the Communist Party, "which must take place next year at the latest" (it was actually held nine years later!), there would be full debate "on whether to have moral or material incentives. . . . Everyone will speak his mind and the Congress will decide." On all these problems, he said, "I have my ideas, but I've never wanted to use the influence of my office, or the esteem of the people for the words I utter, in order to impose my view. . . ." After this astonishing statement, he went on to chide the skeptics. "It would be the greatest injustice," he added, "to claim that the revolutionary leadership [euphemism for "I"] practices any kind of exclusion, intolerance, discrimination. . . . Some make this imputation in order to defend their lack of capacity, to defend their incompetence."

It is doubtful whether this statement added to the comfort of the many people who were concerned about the specific incidents which prompted Fidel to make the statement in the first place. The statement was, in fact, Fidel's hollow explanation for (1) the sacking, two months earlier, of Pelegrín Torras, first vice-minister of foreign affairs and an "old" Communist, as well as (2) the "election" at the very congress he was addressing of a new secretary-general of the CTC-R to replace an "old" Communist stalwart, Lázaro Peña. Both men, incidentally, were returned to their respective posts after Fidel's reconciliation with the Kremlin; and Peña, following his death from cancer in 1975, was elevated to the ranks of the immortal heroes of the Revolution.

It was one of those occasions when Fidel would sense the need to explain that he never sought personal power, that it was thrust upon him by history, that he himself was incapable of abusing power, that personal power as a rule was dangerous, that he looked forward to the day when he could divest himself of power, and so on. "We have always been and shall remain enemies of any abuse of power," he declared. Whether this was pure self-deception or an elaborate charade was difficult to determine. "It does not mean," he continued, "that we can prevent an isolated abuse or error here and there; but within our revolutionary consciousness we have never deliberately tolerated anything that might be considered an abuse of power. . . . Hopefully our country . . . will never have to endure any abuse of power. . . . In the future . . . no man will have the authority which we [I] who have initiated this Revolution have had, because it is dangerous for men to have so much authority."

An Exercise in Demagogy

For sophisticated Cubans, this must have been a startling, if not grotesque, performance by one who came closer to wielding absolute power than any other living head of government in any civilized nation on earth. For other Cubans, to whom Fidel was always able to project the image of complete candor and sincerity, the speech had a different meaning. Yes, he was saying, there had been some abuse of power, but by "others," and he had always tried to prevent it, with the help of the people. "From my revolutionary experience," he declared, "I have never been better informed than when I speak with the people, when I meet with workers, students, and country folk." And here, precisely, was the greatest source of protection for the people, he went on to explain. It came from the intimate ties which he had established with them. Thus, the "conscience, . . . the solid judgment of the people will be the impassable barrier for the ambitious, the opportunists, the fakers, the abusers of power." It was unadulterated demagogy, and it was effective.

26

■

Concerning Money, Ice Cream, and Dogma

An Evil Obsession

CASTRO'S THIRD MAJOR PRONOUNCEMENT on Cuba's new road to socialism and communism came a month later. Addressing a mass meeting in Havana's Plaza de la Revolución on September 28, 1966, he heaped scorn on the "pure" economists, the "metaphysicians" of revolution who would judge every measure designed to benefit the people by the amount of money it would cost. "These individuals are obsessed with the idea of money . . . and we want our people to remove the idea of money from their minds and hearts," he exclaimed. If we had operated on the basis of their principles, counting the pennies before giving the people free education and free health services, he continued, "we could never have aroused the enthusiasm of the masses. . . ." Fidel neglected to mention that his uninhibited spending on education and health was made possible only because the Cuban economy was heavily subsidized by the Soviet Union. And as for socialism and communism, he continued, they can never be created with the "mentality of a shopkeeper."[1]

However, it turned out that there were also practical reasons to abolish the fixation on money in a revolutionary society. By way of illustration, Fidel cited a projected amendment to the 1959 Urban Reform Law, which had nationalized all urban real estate and set the rental fee for tenants at a very modest ten percent of wages earned. The amendment, planned to go

1. *Política Internacional*, 15 (third trimester, 1966), 178 and 179.

into effect in 1970, would abolish rents for practically the entire urban population, that is, some three-fifths of all Cuban families. As Fidel went on to explain, eliminating rent would not only fulfill the social objectives of the revolution. "It would mean," he said, "the dismantling of a whole government agency" and the release for productive labor of a "considerable number of office employees" engaged in collecting rent and keeping records. As for the "financial aspects of this type of revolutionary law," he added, as if to further confound the "metaphysicians," he was confident that "the approximately seventy or eighty million pesos of lost government revenue [in 1970 and thereafter] will mean practically nothing . . . [compared] with the many times greater income which the [successful] development of our economy will provide."[2]

Predictably, nothing, including Fidel's free-rent fantasy, worked out as he expected. One of the reasons was that most Cubans were not philosophers and responded poorly to "moral" incentives and the "laws" of the simultaneous construction of socialism and communism. Money had already lost a good deal of its capitalist glamour, not for ideological reasons but because there were so few goods to spend it on. Thus, an announcement that admission to athletic events would henceforth be free created much less satisfaction than the inauguration of the giant *Coppelia* ice cream emporium, where customers lined up day and night eager to pay money for its new and delectable concoctions.

The Function of Ice Cream

As a showpiece of "people's luxury," *Coppelia* could be compared with the palatial subway stations which Stalin built in Moscow. Covering a fair-sized plaza opposite the Habana Libre hotel and seating four hundred customers at a time, it was opened to the public in June 1966. It was, and most likely remains, the largest and most elaborate dispenser of ice cream in the world. Built of wood, glass, and concrete in a style recalling the conical structure of a pre-Columbian Indian dwelling, the construction, equipment, furnishings, waitress uniforms, and other incidentals easily involved an investment of several million pesos. This extravagance was matched by the richness of the ice cream (eighteen percent butter fat, with two or three dozen natural fruit flavors), at a time when milk and milk products were in very short supply in Cuba. Hailed as a demonstration of the superiority of Cuban socialism over Yankee imperialism, the *Coppelia* was glorified in the

2. Ibid., p. 177.

press as surpassing "Howard Johnson" in the quality of its product (this was true) and the quantity of its flavors (this was debatable). As with the regal decor of the Moscow subway stations, the ice cream emporium combined economic irrationality with political astuteness. In hard times, a banana split topped with crushed strawberries, pineapple, and whipped cream, and served in elegant surroundings, could soothe feelings and pacify tempers.

About this same time, coin-operated public telephones were declared to be a free service. However, there was some skepticism about the government's ideological motives. The coin mechanism in most telephones had already broken down and ceased to function. Then came the law abolishing payment for funerals, another step in the transition from socialism to communism, but the prospect of being buried free of charge was a communist benefit which everybody hoped to postpone as long as possible.

Meanwhile, Cubans were constantly exhorted to work harder and for longer hours for intangible rewards. In industry and on the docks, for example, overtime pay was declared to be morally incompatible with communism, and hence was abolished. The result was a sharp decline in productivity and an increase in absenteeism. On the state farms, the notoriously relaxed pace of work remained unchanged, while small private farmers diverted as much of their produce as they could from government collection depots to home consumption and the black market. Urgent appeals for "voluntary" agricultural labor brought out great hordes of students and office employees; but with little aptitude for their tasks and even less dedication, the value of their labor often did not exceed the costs of transporting and feeding them. Eventually, several thousand soldiers were put to work in the fields under military discipline.

On another level, the administration of the economy became less and less efficient. With capital and operating expenditures of most enterprises directly allocated from an all-embracing national budget, and with profits and losses pooled in a single national accounting system, the absence of financial autonomy reduced managerial incentives for efficiency. At the same time, decision-making on even minor administrative details throughout the island was centralized in Havana. Adding to the normal difficulties inherent in over-centralization was the lack of an adequate system of statistics and communications. As a result, gross errors in the allocation and utilization of resources and in the calculation of anticipated production became commonplace. Under these circumstances, integrated planning of the economy was practically abandoned, to be replaced by a series of crash programs, primarily in agriculture, and first and foremost in sugar.

An Ominous Note

To return to Fidel's speech of September 28, it essentially reiterated, amplified, and exalted basic themes which he had stressed earlier and which were principally aimed at one goal: to mobilize the population, or as he put it this time, to instill "a warlike attitude"[3] toward the glorious and unprecedented tasks on which the revolution had embarked. There was, however, an ominous note that was lacking in his previous speeches. Again castigating the "servile" and "domesticated" doubters "in our midst," this time he warned that those "who do not want to make our kind of Revolution will suffer the fate of pseudorevolutionaries, or counterrevolutionaries, . . . because their criticism of the Revolution is the same which the counterrevolutionaries make, because they use the same arguments against the Revolution which the counterrevolutionaries use."[4] While Fidel rarely tolerated any kind of dissent from his own views, never before had he equated dissent by those loyal to his regime with counterrevolution.

What prompted him to do so can only be surmised. Only a month earlier, at the CTC-R congress, he had vehemently denied any intention to impose his views on anybody. Had more cadres taken him at his word than he anticipated? Had it come to his attention that the many hundreds of Russian and other East European technical experts scattered through the ministries and university faculties were making common cause with their more sober Cuban colleagues? Whatever it was, to all intents and purposes Fidel had formally proclaimed the beginning of a new era. Whereas he had hitherto generally applied the principle that "within the Revolution" those who were not against him were with him, from now on the principle would be that those who were not with him were against him. Thus, in the process of liberating the Cuban revolution from the shackles of Soviet dogma, Fidel imposed a new dogma, equally infallible, from which deviation was tantamount to treason.

A couple of months after the speech, Castro told a foreign interviewer that there were twenty thousand political prisoners in Cuba. In early July 1964, as previously noted, he had put the figure at fifteen thousand in his discussion with Richard Eder of the *New York Times*. If Castro is to be believed (it is unlikely that he would exaggerate on either occasion), his later figure could well have been an indicator not so much that disaffection had increased so dramatically as that tolerance for it had notably diminished.[5]

3. Ibid., p. 186.   4. Ibid., p. 188.
5. The 20,000 figure was cited in *Playboy*, January 1967, p. 74. In late 1978, Castro announced that he was prepared to release three thousand political pris-

In any event, what could easily be observed in Havana was that in the various bureaucracies which administered the economic, social, and cultural activities of the country, audible dissent vanished while opportunism flourished. Ambitious *Fidelista* firebrands rapidly moved up the ranks. Competence was downgraded. It was largely a subtle process of repression and forced conformity that outsiders could not detect. But it was a deadly process nonetheless. There was no way to rectify Fidel's colossal blunders, which in a short time would bring the Cuban economy to the brink of disaster—and paradoxically would lead to the resurrection of old dogma.

---

oners, among whom were six hundred who had tried to leave the island illegally, if the United States would accept them. He estimated that this would amount to eighty percent of the total number of political prisoners still in jail (*Boston Globe*, November 22, 1978). This would mean that some sixteen thousand persons in prison at the time of the *Playboy* interview (and probably others apprehended later) had already been released, presumably having served their sentences, as there had been no amnesty since Fidel took power. The proposal to release three thousand prisoners was related to Castro's efforts at the time to win over the exiled Cuban community in the United States, which represented a political obstacle for the Carter administration in moving toward an improvement in relations with Cuba. The proposal would also improve Castro's "human rights" image, another factor in easing the obstacles to normalization of relations. By late 1979, 3,200 prisoners had been released (*Granma Weekly Review*, November 4, 1979).

27

■

The State of Revolutionary Consciousness

Greater and Lesser Achievements

ON JANUARY 2, 1967, the eighth anniversary of the Revolution, Fidel once again addressed the multitudes in the Plaza de la Revolución. The celebration had actually begun on New Year's Eve with a mammoth communal supper, even more elaborate and profligate than the one a year earlier. As reported in *Granma*,[1] there were over one hundred thousand paying customers. It was to be the last feast of its kind in Cuba, and no doubt anywhere in the world, for at the year's end, harsh austerity, unrelenting labor, and mourning for Ché Guevara were to grip the nation.

As was his custom on these occasions, Fidel reviewed the achievements of his regime: a significant decline in infant mortality; the doubling of hospital beds; an enormous expansion of educational facilities; the outstanding performance of the Cuban athletes in international competition; the thorough modernization of the armed forces; the vastly increased tonnage of the merchant marine; a "gigantic fishing fleet . . . operating off the coast of Patagonia, 5,000 miles from home . . . gathering cod in the glacial waters near Greenland . . . only eight years after the Revolution! Cuban fishermen in the Pacific Ocean! Who could have imagined it?"[2]

Concerning progress in agriculture he had less to report, and in industry, still less. There was an abundance of eggs, which for the time being were no longer rationed. This was the result of an exceptional, indeed

1. January 3, 1967.
2. *Política Internacional*, 17 (first trimester, 1967), 174.

amazing, case of sound planning and management, although production later faltered, since it was based on imported feed for the laying hens. A program of artificial insemination of livestock was in full swing, "which will unbelievably improve our herds in a few years" and consequently "the level of meat and milk production" (a decade later, rations for the population were still scanty). With respect to sugar, Fidel declared that "we shall have a good harvest this year; we shall produce more sugar than in any of the past five years." This time, uncharacteristically, his forecast turned out to be correct. However, the 6.2 million tons that would be produced in 1967 were far less than the 7.5 million called for by the five-year plan inaugurated the year before. In fact, this would be the second year in a row in which production would lag dangerously behind the plan by virtue of which the mythical ten-million-ton harvest would supposedly be reached in 1970.[3] Since the extent of the fulfillment of the annual plan was a realistic indicator of the prospects for achieving the goal set for 1970, it was a topic which Fidel, who was projecting optimism, preferred to avoid.

Mobilization for Production

Thus, in Fidel's view, there was nothing to cloud the great prospects and enthusiasm for the tasks that lay ahead. "We are engaged in an enormous effort to develop the economy of the country," he declared, "concentrating primarily on agriculture. This spring we shall mobilize 150,000 young people to work in the fields for six weeks; but we shall also mobilize tens of thousands of soldiers."[4] Equally impressive would be the mobilization of agricultural equipment, and here he boasted that "Cuba alone has received foreign credits for agricultural development equal to the amount received by all the other countries of Latin America put together."[5] The figure he gave was $125 million, but he did not say for what period or from where the credits came. The bulk, of course, came from the Soviet Union, and the rest came from capitalist sources which took the risk in view of the

3. See chapter 35, below, for more complete data on planned and real sugar production, 1966–1970.

4. *Política Internacional*, 17 (first trimester, 1967), 187. Apparently, some 45,000 soldiers were mobilized in 1967. By 1970, the figure reached 70,000, "about 65 percent of all military personnel. . . . [they] cut between 18 and 20 percent of all cane harvested and supervised the harvesting of most of the rest" (Jan Knippers Black et al., *Area Handbook for Cuba*, 2nd edition [Washington, D.C.: U.S. Government Printing Office, 1976], p. 479).

5. *Política Internacional*, 17 (first trimester, 1967), 180.

Soviet commitment to sustain the Castro regime. But these were not details that concerned Fidel at the moment.

What Fidel meant to convey to his listeners was proof that their "voluntary" labor in the fields was backed up by enormous mechanical and technical resources which insured his promise of the spectacular growth of Cuban agriculture. Inadvertently, the comparison with the rest of Latin America had revealed a measure of the external assistance available for Cuban development, as well as a measure of the extent to which Fidel had thus far squandered the resources at his disposal. However, few of those present would have noticed the slip. In any event, for Fidel the future was never brighter. "We expect that by 1970 we shall double agricultural production compared to what it was in 1959 when the Revolution triumphed," he predicted, "and the whole population will share equally in the benefits of this production."[6] Little did he imagine that, by 1970, agricultural production, excluding sugar, would in the aggregate and in per capita terms, by any reasonable method of calculation, be closer to one-half than double that prior to 1959, and that what was to be "shared equally" would be the most acute scarcity of consumer goods since the Revolution came to power.

The Importance of Vietnam

As for the rest of the speech, there was the predictable denunciation of the United States, the reaffirmation of undying support for revolution throughout the planet, and a special message of greeting to Ché Guevara and his comrades, "of whom we shall some day have very definite news." Finally, there was "our fervent solidarity with Vietnam, . . . so natural and logical for a country like [Cuba] threatened with the same dangers. . . . And Vietnam is in the midst of a struggle to the death. . . ."[7] No one could doubt Fidel's passionate sincerity about the fate of Vietnam, although he also exploited Vietnam as a tool for sharpening Cuban patriotism, "threatened with the same dangers," as he was careful to explain. Thus, it came as no surprise that he ended his speech by proclaiming 1967 to be the "Year of Heroic Vietnam."

Revolutionary Consciousness: The Claim and the Evidence

A recurrent theme in Fidel's eighth anniversary speech was the "increasing enthusiasm and revolutionary fervor" of the people, year after year. As his own "enthusiasm" mounted, he reached a climax. "The most extraordi-

6. Ibid., p. 180.   7. Ibid., p. 191.

nary consequence of this Revolution," he exclaimed, "is the incredible revolutionary consciousness which has developed among the people!"[8] However, as the year wore on, the evidence would not support his claim, and some of the evidence he would himself supply when it seemed to him urgent to face the disagreeable facts in the open. Less than a month after extolling the "incredible revolutionary consciousness" of the people, he inveighed in another speech against the continued "squandering of human and material resources," which he attributed to the persistence of a "petty bourgeois" attitude toward society. Bureaucracy, which he defined as a "massive, useless, parasitical, and unproductive concentration" of human resources, was a prime example of nonrevolutionary spirit. The battle against bureaucracy, he declared, "is almost as difficult as the battle against imperialism." Another outrageous example of nonrevolutionary spirit was the "wasting of material resources" by those who "show no interest in the care and maintenance of machinery or in saving raw materials such as fuel. . . . They are not conscious of the value of these things. . . . Therefore we must be inflexible against this criminal, antisocial, and unjustifiable waste. . . ."[9]

A month later, Fidel returned to the same theme. He complained bitterly about a recent incident in which lack of interest in distributing an unexpected surplus of produce resulted in "great quantities of vegetables rotting in the grocery stores." Then there was the problem of excessive office personnel in the factories. "There are factories," he declared, "where the capitalist owner had three or four [employees] in the office and we have twenty-five or forty." What was especially alarming, he continued, was that "*burocratismo*" was on the offensive: "Practically eighty-five percent of work centers recently investigated had violated the norms established in the struggle against bureaucracy. . . . The Committees for the Struggle Against Bureaucracy have themselves become bureaucratized and are in full retreat." The Revolution, however, was determined to win this "decisive battle," he promised, and "without bloodshed, . . . but there will be sanctions! Possibly hundreds of administrators will be fired and assigned to nonadministrative jobs at reduced salaries." There was still another culprit lagging in "revolutionary consciousness," the technician addicted to "technocratic criteria." Frequently, according to Fidel, "technicians make truly stupid decisions. . . . Sometimes you begin to suspect that they do it in

8. Ibid., p. 182.
9. Ibid., p. 224. The speech took place on January 30, 1967.

bad faith." He then went on to define the "technocratic criterion" as a form of "mystical faith" in the wisdom of the technician whose answer to an appeal for more production is that "it can't be done." [10]

Speculation in the Countryside

Fidel's wrath, however, was not confined to uncooperative administrators, factory managers, technicians, and the vast number of "slackers" who dodged productive labor by securing office jobs. There were also those among the common people who failed to respond to the great ideals of the Revolution, and their numbers were large enough to warrant public reprimand. Speaking in May at a congress of the National Association of Small Farmers (private producers legally obligated to sell to the state at officially set prices what they did not consume), Fidel said that it would be "hypocritical" to extol their virtues and patriotism without mentioning "at least some of the defects of some of our farmers." He was referring to those who speculated with their produce "without the slightest pangs of conscience." They get out on the highways and sell their milk and chickens to city folk who drive out to the country and are willing to pay "five times what the stuff is worth." But, he added, we are not going to throw anybody into jail for speculating (a prudent policy, since it could provoke active disaffection). We can afford to wait, he declared. "And do you know why?" he asked. "I'll tell you why. The day will come when fruits, vegetables, even milk, will be distributed free of charge to all the people!" [11] Statements like these would cost Fidel credibility even among the simplest of citizens.

The Persistence of Evil

Fidel's campaign against the evils of speculation, combined with what he termed "parasitism," was renewed in his speech on July 26, commemorating the anniversary of the aborted attack on the Moncada garrison in 1953. In the revolutionary annals, the date marked the beginning of Castro's struggle against Batista. Thus, it was one of the two most memorable days of the year (the other being January 2, celebrating the victory of the Revo-

10. Ibid., p. 232, 233, and 238. The speech was delivered to factory workers on February 20, 1967.

11. *Política Internacional*, 18 (second trimester, 1967), 264 and 265. The speech was given on May 18, 1967. At the time, there were about 200,000 private farms (reduced to 160,000 by 1975), cultivating some thirty percent of all farmland and accounting for a considerably larger proportion of all food (excluding sugar) produced in Cuba. See Black et al, *Area Handbook for Cuba*, pp. 390–391.

lution), when he delivered his most important speeches addressed to the entire nation. Accordingly, it was significant that he would use this occasion to ventilate his concern with the stubborn persistence of negative attitudes toward the aims of the Revolution.

After expressing his customary shrill optimism concerning the revolutionary virtues of his people, Fidel confessed that "in many towns we see loafers who produce nothing, . . . we see strong men who spend their time making fried meat patties. . . . And why? Because anyone who sells fried patties or fruit drinks or fried cracklings on the street [getting his materials on the black market] is going to earn ten times more than a man working [in the fields] under a blazing sun." Then he went on to cite similar examples of people whose "ideas and activities are completely removed from serving the collective interest. . . ."[12] For anyone living in Cuba at the time, the perversity of human nature was not hard to understand. The "parasites," that is to say, all the petty entrepreneurs and black marketeers of town and country, had accomplices: namely, a great mass of customers in all walks of life for whom there was no other way to obtain the simplest services or satisfy some of the most elementary needs.

A Sober Appraisal

Unexpectedly, Fidel paused in his attack on the "parasites" to explain the circumstances which produced them: in his words, "the deficiencies in the state economy." As one example, he described a typical situation involving lemonade. "If in some place where it is very hot and lots of people congregate," he said, "and the appropriate state authorities—whether municipal, regional, or national—can't manage to provide a little lemonade with some ice in it, the parasite springs up. He buys sugar in the grocery store and the lemons wherever he can, and sets up a stand selling ice cold lemonade." In another example, he dealt with the shortage of brooms: "If our industries forget to produce brooms, and hundreds of thousands of families have to sweep out their homes every day, and there aren't any brooms, then a multitude of people start making brooms. They sell them at any price they can get," and make enormous profits. There would be no need to outlaw this business, he added, "if our light industry would manufacture brooms. . . . The private broom makers would have no market."[13] It was still too early for Fidel to understand that a little capitalism could do wonders in helping socialism to function.

12. *Política Internacional*, 19 (third trimester, 1967), 45.
13. Ibid., pp. 46 and 47.

The New Exploiters

A month later, on another solemn occasion, Fidel again voiced his indignation over the great numbers of "exploiters" who remained immune to the revolutionary fervor which, paradoxically, he claimed was sweeping the country. It was clear that he perceived the problem to be increasingly serious and that he was losing his patience. This time he failed to mention the "deficiencies in the state economy" as extenuating circumstances for perpetuating the evils which he was determined to eradicate. "Multitudes of new merchants have sprung up," he declared, "the great majority without authorization, but some with the authorization of an idiotic municipal functionary . . . without a vigilant revolutionary consciousness, authorizing and legalizing activities promoting parasitism." Thus, he said, while the masses are being mobilized to produce much more food and everything else, "tens of thousands of . . . new merchants have appeared since the triumph of the Revolution. . . . Hence, instead of a minority of [large] exploiters [whom we have expropriated], we shall have tens of thousands of small exploiters living off the sweat of the people." Then came a warning: our patience thus far does not imply "that we are going to do nothing about the proliferation of small businesses. . . . I'm not talking about waiting thirty or twenty years but very much sooner."[14]

The following March (1968), Fidel made good his threat. In what he called the "Profound Revolutionary Offensive," some 58,000 miniscule enterprises were expropriated or otherwise eliminated. Since the "deficiencies of the state economy" continued or grew more pronounced, the complete destruction of the nonagricultural private sector increased the daily hardships borne by the urban population in particular. As my wife was told by a disgruntled young housewife who came to "borrow" a tablespoon of unobtainable cooking oil: "You know that as a practicing Catholic I could never be a communist. But this revolution has become sheer lunacy. If we could only have communism, I'd be happy now." (More about the "offensive" later.)

Education Thwarted

In the same speech of late September 1967, Fidel thundered against another evil, which he said was worse than a "vice," such as parasitism, but a real

14. Ibid., pp. 155–157. The speech was given at a mass meeting in Havana on September 28, 1967, the seventh anniversary of the founding of the Committees for the Defense of the Revolution (CDR), neighborhood vigilance groups set up by the thousands throughout the island.

"crime." It was a fact, he declared, that "many young people are neither working nor studying." In the past, he noted, we had children without schools and without teachers. This was deplorable, but now there were teachers and schools without pupils. How is this possible in our society, he asked, and then placed the blame on the parents. No one has the right, he insisted, "to permit his son to be an idler, a vagabond, a future delinquent. . . . Perhaps it is not a crime under capitalism, but a society which aspires to satisfy human needs through work and the application of technology cannot be indifferent when [youth are permitted to be] ignorant and illiterate. . . ." The remedy he proposed was drastic. "We shall have to have laws," he exclaimed, "which severely punish parents who do not comply with the elementary duty of sending their children to school. . . ."[15]

The "El Purio" Report

In his conflicting claims and revelations concerning the state of revolutionary consciousness in Cuba, Fidel had only exposed the more conspicuous and more critical gaps in the dedication of the population to the new ideals which were to transform society. In fact, what could be termed revolutionary apathy was more widespread than he admitted, particularly in the countryside. Some indications of the dimensions of this apathy came to public light in one of those increasingly rare indiscretions in the tightly controlled press. On November 28, 1967, the daily *Granma* reported on a pilot project in which "advanced" methods of social research were used "for the first time" by university students and professors "in coordination with the Party." The purpose, it was stated, was to obtain the data for "developing concrete plans for improving the quality and standard of living in rural areas." In the course of the study, *Granma* revealed some of the findings of the project.

As I later learned, it was a standard in-depth community study adapted to Cuban conditions. It was designed and led by a husband-and-wife team of western sociologists. *Granma* explained that they had initiated the proposal and, upon its acceptance, had come to Cuba, where they "were provided with all the necessary facilities." After a preliminary survey of the countryside, in January 1966, they selected and installed themselves in El Purio, a settlement of some two thousand inhabitants located in the northwestern part of the central province of Las Villas. According to what the newspaper revealed of their report (which was apparently submitted to the authorities in May 1967), their conclusions were all negative:

15. Ibid., pp. 160 and 161.

The inhabitants . . . lack a sense of community and stability. . . . There were two television sets, neither of which was functioning. There was a lack of any kind of cultural or sport facilities. . . . The town received no books or magazines. Distribution of necessities was irregular. . . . There was no mail or telegraph service. There were difficulties in taking children to a doctor [situated in another town]. . . . There was no pharmacy.

By way of summary, *Granma* stated that the inhabitants "participate to a minimum degree in political, social, and cultural activities; there is little or no effort at community planning for the cultural and social needs of children, youth, and adults."

One member of the husband-and-wife team (both were competent professionals as well as Communists in good standing for many years) told me that conditions in El Purio and neighboring communities were "appalling. Do you know what I would do if I were young and a Cuban? I would be a *gusano* [literally "worm," epithet for a counterrevolutionary]."

The Revolution in the University

Toward the end of April 1967, the teaching staff and students of the faculty of geography at the University of Havana were summoned to an urgent meeting. Some one hundred of us, as I recall, assembled to hear the director announce that the whole faculty, lock, stock, and barrel, was to move the following week to the Sierra Maestra, the mountain wilderness made famous by Fidel's guerrilla exploits. The director, recently appointed, was a young journalist whose "revolutionary consciousness," probably not unmixed with personal ambition, compensated for his academic inexperience. He arrived late in a state of great excitement, unshaven and unkempt, accompanied by the equally disheveled president of the student federation and a Party functionary, both of whom mounted the platform with him.

The director made a rousing speech. The three men on the platform, he exclaimed, had just been in the country with Fidel, who had decided on the move. (No enterprise, including the university, was immune from Fidel's personal intervention.) The faculty would combine book learning with firsthand research on the flora and fauna of the Sierra, the soil, climate, and peasant communities. Fidel had selected the area, and there was no need to waste time planning. Once installed, the geographers could decide, as Fidel expressed it, "whether to explore toward the north, the south, east, or west." The task of the Marxist geographer, Fidel wished to remind them, was not merely to study nature but to transform it.

The press reported that Fidel's message to the faculty of geography had been greeted with joy, enthusiasm, and pride at having been chosen by the Commander-in-Chief as the vanguard prepared to make all sacrifices in the task of transforming the university into a truly revolutionary institution. The actual response was quite different. When the director finished, his two companions on the platform broke out with vigorous applause, but not a single person in the audience followed suit. They all sat in stony— and dramatic—silence under the watchful eyes of the leaders. Then a bold young woman stood up and said that she was ready to go into the mountains, but that neither students nor instructors had any previous experience in field research. Wouldn't it be better if the move could be postponed until they acquired sufficient technical preparation to make an effective contribution in the Sierra? The director shouted her down with a single word: "*Derrotista!* [defeatist]." Others then asked about practical arrangements such as clothing, lodging, special diets for diabetics, facilities for nursing mothers, and so on. The answer was simple: the Party would take care of everything, and it would be ready for them when they arrived.

Predictably, the expedition was a complete disaster. The rainy season had begun, shelter was primitive, food and other supplies were insufficient, books and paper transported from Havana became waterlogged, and "research" for these city-bred scholars consisted of trying to survive in the jungle. There were accidents, and some people with broken bones had to be evacuated, along with others suffering from gastrointestinal ailments and exposure. At the end of three months, the faculty of geography moved back to Havana. Understandably, it was not greeted by Fidel on its return, nor were its exploits mentioned in the press.

Don Quixote in Cuba

Thus, in 1967, the "Year of Heroic Vietnam," the best that could safely be said for vast numbers of Cubans in many walks of life—almost certainly the majority of the people—was that they tolerated the Revolution, with varying degrees of equanimity or reluctance, hoping for better days. In one sense, there was no alternative, since along with the utopian carrot which Fidel dangled before their eyes, he offered the credible threat of punishment for those who might seek an alternative. Or to take a more positive view, one could borrow an analogy from Cervantes. Fidel was, so to speak, Don Quixote, the noble visionary, and the Cuban people were a collective Sancho Panza, his down-to-earth peasant squire. Although Sancho Panza was unmoved by the idealism of his master, and at times doubted his sanity, the reward which the obsessed knight-errant promised him—an island kingdom—was so tempting and otherwise so far out of his reach that, against his better judgment, he continued to serve him, accompanying him from one mad adventure to another. In any event, from either perspective, the Cuban attitude was a far cry from the enthusiasm proclaimed by Fidel and echoed by his excited and gullible following abroad.

28

■

The Conflict with the Venezuelan Communist Party

A Kidnaping and Murder

WHILE CASTRO GRAPPLED with revolutionary backsliding on the domestic front, there had been no lack of revolutionary business to attend to on the external front. For some time, it will be recalled, relations between the Cuban leader and the major Latin American Communist parties had been less than cordial, but both sides had managed to avoid an open break. On March 1, 1967, an event in Caracas unexpectedly escalated the discord and brought it into the open. This was the kidnaping and murder of the brother of the Venezuelan foreign minister, for which the Cuban-backed guerrilla movement, in handbills scattered in Caracas, assumed responsibility.

Government officials immediately seized the opportunity to implicate Castro in the crime and call for international sanctions against Cuba. This, in turn, made it imperative for the Venezuelan Communist Party to publicly define its position. Months earlier, the party had quietly conceded the defeat of the guerrilla movement and withdrawn its support, and it was now trying to persuade public opinion that it was a legitimate political party. Accordingly, it categorically condemned the terrorist atrocity, declaring that it was incompatible with revolutionary principles. At the same time, it sent condolences to the family of the victim. In addition, by studiously avoiding any mention of Cuba, and leaving unchallenged the alleged Cuban involvement in the crime, the party implicitly reinforced the Venezuelan government's linking of the crime with the Castro regime.

Castro Condemned

More than likely, the intention of the Venezuelan Communist Party was not to provoke Castro, although its actions could not have failed to do so. With his guerrilla disciples earlier disowned by the party, and, in a larger sense, with his leadership of the Latin American revolution disputed (preparations for the forthcoming Havana assembly of the Organization of Latin American Solidarity were well under way), some response by Castro was required. On March 6, *Granma* prominently displayed a formal statement by a leading official of the Venezuelan guerrilla movement which acknowledged, in the familiar language of ultraleft extremists, responsibility for the "execution," which was carried out according to the principles of "revolutionary justice," and so on. It was the same message already broadcast in Caracas, but with the important difference that it was signed and dated in Havana. This flagrant demonstration of solidarity (it is safe to assume that Fidel personally approved, if he did not himself suggest, the *Granma* statement) was eagerly acclaimed by the Venezuelan authorities as proof of its earlier claim of Cuban complicity in the assassination. Predictably, the statement also again placed the Venezuelan Communists on the spot. Constrained like all Kremlin affiliates to maintain a posture of public support for the Soviet-subsidized Havana regime, this time, in order to preserve the credibility of its own new posture, the Venezuelan party was compelled to openly denounce Castro's moral involvement in the crime.

The Polemic Intensified

The denunciation in turn prompted Fidel to rise to the challenge in his characteristic manner. Using the occasion of the traditional student mass meeting on March 13, the anniversary of the suicidal attack on Batista's palace, he leveled a vitriolic attack on the Moscow-backed leadership of the Venezuelan party, and, for good measure, he delivered a stinging rebuke to the Soviet Union. To begin with, he underscored the identity of the positions taken by the Venezuelan party and the "imperialistic puppet" government of Venezuela, citing numerous foreign press dispatches to prove his point. In contrast, he declared, although "we consider that it is a mistake [by the guerrilla movement] to use this type of procedure which the enemy can exploit before public opinion," we would never "join the hysterical chorus of the hangmen who govern Venezuela to condemn the revolutionaries." Later in the speech, he went further and in effect justified the action of the terrorists by placing the "main responsibility for the death" on the Venezuelan government because it "unleashed repression . . . and violence . . . in the service of its imperialist master."[1]

Much of the speech was devoted to an exposure of hitherto secret information concerning the internal struggle within the Venezuelan Communist Party, the "duplicity" of the leadership as it sabotaged the guerrilla movement, and its "infamous campaign" against Cuba, which "for many months we suffered in silence . . . while communications were sent to the various Communist Parties of Latin America accusing Cuba of interfering in their internal affairs and supporting and fomenting factionalism."[2] In short, as in his great polemic with the Chinese a year earlier, Castro defended himself by once again engaging in a scandalous washing of dirty Communist linen in public.

The Soviet Union Denigrated

While the Russians must have derived considerable satisfaction from Fidel's exposure of the skeletons in the Chinese closet, this time his reckless "spilling of the beans" could only have aroused their anger and indignation, and all the more so since he went out of his way to drag them into what he portrayed as a cesspool of deceit and dishonor. At one point, he noted that, a few months earlier, the Soviet ambassador to the United States, "in a friendly spirit," had attended the New Year's Day reception at the Venezuelan embassy in Washington, "despite the fact that the Soviet Union and Venezuela have no diplomatic relations."[3] Later in the speech, he singled out a more flagrant example of recent Soviet misconduct in Colombia: "At six o'clock in the morning, the [police] arrested the Secretary-General of the Communist Party and all the members of the leadership, . . . all of whom were in their usual places of residence. Not the slightest attention was paid to the fact that at that very moment a delegation of high Soviet functionaries was [in Bogotá] to sign a commercial, cultural, and financial agreement with the government, and on that very day, it was reported, was to meet with Lleras Restrepo [the Colombian president]. . . . And again, on the same day, [the police] stormed the offices of the TASS agency. . . ."[4] As Fidel reported these incidents, the clear implication was that the Soviet delegates took the abuse "lying down."

It was the kind of speech to which young Cubans, and others as well,

1. *Política Internacional,* 17 (first trimester, 1967), 270 and 275.
2. Ibid., p. 260.   3. Ibid., p. 256.   4. Ibid., p. 272.

responded with great enthusiasm and which created the kind of "revolutionary consciousness" that Fidel failed to arouse on domestic issues. They admired his courageous defense of Cuban integrity, they applauded his fearless challenge of the imperialist enemy and its puppets, they shared his outrage at the betrayal of guerrilla fighters inspired by the Cuban model, and they savored his denigrating remarks about the Russians, who at the time were distinctly unpopular in Cuba.

The Priority of Humanity

On April 19, the date of the annual celebration of the Bay of Pigs victory, Fidel was again in top fighting form, defying Yankee imperialism, denouncing the "pseudorevolutionaries," exalting armed struggle—"the only road to liberation"—and introducing a new slogan drawn from the noblest of Marxist principles. We love our country, he exclaimed, and are devoted to the welfare of our people, but "humanity comes first, before the fatherland!"[5] Not even Lenin had so clearly defined the priority of humanity.

A month later, three Cubans were discovered among a small group of Venezuelan guerrillas captured with their weapons as they attempted to make a clandestine landing on the Caribbean coast. One Cuban was killed in the brief struggle that took place. It was a case of being caught in *flagrante delicto.* In reply to the Venezuelan government's outcry, *Granma* carried a full-page inventory of the worldwide criminal activities of imperialism. At the end, in the spirit of "humanity comes first," the statement proclaimed "deep solidarity" with the martyred young Cuban, "with his altruistic, revolutionary, internationalist, and heroic gesture . . . within the purest Marxist-Leninist conception." Curiously, under a bold headline, the statement was attributed to the Central Committee of the Communist Party of Cuba,[6] which at the time had only a nominal existence. The deception, not particularly of the "purest Marxist-Leninist conception," was of course transparent. It was meant to shield the Cuban government from indictment for a criminal offense under international law while maintaining Cuba's "internationalist" revolutionary image.

5. *Política Internacional,* 18 (second trimester, 1967), 200.
6. "Declaraciones del Comité Central del Partido Communista," *Granma,* May 18, 1967.

29
■

Fidel Castro and the Jews (I): Before the Break with Israel

A Classical Riddle

THE SIX-DAY WAR IN THE MIDDLE EAST in early June 1967 presented Castro with the problem of solving the classical riddle of how "to eat one's cake and have it too." On the one hand, the defeated Arab countries were members of the Third World, which Cuba was pledged to support, while victorious Israel was closely allied with the United States, Cuba's deadly enemy. On the other hand, Cuba had maintained friendly relations with Israel before the war. To break relations after the war, as the Soviet Union had done, would have demonstrated the proper solidarity with the Arabs but would not have demonstrated Cuban independence vis-à-vis the Soviet Union, at the time a matter of considerable importance to Castro.

For the short run, he solved the problem by (1) condemning Israeli aggression but placing the major onus, oddly enough, on the United States; (2) chastising the Arabs for political ineptitude and not resisting to the bitter end; and (3) refusing to break Cuba's diplomatic relations with Israel. In the long run, however, he moved all the way into the Arab-Soviet anti-Israel camp. Early in September 1973, a month before the Yom Kippur War, he broke relations with Israel. Cuba soon emerged on the international scene as a leading spokesman of hard-line Arab propaganda against Israel and "Zionist racism" and later of the Arab-Soviet "rejectionist" coalition against the Egyptian-Israeli peace process. However, a number of factors other than realpolitik played a role in determining the course of Cuban-Israeli relations, including the presence of a Jewish community in Cuba and Fidel's personal attitude toward the "Jewish question."

The Jewish Community

It is estimated that in 1959, when the Batista government fell, there were some twelve thousand Jews in Cuba.[1] A small number of Spanish-speaking Sephardim from the Balkans and Palestine, the latter then under the Turkish rule, had settled prior to World War I. However, the great bulk of the Jewish population were Yiddish-speaking immigrants who came principally from Poland in the early 1920s. Denied admission to the United States under the postwar restrictive quota system, they first looked upon Cuba as a temporary refuge while they awaited their turn for American visas. The latter were hard to come by, while Cuba turned out to be a hospitable country with reasonable opportunities for earning a living. The result was a permanent Jewish community, concentrated in Havana. By the time of Castro's insurrection, it was a fairly prosperous community consisting predominantly of merchants and manufacturers of consumer goods, such as clothing and shoes.

At the time that Castro came to power, there had been no significant anti-Semitism in Cuba, unlike other Latin American countries containing visible Jewish settlements, such as Argentina, Brazil, Chile, and Mexico.[2] During the 1930s, Nazi-subsidized publications in Havana attempted to create a "Jewish problem," but with very little effect. Otherwise, systematic anti-Semitic propaganda was unknown to Cuba. Probably without precedent in the Christian or Moslem world was the absence in Cuba of slur terms for Jews—or, for that matter, for other foreigners, including Americans. The word "gringo," for example, invented in Mexico, was not used in Cuba. East European Jews were popularly known as *polacos* ("Poles"), and others as *turcos* ("Turks"), but no stigma was attached to these terms.

1. See Dona Katzim, "The Jews in Cuba," *The Nation*, May 25, 1974, pp. 658–660.
2. "Catholicism, historically . . . identified with Spanish domination, . . . never won great influence [among] the Cuban population. Thus, religious distinctions did not antagonize the Cubans against the Jews, and still less so since, by disposition, the Cubans are a friendly and hospitable people" (Boris Sapir, *The Jewish Community of Cuba: Settlement and Growth* [New York: J.T.S.P. University Press, 1948], p. 55).

Ché Guevara, beyond suspicion of any kind of racial prejudice, adopted the Cuban custom of referring to the main body of Cuban Jews as *polacos*.

Nevertheless, a migration of young Cuban-born Jews to the United States began in the 1950s. Many went to study in American universities and remained in the United States. This was largely a matter of seeking better opportunities for advancement, as well as escape from the parochial confinement of the Cuban Jewish community. There was little inducement to assimilate into the mainstream of Cuban life, while the structure of social and political institutions, as in most Latin American countries, made it difficult to do so. A mere handful of the early immigrants, who had been Socialists or Communists in Poland, joined the Cuban Communist Party. Otherwise, there were no Jews to speak of in "politics," until Castro began his armed struggle. One Jew joined the July 26 Movement and was possibly the only active Jewish recruit. This was Enrique Oltuski, who, as previously noted, became a leader of the underground and then Castro's first minister of communication.

The Impact of the Revolution

Thus, the Jewish population was already declining when Castro assumed power. However, by the end of 1960, when the government began to nationalize privately owned commerce and industry, what had been a modest emigration became a large-scale exodus, mainly to the United States and Israel.[3] By 1967, the Jewish population had probably dwindled to less than two thousand. Those who remained shared the discomforts of other middle-class Cubans, but there was no discrimination against them as Jews. On the contrary, in some respects they were given favored treatment. They were permitted to keep the large and elegant Jewish social center, known as the *Patronato de la Comunidad Hebrea*, located in Havana's fashionable Vedado district. The kosher restaurant in the building continued to operate with generous allotments of supplies. At Passover, the government permitted the several synagogues to receive and distribute duty-free shipments of matzot and other ceremonial foods, as well as Israeli wine and locally hard-to-come-by cooking oil, donated by the Canadian Jewish Congress. Although the Albert Einstein School, a Jewish day institution, became a neighborhood public school, two classrooms were set aside for Jewish studies in the late afternoon, and children living at a distance who wished to

3. The *New York Times* (March 26, 1969) reported that some six thousand Jews from Cuba were living in the Miami area.

attend were provided with free government transportation.[4] In addition, the long-established Zionist Association continued to hold meetings from time to time.

Conspicuous during the middle and late 1960s was the attention given by the media to Jewish holidays and cultural events, all out of proportion to the size of the Jewish community. Passover was portrayed as commemorating Jewish "national liberation"; while on the anniversary of the Warsaw ghetto uprising, Jewish resistance was praised as an example of heroic "armed struggle."[5] Lectures by a local Jewish writer on such topics as "The Bible and Hebrew Influence in the Life and Work of José Martí";[6] Mendele Mocher Sforim, "grandfather of Jewish literature"; and the twelfth-century Jewish sage Abraham Iba Ezra, were duly commented on in the press.[7] Also noteworthy were the weekly half-hour radio talks in the Yiddish language, the only regular foreign-language program on the air.[8]

Castro's Motivation

The extraordinary solicitude for the remnants of the Jewish community, which moreover had largely remained aloof from the revolutionary process, could not be attributed solely to the absence of anti-Semitism in Cuba or to the regime's relatively tolerant attitude toward most religious congregations. It was a matter of deliberate policy on the highest level,

---

4. Concerning the curriculum (as of 1968): "Strictly speaking, religion is no longer taught in the public schools, and we observe this regulation; so we teach only Hebrew, Yiddish, Jewish history, and Jewish culture" (from an interview reported by Everett Gendler, "Holy Days in Havana," *Conservative Judaism*, 23:2 [Winter 1969], 19).

5. For example, the April 14, 1968, Sunday supplement of *El Mundo* carried a full page, amply illustrated, on the twenty-fifth anniversary of the "epic struggle . . . to the death against the Nazi-Fascist oppressor in the Warsaw ghetto."

6. On this occasion, a caption under a photo identified a figure on the platform as "His Excellency Shlomo Levav, Minister of Israel in Cuba" (*El Mundo*, February 1, 1968).

7. *El Mundo*, December 24, 1967, and February 20, 1968, respectively.

8. Russian technicians and military personnel vastly outnumbered the Yiddish-speaking community. Among the permanent residents speaking a foreign language were numerous Chinese, perhaps ten thousand or more, who maintained their ethnic identity, lesser groups of relatively assimilated Jamaicans and Lebanese, and a few hundred Japanese. For the history of the Chinese presence in Cuba, see Clough Corbitt, *A Study of the Chinese in Cuba, 1847–1947* (Wilmore, Kentucky: Asbury College Publications, 1971). The Tokyo *Asahi* carried a brief account on February 13, 1979 of Japanese immigration to Cuba and a photo of an elaborate Japanese mausoleum in Havana's *Colón* cemetery.

which brings us to Fidel Castro. It is more than likely that, as in the case of his attitude toward Israel, Fidel felt the need to demonstrate that Cuba was not a Soviet satellite. From a humanitarian point of view, as well as from the point of view of respect for Marxist principle, the contrast between the Cuban and Soviet treatment of Jews provided convincing evidence. At the same time, Fidel's personal views toward Jews reinforced his political motivation.

In common with many other young Cubans of his generation, Fidel had been strongly influenced by the nineteenth-century humanism of José Martí and the anti-fascist heritage of the Spanish Civil War, in which Cubans formed the largest of the Latin American contingents fighting in Spain against Franco and his Nazi-Fascist allies.[9] In the late 1940s, when Fidel began his political career, the then fresh revelations of the Nazi atrocities against the Jews created widespread sympathy for the Jews which he undoubtedly shared and which could only have confirmed his humanist and anti-fascist convictions. Moreover, Hitler's lethal anti-Semitism provided striking evidence that the treatment of the Jews could be a significant indicator of a government's overall guiding principles and aspirations. After the triumph of the Cuban Revolution, as Fidel's frequent public reminders of the Nazi iniquities suggested, this could well have been one of the considerations that shaped his policy toward the Jews. As for the new state of Israel, although there is no record of his reaction at the time it was created, everything, including his subsequent attitude, would indicate that he held it in esteem.

There is yet another element which might have played a part in shaping Fidel's approach to the "Jewish question." He apparently was convinced that some of his ancestors were Marranos, Spanish Jews who converted to Christianity in the sixteenth century to escape being burned at the stake by the Holy Inquisition. He told this privately to an elderly Jewish friend, a well-to-do chemical engineer and financial contributor to the July 26 Movement, whom he rewarded with an appointment as minister to Israel in 1960.[10] In any case, when Fidel came to power, there was nothing

9. In a message from the Communist Party of Cuba to the ninth congress of the Spanish Communist Party, there was a reference to "more than 1,000 . . . Cuban fighters who served in the International Brigades and the Republican Army . . ." (*Granma Weekly Review*, May 7, 1978).

10. The minister was Ricardo Subirana y Lobo, who mentioned Fidel's remarks on his ancestry to Shlomo Levav, Israeli minister to Cuba from 1965 to 1968. I interviewed Mr. Levav in Jerusalem in the spring of 1975. There is historical evidence that Castro is one of several Marrano-descended family names, in-

in his background to indicate the slightest prejudice against Jews, in either Cuba or Israel, and much to predispose him in their favor.

Relations Before the Six-Day War

Almost from the beginning of his regime, as has been noted, Castro looked to the Third World as a source of support in his confrontation with the United States. During the early 1960s, Cuba's closest relations with the Third World (excluding China) were Nasser's Egypt and Ben Bella's Algeria, leaders of Arab nationalism and unreservedly opposed to the existence of Israel. Nevertheless, Castro ignored this burning issue in his public dealings with both countries. For all the Cuban people could gather from his speeches and the media, the "Palestine question" did not exist. In effect, seen from an Arab point of view, his position amounted to one of benevolent neutrality toward Israel.

Thus, in 1961, as the result of an unpublicized, though not secret, policy, Cuban Jews emigrating to Israel were classified as *repatriados*, that is, persons returning to their homeland, although most, if not all, had originated in eastern Europe and had never lived in Israel or Palestine. This was in total contradiction with Arab policy. Several hundred Cuban Jews, with all their movable property, were transported to Israel by *Cubana de Aviación*, the national airline, in several flights.[11] This was indeed exceptional treatment. All other Cuban emigrés were considered to be *gusanos*, antirevolutionary scum, and could take with them only the clothes on their backs and a change of underwear.

Relations with Israel received little public attention in Cuba. This was partly because trade and other transactions between the two countries were minimal, and partly, one would suspect, a matter of political discretion. However, a conspicuous demonstration of Cuba's friendly relations with Israel occurred on the occasion of the death of Israeli President Yit-

---

cluding Mendes, Franco, Meléndez, and others. Among the judicial records of hearings or trials by the Holy Inquisition of suspected backsliding Jewish converts, persons named Castro appear several times. See Seymore B. Liebman, "Summaries of *Procesos*, 1500–1810," and Bibliographical Guide, in *The Inquisitors and the Jews in the New World* (Coral Gables, Florida: University of Miami Press, 1974), passim.

11. Yoram Shapira and Edy Kaufman, "Cuba's Israel Policy: The Shift to the Soviet Line," *Cuban Studies* (University of Pittsburg), 8:1 (January 1978), 22. See also chapters by each author in Michael Curtis and Susan Aurelia Gitelson, eds., *Israel in the Third World* (New Brunswick, N.J.: Transaction Books, 1976), pp. 120–146; and 147–181.

zhac Ben-Zvi, in late April 1963. An official three-day mourning period was declared, and all Cuban flags on public buildings in Havana were flown at half-mast. Although this was no more than the customary courtesy paid to a deceased head of state with whose country Cuba had normal relations, it was extremely irritating to Cuba's Arab friends. One source later reported that it provoked Ben Bella into canceling a proposed formal visit by Castro to Algeria.[12]

Shortly after the Ben-Zvi incident, an interview with an Israeli journalist visiting Cuba was published in *Revolución*.[13] He had some flattering things to say about Cuba. "For us leftists," he was quoted as saying—he was a member of MAPAM, on the far left of the Zionist political spectrum— "this revolution is also a symbol, because, while it is socialist, at the same time it is free of some of the negative phenomena which in the past accompanied the development of socialism in some countries." Such a statement normally would have been prominently displayed in *Revolución*, but the journalist went on to say that we "Israelis are very patriotic and are proud of our national rebirth, and we hope that your revolution will be able to understand that the efforts put forth in Israel's national struggle are an expression of the Jewish people." This more than likely explained why the interview was discreetly printed on page fourteen. Nonetheless, something was gained in promoting goodwill for Israel.[14]

In its relations with Cuba, Israel also had to use discretion, in view of its considerable dependence on economic and military support from the United States. At the same time, it hoped that friendship with Cuba would be an asset in countering Arab pressures to isolate Israel from other Third World countries (which eventually proved to be a miscalculation). Hence, in March 1964, the Israel-Cuba Friendship Society was created in Jerusalem, oddly enough recalling the ubiquitous and supposedly autonomous

12. *Latin American Jewish Congress Information Bulletin* (Buenos Aires), No. 186 (September 12, 1973); cited by Shapira and Kaufman, "Cuba's Israel Policy," p. 31, note 5.

13. May 6, 1963. The journalist was Mordejai Nahumi (Spanish spelling), who wrote for *Al Hamishmar* of Tel Aviv.

14. The delicate nuances that came into play when the Cuban press dealt with Israeli topics were further illustrated by the front-page account in *Revolución* (August 25, 1965), complete with photo, of the ceremony in which Shlomo Levav, newly-appointed Israeli minister to Cuba, presented his credentials to President Osvaldo Dorticós. It was the customary treatment of such an occasion, and, like the mourning period for Ben-Zvi, not to have adhered to custom would have signaled less than normal consideration for a country with which Cuba maintained normal relations.

"friendship societies" functioning in most Communist countries. It was ostensibly a private organization through which technical aid could be channeled to Cuba without involving the Israeli government.

Until the beginning of the 1970s, notwithstanding the hardening of Cuba's public attitude toward Israel after the 1967 war, a modest unofficial flow of Israeli technical experts to Cuba took place, mainly from the *kibbutzim*. Some Israeli citrus specialists spent as much as two years in the Cuban countryside. Other activities for which Israeli expertise was provided included irrigation, sorghum cultivation, and freshwater fisheries. Perhaps a score of Israeli technicians at one time or another worked in Cuba, while a much smaller number of Cubans spent brief study periods in Israel, mainly in the citrus groves. Israeli technical aid to Cuba was practically unpublished in either country, reflecting the international political constraints that affected their relationship.[15]

At the Havana tricontinental conference in January 1966, the Cuban delegation voted for the extreme anti-Israel and anti-Zionist resolutions, as well as for support of the Palestine Liberation Organization, approved by the assembly. However, the Cubans played a passive role during the formulation of the resolutions, in contrast to the militant pro-Arab stand of the radical *Fidelista* Latin American delegations. The Cuban explanation for its voting record, privately given at the time to a disturbed Israeli diplomat in Havana, was that Cuba did not consider itself bound by the vote, since the delegations at the conference represented parties and organizations, not governments. In this connection, it was significant, as one pro-Israel source pointed out, that "the texts of the Conference in Cuban publications distributed in Mexico and other Latin American countries systematically omitted the resolutions adopted against Zionism and the state of Israel." The same source concluded: "Cuban-Israeli relations continue to be satisfactory."[16]

Repercussions of the Six-Day War

Surprisingly, these relations continued to be more or less "satisfactory" despite the Six-Day War, although it must have been a matter of conjecture in Israel as to how long they could remain so. The crisis began, it will be recalled, on May 19, 1967, when the United Nations Emergency Force,

15. Data supplied by former minister to Cuba, Shlomo Levav, in my intervew with him in 1975.

16. *Israel: Un Tema para la Izquierda* [Israel: A Theme for the Left] (Buenos Aires: Editorial Nueva Sion, February 1967), p. 290.

on Nasser's demand, withdrew from the Gaza Strip, where it had been stationed to supervise the truce between Egypt and Israel after the 1956 war. Egyptian troops immediately reoccupied the Strip and closed the Gulf of Aqaba to Israeli shipping. With tensions mounting and Arab and "progressive" Third World countries aligning themselves with Egypt, Cuba felt compelled to define its position. On May 30, President Dorticós sent a brief message to President Nasser expressing the "militant and solid revolutionary support of the Cuban people for the Arab peoples," determined to resist the "maneuvres, provocations, threats, and aggressions of Yankee imperialism in the Middle East." It was, in one important respect, a model of lofty evasion, for there was no mention of Israel at all.[17]

Two days after hostilities began on June 5, the Havana press carried a 500-word official declaration by the Cuban government "on the war in the Near East." It condemned the "aggression . . . by the armed forces of Israel . . . instigated and supported by imperialism. . . ."[18] This was the only mention of Israel—that is to say, in a statement of five hundred words, Israel was referred to by name only once. The villain was "imperialism," and almost as much space was devoted to its nefarious deeds in Vietnam, Laos, Santo Domingo, Korea, and so on, as to the Middle East. The reluctance to focus on Israel was indeed impressive.

Cuban public reaction to the war, so far as could be determined, was to a large degree favorable to Israel.[19] Cubans tended to identify with a small country fighting for survival against vastly superior numbers, and winning.[20] They got long well with their Jewish neighbors and had little direct experience with Arabs. Besides, government propaganda had not prepared them to be hostile to Israel. These circumstances no doubt further complicated Castro's problem when, shortly after the Arab débacle, he could no longer avoid joining the angry Third World chorus with an unequivocal comdemnation of Israel.

17. *Política Internacional*, 18 (second trimester, 1967), 277.
18. Ibid., p. 299.
19. This was my impression at the time from conversations with Havana acquaintances in various walks of life. One high-placed person, putting on a long face, told me that "our side" suffered a serious setback. Then he winked and chuckled. A filling station attendant asked if the rumor was true that the "Israelitas" had won the war. When I answered in the affirmative, he was obviously pleased. Foreign residents who talked with Cubans confirmed my impression. My sampling was meager and spotty, but in the absence of opinion polls in Cuba, as in all Communist countries, there was nothing better to go on.
20. Prior to the war, Castro told Shlomo Levav that he could see a parallel between Israel's struggle to survive and the Cuban experience.

The Cuban Statement at the United Nations

On June 23, at a special session of the United Nations General Assembly, Ricardo Alarcón, Castro's permanent UN ambassador, in a lengthy statement accused Israel of "armed aggression against the Arab peoples . . . by a most treacherous . . . surprise attack, in the Nazi manner," and went on to condemn Israel's "[brutal] proposal to annex the territory occupied by force of arms." [21] Thus, he met the main requirements of "solidarity" with the Arabs, including the repulsive analogy between Israeli and Nazi behavior. This also marked the first time that any Cuban statement at the United Nations explicitly condemned Israel. [22]

Nevertheless, Arab satisfaction with the Cuban declaration was less than complete. The denunciation of Israel was blunted by a remarkable preface with which Alarcón had opened his address. Cuba, he declared, "as a matter of principle, [is] opposed to every manifestation of religious, national, or racial prejudice, from whatever source, and also objects to any political proclamation which advocates the destruction of any people or State. This principle is applicable to the Palestinian people . . . unjustly deprived of its territory, as well as the Jewish people, which for two thousand years has suffered racial prejudice and persecution, and during the recent Nazi period, one of the most cruel attempts at mass extermination." The Soviet position, while unreservedly hostile to Israel, also conceded its right to exist (consistent with the Soviet vote at the United Nations when the new state was created), but the Cuban reminder of the historic context which justified the existence of Israel was unique.

Cuba also had its own special axe to grind, which relieved Israel of the full, or even the main, guilt for its seizure of Arab territory. "Our position with respect to the State of Israel," Castro's spokesman declared, "is determined by [its] aggressive conduct . . . as an instrument of imperialism against the Arab world. . . . It is in the context of the global strategy of imperialism that the true meaning . . . of the aggression . . . is revealed. . . . The criminal war unleashed by the imperialist Government of the United States against the people of Vietnam, with absolute impunity, demonstrates this affirmation, if the experience of Korea, the Congo, and Santo Domingo . . . are not sufficient proof."

21. *Granma*, June 24, 1967.
22. A typical previous Cuban response to the Arab-Israeli controversy was foreign minister Raúl Roa's statement on October 15, 1965, at the twentieth United Nations General Assembly, that Cuba "supports the position of the Arab States in the pathetic case of Palestine" (*Política Internacional*, 11–12 [third and fourth trimesters, 1965], 259).

Here was Fidel's familiar obsession with the implacable American adversary, but this time there was also something more. Indirectly, the emphasis on American culpability helped to justify his refusal to break relations with Israel. More directly, he was sending a message to the Kremlin. The Soviet Union had severed diplomatic relations with Israel and had forced its satellites, excepting Rumania, to do likewise, while it continued to practice and preach peaceful coexistence with the country held responsible for armed aggression on a world scale, including the Middle East.

By coincidence, a glaring—and for Fidel an extremely offensive— example of Soviet-American coexistence occurred at about the time of Alarcón's speech at the United Nations. It was the meeting between Prime Minister Kosygin and President Johnson in Glassboro, New Jersey. To Fidel's chagrin, Kosygin came directly from Glassboro to Havana, arriving there for a brief visit on June 27. Cuban sources leaked the information that Kosygin had pressed Castro to break relations with Israel. Castro responded that he would do so when Moscow broke its ties with Washington.[23]

A Critique of Arab Policy

A final Cuban "twist" enlivened Alarcón's statement at the special UN session. Condemning the Security Council for having imposed an "unconditional" cease-fire on the belligerents, thereby condoning Arab "surrender in the face of imperialist aggression," Alarcón declared that "our Revolutionary government believes, as a question of elementary dignity and patriotism, that there can be no cease-fire while a single inch of territory is in the hands of [the enemy]. Death until the last citizen of a country perished is preferable to accepting such ignominy. . . ." Ostensibly directed against the Security Council, this was a scarcely concealed indictment of Arab debasement and cowardice, as contrasted with the unquenchable patriotism and heroism of the Cubans. On several occasions, Fidel would later say that in case of an invasion of Cuba, anyone in favor of accepting a cease-fire while the tiniest bit of Cuban soil was occupied by the enemy, would be summarily shot.

A few months later, Fidel was severely critical of the Arabs on another score. "True revolutionaries never threaten to exterminate a whole country," he told K. S. Karol in an interview published in the Paris *Nouvel Observateur*. "This kind of propaganda . . . helped the Israeli leadership to mobilize the patriotism of their people."[24] It was, of course, another way of

23. According to former Israeli minister to Cuba, Shlomo Levav.
24. Cited in *Le Monde*, September 21, 1967.

justifying the Cuban position on the existence of Israel. Later it would not stand in the way of Cuba's militant support of Arab "revolutionaries" committed to "exterminate a whole country." In any event, this was to be Fidel's last public disparagement of Arab conduct. As time went on, the reporting of the Arab cause, with belated praise for the Fatah commando raids in Israel, received more frequent and positive mention in the Cuban media, as well as in official statements. Meanwhile, there was no yielding to public and private pressures to break relations with Israel. First, break with the United States, Castro would reply to his socialist critics; and to others he would argue that it had never been Cuban policy to break with any country which did not first break with Cuba.[25]

At the same time, there was no change in Fidel's policy toward Cuban Jews. Matzot and sweet wine, shipped from Montreal, arrived as usual in time for Passover, while Havana's Zionist Association continued to hold its meetings. In 1970, for example, a visitor to Havana reported that a memorial meeting on the occasion of the death of Samuel Agnon, Israeli Nobel Prize laureate in 1966, drew nearly one hundred people.[26]

25. Until 1973, the record bears Castro out. The Western Hemisphere nations hostile to Cuba (i.e., all except Mexico and Canada) took the first step in breaking relations. Likewise, the German Federal Republic initiated the break with Cuba when the latter recognized the German Democratic Republic. Despite early friction with the Franco regime in Spain and with the Roman Catholic Church, Castro's government maintained traditional relations with Spain and the Vatican. Nor did Castro follow suit when the Soviet Union broke relations with Albania. In the case of Chile, which had renewed relations with Cuba when Allende was elected president in 1970, the generals who overthrew Allende initiated the second Chilean rupture with Cuba on September 13, 1973 (as reported by the *New York Times* on the following day).

26. *Jewish Western Bulletin* (Vancouver, British Columbia), June 5, 1970.

30
■

Fidel Castro
and the Jews (II):
1973 and After

The Conference in Algiers

THE CIRCUMSTANCES UNDER WHICH Fidel Castro broke relations with Israel
were, to say the least, improbable. He had arrived in Algiers on September
5, 1973, to attend the Fourth Conference of the Heads of State or Government of Non-Aligned Countries.[1] On his way, his plane had stopped to
pick up his newly won Caribbean admirers, Prime Minister Michael Manley in Jamaica and Prime Minister Forbes Burnham in Guyana. There was
another detour to Conakry, Guinea, where President Sékou Touré joined
Castro's party for the final leg of the flight to Algiers. After the meeting in
Algiers, Fidel was scheduled to visit Baghdad, New Delhi, and Hanoi before returning to Havana.

The days of exporting revolution to Latin America, and of his great
quarrel with the Soviet Union, were long behind him. In Algiers, where
representatives of seventy-six "nonaligned" countries, as well as more than
one thousand journalists,[2] were to assemble, he would enhance his emerg-

1. Previous summit meetings, in all of which Cuba was a voting member,
took place in Belgrade (1961), Cairo (1964), and Lusaka (1970). The Algiers meeting was the first attended by Castro.
2. According to Le Monde, September 11, 1973. Including members of the
delegations, observers, and journalists, the newspaper estimated that some seven
thousand persons attended the conference. The term "nonaligned," as originally

ing role as a preeminent spokesman for the entire Third World. He would
also have a special task to perform: the defense of the Soviet Union. Brezhnev had already sent an open message to Algerian President Boumediène,
chairman of the conference, politely but firmly warning the participating
countries against accepting the Chinese thesis linking the Soviet Union
with the United States as the "two imperialisms."[3] Thus, the last thing on
Fidel's mind when his turn came to address the assembly, on September 7,
was Israel.

The Soviet Union Defended

Fidel spoke for only a half-hour—possibly the shortest speech in his career, but long enough to display the full range of his polemical talent.
"The theory of 'two imperialisms,'" he declared, ". . . has been echoed
. . . by leaders and spokesmen of nonaligned countries. . . . In certain political and economic documents drafted for this Conference, we have seen
that current come to the fore. . . . Cuba will always oppose that current in
all circumstances. That is why we find ourselves obliged to deal with this
delicate matter as an essential issue."[4]

The rest of the speech illustrated the "unbridgeable abyss between the
imperialist regime and socialism" and expounded the great virtues of the
Soviet Union, "the glorious, heroic, and extraordinary services rendered
to the human race by the Soviet people. . . ." If it were not for the impression of total sincerity which he rarely failed to project, one could have
suspected that he was determined to pay back a major portion of Cuba's as-
tronomical debt to the Kremlin with thirty minutes of impassioned elo-
quence.[5] In any case, as he further developed his theme, he reviewed the

---

used, referred to nonaffiliation with either camp in the cold war of the 1950s and
early 1960s, and, more specifically, to nonmembership in either NATO and other
western-dominated security alliances or the Warsaw Pact. Technically, Cuba was
deemed to qualify as a nonaligned country because it was not a member of the
Warsaw Pact, although it was otherwise "aligned" with the Soviet Union. By the
time of the Algiers meeting, nonalignment had lost much of its original meaning
and had become largely synonymous with the status of a developing or Third
World country. This conformed with the shift in interest from the political problems of the cold war to issues affecting the common economic aspirations of developing countries.

3. *Le Monde*, September 9–10, 1973.
4. *Granma Weekly Review*, September 16, 1973.
5. There was no lack of appreciation in Moscow for his performance. A
prominent Soviet journal described Fidel's speech as "fiery" and declared that his

areas of the world where good and evil were locked in struggle, contrasting
the benevolent role of the Soviet Union with the malevolent role of the
United States. Everywhere, he asserted, the "culprit is the same: United
States imperialism." The lesser "culprits," such as Portugal, South Africa,
Brazil, and Bolivia, came in for their share of blistering censure, but Israel
got off lightly. It was mentioned only once, and with relative restraint: "Israel mocks the United Nations resolutions and refuses to return the territory it occupied by force." This could hardly have satisfied the numerous
Arab delegations at the meeting, who were divided on a number of issues
but united against Israel.

Castro Challenged

Not unexpectedly, Fidel's speech caused an immediate commotion. Exiled
and Peking-based Prince Norodom Sihanouk, recognized by the conference as the legitimate representative of Cambodia, took the floor, over the
objections of Chairman Boumediène. Sihanouk attacked Castro's thesis,
citing his own case as an example of the collusion between the "two imperialisms." His government, he pointed out, had been overthrown by the
American-backed reactionary Lon Nol, and the new regime was then recognized by the Soviet Union.

There was more recrimination when the Brazilians and the Bolivians,
who had only observer status at the conference, insisted on replying to
Castro. Boumediène yielded to their demands over Castro's objections.

More serious was a direct challenge to Fidel by an important Arab
leader, Colonel Moammar Khadafy of Libya, on the far left of the Arab
political spectrum. In his formal address at the meeting the day before,
Khadafy had criticized the Soviet Union. A few hours after Fidel's speech,
he held a press conference in which he lashed out against Castro and declared that Cuba had no right to belong to an organization of nonaligned
states. Not wholly implausibly, he maintained that Cuba was like "Uzbeki-
stan and Czechoslovakia," a part of the USSR. "In the beginning," he said,
"the aim of the revolution was to obtain Cuba's freedom. This freedom has
no meaning if it consists of moving from the domination of one power to
that of another power. . . . I am nonaligned and Castro is aligned."[6]

For nearly two days after Khadafy's blast, frantic efforts were made to
patch up the Cuban-Libyan quarrel, which had split the conference and

---

defense of socialism and the Soviet Union "had successfully shattered the false theories planted by the Chinese" (*New York Times*, November 9, 1973).

6. *Le Monde*, September 9–10, 1973.

threatened to prevent an orderly adjournment. Finally, at a closed session only one hour before Boumediène was scheduled to appear at a public session to make the closing speech, Castro announced that Arab arguments had just convinced him to sever relations between Cuba and Israel. Whereupon, according to an eyewitness, Khadafy rushed over to Fidel and embraced him.[7] Thus, almost miraculously, harmony reigned when Boumediène convened the final session and pronounced the conference to have been a resounding success.

The Scapegoat

In a strange way, uninvited and deprecated Israel emerged as the savior of the unity of the stormy meeting in Algiers. Evidently, Castro had been privately under great Arab pressure before and during the conference. Israel thus became the scapegoat and main bargaining chip in a crucial political poker game. In exchange for breaking relations with Israel, Castro purchased Arab tolerance for the Soviet position and his defense of it, safeguarded his new role as the foremost "nonaligned" champion of the Kremlin, and improved his own leadership aspirations in an increasingly important sector of the Third World. Needless to say, there could be no objections from Moscow, which had broken relations with Israel in 1967. Later, when Russo-Egyptian relations deteriorated, the USSR would find Castro a valuable asset in promoting a new pro-Soviet alignment with Libya and the other "progressive" Arab states.

There was an amusing epilogue to Fidel's performance in Algiers. The news of the break with Israel, instantly transmitted by the western press, caught both Cuban and Israeli diplomatic services by surprise.[8] Fidel had given Havana no warning of his decision. Belatedly, an official statement was issued in Havana announcing that the "Revolutionary Government of Cuba" had decided to break diplomatic and consular relations with the State of Israel. . . ."[9] It was, of course, already widely suspected that the "Revolutionary Government of Cuba" generally was a euphemism for Fidel Castro. In this case, there could be no doubt.

7. *Le Monde*, September 11, 1973. *Granma* reported that Castro's announcement was "greeted with a standing ovation that seemed to last forever. . . . Yasser Arafat . . . ran across [the hall] to embrace Fidel, and the applause lasted for minutes" (*Granma Weekly Review*, September 16, 1973). All information relating to Khadafy's presence at the conference was suppressed.

8. *Le Monde*, September 11, 1973.

9. *Granma*, September 10, 1973; the citation is from *Granma Weekly Review*, September 16, 1973.

The Escalation of Hostility

A month later, with the outbreak of the Yom Kippur War, there was also no doubt that the break in relations with Israel was no mere formality. Under the heading of ZIONIST BARBARISM IN SYRIA, a full page of *Granma* was taken up with photos of scenes identified as atrocities committed by Israeli bombardment of Damascus and other populated centers.[10] This set the tone of Fidel's new commitment, and in a short time Cuba became one of the leading exponents, outside the Arab League, of intransigent hostility toward Israel. A landmark in this process was Cuban sponsorship, accompanied by extensive lobbying, of the notorious "Zionism-is-racism" resolution adopted on November 10, 1975, at the thirtieth United Nations General Assembly. *Granma's* comments on "this forward step by the peoples of the world" went beyond the text of the resolution, explaining that the latter "left no doubt about the identical imperialist origins and racist structure of the Israeli Zionist regime that is occupying Palestine and the one that is exploiting the black masses of Zimbabwe [Rhodesia] and South Africa. . . ."[11] This was a far cry from the Cuban acknowledgment at the United Nations in June 1967 of the centuries of Jewish persecution and of the right of the Jewish state to exist in part of Palestine.[12]

In April 1974, Cuban troops were detected on the Syrian-Israeli front, a fact that was later confirmed by Castro.[13] The following November, Yasser

10. *Granma Weekly Review*, October 28, 1973. The photos were supplied by the Syrian news agency SANA.

11. *Granma Weekly Review*, January 18, 1976. Under Arab pressure, most African states had broken relations with Israel. Cuba lost no opportunity to reinforce African hostility against Israel, even to the extent of joining the Arab-African chorus at the UN Security Council in July 1976 which condemned Israel's rescue of the hijacked prisoners at the Entebbe airport as a criminal violation of Uganda's sovereignty, consistent with Israel's racist policy.

12. Cuban journalism subsequently adopted the Soviet formula concerning the identity of the victims of Nazi genocide. In a full-page, illustrated account of a visit to Auschwitz, there was no reference to Jews. The writer, returning from a tour of the death camp in Poland, informed his readers that between "June 14, 1940 and January 27, 1945, more than four millions persons . . . died in Auschwitz. . . . Confined in this vast prison were people of different nationalities, different languages, different customs, and different ideas" (*Granma Weekly Review*, March 2, 1980, p. 12).

13. In his speech at the closing session of the First Congress of the Communist Party of Cuba, on December 22, 1975, Castro said: "And it is no secret to anyone that at a given moment of danger and threat for the Republic of Syria, our men were in Syria" (*Granma Weekly Review*, January 11, 1976). Castro gave no further

Arafat was enthusiastically received in Havana with all the honors due a
head of state, and he also had the special distinction of being awarded
Cuba's foremost decoration, the Order of Playa Giron (Bay of Pigs). On Arafat's departure, a joint Cuban-Palestine Liberation Organization communiqué was issued.[14] A year later, in his opening report to the First Congress of
the Communist Party of Cuba, Fidel again accused Israel of being an instrument of Yankee imperialism, but this time in the context of Cuba's complete
identification with the Kremlin's strategic interests in the Middle East. The
United States, he declared, "through the Zionist State of Israel, is seeking
. . . to threaten the southern flank of the Soviet Union. . . ."[15] Finally, the
congress resolution on foreign policy solemnized the condemnation of Israel and support for the PLO, which was "leading the Arab peoples of Palestine" in the struggle for "their national rights."[16]

The Sacrifice of Principle

If Fidel's abrupt shift in policy toward Israel troubled his conscience, more
than likely it was not for long. He was always able to rationalize the sacrifice of one principle as a necessary means of advancing another, and higher, principle, although in fact the question of principle might not have
been involved in his decision at all. In this practice, to be sure, he was no
different than others who wield arbitrary power in the name of an exalted
ideology. In any event, the circumstances which led him into active hostility against Israel left no doubt that he was moved by pure opportunism;
and once having changed his course, he was determined to make the most

details. Israeli sources, however, claimed that the Cubans consisted of an armored
brigade ("Why Cuba Broke with Israel," an interview with Chaim Herzog, Israeli
Ambassador to the U.S., in *The Canadian Jewish News*, National Section, September 9, 1977).

14. *Granma*, November 17, 1974; reproduced in *Granma Weekly Review*,
December 1, 1974.

15. *Granma Weekly Review*, January 4, 1976.

16. Resolution adopted on December 21, 1975; reproduced in *Granma
Weekly Review*, January 25, 1976. On October 12, 1979, in his speech to the 34th
session of the UN General Assembly in New York, Castro took the final step in
condemning Israel. He accused it of practicing "genocide" against the Palestinian
people, similar to the "genocide that the Nazis once visited on the Jews." The Pal-
estinians, he added, were "living symbols of the most terrible crime of our era"—
by inference, more "terrible" than the massacres that had taken place in Uganda
and Cambodia and the fate of the "boat people" fleeing from Vietnam, countries
which he did not mention (*Granma Weekly Review*, October 21, 1979).

of it. Here he was eminently successful, bolstering his ambition for leadership in the Third World and at the same time earning the gratitude of the Soviet Union. A well-earned tribute to his political competence was the decision taken at the Fifth Conference of the Heads of State or Government of the Non-Aligned Countries, held in Sri Lanka in 1976, to convene the next summit meeting, scheduled for September 1979, in Havana.

For the Jews in Cuba, the "good old days" slowly but surely gave way to a new environment. A visitor in 1977 reported that Havana's largest and most elegant synagogue was in a state of disrepair, with "tattered curtains and a ruined ceiling." The kosher restaurant for the community, which still numbered some fifteen hundred individuals, had been closed for a year, allegedly because of "labor troubles." The daily Hebrew classes for children were "down to once a week, the lessons being given by a non-Jewish teacher from Spain."[17] Meanwhile, the sense of insecurity among Jews which followed the change in policy toward Israel gave way to resignation. The retrenchment in services could be attributed as much to the prolonged austerity which affected the entire Cuban population as to a change in attitude toward the needs of the Jewish community. Otherwise, there was no detectable spillover of enmity toward Israel in the treatment of Cuban Jews.

17. *New York Times*, December 12, 1977. A later visitor reported that government busing of children had ended in 1975 (*Women's American ORT Reporter*, January–February 1979, p. 11).

31

■

"De l' Audace, Encore de l' Audace, Toujours de l' Audace"

The Salon de Mai

IN MID-1967, CASTRO further demonstrated his capacity to dazzle the world with the sheer audacity and flamboyance of his leadership aspirations by mounting two elaborate international meetings in Havana. They were followed by a third such meeting in early January 1968, but were destined to be the last of their kind before the near collapse of the Cuban economy and Castro's subsequent domestication by the Kremlin. The next events of comparable magnitude to take place in Cuba, the Eleventh World Festival of Youth and Students (a Soviet invention) in 1978 and the Sixth Summit Conference of Non-Aligned Countries in 1979, followed the standard patterns established at previous youth festivals and summit meetings and provided Castro with only marginal opportunities to display his impressive innovative talents.

It was in late July, at an undisclosed cost to the declining Cuban economy, that the Paris *Salon de Mai*, a prestigious annual exhibition of ultra-avant garde painting and sculpture, was transported to Havana for its first appearance in the Western Hemisphere, accompanied by scores of prominent leftist-libertarian artists, writers, and assorted intellectual fellow travelers. The display was the ultimate insult to the Soviet school of "so-

1. "Audacity, more audacity, always audacity" (Georges Danton, September 2, 1792).

cialist realism." It was a major demonstration of Fidel's challenge to the Soviet cultural and ideological model and was designed to cultivate the support of the independent radical and revolutionary intelligentsia in western Europe and Latin America.

The Cultural Congress

Considered to be a resounding success by all who participated, including Fidel, the exhibition was followed in early January 1968 by an even more elaborate and expensive "cultural congress," attended by five hundred intellectuals from seventy countries, according to the official count. Here Fidel distinguished himself by an exceedingly bold and provocative attack against Soviet dogmatism and revolutionary retrogression. But he had woefully miscalculated. The cheering intellectuals could flatter him and spread the good word among the restricted circles in which they moved, but from any practical point of view they were powerless. They were no threat to the Kremlin and its network of loyal Communist parties; nor could their wild applause conceivably persuade the Kremlin to step up delivery to Cuba of petroleum, at the moment a matter of critical importance for the incessantly proclaimed "impetuous advance of the Revolution," as will shortly be explained.

Then, in 1971, after Soviet orthodoxy had firmly gripped the Revolution and Fidel had repented his heresy, the mutual admiration displayed at the *Salon de Mai* and the cultural congress was reversed. The arrest in March of the poet Heberto Padilla, accused of writing counterrevolutionary poetry, brought public protests in April and May by several score of the most prominent western leftist intellectuals. The treatment of Padilla, they wrote, recalled the "most sordid moments of the era of Stalinism."[2] The reply from Havana denounced the "apparent ideas of freedom as a disguise for . . . counterrevolutionary poison."[3]

The Latin American Solidarity Conference

The *Salon de Mai*, for all its pretensions, had modest objectives compared with the meeting of the Latin American Solidarity Organization that immediately followed the closure of the exhibition. OLAS (acronym for

2. *New York Times*, May 22, 1971. Padilla was finally allowed to emigrate in March 1980.

3. *Granma Weekly Review*, May 9, 1971. For a fuller account of the *Salon de Mai*, the cultural congress, and the Padilla affair, see my *The Rise and Decline of Fidel Castro* (Berkeley and Los Angeles: University of California Press, 1972), pp. 352 ff.

Organización Latinoamericana de Solidaridad), as was mentioned earlier, was set up in January 1966, at the close of the tricontinental meeting. At the time, it was envisaged by Fidel as his trump card in securing wide acceptance of his "armed struggle" thesis, and with it his uncontested leadership of the anti-imperialist struggle in Latin America. It was to be a formidable challenge both to the United States and the Soviet Union, not without its risks, but promising commensurate rewards: in the short run, leverage vis-à-vis the imperialist enemy and the Communist benefactor; in the long run, the "liberation" of Latin America and the confirmation of Fidel's role as the Bolívar of the twentieth century.

Looking back at the OLAS conference, held in Havana from July 31 to August 10, 1967, one is astonished by the extraordinary illusions that it created. All the evidence since early 1966 had pointed to the increasing ineffectiveness of Cuban-style guerrilla warfare in Latin America and to the growing isolation of *Fidelista* political activists from the broad sectors of the Left. The last of the guerrilla movements in Peru had been crushed in early 1966. In Guatemala, factional struggles had reduced the remnants of Castro's following to impotence. In Colombia, sporadic guerrilla activity continued in remote inaccessible areas, but with no prospect of spreading to populated centers. In Venezuela, as has been noted, Fidel suffered a major defeat when the Communist Party withdrew its support from the FALN (Armed Forces of National Liberation) and thus effectively sealed its doom. Earlier optimism in the Cuban press concerning Bolivia had been followed by an ominous news blackout shortly before the OLAS conference was convened.

In other countries, such as Argentina and Brazil, Cuban-backed armed struggle had died in its infancy. In the Dominican Republic, American intervention in the civil strife of 1965 had eliminated the likelihood of successful leftist insurrection in the foreseeable future. In Puerto Rico, despite the constant aggressive propaganda emanating from Havana, the puny independence movement had made no headway. And everywhere in Latin America, the Moscow-chartered Communist parties had easily held their own against the militant fringe groups, including not only the Castroites but also the Trotskyists, Maoists, and anarchists. As for the Soviet Union, it continued to push ahead with its efforts to promote trade and political relations with governments denounced by Fidel as puppets of Yankee imperialism.

All of this notwithstanding, Havana once more became a center of world attention. Some one hundred and sixty delegates from the Latin

American and Caribbean countries, among them a scattering of guerrilla veterans, were accredited to the OLAS conference. They made impassioned speeches and adopted predictable resolutions—some of them predictably opposed by a handful of Moscow-leaning participants—in the presence of several scores of accredited observers from most of the socialist countries and a dozen or so leftist international organizations.

A Conspicuous Provocation

Also present at the conference were a hundred or so journalists from many parts of the world, including the United States and other western countries. Impressed by the lavish setting and the sheer temerity of the meeting, underscored by Fidel's superb showmanship and the audacity of his scathing rebuke to the Kremlin for the betrayal of revolutionary principles in Latin America,[4] the western reporters produced bales of copy on the proceedings, as well as corridor gossip and interviews with the more uninhibited delegates and guests. Among the latter was the handsome young Stokely Carmichael, a West Indian who at the time was a prominent spokesman of the "black power" movement in the United States, although he was shortly to fall into almost complete obscurity, one among many ironies of the conference. In his incendiary remarks, opportunely coinciding with massive riots in Detroit, Carmichael urged the American black population to continue burning and pillaging in order to create, as he put it (borrowing from Ché Guevara's much quoted message to the tricontinental organization), "50 Vietnams in the United States."[5] At another point, he promised that "[we blacks] are ready to destroy United States imperialism from within as you are ready to do it from without. We can't wait for them to murder us—we must be prepared to be the first to kill."[6] Car-

---

4. In his closing speech, clearly alluding to Moscow's offer of assistance to the Venezuelan and Colombian governments, Fidel said that "if internationalism exists, if solidarity is a word worthy of respect, the least that we can expect of any state of the socialist camp is that it refrain from giving any financial or technical aid to those regimes" (*Granma*, August 20, 1967; cited by Edward González, *Cuba Under Castro: The Limits of Charisma* [Boston: Houghton Mifflin, 1974], p. 187).

5. William R. Ratliff, *Castroism and Communism in Latin America* (Stanford, Calif.: Hoover Institution Press, 1976), p. 204. See Ratliff's Appendix B, pp. 199–208, for a convenient summary of the OLAS conference. For Castro's closing speech and the "General Declaration" issued by the conference, see *Granma*, August 11, 1967.

6. Cedric Belfrage, "Solidarity in Havana," *The Minority of One*, October 1967, p. 24.

michael's presence as an "honorary delegate," singled out for special attention by Castro, was one of the highlights of the conference and its most
conspicuous provocation.

The Appraisal of OLAS

There was little sober appraisal of the meeting. Reactions by proponents
and opponents of its objectives were largely subjective, corresponding to
their respective hopes, fears, and propaganda needs. In Cuba, of course,
the conference was hailed as a great political and ideological victory.
Equally enthusiastic were the "new left" western radicals, impressed by its
"profound significance," and in one instance unabashedly proclaiming it
to be "the birth of a new International, . . . the Fifth International."[7] At
the same time, many Latin American governments denounced it as if it
were a real threat and called for more sanctions against Castro.

Moscow was officially silent, but its spokesmen in the world Communist press bitterly complained that the conference was dominated by
"ultraleft splinter groups given to anti-Communist and anti-Soviet di-
atribes,"[8] in this case a fair assessment of the facts. As for the major western
press, it was distracted by Stokely Carmichael, by speculation concerning
Russian reprisals against Castro, and by an unexpected sideshow that took
place at the height of the conference. This was a display of newly captured,
live Cuban counterrevolutionaries, who told how they were trained by the
CIA for various missions, including the assassination of Fidel.[9]

In short, it appears that few, if any, of those praising, condemning, or
otherwise reporting on the conference realized that it was essentially a carnival of absurd revolutionary rhetoric. In only a matter of weeks, the Latin
American Solidarity Organization faded away and silently expired.

7. John Gerassi, "Havana: A New International Is Born," *Monthly Review*,
October 1967, pp. 22 ff.

8. *L'Humanité*; cited in *The Worker* (New York), August 20, 1967.

9. The evidence presented was highly credible, but was generally treated
with skepticism in the U.S. press. Later investigations of the CIA by the U.S. Senate confirmed the evidence and revealed the full extent of clandestine operations
against Cuba. See Daniel Schorr, "The Assassins," *New York Review of Books*, October 13, 1977; and Tyrus G. Fain et al., eds., *The Intelligence Community, Public
Document Series*, with an introduction by Senator Frank Church (New York and
London: R. R. Bowker, 1977).

32

■

The Death and Resurrection of Ché Guevara

Homage in Absentia

AMONG THE MYTHS FOSTERED by the OLAS conference was that of an invincible Ché Guevara soon to emerge from a distant hideout to ignite the eagerly awaited Latin American revolutionary conflagration. In anticipation of his reappearance, the opening session elected Ché "Honorary President" of the conference, and the final plenary session acclaimed him to be an "Honorary Citizen of Latin America."[1] On the wall behind the podium, a mammoth portrait of the absent hero dominated the auditorium. Almost certainly none of those present, with the possible exception of Fidel and his most intimate associates, knew that even before the conference began, Ché and his decimated guerrilla band were in a desperate situation in the Bolivian wilderness. Even Fidel might not have known the full extent of Ché's predicament, because of recurring breakdowns in radio communications between Havana and the constantly shifting position of the guerrillas.

Prelude to Disaster

Ché's first skirmish in Bolivia took place in late March 1967, less than two months after his group had emerged from its well-concealed base and had stealthily begun to explore the surrounding area in some depth. Unexpectedly, they had come across a Bolivian army patrol, which they successfully

1. *Granma*, August 11, 1967.

ambushed. Paradoxically, the encounter turned out to be what one writer described as the "prelude to disaster."[2] The ambush had been premature and had alerted the Bolivian government, and indeed the world, to the existence of the guerrillas. In Havana, the skirmish was hailed as a major victory for what was termed the Bolivian Liberation Army, but without revealing Ché's presence. In La Paz, the government mobilized its troops to meet the challenge. By mid-summer, the guerrilla base had been seized, and Ché, encircled by the army, was aimlessly wandering with his men in the difficult mountain and jungle terrain. Supplies of food and medicine were dangerously low, and half of the original forty-three guerrillas were either dead or missing.

On July 31, the very day on which the OLAS conference opened, Ché recorded in his diary the loss of men and equipment in a skirmish with government troops, and then added his customary monthly analysis: "The negative aspects of last month prevail, including the failure to make contact with Joaquín [leader of the permanently strayed rear guard] and the outside, and the loss of men; we are now 22 men, three of whom are disabled, including myself. Thus, our mobility has decreased. . . . The peasantry still is not joining us." Nor did the situation improve during the period of the conference. On August 8, Ché wrote that he was physically "a mess" and that he told his men that "we are in a difficult situation. . . This is one of those moments in which great decisions must be made. . . ." He then invited those unable to endure further sacrifice to say so "and abandon the struggle."

Disaster Confirmed

Three days after being triumphantly hailed in Havana as an "Honorary Citizen of Latin America," Ché wrote (August 14), apropos the loss of a cave and its contents: "A black day. . . . It is the hardest blow they have ever given us; somebody talked. Who?" And so it went during the remaining few weeks of the doomed guerrilla band: "We are in a period of low moral and revolutionary spirit . . ." (August 31). "Helicopters have flown over the area. . . . They may be leaving men in ambush . . ." (September 10). "Defeat. . . . The sound of firing . . . told us that our men had fallen

2. Daniel James, *Ché Guevara: A Biography* (New York: Stein and Day, 1969), p. 234. Along with James's *The Complete Bolivian Diaries of Ché Guevara and Other Captured Documents* (New York: Stein and Day, 1968), this book provides the most fully researched account of Ché's Bolivian campaign and its aftermath.

into an ambush" (September 26). "It was announced on Radio Balmaceda in Chile that top [Bolivian] Army sources revealed that they had Ché Guevara cornered in a jungle canyon" (September 30). Ché's last entry was dated October 7: "The eleventh month of our guerrilla inauguration. . . . The 17 of us set out [under] a very small moon. . . . The Army [informed over the radio] about the presence of 250 men . . . to keep the encircled group . . . from getting out." The next day, the final skirmish and disaster took place. Ché was captured and then was executed twenty-four hours later. He was thirty-nine years old.[3]

Reminiscence

Ernesto Guevara—the footloose Argentine doctor who joined Fidel's near-suicidal "Granma" expedition; the asthmatic warrior-hero of the Cuban insurrection; the renowned theorist of guerrilla warfare; and now Fidel's economic planner and roving ambassador—Ché was already something of a legendary figure when I knew him in Moscow in late October 1960. News of his arrival, en route to Peking, reminded me that an old friend of mine, a prominent Mexican agronomist who had recently been to Cuba, told me that he had given my name to Ché as a blacklisted American academic who could be useful in Havana. I mentioned this to a friend in the Cuban embassy, who shortly thereafter phoned me that Ché would come to my apartment that evening. Accompanied by two embassy officials, Ché arrived soon after midnight, thus confirming another part of the legend about him: that, unlike most Latin Americans of his status, he was meticulous about meeting a commitment, however inconsequential; and that he never went to bed before dawn.

I recall that Ché appeared to be of medium height and well-built. He was wearing his familiar beret, jump boots, and crumpled olive-green fatigues, but without a side arm. At first sight, his sparse, unkempt beard gave a somewhat comical cast to his otherwise unexceptional features, an impression that disappeared when he began to speak and his expressive eyes livened up his countenance. That evening, at least, he was relaxed, completely informal, and frequently displayed his reputed wry sense of humor. His Spanish, as expected, was typically Argentine; but unlike compatriots of

---

3. Citations from James, *Complete Bolivian Diaries*, as follows: July 31, p. 190; August 8, p. 193; August 14, p. 195; August 31, p. 202; September 10, p. 209; September 26, p. 216; September 30, p. 219; and October 7, p. 223. There were five survivors, three Cubans and two Bolivians, who managed to escape and make their way to Chile.

his generation, his foreign language was French rather than English. He was unquestionably an attractive personality. My wife later claimed that he "illuminated" our cramped apartment on Kutuzovsky Prospect, but that could have been a special female reaction or the result of the deference which his Cuban companions showed him.

We talked for an hour or so, then had tea, and continued our conversation for another hour. Ché was interested in my experience at the Nacional Financiera, the Mexican government's industrial development bank, where I had been an economic consultant on several major projects before coming to Moscow, and in my earlier research on development problems for the government of the state of São Paulo, in Brazil. But our conversation strayed from purely professional matters to broader political and ideological issues.

What impressed me at the time, apart from his wide reading and nimble intellect, was a questioning attitude toward prevailing Marxist dogma and a genuine modesty concerning his own doubts and speculations. I gathered that he was groping for a way to make a fresh start in building a socialist society, perhaps on the order of what came to be known during the "Prague spring" of 1968 as "socialism with a human face." All in all, we seem to have hit it off fairly well, because, before leaving, he invited me to come with my wife to Havana as guests of the Cuban government.

Ché's visit with us in Moscow flashed through my mind as I listened on the night of October 18 to Fidel delivering the final eulogy for his departed comrade in front of more than half a million solemn-faced Cubans gathered in the Plaza de la Revolución. In the intervening seven years, the Marxist dogma which Ché questioned had been replaced by an even more rigid conception of Marxism, the modesty with which he expressed his views had been replaced by a righteous arrogance, and his gentle skepticism had been replaced by a shrill fanaticism. It occurred to me that he had become the victim of his own legend and of the conceit which the exercise of arbitrary power frequently induces.

The Record of Failure

The sad truth was that Ché's defeat in Bolivia was the last of an unbroken series of failures, domestic and foreign, although the ultimate responsibility lay with Fidel. Ché had been the chief promoter of rapid industrialization and a restructuring of agriculture, both of which were intended to reduce Cuba's dependency on sugar exports. These policies quickly proved to be costly errors and had to be reversed, with agricultural investment given preeminence over industry and top priority allocated to sugar production. Early in 1963, I was among the guests invited to the inauguration of a much heralded Cuban Institute of Automation, Ché's brainchild. Ché was the smiling and confident host as we were guided among a profusion of expensive instruments and specialized machinery imported from a half dozen countries. The Institute, clearly an irrational "leap forward" at the time, expired in a few months without benefit of ceremony.

Ché created and headed the gargantuan and unmanageable ministry of industries, which incorporated factories, mines, and workshops of every size and description. It had to be partially dismembered while Ché was still minister, and was later totally dismantled. What remained of Ché's inventions, such as the centralized state budgetary system, the primacy of moral incentives in stimulating the productivity of labor, and the forging of the "new socialist man," vanished with the reorganization of the economy on the Soviet model in the 1970s.

Ché, who became a highly competent guerrilla commander under Fidel's leadership and then wrote a highly regarded treatise on the theory of guerrilla warfare, was later singularly inept as a guerrilla strategist and leader outside Cuba. As Fidel's chief of staff for external guerrilla activities, an undercover function he performed until he resumed his career as an active combatant, Ché probably shared some of the blame for the ill-conceived interventions in Peru, Colombia, Venezuela, and Guatemala. However, there is no way to assess the precise role he played in each instance. On the other hand, he was clearly responsible for planning and organizing the guerrilla operation led by his compatriot Massetti in northwestern Argentina, which was wiped out in short order in the spring of 1964.[4] How Ché could have so completely miscalculated the geographic and political factors in his own country, which doomed the expedition from the start, remains a mystery.

We have already dealt with Ché's misadventures in the Congo, the prelude to the disaster in Bolivia. The strategy of the Bolivian campaign was based on a fantasy of Napoleonic dimensions, and hence was more likely to have originated with Fidel. The struggle would begin in Bolivia, the South American "heartland," encircled by Peru, Brazil, Paraguay, Argentina, and Chile. Once the guerrilla band was firmly established, it would trigger a Bolivian upheaval which in turn would ignite a series of triumphant revolutions in the rest of the continent. In fact, however, the

4. For the details, see my *The Rise and Decline of Fidel Castro* (Berkeley and Los Angeles: University of California Press, 1972), pp. 333–335.

odds against mere survival in the Bolivian jungle, to say nothing of the events that were to follow, were overwhelming.

Fidel's Assets

A comparison between the situation which Ché faced in the southeastern Bolivian highlands and the one which confronted Fidel when he reached the Sierra Maestra at once reveals the enormous disadvantages under which Ché labored. The Cuban peasants encountered by Fidel (unlike the small Cuban farmers in the rest of the island) were disaffected and readily cooperated with him, thus insuring his initial survival. In this connection, Fidel wisely permitted only one foreigner, Ché, whom he needed as a doctor, to join his expedition.[5] Thus, the intruding guerrillas were Cuban, spoke "Cuban," and were engaged in a traditional type of Cuban insurrection. Fidel was already a well-known political opponent of the Batista dictatorship and had the support of an extensive underground network with an important unit in Santiago, a large city situated at the base of the Sierra. This meant that new recruits and supplies could reach him in a matter of a few hours. The effectiveness of Batista's army was undermined by corruption and low morale. Fidel's announced objectives—the restoration of democracy accompanied by social justice and economic reform—enlisted wide support among all classes of the population and provided immunity against United States intervention. The American "hands off" policy was further reinforced by the position adopted by the Cuban Communist Party, which dismissed Fidel as a "petty bourgeois adventurer."

Ché's Burdens

As for Ché, the area which he chose as his initial zone of operations was not only extremely rugged but far removed from all potential sources of supplies and recruits. The peasants with whom Ché's band came in contact were either suspicious or downright hostile. One of the reasons for this was that there had been a genuine agrarian reform in Bolivia in 1954, as a result of which the pesants were loyal to the government. In addition, they looked upon the guerrillas as foreign invaders, since nearly half of thém

---

5. As Ché himself explained: "Fidel did not want to involve any more foreigners in this project of national liberation. . . . Fidel did not want our army to become a mosaic of nationalities" (*Pasajes de la Guerra Revolucionaria* [Havana: Ediciones Unión, 1963]; reprinted in *Ernesto Ché Guevara: Obra Revolucionaria*, ed. Roberto Fernández Retamar [Mexico City: Ediciones Era, 1968], pp. 280–282).

were Cubans and other outsiders. The peasants knew nothing about the legendary hero in their midst, whose renown in Bolivia was restricted to urban-based intellectuals and a scattering of militant leftists in the mining centers—as well as to the Bolivian and American intelligence services—altogether an infinitesmal proportion of the population.

Ché had expected support from the Bolivian Communist Party but refused to meet the party's condition that so long as the fighting took place on Bolivian soil he was to be subordinate to the party, and not vice versa. Once more a victim of his "internationalist" illusions, and his vanity, Ché found himself completely isolated. Finally, as soon as the guerrilla band was discovered, an American trained and directed counterinsurgency battallion immediately went into action. Unfortunately, Ché was killed after his capture. Had he been permitted to survive, in due course he might have written perceptively, eloquently, and honestly about the reasons for his failure. His legend in one sense would have been diminished, but in another sense enhanced.

Apotheosis

In his eulogy, Fidel spoke with great feeling about the virtues of Ché, whom he enshrined as "the most extraordinary of our revolutionary comrades." His one fault was his "absolute disregard for danger," which might have contributed to his untimely end. However, "it was not at all strange that a warrior should die in combat." Our "enemies believe that they have defeated . . . his conception of guerrilla warfare, . . . his views concerning revolutionary armed struggle. What they succeeded in doing was, by a stroke of luck, to eliminate his physical being, . . . to take advantage of an accident, which can happen in war."

Thus, with his accustomed self-serving skill, Fidel mourned the loss of the man ("a tremendous blow for the revolutionary movement") but rescued the lethal delusion which he and Ché held in common. "The political and revolutionary thought of Ché," by which he meant his own as well, "will have permanent value in the Cuban and Latin American revolutionary process." Fidel then moved on to transform the martyred Ché into an object of near-worship by the Cuban people, and by rebels and dreamers in many parts of the world. "The example of Ché," he exclaimed, "must be the ideal model for our people. . . . Ché raised to its highest expression the stoicism of a revolutionary, the spirit of revolutionary sacrifice, . . . the spirit of revolutionary labor. . . ."[6]

6. Citations from the eulogy are from *Granma*, October 19, 1967.

Soon, thousands of photographs, paintings, etchings, and lithographs of Ché decorated the Cuban landscape like so many icons. Along with the granite and marble monument to Martí, the Plaza de la Revolución was now dominated by the likenesses of Ché and Lenin, each four stories high and attached to a wall of a government office building. At the same time, Ché's brooding features proliferated on magazine covers, posters, and T-shirts on sale in bookshops and youth centers in Toronto and Tokyo, Baghdad and Bombay, and scores of other cities (but not in Moscow or Peking). And from Havana came a vast outpouring of literature on the life and death of Ché, which made its way in translation, or otherwise reworked, around the globe (excepting eastern Europe and China).

It was in this manner that Fidel intensified, and thereafter nurtured, the cult of Ché. In Cuba, paradoxically, the cult continued long after Fidel's conversion to Soviet-style socialism all but obliterated every vestige of Ché's conception of a socialist society. Beyond Cuba—again paradoxically—the cult was kept alive in later years principally by an international community of terrorists,[7] although Ché in action and thought always opposed terrorism. Terrorism, he once wrote, "is of negative value. . . . It can turn a people against a revolutionary movement. . . ."[8]

7. "Mogadishu, Somalia—A Palestinian woman, . . . the only surviving hijacker of a Lufthansa airliner, . . . was convicted of air piracy and terrorism. . . . [She] was wounded when West German commandos stormed the hijacked plane at Mogadishu Airport last October 17, [1977] . . ." *Province* [Vancouver, British Columbia], April 27, 1978). A photo taken when she was removed from the plane on a stretcher revealed that she was wearing a T-shirt decorated with the features of Ché Guevara.

8. *Guerrilla Warfare*; cited here from John W. Sloan, "Political Terrorism in Latin America: A Critical Analysis," in *The Politics of Terrorism*, ed. Michael Stohl (New York and Basel: Marcel Dekker, 1979), p. 304.

33

■

Escalation of Dispute: Soviet Pressure and Domestic Treason

The Petroleum Squeeze

IT WILL BE RECALLED that in 1960, when the Cubans took possession of the foreign oil refineries and, in reprisal, were cut off from supplies of Venezuelan crude, it was Soviet petroleum that providentially filled the gap and assured the survival of the Castro regime.[1] In 1968, Soviet petroleum again played a significant role in Cuban history, but this time—no doubt with the Soviets particularly annoyed by the extreme provocation of the OLAS conference in August 1967—as a weapon designed to bring the Castro regime under control. Fidel explained how this came about in his speech on January 2, 1968, commemorating the ninth anniversary of the Revolution.

Petroleum consumption, he said, had been increasing for several years as a consequence of the phenomenal growth of the economy. The largest increase was due to the spectacular achievements in preparation for the ten-million-ton sugar harvest of 1970: hundreds of thousands of acres had been cleared for new planting in which thousands of imported tractors, bulldozers, and other oil-burning equipment was used. Supplies of petroleum began to run short in 1966 and especially in 1967, when, even with supplementary shipments, it was necessary to dip into the reserves of

1. See my *The Rise and Decline of Fidel Castro* (Berkeley and Los Angeles: University of California Press, 1972), pp. 78–79.

the armed forces, "which are practically sacred," since our country is "constantly threatened by Yankee imperialism."

Nevertheless, Fidel added with simulated politeness, although Cuba's needs for 1968 will increase again, the Soviet Union "apparently" will not be in a position to meet our requirements.[2] Therefore, it will be necessary to impose strict controls on the consumption of fuel, including the rationing of gasoline for private motor vehicles. "Our economic development," he continued, "must not slow down, much less be paralyzed. . . . Nothing would please the imperialists more. . . . Imperialism knows that fuel is a basic strategic item in the development of our economy . . . and in defense of our country."[3] The target of these sinister warnings was, of course, the Kremlin. The purpose, however, was not to remind the Kremlin of the risks which it must have already calculated, but to mobilize the support of leftist public opinion abroad and of the Cuban people, always responsive to external danger, in Fidel's increasingly bitter confrontation with the Russians.

It was, moreover, a confrontation of rare complexity, since there were limits beyond which neither side could afford to go. The Soviet dilemma was a difficult one. On the one hand, their wayward Cuban client was using the resources placed at his disposal by the Soviet Union to undermine Soviet relations with the rest of Latin America, to threaten their policy of détente with the United States, to challenge their Marxist ideological hegemony, and to engage in increasingly irrational and costly economic experiments. On the other hand, at a distance of six thousand miles from Cuba, which in turn was less than one hundred miles from the United States, the Soviets could not easily discipline Fidel Castro without endangering their enormous political and economic investment in the Cuban Revolution. For Fidel, the constraints were also difficult to overcome.

2. On February 13, with malice aforethought, *Granma* carried a glowing account of progress in Soviet oil production, translated from an article in *Pravda* on February 6, 1968. Entitled "The Torrent of Petroleum Increases," the *Granma* version reported the overfulfillment of the production plan by close to ten percent in 1967, and predicted a further increase of more than nine percent in 1968 over the 1967 total. What the Cuban press had carefully overlooked was an earlier *Pravda* article (noted in *Le Monde*, December 30, 1967) entitled "Petroleum Bridge Across the Ocean." It told of the extraordinary effort required to supply Cuba with oil since 1960, and claimed an unblemished record in meeting delivery commitments. "At the present time," *Pravda* added, "Cuba is the largest consumer of Soviet petroleum among socialist countries."

3. *Granma*, January 3, 1968.

Fully aware of his geopolitical value to the Soviets, he had in effect black-mailed Moscow over the years to underwrite the costs of his guerrilla in-cursions in Latin America, his economic eccentricities in Cuba, and the worldwide promotion of his Marxist heresies. At the same time, his immu-nity from Soviet pressures was not absolute, as he realized. He could not push his provocations to the point where the Russians, as the lesser of two evils, might apply sanctions even at the risk of crippling his regime.

A New Soviet Ambassador

In mid-January, Moscow announced that it was replacing Alexandr Alex-eiev, Soviet ambassador to Cuba since 1962, with Alexandr Soldatov.[4] This was another signal that the Kremlin's attitude toward Castro was hard-ening. Alexeiev was a journalist and one-time press attaché at the Soviet embassy in Montevideo. He was fluent in Spanish and immediately on ar-rival in Havana had flattered the Cubans by adopting an informal, shirt-sleeved, backslapping, "revolutionary" style of diplomacy—unconven-tional behavior for a Soviet diplomat, to say the least. Soldatov, on the other hand, was a high-ranking, no-nonsense professional, who had only recently completed a tour of duty as ambassador to Great Britain.

The Microfaction Exposed

On January 28, almost as if in response to the Soldatov appointment (he did not assume his post until May), Havana was startled by the news of the expulsion of two prominent members from the Cuban Communist Party's central committee, one of whom was also expelled from the party along with nine rank-and-file members. This was followed on February 3 by the more ominous announcement that thirty-four individuals, including seven of the expelled rank-and-file Communists, had been sentenced to prison terms ranging from three to fifteen years.[5] They had been convicted by a "Revolutionary Tribunal" of belonging to a "microfaction," as it was called, engaged among other crimes in "clandestine propaganda against the line of the Party" and efforts to "undermine Cuba's international relations with other governments." What gave special importance to their crimes, it was stated, despite the fact that the culprits "are unknown to the people and to-tally divorced from the great tasks . . . of the Revolution," was the fact that

4. *El Mundo*, January 17, 1968 (TASS dispatch of January 15).
5. Another defendant was placed under house arrest for two years, making thirty-five convictions in all.

"their arguments and positions coincided with those adopted by the pseudo-revolutionaries [pro-Soviet Communist parties] of Latin America and the CIA," thus placing the group "within the context of those who oppose the Revolution."[6] Apparently to underscore the international implications of the punishment inflicted on the microfaction, it was simultaneously announced that Cuba would not participate in the forthcoming Soviet-sponsored meeting of Communist parties to be held in Budapest.

The criminals were not exactly "unknown to the people," as the central committee claimed. The leader of the group was none other than the notorious Aníbal Escalante, a key figure in the "old" Communist Party and the PSP, whom Fidel entrusted in 1961 with the task of organizing a new party that would "integrate" the membership of the PSP with that of Fidel's Movement of July 26 and the revolutionary student Directory. In March 1962, in a public scandal of major proportions, Castro accused Escalante of placing control at all levels of the new organization in the hands of the "old" PSP Communists and attempting to establish Soviet-style supervision over the government bureaucracy. His crime at that time was described as "sectarianism," and his punishment, without benefit of trial, was banishment from Cuba. Not unexpectedly, Escalante found comfortable shelter in Moscow. After his departure from Havana, a discreet purge of "old" Communists took place in the upper levels of the bureaucracy.

The Escalante affair of March 1962 revealed the first symptoms of Cuban-Soviet friction. This was followed by even greater friction at the time of the October 1962 missile crisis, when Khrushchev, bowing to President Kennedy's demand, agreed to remove his lethal weapons from Cuba without consulting Castro. Then came the reconciliation between the two Communist leaders, highlighted by Castro's trips to the USSR in May 1963 and January 1964. It was after Castro's second visit that Escalante was permitted to return to Cuba to work as the manager of an experimental poultry farm near Havana.

Now, in early 1968, still firm in his orthodox Marxist-Leninist convictions and unresigned to the ruinous heresies of Castro's regime, Aníbal Escalante was once more in the limelight (he received the maximum fifteen-year prison sentence), sharing it with a group of faithful "old" Communists who had survived the purge of 1962. However, more was at stake for Fidel than in 1962. Internally, the near-total mobilization for agricultural labor of an increasingly weary and deprived population required drastic disci-

6. "Report of the Central Committee of the Communist Party of Cuba," *Granma*, January 28, 1968.

pline as well as unending exhortation. Externally, relations with the Soviet Union had deteriorated substantially. Although belittled as a "micro" faction, Escalante and company had "macro" potentialities. Hence the elaborate trial and severe punishment of the dissenters, and the public exposure given to the proceedings.

The Evidence Presented

As related in the press, prior to the convening of the Revolutionary Tribunal, the "Central Committee of the Communist Party of Cuba" met to hear the evidence and deliberate on the case, a task on which it spent three full days. Never before had the public been informed that a meeting of the central committee had taken place since that body had first been created, handpicked by Fidel in October 1965. In fact, this might well have been the first meeting after that date, since the central committee's role in Fidel's scheme of things was at the time largely decorative.

The report released to the public was a document of some fifty thousand words, featured in three installments in *Granma* on three consecutive days (January 29–31). It had been presented by Fidel's brother Raúl, in his capacity as chairman of the central committee's commission on the armed forces and state security. Fidel himself had spoken for an all-time record of twelve hours on the last day of the meeting;[7] but in an unusual deviation from custom, not a word of what he said appeared in the press. The presumption was that he had dotted the "i's" and crossed the "t's" of Raúl's exposure of Soviet complicity with the microfaction and had otherwise brought to light details of Soviet misconduct which, if made public, could have forced the Kremlin to risk an open and severe reprimand of the Castro regime, or even a break in relations.

A Critique of the Castro Regime

Nevertheless, what Raúl revealed was damaging enough. During more than a year that the group had been under systematic electronic and photographic surveillance by security agents, the defendants had held numerous clandestine meetings with Soviet and East German officials stationed in Havana. To summarize Raúl's voluminous accounts of what transpired at the meetings, it appeared that the defendants gave detailed information on the state of the Cuban economy and warned of approaching disaster. They condemned both the domestic and international policies of the Cas-

7. He began at "12:20 P.M. and, with brief recesses, finished after midnight" (ibid).

tro regime as fundamentally anti-Communist and anti-Soviet. Furthermore—and even more unpardonably—they urged the Russian and German comrades to impress on their governments the seriousness of the
Castro aberrations and the need to apply corrective measures against the
Cuban leadership.

From the evidence presented, it seemed clear that with the exception
of Aníbal Escalante, who might also have had ambitions to be restored to
leadership after a crackdown by the Soviets, the members of the microfaction had been motivated by a genuine conviction that the Cuban Revolution had abandoned Marxist-Leninist principles and was heading toward
political and economic bankruptcy. "The likelihood of producing 10 million tons [of sugar] in 1970," they were quoted as having advised the Kremlin, "is almost impossible. . . . The financial system, . . . combined with
moral [work] incentives, with absolute disregard of material incentives,
. . . results in stagnation of production. Voluntary labor is called upon to
increase production goals, [leading] to production of inferior quality. The
role of the trade unions in this stage of the construction of socialism is ignored. . . . As a consequence, all of this induces a general sense of uneasiness in the working class."[8]

Leftism, Adventurism, and Personalism

At a luncheon with the captain and the political commissar of a Soviet
fishing vessel, a defendant was reported to have said: "Tell them [in Mos-
cow] that the principal leaders of this Revolution and the Party have no
Communist education. The majority were [originally] anti-Communists.
The Party is penetrated by the petty bourgeoisie. There is a leftist, adventur-
istic deviation . . . running the country; they think that Cuba is the hub of
the universe. . . . They are investing the dollars we earn . . . through the
daily efforts and sacrifices of our workers . . . in supporting anti-Communist policies in all of Latin America and in other continents, in attacking
the Soviet Union and Communist Parties of every country."[9]

The most imprudent "revelations" concerned Fidel himself and the
departed and revered Ché Guevara: "The problem is that Fidel wants . . .
to rise to a higher stature . . . than that of Marx, Engels, and Lenin. . . .
Hence, we have to invent new propositions in philosophy, economics, and
politics. . . . [The Central Committee] never meets. . . . Policy is decided
by one man, Fidel Castro. . . . There is no opportunity for discussion or
expressing opinion." At another point, Raúl noted that one of the mis-

8. *Granma*, January 30, 1968.   9. Ibid.

creants declared that "Ché had crippled the economy, . . . had installed a technocracy in the country . . . with Trotskyist technicians from Latin America, that the best thing he did was to leave [Cuba]. . . . Fidel Castro, after censuring Ché, adopted his line. . . . No one could understand Fidel, he was crazy."[10]

The Definition of Treason

Part of Raúl's report was devoted to confessions by some of the microfactionists. The credibility of the report—and of the state security system's efficiency—was further buttressed by a full page of pictures described as "photos of the activities of the microfaction taken during the investigation."[11] Moreover, many sophisticated Cubans with no affection for the Soviet Union could not doubt that the views expressed by the microfaction were genuine, because these views voiced doubts and apprehensions about Fidel's rationality which at the time they themselves shared to one degree or another but prudently kept to themselves. Perhaps this explained Castro's decision to expose to public view a detailed account of the microfaction's blistering critique of his governance: such an account catalogued the full range of dissenting opinion, ostensibly "within and for the Revolution," but deemed to be treasonable. Henceforth, there could be no mistake that only total and unquestioned conformity with Fidel's "line" and authority would be tolerated.

As far as Moscow was concerned, with several thousand Russian and East European technicians working in Cuba and scores of KGB operatives roaming at will, it is doubtful whether the microfaction revealed anything of importance about the state of affairs on the island which the Kremlin did not already know. The purge, however, must have helped to convince the Soviets that Fidel's KGB-trained secret service was highly competent, that the Maximum Leader's grip on the country was as firm as ever, and that any encouragement of subversion would be counterproductive.[12]

The Paradox of the Microfaction

In retrospect, there is no lack of irony in the fact that perhaps the main crime of the microfaction was that its indictment of Fidel Castro was pre-

10. Ibid.   11. *Granma*, February 3, 1968.
12. Prior to the incident of the microfaction, I recall speculation in Havana that the KGB might attempt to eliminate Fidel, physically or otherwise, and have him replaced by Raúl (always considered to be closer to the "old" Communists than his brother) or by some other military figure more amenable to Soviet guid-

mature. It correctly predicted the outcome of the 1970 sugar harvest and the near collapse of the Cuban economy. Shortly thereafter, Fidel himself implemented the objectives of the microfaction by abjuring the heresies which it attacked and surrendering to Soviet economic, political, and ideological orthodoxy. It is even more astonishing that Castro later described the source of his errors in terms reminiscent of the microfaction's critique of his personal shortcomings. As noted in an earlier chapter, at the first congress of the reconstituted Cuban Communist Party, held in late December 1975, he admitted that in running our economy "we [*sic*] have unquestionably fallen into errors of idealism, and on occasion [*sic*] we have ignored the existence of objective economic laws. . . ." He further acknowledged that he had been infected by the "germ of chauvinism and petty bourgeois spirit . . . [which] foster attitudes that might be labeled arrogance and an overdose of self-esteem."[13]

---

ance. The trial demonstrated that the Cuban security apparatus was fully capable of protecting Fidel and that neither Raúl nor a suitable substitute was available. Juan Arcocha, a novelist who abandoned Cuba in the late 1960s, wrote an amusing "thriller" in which the CIA, assisted by the head of Cuban security, foiled a plot by the KGB to assassinate Fidel (*Operación Viceversa* [Madrid: Ediciones ERRE, 1976].

13. *The First Congress of the Cuban Communist Party*, Information Roundup, *Prensa Latina* (Havana), n.d., p. 22.

34

■

"The Profound
Revolutionary Offensive"

An Awkward Speech

WITHOUT GASOLINE, ON FOOT, AND WITH DIGNITY. EVERYBODY AT THE
UNIVERSITY PLAZA. MARCH 13 AT 7 P.M. This was the portentous legend
printed on fliers distributed in the street and in public buildings of Havana
on the eve of the mass meeting in March 1968. As always, Fidel would
speak on this anniversary of the day in 1957 when the Student Revolutionary Directorate launched a suicidal attack on the presidential palace in a
vain attempt to assassinate Batista.[1] Fliers, however, were scarcely needed
to assure a large audience for Fidel's speeches. Although spontaneous attendance had declined over the years, the mass organizations could be re-

---

1. Had the coup been successful—and it very nearly was—it almost certainly
would have changed the course of Cuban history. The Directorate, led by the charismatic José Antonio Echeverría who lost his life on that day, and Fidel's movement had been arch-rivals. Fidel, recently arrived in the Sierra Maestra and struggling to survive, issued a statement condemning the "putschist" tactics of the
Directorate, although he must have been relieved at the failure to eliminate Batista. Otherwise there would have been no credible reason for him to carry on his
guerrilla campaign. Far away from Havana and with only a handful of ill-equipped
and inexperienced armed followers, he would have been ignored by the Directorate as it negotiated to set up a new regime with anti-Batista political and military
leaders. When Fidel finally triumphed, he astutely incorporated the remnants of
the Directorate into subordinate government positions and assimilated the
"putsch," now remembered as a supreme example of revolutionary heroism, into
the official celebration of Cuba's revolutionary history. For a full account of this period, see Ramon L. Bonachea and Marta San Martín, *The Cuban Insurrection
1952–1959* (New Brunswick, N.J.: Transaction Books, 1974): 451 pp.

lied upon to guarantee the proper turnout to fit the occasion and the available space. Hence, the function of the fliers was to prepare the people for an exceptionally important announcement by the Maximum Leader, and the legend clearly suggested that more discipline and greater hardship were in store for the population. And so it turned out to be.

Fidel began his address at 9 P.M. and finished at 3 A.M. with the inevitable slogan "Patria or Muerte, Venceremos" (Fatherland or Death, We Shall Overcome). Not for years had he spoken at a public meeting for so long and so far into the night. In the early days, when both he and the Revolution were younger, these marathon performances were remarkable for his unflagging virtuosity and the sustained enthusiasm which he aroused. Now, he and his listeners grew visibly weary as the hours rolled by. There were moments of sharp attention when he announced the end of all private enterprise or when he spoke of the recent discovery of oil (which turned out to be a mere trickle) a few miles from Havana,[2] but boredom set in when he recited mountains of economic statistics and fumbled among the papers from which he read. Now and then, he strained to inject revolutionary fervor and optimism into the generally dark picture of unrelieved

2. "There is petroleum in the subsoil of our country," he said. "Our problem is to drill [more wells] and this we are making a determined effort to do." With the Russians at this time unwilling to become involved, Fidel struck a deal with Rumania to provide the necessary funding and technology. This led to a surge in "fraternal" relations with Rumania, signaled by the first visit to Havana, in February 1968, by a high-level delegation of the Rumanian Communist Party (*Granma Weekly Review*, February 9 and 20, 1968). In a speech on April 19, Fidel praised Rumanian drilling equipment and generosity in granting Cuba a "credit of 30 million pesos [at the time the equivalent of $30 million] . . . in very favorable conditions for our country" (*Bohemia Havana*, 17 [April 26, 1968], 48). It was the first Rumanian credit to speak of, since Rumania, alone among Soviet-bloc countries, had always resisted Moscow's pressure to contribute to subsidizing the Cuban economy. The shift in Rumania's attitude at this time was a function of its independent stance vis-à-vis Soviet foreign policy. Solidarity with Cuba now meant non-conformity with the Kremlin. The Cuban-Rumanian honeymoon, however, was short-lived. The following August, Cuba supported and Rumania opposed the Russian invasion of Czechoslovakia, and in due time drilling for oil was abandoned. Production was statistically insignificant. After the post-1970 Soviet-Cuban reconciliation, the Russians conducted unsuccessful onshore and offshore explorations. In 1975 it was announced that the Soviet Union would build a nuclear power plant in Cuba, due to go into operation by 1985. See *Area Handbook for Cuba*, pp. 23, 403, 410. For a full account and analysis of the nuclear power project, see Jorge F. Pérez-López, "The Cuban Nuclear Power Program," *Cuban Studies* 9, no. 1 (January 1979), 1–42.

shortages of consumer goods which he projected, but those who faced him seemed to be less moved than usual by the familiar exhortations—and in need of sleep. For the first time, perhaps, listening to Fidel was an ordeal.[3]

A Difficult Assignment

In fairness to Fidel, his task on that evening was unusually difficult. It was the tenth year of the Revolution, the "Year of the Heroic Guerrilla," so named to arouse emulation of Ché Guevara's revolutionary dedication, but public morale in Havana was visibly declining. First, there was the shock of gasoline rationing (in "underdeveloped" Cuba, there were still many thousands of ingeniously patched-up American cars congesting the streets and highways), followed by the microfaction trauma. At the same time, deliveries of supplies to grocery stores were becoming erratic. As a result, there was not enough to satisfy rationing commitments, causing long lines of customers to form before dawn waiting for the stores to open. Then, in late February, the already skimpy rations of milk for Havana's adult population were officially suspended for an indefinite period. Meanwhile, there was no relief in sight from the increasingly heavy burdens of "voluntary" labor in the cane fields, to which was now added a massive coffee planting project (destined to produce no coffee) on the outskirts of Havana.

Nor was there anything in Cuba's foreign relations to inspire confidence in the future. *Granma* continued to beat the drum of guerrilla warfare in Guatemala, Colombia, and Venezuela; but after the debacle in Bolivia, most Cubans were skeptical about further commitments to what appeared to be a lost cause. Much was made in the press of Cuba's success in obtaining credits in Britain and France for the purchase of industrial and transport equipment. To be sure, this represented a victory over the Ameri-

---

3. It was the last time I heard Fidel speak, having left Cuba six weeks later. In my notes I wrote: ". . . in contrast to importance placed on event and impressive mobilization of the masses, the speech was poorly organized and excessively rambling . . . extravagant use of time and effort . . . especially symptomatic of organizational and administrative shortcomings was presentation of economic data . . . perhaps Fidel doesn't have people capable of putting data together properly . . . or he doesn't give them time . . . or he is unaware of the mess he is handling . . . or there is no one sufficiently bold to explain these matters to him . . . or he is basically unteachable in this area . . . after nine years of speeches improvised or semi-improvised, despite the benefits of spontaneity, the law of diminishing returns is beginning to operate." I was wrong about the "law." Fidel recovered nicely and went on giving spell-binding speeches, in Cuba and abroad, for many years.

can trade boycott.[4] However, these credits would not significantly reduce Cuba's overwhelming dependence on the Soviet Union for petroleum, wheat, and a host of other edible and consumer goods, as well as machinery and equipment. The Russians were not popular in Cuba, and Fidel could be applauded for insulting the Russians so long as there were no reprisals. Now there was concern that Fidel was pushing things too far. The harsh punishment of the microfaction raised little sympathy for the victims, discredited by their allegiance to Moscow, but it revealed an ominous sharpening of Fidel's conflict with Cuba's indispensable benefactor.[5]

The Problem of Milk

Thus, Fidel felt constrained to assume a defensive posture when he began his speech. He explained that he proposed to deal with what he bluntly called the "circumstances of protest . . . discontent . . . confusion . . . malaise . . . anxiety . . . [and] uncertainty" which he observed in the population.[6] These he attributed partly to rumors but also partly to "real difficulties." It was the latter that led him to a formidable exposition of statistical data on the "problem of milk": he talked about whole milk, powdered skim milk, condensed milk, production, imports, and consumption; some figures he cited in millions of litres, others in tons, and still others in cartons; and some items he listed by years since 1959, others by provinces, and still others in terms of daily rations by age groups. It is doubtful whether Fidel himself (or those who supplied him with the data) fully understood the "problem of milk," except that there was not enough of it, since at no point were the various types and quantities converted into the equivalent of a common substance, such as whole milk, with a common standard of measurement in either volume or weight. As a result, the great mass of data was wholly unintelligible.

But this was probably overlooked by an audience largely unsophisti-

4. The United States, for example, unsuccessfully protested a British grant of an export credit of $45 million for the construction of a fertilizer plant (*New York Times*, February 7, 1968). Among other items breaching the boycott were French trucks and bulldozers, Japanese port equipment and passenger buses from England and Spain.

5. In his speech, Fidel specifically referred to the trial of the microfraction. "It is possible," he said, "that the need to ration gasoline . . . combined with the meeting of the Central Committee . . . which severely condemned the microfractional elements . . . contributed in creating a certain feeling of uneasiness and uncertainty."

6. All citations are from *Granma Weekly Review*, March 15, 1968, which carried the full text as well as nearly a score of tables.

cated in matters of statistics, and hence the bewilderment and boredom which Fidel inflicted on his listeners could be tolerated as an earnest demonstration of the complexities of a "real problem," his untiring efforts to grapple with them, and his complete candor in exposing them. While Fidel's excursion into statistics was not a deliberate effort to confuse his fellow countrymen, its essential purpose was to appeal for continued confidence in his leadership. At one point in the speech, he said: "To what extent are we [am I] responsible . . . for these real difficulties? Only in the future will it be possible to tell. The important thing is the conviction by all of us . . . that at every moment and in every circumstance . . . we [I] have tried to do the best possible." Over the years, it was this conviction, to a considerable extent induced by the sheer magnetism of his personality, which helped enormously in binding the Cuban people to him.

More Statistics

There were more columns of figures that Fidel inflicted on his audience: rainfall in fractions of millimeters, by province and season, to show the effect of drought on the current milk crisis; the price of sugar on the world market from 1952 on, revealing a sharp decline since 1963 and consequently the need to curtail the purchase of milk products available only in the capitalist market.[7] Then he turned to eggs, beans, coffee, and other commodities; population growth by age groups; and government investment figures. This was followed by a lengthy dissertation, bulging with statistics, comparing production and income in the Third World and the developed capitalist countries.

For his weary and confused listeners, the upshot of this gargantuan

---

7. As Fidel pointed out, the average annual price of raw sugar, which had reached until then the all-time high of 8.48¢ per pound in 1963, steadily declined thereafter, falling below 2¢ in 1966 and remaining at approximately that level at the time of his speech. More than 90 percent of Cuba's convertible currency earnings depended on sugar exports. Prices began to rise again in 1969, at first gradually and then made a spectacular jump in 1974 to an annual average of nearly 30¢, declining rapidly in the following years (*Sugar Year Book*, [London: International Sugar Organization, 1976], p. 364). By early 1979, the level of daily price quotations was running under 8¢. While Cuba profited from the bonanza of the mid-1970s, the gains were less than they appeared to be because prices of imports were also inflated. By the end of the 1970s, the purchasing power of Cuban sugar exports in capitalist markets was probably close to what it was at the end of the 1960s. Despite some diversification of exports in the late 1970s, it is a safe assumption that Cuba's dependence on sugar for convertible currency has not diminished appreciably.

exposition of the domestic and world economies was nevertheless comprehensible, if not crystal clear: Cuba's "real difficulties" were due to weather conditions, the drastic decline of sugar prices on the world market, the state of underdevelopment which capitalism and imperialism had imposed on the country—and the heavy investment of resources destined to create a prosperous and just society in the not-too-distant future. For all his display of candor, and for all his modesty concerning history's later assessment of his contribution to Cuba's "real difficulties," Fidel gave no hint that, as of March 1968, mismanagement might have played a part in creating these difficulties (he would make the confession two years later).

A Great Leap Forward

It was long past midnight when Fidel's mood abruptly changed as he announced that the Revolution was about to make a great ideological leap forward. All remaining private commercial enterprise was to be abolished. "If there is something for which this Revolution can be reproached," he exclaimed, "it is not that it has been extremist . . . but that it has not been sufficiently radical. There is not a moment to lose in further radicalizing this Revolution. We must once and for all create a revolutionary people." Capitalism, parasitism, and exploitation of man by man, he said, had to be "dug up by the roots." This is what we understand Marxism to be, "the Marxism of Karl Marx." This is the kind of communism that "we are proclaiming here, . . . true communism." Two days later, the process of nationalizing what remained of the private business sector was under way.

A month later, *Granma* published a summary of the results thus far: 57,280 enterprises had been expropriated, including some sixty categories of establishments, among which were pushcarts dispensing fritters, bars, barbershops, hardware stores, laundries and cleaners, shoe repair shops, clothing stores, rooming houses, owner-operated buses, and various businesses classified under "industry."[8] They were all miniscule in size, owner-operated, and with few exceptions employed no help. Calculated as a proportion of the total value of the country's economic activity, their importance was statistically negligible. In terms of the effect on the victims and their customers, however, the expropriation was another story.

This was the first wholesale confiscation of private properties since the land seizures of 1963, and it was to be the last. A sector of capitalism, however, survived. It consisted of nearly 200,000 small farms which Fidel conveniently overlooked when he invoked his dedication to the "true com-

8. *Granma Weekly Review*, April 15, 1968.

munism." And with good reason. Although their efficiency suffered under state regulations, they still accounted for nearly all of the nation's tobacco, a diminished but still important export commodity, and a major proportion of domestic food production other than sugar. Besides, Fidel understood the attachment of a farmer to his land, and hence the political hazard of still another and total agrarian reform. Nevertheless, as far as the ownership of the means of production and distribution was concerned, *Granma* could boast that Cuba was now the most completely socialist or communist country in the world.[9]

The Motivation of the Revolutionary Offensive

No doubt, Fidel's "profound revolutionary offensive," as he described the measures taken against Cuba's remaining "mercantilist infrastructure," helped to reinforce his image as the world's paragon of Marxist conviction and leadership, and thereby further inflated his enormous self-esteem. Nevertheless, the "offensive" was not motivated by pure idealism, as he himself at one point revealed. What about the "famous subject of incentives," he asked. "We don't believe that you can create a communist man by encouraging his ambition [to satisfy] his individual appetites. . . ." Then, as if in an afterthought, he added: "For us it is not only a question of principle, but a real and objective question. . . . Are we going to provide incentives for people by giving them money when there is nothing to buy with the money?" This was a fleeting, but revealing, digression as he resumed his sermon on "moral values," stressing "dignity" and "honor" and reiterating his challenge to the powerful and cynical benefactor. Let us struggle valiantly, he declared, "to reduce to the minimum our dependence on everything that comes from abroad," which no one failed to understand meant the Soviet Union. "We have had the bitter experience of how this can be converted into a weapon against us," he added, without needing to mention petroleum.[10] Let us struggle, he repeated, "to obtain our independence to the maximum degree, whatever the cost may be!"

It was in this context, in which the "ideal" and the "real" were adroitly merged, that Fidel had finally decided to move against the petty mer-

9. In a front-page editorial, March 29, 1968. Petty private enterprise was restored in the 1970s.

10. Elsewhere in the speech he explained that "great efforts" were being made to save fuel with the result that "we have been able to divert a considerable [amount] . . . to the enormous task under way in agriculture." However, he added, the "situation is tense: our machines working around the clock are in a tight situation with respect to fuel and [lubricating] oil, but we are making maximum use of what we

chants. They were not simply an ideological eyesore on the Cuban scene. The services which they managed to perform, by "hook or crook," as it were, undermined the norms of austerity, sacrifice, and spartan discipline which the regime promoted for eminently practical reasons. It was imperative to maintain the kind of environment which helped to legitimize the mobilization of the population for unpaid labor in the field, for unpaid overtime in the factories and on the docks, and for enduring the vicissitudes of the confrontation with the Soviet Union. During the previous months, Fidel had on several occasions threatened to crack down on the "parasites," but it was a risk which he apparently hesitated to take. Experience had proved that substituting a state network for private enterprise would mean an immediate and sharp decline in services. Now, however, having faced up in his speech to the decline of public morale, he badly needed a scapegoat on which to place the major blame and inflict exemplary punishment. The time had come to make good his earlier threat.

Accordingly, with rising indignation buttressed by a great mass of data assembled by "party investigators," he lashed out against an "unbelievable" state of affairs: in Havana, "28.2 percent of private business is illegal [that is, unlicensed]. . . . 61.9 percent of fried-food stands are unsanitary. . . . Two-thirds of proprietors are in good physical condition [that is, are able to do manual labor]. . . . 18 percent obtain their raw materials on the black market or by theft. . . . Omelettes: cost of production, 11 centavos each; price charged, 30 centavos; profit, 173 percent." And so on. In Havana alone, he claimed, there were still "955 private bars, making money hand over foot. . . . And every day truckloads of women pass by [these bars] on their way to work in the Havana greenbelt [planting coffee] or to pick tomatoes in [nearby] Güines or somewhere else. . . ." A shameful and intolerable situation! The fact was that "we still have a whole layer of privileged people in our society who prosper on the labor of the rest of the population, who live considerably better than the rest, and who stand by while others work."[11]

---

have. . . . We are also making massive use of oxen, animal traction, and we must train oxen and learn how to handle them . . . if some day we'll have more problems with the supply of fuel, then part of the work done with machines we'll perform with oxen."

11. Running a small private business under Cuban conditions was also "work," and often hard work, but not by Fidel's definition. The really privileged sector of Cuba's socialist society, "living considerably better than others," was the upper bureaucracy, mostly hard working but inefficient.

The Comparison with China

Fidel's "profound revolutionary offensive" has sometimes been compared with Mao Tse-tung's "proletarian cultural revolution," which was nearing its climax at the time. Actually, the resemblance was superficial. The Chinese process was a great ideological and political upheaval (counterproductive, as it turned out) aimed at overhauling the basic institutions created by the revolution, including first and foremost the Communist Party itself, which underwent an extraordinary purge and loss of authority. Millions of people were involved in a struggle which took on some of the characteristics of a civil war. In Cuba, on the other hand, the masses were not consulted, much less participants, in Fidel's "profound revolutionary offensive." Not a shot was fired, not a drop of blood spilled. The expropriation of unorganized, defenseless petty entrepreneurs was accomplished by a simple decree. Within the context of Cuba's already excessively centralized state economy, an essentially minor adjustment was imposed by an entrenched and unchallenged dictatorship, with the importance of the adjustment inflated by rhetoric.

35
■

A Precarious Situation

A Wave of Sabotage

In April 1968, with the "profound revolutionary offensive" in full swing, Castro came forth with an equally profound historical statement. "The year 1959 marked the triumph of the rebellion," he declared, no more than that, "but the year 1968, . . . when an entire people became conscious of its historic duties, its most sacred obligations, its mission in the world, . . . the year 1968 marked the triumph of the Revolution. . . ." [1]

Paradoxically, it was in April that a wave of sabotage began to spread over the entire island. News of the damage had been largely suppressed in the media until Fidel, in a speech on September 28 (appropriately, the anniversary of the founding of the nationwide vigilance units known as the Committees for the Defense of the Revolution), felt it necessary to confront the problem openly, revealing some of the details, warning that the "class struggle continues," and promising that punishment would be "severe, implacable, and inflexible." [2] Altogether, he mentioned fifteen major incidents, starting with an attempt on April 6 to burn down a large coffee warehouse in Guantánamo, at the eastern end of the island, and concluding with arson on September 7 in the central clothing warehouse in Camagüey, several hundred miles to the west. Among the losses were large quantities of sugar, chemical fertilizer, poultry feed, hides, and leather, as well as the destruction of buildings, various types of machinery, equipment, and building materials. In one plant, he reported, "five acts of sabotage were reported this year, in addition to various suspicious incidents of negligence and other abnormalities." There were a score of lesser inci-

---

1. *Política Internacional*, 22–24 (second, third, and fourth trimesters, 1968), 88. The speech was delivered on April 9, 1968.
2. Ibid., pp. 278–279.

dents, he said, in state-operated retail establishments, hotels, cattle sheds, cigar factories, and coffee seedling nurseries. Finally, he stated that thirty-six schools, scattered across the island, had been set on fire. Significantly, in no case did he attribute the crimes directly to the CIA. Total damage ran into millions of pesos and thousands of dollars worth of goods imported from capitalist countries.

Juvenile Delinquency

There were other disturbing symptoms of demoralization that cast a shadow on the "indescribable enthusiasm"[3] with which the Cuban people were purportedly accepting the sacrifices imposed by the Revolution. In the same speech on September 28, Fidel announced that drastic measures would be taken against youthful dissenters roaming the streets of Havana. "In recent months," he said, "hundreds of young boys in various groups . . . have openly engaged . . . in criminal and intolerable activities." Among these he listed obtaining fourteen- and fifteen-year-old girls for sailors on shore leave from capitalist boats; trafficking in American cigarettes; ostentatiously strolling around with portable radios tuned in to imperialist propaganda; and committing various acts of vandalism such as breaking public telephones, damaging school property, destroying Cuban flags, and—the most outrageous sacrilege—tearing down posters displaying the likeness of Ché Guevara. The boys became so bold, Fidel added, "that they reached the point of gathering [in the center of town and in front of hotels] flaunting their lack of respect for our people. . . . What did they imagine? That we are living in a liberal bourgeois regime? No! There is not an iota of liberalism in us. We are revolutionaries, socialists, collectivists, communists!"[4] In the months to come, "liberalism" was to become one of Fidel's favorite terms of opprobrium in suppressing Cuban, and denouncing friendly foreign, writers who deviated one "iota" from an unconditional approval of his wisdom and management of the Revolution.

The Faltering Sugar Plan

However serious the problems of sabotage and of cynicism among the youth, they were overshadowed by those of the ailing sugar campaign. Thus, in a laconic communiqué on August 13, *Granma* announced the

3. This expression was used by Fidel's brother Raúl, vice prime minister of the nation and minister of the armed forces, in the main speech delivered at the 1968 annual May Day celebration (ibid., p. 124).

4. Ibid., pp. 282 and 283.

replacement of Orlando Borrego as minister of the sugar industry "to insure more efficient coordination in the execution of the sugar plan." The
wording, and the failure to mention that the ex-minister would be assigned
new duties, a customary statement in such a circumstance, clearly indicated that this was more than a routine dismissal. Nor was Borrego a routine bureaucrat. A veteran of the Sierra Maestra, he was handpicked by
Ché Guevara to be his deputy when Ché became minister of industries in
1961. Then, in 1964, in connection with the reorganization of Ché's cumbersome ministry, Borrego was appointed to head the new sugar ministry,
the key administrative post in the all-out effort to achieve Fidel's goal of a
ten-million-ton sugar harvest by 1970. Borrego's reputation over the years
was that of a dedicated, competent, and sometimes outspoken member of
Fidel's cabinet. That he was sent into disgraceful retirement probably had
less to do with his managerial shortcomings than with something like confronting Fidel with a sober appraisal of the shortcomings of the plan. For it
was now apparent that it was an impossible plan.[5]

"On May 28," as *Granma* reported on the next day, "Cuba reached
the figure of 5 million tons of sugar produced. . . ." Since the harvest was
drawing to a close, the final figure would be only slightly higher. What was
not mentioned was that the plan for 1968 called for eight million tons.
Coming after a harvest of a little more than six million tons in 1967 (the
plan called for 7.5 million), the decline was distinctly inauspicious. Altogether, there was nothing to celebrate in the record since 1966, the first
year of the plan, when only 4.5 million tons were produced, two million
short of the plan.[6] In part, the dramatic failure to fulfill scheduled production had been unwittingly built into the plan. The extraordinary diversion
of material and human resources in the process of clearing and preparing

5. Ironically, Borrego had exposed the enormous complexity of the undertaking several months after taking charge of the sugar ministry. In an article entitled
"Problems of a Ten Million-Ton Sugar Harvest" (*Cuba Socialista*, No. 44 [April
1965], 10–30), he identified the major agricultural, industrial, transportation, financial, and manpower bottlenecks to be overcome, as well as the magnitude of
planning and coordinating requirements. As an example of one aspect of what was
involved in the industrial sector, he mentioned that "investments just for [increas-
ing the capacity of] sugar mills represent more than 2,000 individual projects" (p.
22). However, he ended on an optimistic note, quoting Fidel in a speech delivered
six months earlier. "And I, for my part," Fidel had declared, "do not hesitate risking
once more my honor as a revolutionary in this Plan . . ." (p. 30). Unlike Fidel,
Borrego risked both his honor and his job.
6. Castro first announced the schedule of the five-year sugar plan (which was

hundreds of thousands of acres for new cane plantations, combined with the work of upgrading sugar mills, building new roads, installing drainage and irrigation facilities, and so on, meant the neglect of existing cane fields and the under-utilization of much of the newly cleared area. Thus, the original plan was in effect abandoned (after 1968, mention of it was taboo), and all effort was concentrated on a single objective: the harvest of 1970. As *Granma* explained, "conditions are thus being prepared for a tremendous advance in 1969, putting us within reach of our sugar goal of 10 million tons." The "advance" in 1969, as it turned out, further reduced production to 4.5 million tons while "preparing conditions" for a sugar yield of 8.5 million tons in 1970, significantly short of the goal.[7]

The Abuse of Equipment

One of the major obstacles that plagued the sugar campaign was the quality of human resources, which to a considerable extent consisted of poorly trained and insufficiently motivated workers. Neglect and misuse of equipment had been a problem from the start of the massive mobilization of manpower and machinery, but during the course of 1968 they became se-

---

in fact the *only* plan of Cuba's "planned" economy) in a speech on June 7, 1965. His figures were as follows:

Year	Plan (millions of metric tons)[*]	Real Output[†]
1966	6.5	4.5
1967	7.5	6.2
1968	8.0	5.2
1969	9.0 (implied)	4.5
1970	10.0	8.5
	41.0	28.9

[*]*Política Internacional*, 10 (second trimester, 1965), 272.
[†]Junta Central de Planificación, Dirección Central de Estadística, *Anuario Estadístico de Cuba 1973* (Havana, 1975), p. 124. Figures have been rounded. Cuba's first comprehensive five-year plan, on the Soviet model, was inaugurated in 1976.

7. The production figures released in Cuba for 1969 and 1970 were based on calculations which need to be explained. Traditionally, the Cuban harvest began in January and ended in April or May, the period of optimum sugar content of the cane. The crop year and the calendar year thus coincided. Beginning with the crop year of 1964, which saw an increasing reliance on "volunteer" amateur cane cutters, who were less efficient than professionals, the harvest period was gradually lengthened during the 1960s, starting earlier and ending later. As a result, the harvest of the official 1969 crop year actually began in October 1968, and with practically no interruption continued until June 1970. The end of the 1969 crop year

rious enough to impel Fidel to denounce the evil in his speeches. Thus, on one occasion he declared that although "we have a large number of machines, trucks, graders, bulldozers, [and] tractors, there is no doubt that we are still handling these machines . . . with the mentality of the time when the work was done with oxen alone. . . . People underestimate the importance of lubricating the machines, . . . of tightening nuts, things like that." Operators of heavy trucks came in for special mention. Some of them, he said, are "speed crazy," endangering lives. In addition, the vehicles "are not handled carefully, and as a result their productivity is reduced to 50 percent. . . . Often there are collisions, and this equipment is very expensive." Part of the blame he placed on "not high enough levels of technical preparation." The other part he attributed to something even more lamentable. "There are many persons," he complained, "who lack a sense of responsibility."[8]

A few weeks later, Fidel was again berating the abuse of equipment. "There are those who use machinery," he said, "and if a bolt drops out, put it beside the seat; if a cap is removed, they put that beside the seat; the accelerator is soon no longer an accelerator, but instead a wire to be pulled out; if a valve gets lost, a makeshift connection is made. And by the time we see it, a machine that cost 20 to 25 thousand in foreign exchange has become a piece of junk."[9] Further along in the same speech, he boasted that there were forty thousand tractors in Cuba as compared with seven thousand in 1959, an indicator of progress which he was fond of citing and

---

and the start of the 1970 crop year were recorded as falling in July 1969, *hence statistically helping to improve the official performance in the critical year of* 1970, but creating substantial differences between the output of crop and calendar years. In this connection, the authoritative London-based International Sugar Organization reported Cuban sugar production for the *calendar year* 1969 *as* 5.5 *million tons*, as compared with the Cuban figure of 4.5 million tons; and as 7.5 *million tons for* 1970, one million tons less than the Cuban figure. It should be noted that the previous Cuban record of 7.2 million tons in the 1952 crop year was achieved, as normally happened before the Revolution, during the same calendar year. In this case, there was no discrepancy between Cuban and I.S.O. statistics. See G. B. Hagelberg, *The Caribbean Sugar Industries: Constraints and Opportunities* (New Haven, Conn.: Antilles Research Program, Yale University, 1974), p. 134, Table 24, "Cuba: Sugar Manufacturing Data, 1951–1970," and passim. Hegelberg's study of the sugar economy of the region is a major contribution to the subject.

8. *Granma Weekly Review*, November 24, 1968. The speech was delivered on November 15.

9. Ibid., December 15, 1968. The speech was delivered on December 8.

which foreign commentators were apt to accept at face value. How many of the new tractors had become "pieces of junk," or were rusting for months on the docks, he did not say, but he complained about the "transportation bottleneck," which included the lack of "dock space for unloading" imported equipment. "So the problem is no longer a matter of obtaining machinery," he concluded, "but one of transporting it and using it correctly." Actually, the problem could have been more properly defined as conspicuously wasteful mismanagement, that is, a lack of coordination between investment outlay and the capacity to utilize it, for which the final responsibility lay with Fidel himself.

The Lack of Labor Discipline

While Castro condemned the destructive handling of equipment, Captain Jorge Risquet, minister of labor, struggled valiantly with the no less critical problems of the recruitment of agricultural workers and absenteeism. WASTING MANPOWER IS A CRIME AGAINST THE REVOLUTION was the headline in bold type with which *Granma* reported on a speech which Risquet delivered in Camagüey, a key province in opening new land for sugar cultivation. It was urgent, he declared, that "all men of working age [17 to 60 years old] in the rural areas" be incorporated into "stable production units," and he stressed the need for "daily checking . . . of attendance at work and fulfillment of the eight-hour day." With these measures, he argued—bluntly—that "the present production of our labor force will be doubled."[10]

Toward the end of the year, tucked away in the text of a full-page illustrated *Granma* report extolling the phenomenal deeds of the "Ché Guevara Trailblazers Brigade," was a paragraph that unexpectedly provided some idea in more detailed quantitative terms of how the combination of poor handling of equipment and poor work attendance affected performance. Describing the virtues of a new "time-control" board recently adopted, the report cited the daily "record of a certain [unit] . . . for one complete month." The figures revealed that "stoppage of equipment because of breakdown" and "other causes" resulted in the unit having "worked only 1,421 hours—33 percent of the plan—with 114 machines, instead of the scheduled 4,220 hours with 211 machines."[11]

10. Ibid., August 4, 1968.
11. Ibid., December 1, 1968. Fidel himself inaugurated the start of the "Trailblazers" massive land-clearing operation in November 1967 with a grandiose

The Problem of Sugar Exports

In addition to the domestic problems that Fidel faced, the failure to meet his export commitments to the Soviet Union was perhaps even more embarrassing. According to the six-year agreement which he and Khrushchev solemnized in Moscow on January 21, 1964, Cuba was to deliver to the Soviet Union during the first four years (1965–1968) a total of slightly over fourteen million tons of sugar. In return, the Soviet Union was to credit the value of the sugar to Cuba's account at the then premium rate of six cents (U.S.) per pound (for the six-year period, the average world market price turned out to be less than 2.5 cents). With the exception of 1965, the annual deliveries fell far short of the agreement; and by the end of 1967, less than seven million tons had been shipped to the Soviet Union.[12]

For the year 1968, the agreement called for an export of five million tons, which, as has been noted, was the entire production for that year. To meet this commitment would mean that there would be no sugar left for domestic consumption and other markets, both socialist and capitalist. Thus, once more, as he had been forced to do in 1966 and 1967, Fidel had to eat humble pie and persuade Moscow to divert part of the Soviet quota elsewhere, particularly to the capitalist hard-currency market. In 1968, after his polemic with Moscow had become highly acrimonious, it must have been extremely distasteful for him to do so. As for the Russians, they had little choice in the matter. Their objective was not to ruin Castro but

---

display of simulated military fanfare. A year later, according to the *Granma* report, the so-called "brigade" numbered thirty-six units, "operating on six fronts," with five thousand men, some eight hundred and fifty bulldozers, and assorted lesser equipment. It was the most spectacular stunt of the sugar campaign.

12. The text of the agreement is in *Cuba Socialista*, 30 (February 1964), 165–1966. Exports of sugar to the USSR, planned and real, in millions of tons, were as follows:

Year	Planned	Real*
1965	2.1	2.5
1966	3.0	1.8
1967	4.0	2.5
1968	5.0	1.8
1969	5.0	1.3
1970	5.0	3.1
	24.1	13.0

*Hagelberg, *Caribbean Sugar Industries*, p. 116, Table 7: "Centrifugal Sugar Exports of Cuba by Country of Destination, 1950–1972."

to domesticate him. Cuba desperately needed the convertible currency earned in the capitalist market. At the same time, the other East European importers of Cuban sugar had insisted for a number of years on a balanced trade with the island. They were no longer willing to join the Soviet Union in subsidizing the Cuban economy, and on this point Moscow had deemed it wise not to insist.

Hence, the brunt of bailing out Castro fell on the Kremlin's shoulders. Of the total 4.6 million tons of sugar exported in 1968 (leaving approximately half a million tons for domestic consumption), the adjusted Soviet share was only 1.8 million tons (as against 2.5 million in 1967), while 1.4 million tons were allocated to each of the other markets.[13] For the socialist countries, this amount was only marginally less than that of 1967, but for the capitalist countries the reduction was substantial, on the order of twenty percent. Combined with the low price of sugar on the world market, the result for Cuba was an even greater loss of convertible currency earnings. Here again, dependence on the Soviet Union was critical, since, according to a long-standing agreement, the Russians paid for up to twenty percent of their Cuban sugar imports in dollars.

Altogether, the Soviet support of the Cuban economy in 1968, calculated in terms of the Cuban trade deficit, amounted to the equivalent of $325 million, as compared with $213 million in 1967. This raised the grand total of the Cuban trade debt to the Soviet Union beginning with 1962, the first year of large-scale deficits, to close to $1.5 billion, and the end was not in sight (the deficit in 1969 turned out to be $436 million).[14] Nor was this the full amount of the Soviet investment in the Cuban Revolution at the time. Among other items, the cost of supplying military equipment amounted to $1 billion or more, most if not all of it provided as an outright gift.[15] Thus, more than political and ideological considerations must have motivated the hardening of the Kremlin's attitude toward its

13. Hagelberg, *Caribbean Sugar Industries*, p. 116, Table 7.

14. Sources of data: for the 1968 deficit, *New York Times*, November 18, 1968; for the 1967 deficit, C. Paul Roberts and Mukhtar Hamour, eds., *Cuba 1968: Supplement to the Statistical Abstract of Latin America* (Los Angeles: Latin American Center, University of California, 1970), p. 169; total trade deficit calculated from *Anuario Estadístico de Cuba 1973* (Havana: Dirección Central de Estadística, 1975), p. 189; for the 1969 deficit, ibid.

15. In a speech on April 22, 1970, Castro said that Cuba had received "$1,500 million in armaments" from the Soviet Union (*New York Times*, May 10, 1970).

profligate satellite. For the Russians, financing Fidel's "profound revolutionary offensive" was something like pouring money into a bottomless pit, as he undoubtedly must have been made to understand. It was a ritual which they were not prepared to go on performing without something more than Castro's insults as their reward.

Castro's Dilemma

By mid-1968, if not earlier, Castro could hardly have failed to realize that he was in deep trouble. In the first place, he had lost much of his leverage in his relations with the Kremlin. In Latin America, a revival of Cuban-supported guerrilla warfare could be discounted; and the aftermath of the Cuban missile crisis had effectively removed the threat of an American invasion. Hence, the rhetoric on these issues had lost its credibility. In the second place, planned sugar production had fallen hopelessly behind schedule, and the diversion of resources into the sugar campaign was undermining the entire economy. Finally, the hardships imposed on the population by the frantic mobilization of manpower, the reduction of consumer supplies, and the years of postponement of the promised material rewards of the Revolution were unquestionably affecting morale.

The one hope remaining was that the miracle of a ten-million-ton sugar harvest in 1970 could be achieved. It was more than a hope. It was a political necessity. Desperately striving to impart confidence in his goal and to stimulate the efforts to achieve it, Fidel had again and again, ever more stridently, proclaimed that he had staked his honor and that of the Revolution on the outcome of the 1970 harvest. Fidel, so to speak, had painted himself into a corner. Even at the risk of a Pyrrhic victory—ten million tons of sugar and the rest of the economy in shambles—if only to save face, there was no turning back. However, without continued and even greater Russian help, and especially a larger supply of petroleum, the odds against meeting his goal would be overwhelming. Such was Fidel's precarious situation when events taking place in Czechoslovakia provided him with an opportunity to extricate himself from his dilemma.

36

■

The Complexities
of the Dilemma

A Strange Coincident

ON JANUARY 5, 1968, Antonin Novotny was removed from the leadership of the Czechoslovak Communist Party by a vote of its central committee, which simultaneously elected Alexander Dubček, a prominent figure in the Slovak branch of the party, to succeed him. This was the first formal step in a process designed to democratize and humanize a socialist regime that was characterized by the survival of rigid Stalinist norms of governance and by its notable servility in its relations with the Kremlin. Novotny's ouster thus had more than domestic implications and accordingly marked the beginning of a period of suspicion and then tension between Moscow and Prague. This led to the Soviet invasion of Czechoslovakia on August 20, 1968, and the end of what came to be known as the "Prague spring."[1] By a strange coincidence, Novotny's replacement by Dubček occurred at precisely the time of the most serious quarrel between Cuba and the Soviet Union since the missile crisis of 1962; and by an even stranger quirk of fate, the Soviet invasion of Czechoslovakia would inau-

1. "The Prague Spring can be considered the forerunner of Eurocommunism, and the Czechoslovak reformers . . . its forefathers in their attempt to create a model of socialism that, rooted in the Western tradition, differs from that of the USSR. As [Santiago] Carrillo, [leader of the Spanish Communist Party], . . . later stated: 'If the term *Eurocommunism* had been invented in 1968, Dubček would have been a Eurocommunist'" (Jiri Valenta, "Eurocommunism and Eastern Europe," *Problems of Communism* [Washington, D.C.], 27:2 [March–April 1978], 44–45.

gurate a momentous and lasting reconciliation between Cuba and the USSR.

Almost certainly, Fidel shed no tears when the news of Novotny's misfortune reached Havana. He was sufficiently well informed to know that Moscow would be apprehensive over the emergence of a new and less reliable leadership in Prague. At the time, he must have looked favorably upon a development which offered the prospect of diminishing the Kremlin's grip over one of its more obedient satellites. In addition, Fidel could have had no personal affection for Novotny, under whose regime Cuba had received shabby treatment in the exchange of goods between the two countries, as Fidel was later to reveal in a speech (which we shall examine in due course).

However, it was six weeks after Novotny's removal before the Cuban press provided the first inkling that profound changes were taking place in Czechoslovakia. On March 15, *Granma* published five brief dispatches from Prague, grouped together under a single heading. Citing the official Czech press agency CTK, the Cuban press reported the suicide of one high government official, the ouster of another, sharp criticism leveled against Novotny,[2] and a bitter attack against police brutalities in the past, "violating the fundamental rights guaranteed under the Czechoslovak constitution." The Cuban reports spoke of "progressives" and the "progressive line in the party," enclosing these terms in quotation marks to indicate that it was not *Granma* but the CTK which so defined the dominant trend in the Czech party. Nevertheless, despite the ostentatiously objective style of reporting the news, the Cuban reports apparently favored the "progressives," or at the least were in no way hostile to them. Certainly, Moscow could detect no support for its views concerning the upheaval in the Czech party, and perhaps a hint of Cuban satisfaction at the way things were moving in Prague.

Among the many other developments which *Granma* might have reported on but failed to do so were the already clearly visible problems arising in the relations between the Czechs, on the one hand, and the Russians and their East European supporters, on the other. On March 26, for example, after a meeting held in Dresden between the top leaders of Czechoslovakia, the USSR, Bulgaria, Poland, Hungary, and the German Democratic Republic, Dubček publicly stated that the other countries had collectively ex-

---

2. Novotny was forced to resign as president of the republic on March 22, 1968, and was expelled from the Communist Party on May 29.

pressed dissatisfaction with Czechoslovakia. And on the same day, the first open attacks directed against Czechoslovakia from the Soviet camp took place. In East Germany, a member of the Politburo accused the Dubček regime of "favoring the policies of Bonn"; while in Hungary, a Politburo member declared that the "reformists . . . were supported by right-wing anti-socialist forces."[3]

However, nothing of this—pretty much the heart of the "case" against Czechoslovakia—appeared in *Granma*. Charges of this serious nature by the highest authorities of two fraternal parties could not have been published in Cuba without some comment—that is, they had to be either approved or rejected. It would seem that, apart from the merits of the case, Fidel was in no mood to support Soviet pressures on another member of the socialist family, nor was he prepared to enlarge the area of polemics with the Soviets at a time when he had his hands full in managing his own problems with the Kremlin. Hence, there was silence in the Cuban press; but here again, from the perspective of the Kremlin's needs, the implications of silence could be disturbing.

Soviet Pressure Increased

Meanwhile, the basic issues in the Cuban-Soviet dispute remained unresolved. The long postponed trade protocol for 1968 was finally signed in Moscow on March 22. It called for a ten percent increase over 1967 in the value of the two-way exchange of goods, as compared with a twenty-three percent increase in 1967 over 1966, and with practically no increment in Soviet petroleum exports, as later figures revealed. Considering Castro's needs in 1968, the protocol reflected a punitive attitude on the part of the Russians. The ten percent increase was merely a token that would be useful for public relations purposes. In a statement released by TASS at the time, the Soviet vice-minister of foreign trade was quoted as saying that the USSR is making a sincere effort to satisfy Cuban needs more completely."[4]

In its public polemic with Castro, the Kremlin had invariably used surrogate spokesmen, mainly leaders of Latin American Communist par-

3. The chronology of events relating to the Czech crisis is taken from a report published in *Bohemia* (Havana), 33 (August 16, 1968), 68 ff.
4. *Le Monde*, March 24–25, 1968. There were only insignificant increases in Soviet exports to Cuba of both crude oil and oil products in 1968 as compared with 1967. In rounded figures, the combined total shipped to Cuba each year was 5.3 million metric tons (Arthur Jay Klinghoffer, *The Soviet Union and International Oil Politics* [New York: Columbia University Press, 1977], p. 204).

ties. Their criticism of the Cuban heresies, frequently sharp and direct, would initially appear in publications outside the Soviet Union and would then be reproduced without comment in the Soviet media as "news." However transparent this device might be for sophisticated readers, it avoided overt censure (which in a Communist regime would be tantamount to official censure) of its only protectorate in the Western Hemisphere—and which, therefore, the Soviet Union had to support and defend, willy-nilly. Hence, a departure from this practice would be significant, and that is precisely what occurred shortly before the signing of the commercial protocol.

On March 19, *Pravda* carried an article, written by the director of the authoritative Latin American Institute of the USSR Academy of Sciences, which was highly critical of Cuban efforts to promote armed struggle in Latin America. "Marxists," he wrote, "are convinced of the futility of imposing revolution from abroad." In the context of the article, there could be no doubt about who was the target of the criticism. However, contrary to Soviet convention where Cuba was concerned, the author chose to be explicit. "Cuba itself chose socialism without any foreign intervention," he argued, "and this is the best answer to those who speak of exporting revolution."

After Castro's defeat in Bolivia, this particular issue had lost much of its practical importance, and perhaps it was chosen for this reason. It was more than likely calculated as a warning, like the protocol but more explicit, that the Soviet Union was prepared to confront Cuba openly on other issues of more immediate consequence. Nevertheless, like the protocol, the article ended with the customary affirmation that the Russians were not relinquishing their responsibility toward the Cuban Revolution. The Soviet Union, the author maintained, "has helped and will continue to help Cuba in every way possible, thus insuring the failure of all attempts to strangle the revolution by military means or economic blockade."[5]

Flexibility in Washington

Whether the explicit reference to "military means" and "economic blockade" was merely the stereotyped rhetoric that would normally be used in a pledge to protect Cuba, or whether it carried other implications, is a matter of conjecture. As a matter of fact, the *Pravda* article appeared at a time when the deterioration of Soviet-Cuban relations had received considerable attention in the American press, leading to more than a suspicion that Washington was exploring the possibilities of exploiting this situation. On March 7, for example, the *New York Times* reported that Covey T. Oliver,

5. Cited in *Le Monde*, March 21, 1968.

Assistant Secretary of State for Inter-American Affairs, had discussed Cuban-American relations at a meeting on March 6 of a Senate Foreign Relations subcommittee. Replying to a question by Senator Wayne Morse as to whether or not the time had come for the United States to consider a "cautious resumption of nonstrategic trade" with Cuba, Mr. Oliver reiterated the U.S. government's long-standing policy that there could be no trade unless Cuba severed its military ties with the Soviet Union and abandoned her efforts to subvert other Western Hemisphere governments.

Nevertheless, there was a "hint" of potential flexibility in the American position in other remarks by Mr. Oliver, which led the *New York Times* correspondent to note that "diplomatic sources described Mr. Oliver's reply as having been phrased to promote discussion in Cuban ruling circles. . . . In view of Cuba's worsening economic conditions and strained relations with the Soviet Union, the diplomatic observers regard Mr. Oliver's testimony as more than usually significant." Thus, the final paragraph in the *Pravda* article two weeks later could also have been intended to be a signal to both Washington and Havana that the Soviets were not prepared to relinquish their presence in Cuba.

The Response from Havana

Both the *New York Times* dispatch and the *Pravda* article passed unnoticed by *Granma*, but Fidel responded obliquely a month later to the questions they raised, with no mention of the items themselves. In a speech on April 19, commemorating the seventh anniversary of the Cuban victory at the Bay of Pigs and mainly dedicated to matters of domestic interest, he managed to lead into an attack on Rodomiro Tomic, the Chilean ambassador in Washington. It was plainly a digression contrived for the purpose of striking at another target. The ambassador, he declared, was "a parrot trained by the Yankees [and] whom they are grooming to be . . . a candidate for president in Chile, *together with a little scheme for obtaining the support of the Communist Party of Chile*—a pro-Yankee candidate of the Christian Democratic Party. . . . It is evident that these lackeys of imperialism are doing very well. They have been accomplices of . . . every crime committed against Cuba. . . . Ah, but that doesn't matter! They are treated as decent persons, as progressives. *Reactionary bourgeois and oligarchs have even been pampered and showered with attention by governments which call themselves revolutionary.*" [6]

6. *Política Internacional*, 22–24 (second, third, and fourth trimesters, 1968), 114 (emphasis added).

This was something less than the "export of revolution" to which *Pravda* had objected, but it was precisely the kind of political provocation which Moscow was now trying to control. As Fidel remarked with heavy sarcasm: "We are not supposed to speak about these topics. If we do, then it immediately creates a scandal: 'Cuba is interfering in the internal affairs of other countries.'"[7] Then, on the heels of this message to Moscow, came a message to Washington. It has been suggested, Fidel said, that Cuba might do well to set up "a kind of tropical Titoism." How absurd, how ridiculous, he added, and then identified the source of the suggestion: "If the Yankees are dreaming about seeing a kind of tropical Titoism here, what they are going . . . to see is a real tropical communism. Because we are advancing resolutely toward our goal, . . . [which] we shall reach just as we have been able to withstand the blockade by the United States and the aggressions of imperialism. . . . If they are dreaming about tropical Titoism, they are ridiculous."[8]

The Meaning of the Response

If Mr. Oliver's testimony in early March revealed merely the tip of an iceberg, we have no way of knowing the dimensions of what lay submerged. We can only speculate whether Washington again bungled an opportunity, as it undoubtedly did in 1964, or whether this time, whatever Washington's intentions might have been, no real opportunity existed. Indeed, it is hard to imagine what Washington could have offered at a time when Castro's persistent and intensive exploitation of the American trade embargo and what he portrayed as the everpresent peril of American military aggression played an essential role in identifying his leadership of the Cuban people with a high level of patriotism. Particularly at this juncture, American hostility was a well-nigh indispensable psychological instrument in mobilizing the population for the "heroic" material and ideological tasks of the "profound revolutionary offensive."

7. Ibid. Tomic, candidate of the left-wing of the Christian Democratic Party, obtained his party's nomination for the 1970 campaign, but failed to win the election. With no candidate receiving a majority of the votes, Congress elected Salvador Allende, who was overthrown in 1973 by the military. Had Tomic been elected, Chile might have been spared the brutal dictatorship of General Pinochet. For the setting and results of the 1970 election, see Robert J. Alexander, *The Tragedy of Chile* (Westport, Conn.: Greenwood Press, 1978), p. 125 and passim. Alexander's book is a landmark study of the Chilean crisis.

8. *Política Internacional*, 22–24 (second, third, and fourth trimesters, 1968), 115.

Thus, a truce, let alone a normalization of relations, with the United States would have seriously jeopardized the momentum of the now irreversible "offensive" at a critical moment. At the same time, for Fidel it would have meant an unacceptable loss of face, not only domestically but also internationally. Perhaps the most damaging blow to his credibility would have been to accept an accommodation with the United States while the "monster," as he described it, continued to inflict death and destruction on Vietnam, whose cause he had embraced with extraordinary and unceasing fervor.

Quite likely, this is what Moscow concluded as it pondered over Fidel's statement on "tropical Titoism." Coupled with the derogatory remarks about the Chilean ambassador in Washington, the statement might have appeared at first glance as a signal to the Russians that Fidel had the option of accommodation with the Americans and could use it if the Russians pressed him too hard. If it had been Fidel's intention, however, to signal the Russians in this way, the option lacked credibility, and this assessment would be reinforced by the categorical terms with which he rejected the role of a "tropical Tito." More likely, at this point Fidel's intention was to reassure the Russians that, despite his Chilean digression, he had no intention of deserting the Soviet camp. It was thus a conciliatory gesture. Indeed, there were hints in the following weeks that, behind the scenes, Fidel and the Kremlin were bargaining over the terms for a settlement of their mutually unprofitable quarrel.

37

■

The Management of the Dilemma

Early Symptoms of a Thaw

BEGINNING IN MAY 1968, a significant decline in public manifestations of Cuban-Soviet irascibility could be observed. In the traditional May Day speech, this year given by Fidel's brother Raúl (an infrequent day of rest for the Maximum Leader), there was, surprisingly, nothing said that could irritate the Russians, even on a sensitive issue concerning the need to use petroleum economically.[1] Later in the month, it was reported that a Bulgarian trade mission, headed by the minister of foreign trade, had been in Havana and had advanced credit for the Cuban purchase of agro-industrial equipment. This was more than routinely noteworthy. In mid-January, elaborate preparations had been under way in Havana for the impending visit of Todor Zhivkov, leader of the Bulgarian Communist Party and head of the state.[2] However, the visit failed to materialize (a lame excuse was offered), undoubtedly because of Soviet advice, since the visit would have coincided with the climax of the microfaction scandal. Now, some four months later, the political climate had changed. To further underscore the change in climate, the minister of foreign trade was received by Fidel.[3]

Even more remarkable was the new and unexpected warmth in Cuban–East German relations. In a speech delivered in Oriente Province on May 30, Fidel revealed that the German Democratic Republic had grant-

---

1. *Política Internacional*, 22–24 (second, third, and fourth trimesters, 1968), 138.

2. *Bohemia*, 3 (January 19, 1968), 79.

3. *Granma Weekly Review*, May 26, 1968.

ed Cuba a 25-million-peso credit to acquire hydraulic and construction equipment "under advantageous conditions" for Cuba. Fidel went on to praise the Germans above and beyond the call of duty. "In the German Democratic Republic," he said, "they manufacture magnificent irrigation motors," and then he went on to recall that the "imperialists have tried in every way possible to blockade the German Democratic Republic, in the same way that they have tried . . . to blockade our country." To further emphasize the special status, indeed virtue, shared by both countries, and hence their "close bonds of economic cooperation," he expressed deep gratification that "today there is present among us a delegation of the German Democratic Republic, headed by a First Vice-Minister of Foreign Trade. . . . They have done us the honor of accompanying us today, in spite of the sweltering heat. . . ."[4]

Needless to say, the German Communists, like the Bulgarians, could not resume cordial relations with Cuba without clearance from the Kremlin, or what is even more likely, without the Kremlin's initiative. This, in turn, would not occur without a prior commitment, implicit or explicit, by Fidel to curb his public criticism of the Soviet Union and its affiliated parties in Latin America, as the record would appear to confirm. As for Fidel's solicitude for the East Germans, it was particularly conspicuous since five months earlier they had been specifically singled out as implicated in the crimes of the microfaction. Thus, Fidel's remarks signaled that all was forgiven, and in a sense were addressed to the Russians as well as to the Germans.

Several weeks later, there was further evidence of a thaw in Cuban-Soviet relations. On June 24, a Soviet exhibit on the peaceful uses of atomic energy was inaugurated at the Academy of Sciences in Havana. It was a rare event, and probably few of those present could easily recall when the last display of Soviet achievement had taken place. Ambassador Soldatov opened the show, which included a scale model of a nuclear reactor. This attracted special attention, since it was described as the type of reactor which the Soviet Union expected, at an unspecified date, to be set up in Cuba.[5]

Some Remaining Discrepancies

Despite the events already described, the Cuban-Soviet thaw was not yet complete. Cuba was one of only four countries which on June 10 rejected

---

4. *Política Internacional*, 22–24 (second, third, and fourth trimesters, 1968), 166.

5. *Granma Weekly Review*, June 30, 1968.

a United Nations draft treaty to halt the spread of nuclear weapons. The document had been jointly sponsored by the United States and the Soviet Union. However, Cuba had consistently voiced its objections during the several years that the topic had been under debate. Furthermore, voting with the United States on any issue at that time would undoubtedly have been excluded as a matter of general principle.[6]

In another vote at the United Nations two days later, Cuba's position again differed from that of the Soviet Union. The latter, along with a large majority of member states, supported a resolution concerning the independence of South-West Africa, to be known as Namibia. This time Cuba abstained. The Cuban delegate explained that while his country was in favor of the resolution in general, it could not support a paragraph referring to the eventual participation of the Security Council in obtaining the independence of the territory. As "a question of principle," he said, Cuba could not approve a decision which "tends to create illusions" concerning the effectiveness of the United Nations "as to the achievement of objectives that the Namibian people can win only through struggle."[7] Earlier in the debate, he had stated that "neither the General Assembly nor the Security Council, nor any other United Nations agency—all of which are under the ruinous influence of the United States Government—is in a position to safeguard the interests of the weaker nations."[8] Again, the Cuban vote had no practical significance for the Soviet Union, and Castro's effort to maintain a "revolutionary" image could be overlooked. As it turned out, this would be the last time for more than a decade, and very likely much longer, that Cuban and Soviet voting in the United Nations would not be identical.

Probably a matter of more importance to Moscow was Cuba's refusal to participate in the Ninth World Youth Festival held in Sofia, Bulgaria,

6. *New York Times*, June 11, 1968. The vote came at the end of a six-week debate in the General Assembly's Political Committee. Raúl Roa, Cuba's foreign minister, presented his case on May 17. The final vote was ninety-two in favor, four against, and twenty-two abstentions. In the words of the head of the Soviet delegation, the resolution was approved by "an overwhelming majority." Thus, Cuba's negative vote, shared by Albania, Tanzania, and Zambia, had no practical importance.

7. *Granma Weekly Review*, June 23, 1968.

8. Ibid., June 9, 1968. A few years later, when a coalition of Third World countries and the Soviet bloc created a solid majority in the UN General Assembly and the UN specialized agencies, Cuba changed its tune about UN intervention on behalf of "weaker states."

during the first week of August 1968. The decision, announced on June 28, stated that the Cuban Communist youth organization could not accept the orientation adopted by the festival authorities. Cuban youth, it was pointed out, supported the principle of revolutionary armed struggle as exemplified by the "spirit, teaching, and example" of Fidel Castro and Ché Guevara.[9] Although by this time the "principle" had become largely a matter of rhetoric, apparently Fidel, who undoubtedly made the decision, considered that Cuban participation would imply a reversal of a position that he was not ready to abandon at this time, at least not publicly and bluntly. Nor could he afford the risk of contaminating the militant "guerrilla" psychology with which he had mobilized Cuban youth in the drive for the giant sugar harvest of 1970. It was Cuba's first, and was very likely destined to be her last, withdrawal from the Moscow-backed international youth holiday. Nor could it have been predicted at the time that Cuba in due course would be host to one of these gatherings. The Eleventh World Youth Festival, as was noted earlier, was held in Havana in July 1978, with huge poster-portraits of Ché Guevara as the only remnant of the "spirit, teachings, and example" of bygone days.

A Significant Speech

Thus, areas of friction remained in Cuban-Soviet relations, although greatly reduced in scope and intensity. Meanwhile, it could be reasonably assumed that behind the scenes the two parties were engaged in some form of exchange of views concerning the basis for a mutually satisfactory and durable understanding. What transpired during this exchange was not public knowledge. However, a prefiguration of the terms on which Fidel proposed to settle his quarrel with the Kremlin could be detected in a speech which he delivered in Santa Clara, capital of Las Villas Province, on July 26, 1968. Always the occasion for a major pronouncement by the Commander-in-Chief, this year the date had special significance. It was the fifteenth anniversary of his attack on the Moncada barracks in Santiago, deemed to be the start of his insurrection and now enshrined in history. Hence, it was the appropriate moment to sum up the great achievements of the Revolution and its continued dedication to the unswerving and self-sacrificing support of the peoples of Latin America and elsewhere engaged in armed struggle against native tyranny, foreign domination, and imperialist aggression.

9. Havana Radio, as reported in the *New York Times*, June 29, 1968.

A Silent and an Audible Message

In part, Fidel followed the anticipated script. The extraordinary transformation and progress of Cuba since Moncada, he declared, proved that our "Revolution 's the most profound ever achieved by any people of [Latin] America. . . . And we accomplished this face-to-face with Yankee imperialism, the most powerful and aggressive bulwark of world reaction."[10] But what he did not say was more noteworthy. Missing was the invariable assertion of the universal validity of the Castro-Guevara armed struggle thesis, one of the pillars of Cuban revolutionary doctrine. There was no mention of guerrilla warfare or of the existence of guerrillas anywhere in Latin America—or in the rest of the world, for that matter. Even Vietnam was conspicuously absent from Fidel's speech. In short, he said nothing that even by implication could be construed as critical of the Soviet Union or the Communist parties in Moscow's orbit; and as if to balance this omission, he said nothing supportive of the Soviet Union either, omitting even the customary pro forma acknowledgment of Soviet assistance to the Revolution.

It was, so to speak, a silent message to the Kremlin, but it was also accompanied by an audible message. It amounted to an appeal for, and an offer of, mutual tolerance:

> Every people, every country, has its own way of making its revolution, . . . of interpreting revolutionary ideas. We do not claim to be the most perfect revolutionaries, . . . the most perfect interpreters of Marxist-Leninist ideas. But we do have our own form of interpreting these ideas, . . . of interpreting socialism, . . . of interpreting Marxism-Leninism, . . . of interpreting communism.[11]

The full message, deciphered, could read as follows: We are prepared to respect Soviet ideology and foreign policy in return for Soviet respect for our ideology and material support of our domestic goals.

This, indeed, turned out to be the basis for initiating the Soviet-Cuban reconciliation, but only after Fidel had to grapple with an issue of extraordinary complexity and urgency.

10. *Política Internacional*, 22–24 (second, third, and fourth trimesters, 1968), 232.
11. Ibid., p. 227.

38

■

The Dilemma Resolved

Unprecedented Coverage

SOME THREE WEEKS before Fidel's speech in Santa Clara, *Granma* began to give extraordinary coverage to the rapidly deteriorating relations between Czechoslovakia and the Soviet Union. During the month of July, for example, close to one hundred dispatches were published. As in the brief March series, they were short, factual, presented with studied objectivity, and without comment. The main sources were TASS, the official Soviet news agency, and CTK, the corresponding Czech agency, with a scattering of items originating in other East European countries. The numerical balance favored Czech and Czech-oriented (Rumanian and Yugoslav) dispatches by a considerable margin, and for the Cuban reader the balance of the information as presented almost certainly evoked more sympathy for the beleaguered Czechs than for their Soviet and pro-Soviet accusers.[1] Cubans could easily perceive the threat to the sovereignty of a small socialist country. They could only respond favorably to the Czech appeal for the right to choose their own road to communism, a principle which Fidel had frequently invoked and had emphatically reiterated in his

1. An enumeration of dispatches, with summaries of contents, appeared in the *Granma Weekly Review* on July 28 and August 4, 1968. A total of ninety-three items were listed. Their sources were as follows: TASS, 29; pro-Soviet Warsaw Pact countries, 6; CTK, 43; TANJUG (Belgrade), 7; AGERPRESS (Bucharest), 4; and PRENSA LATINA (Havana, originating in Prague and Bucharest), 4. Major coverage also appeared in the popular weekly magazine *Bohemia*, less than a week before the denouement of the crisis. The issue of August 16, 1968 (No. 33, pp. 68–74) carried a detailed summary of events starting with Novotny's removal from the leadership of the Czech Communist Party at the beginning of January. For the Cuban reader, the summary could only reinforce the impression created by *Granma*.

speech on July 26. The Soviet position that the Dubček regime was in the process of abandoning socialism and conniving with imperialism was unsubstantiated in the summary statements appearing in *Granma*, and hence unconvincing. In addition, the background of the controversy between Cuba and the Soviet Union would predispose the average Cuban against the Russians.

One can only speculate about Fidel's intentions, for on this issue of critical importance only he could issue instructions to the press for providing the Cuban population with this unprecedented access to information —unprecedented in volume, sobriety, and freedom from commentary. Was he acting in anticipation of a possible or probable Soviet determination to put down the Prague "mutiny" by whatever means were required? In this event, he would have to define Cuba's position and explain his decision to the Cuban people. Hence, the exhaustive coverage of the impending crisis can be viewed as preparing the population to support his decision. This might be a reasonable hypothesis. However, in view of the tilt of the news coverage, as it would have been perceived by the Cuban public, a position condemning the Russians is what would be expected from Fidel. The Cuban people would certainly have been much less prepared to approve a breach of Czech sovereignty. Since we know that in the end he supported the Soviet invasion, one wonders what he was really up to. Was he, for example, applying pressure on the Russians as part of an explicit or implicit bargaining process? Such an hypothesis cannot be discounted. In any case, Moscow must have been extremely unhappy with the performance of the Cuban press, and on the face of it could expect the worst if and when the showdown came.

The Invasion

Shortly before midnight on August 20, Prague time, Soviet troops and the armed forces of its Warsaw Pact allies (excluding Rumania) crossed the Czech frontiers, and a few hours later Russian tanks were in the center of Prague.[2] Because of the difference in time zones, the news reached Cuba shortly before dawn on Wednesday, August 21. However, it was not until

2. For a detailed account of the Czech crisis and its international repercussions, see Vojtech Mastny, ed., *Czechoslovakia: Crisis in World Communism* (New York: Facts on File, 1972). Also useful is A. G. Mezerik, *Invasion and Occupation of Czechoslovakia and the United Nations* (New York: International Review Service, 1968).

Friday night, August 23, more than sixty hours later, that Fidel pronounced judgment on the event over a national radio and television hookup.

Again, one can only speculate concerning the reason for the long delay, particularly since, up to the last moment, Cubans were given no inkling of the surprise that Fidel had in store for them. On the contrary, Thursday's edition of *Granma*, for example, carried a long statement of protest submitted by the Czech embassy in Havana, while Cuban radio and television transmitted the full statement of Rumanian President Nicolae Ceauşescu attacking the Russians, defending the right of the Czechs to build socialism their own way, and announcing that special measures of a military nature had been taken to safeguard Rumanian independence and security.[3] It will be recalled that at this moment Rumania enjoyed considerable prestige in Cuba. On the same day, some two hundred Czechs employed as technical experts in Havana, accompanied by a fair number of Cubans, paraded in the center of the city with banners reading: "Russians Go Home From Czechoslovakia." Cuban police cleared the way for the procession, which ended up at the Czech cultural center, where the Czech ambassador addressed the meeting.[4]

The regular edition of the popular weekly *Bohemia*,[5] on the street the day before Fidel's speech, added to the disorientation of the Cuban reader. It included an extraordinary sixteen-page supplement, inserted after the edition had closed early Wednesday morning. Interrupting the normal pagination of the magazine, the editors asked the forebearance of their readers because of the "urgency . . . of this international development which has such great importance for the world and Cuba."[6] The supplement, in addition to a brief factual summary of events from August 3 to the eve of the invasion, carried scores of postinvasion dispatches, mostly from Prague but also from Moscow and other capitals in various parts of the world. Again the tilt, as it surely would have been perceived by the Cubans, was predominantly anti-Soviet, reinforced by a whole column set off by a heavy black border detailing the Rumanian position, and by an Agence France Presse dispatch reporting that the Communist parties of France and Italy, "the most powerful in the west, condemned the occupation of Czechoslovakia."[7]

3. *Le Monde*, August 24, 1968.
4. *New York Times*, August 23, 1968; and *Le Monde*, August 24, 1968.
5. No. 34, August 23, 1968.
6. Supplement, p. 2.   7. Ibid., p. 13.

Likewise, an item from Montevideo, reproducing the Uruguayan Communist Party's statement of support for the Soviet Union, would only confirm the normal Cuban antipathy to Soviet aggression, since the Uruguayan party, along with the other Latin American Communist parties, had long been discredited in Cuba as Soviet puppets. There was some irony here, for the Uruguayan defense of the Soviet action was very close to the one that would be adopted by Fidel. On the other hand, there were a few details that probably puzzled some Cubans, such as the coincidence that there were Communist countries (Albania and Rumania, China having not yet been heard from) and important nonruling Communist parties (French and Italian) which shared the views of the United States and other "imperialist" countries. Cubans might also have been perplexed, if they were careful readers, by two small items near the end of the coverage, to the effect that the "Voice of Vietnam" (Hanoi) had transmitted and endorsed the official TASS statement justifying the occupation of Czechoslovakia.[8]

A Belated Speech

It was against this background that Fidel, on Friday night, August 23, finally presented what he termed his "analysis" of the "situation in Czechoslovakia . . . in the light of the revolutionary position and international policy maintained by our Revolution and our Party." He was seated at a desk facing a studio audience and the television cameras. Behind and above him hung an enlarged photograph of the head of Ché Guevara.[9] Serving as a holy image since his death, Ché's melancholy countenance was not a casually chosen prop, for Fidel's task was a difficult one, as he himself conceded in his opening remarks. "Some of the things we are going to say here," he began, "will be in contradiction with the emotions of many."[10] He also acknowledged that although "our people have a good deal of information about these events," they had thus far received "no . . . exposition of the position of our Party regarding these events—among other reasons because the events were still in progress, and we are not obliged to analyze each thing going on in the world every day. . . ." It was an awkward explanation both for the delay (the "other reasons" were left in the dark) and for the circumstance, which he neglected to mention, that the people had been given too much of the wrong kind of information. He then launched into a

8. Ibid., pp. 14 and 16.
9. Photo in *Bohemia*, 35 (August 30, 1968), 37.
10. All citations from the speech are from the complete text in *Granma Weekly Review*, August 25, 1968.

rectification of the information and the startling conclusion to which it led.

He had noted, Fidel said, as he studied the unfolding of the crisis, the "beginning of a 'honeymoon' between the Czech liberals and imperialism." At the same time, a "real liberal fury was unleashed: a whole series of political slogans in favor of [permitting] opposition parties to develop, in favor of openly anti-Marxist and anti-Leninist theses," amounting to the repudiation of the "governmental form known as the dictatorship of the proletariat." In addition, "certain measures were taken such as the establishment of a bourgeois form of 'freedom' of the press." Of course, he added, "all of this was linked to a series of unquestionably correct slogans," such as "democratization" and "the need to create their own forms for the development . . . of the socialist system in Czechoslovakia." This confused many people, he said, even "some European Communist Parties." By implication, perhaps, his explanation was a way of excusing the "confusion" of the Cuban people, though it raised the question of why the Cuban press had abetted, if not reinforced, the "confusion" for so many weeks.

Turning now to matters of foreign policy, Fidel said that there was clear evidence of "open rapprochement . . . toward the West." He read several press dispatches (hitherto kept from the Cuban people), such as one from early June mentioning discussion of a possible American loan to Czechoslovakia, and another from mid-June quoting the West German weekly *Spiegel*, which reported that "Prague, fearing economic reprisals from Moscow, turned recently to Bonn for a credit," and that there was a "possibility of a normalization of diplomatic relations between the two countries at the beginning of next year." Bonn, he reminded his listeners, "following our recognition of the German Democratic Republic, . . . promptly broke relations with us. . . ." In short, the Czech leadership was "in camaraderie with pro-Yankee spies, . . . with the agents of West Germany and all that fascist and reactionary rabble. . . ."

The Invasion Defended

From this and similar evidence, the conclusion was inescapable: "*Czechoslovakia was moving toward a counterrevolutionary situation, toward capitalism and into the arms of imperialism.*" As a result, "*we consider that it was absolutely necessary, at all costs, in one way or another, to prevent this eventuality from taking place. . . . Our point of view is that . . . the socialist camp has a right to prevent this in one way or another. . . . We look upon this fact as an essential one*" (emphasis added).

This was a faithful paraphrase of the heart of the "Brezhnev doctrine" as formulated in a long statement appearing in the *Pravda* of August 22.[11] To put it unkindly, it was one of Fidel's less decorous exercises in deceptive demagogy. Fidel was blunter than Brezhnev in admitting that the "sovereignty of the Czechoslovak State was violated" and could not be justified "from a legal point of view"—a shrewd diversion to bolster his credibility—but he accepted the Russian sophistry that the transgression was morally justified "from a political point of view." This was a cynical denial of bedrock principle concerning the inviolability of the sovereignty of small nations, Cuba first of all, which he had defended since the beginning of his regime, and which he again invoked years later to legitimize his military support of Angolan sovereignty endangered by South Africa and Ethiopian sovereignty trampled underfoot by Somalia.

For sophisticated Cubans, Fidel was no more convincing than for the world at large, and concerning the validity of some of his arguments they were apt to be more informed. After all, he had been no less guilty of obtaining credits from capitalist countries, such as England, France, and Italy, and in particular from fascist Spain, which had become Cuba's third largest trading partner, after the Soviet Union and China.[12] In fact, the Franco regime for many years had enjoyed complete immunity from unfavorable mention in the Cuban media. As for relations with the Bonn government, it was not Cuba that initiated the break,[13] as Fidel admitted, and had it not occurred there would have been no reluctance to accept West German credits. Some Cubans could probably remember that four years earlier Fidel had publicly offered to normalize relations with the United States.

11. The statement was entitled "Defense of Socialism: Supreme International Duty"; the English version was distributed in pamphlet form by Novesti Press Agency Publishing Press, Moscow, n.d., 26 pages. Fidel may or may not have seen the statement before his speech, but he undoubtedly had the gist of the argument even before the invasion.

12. By 1966, the volume of Cuban trade with Spain ($107.7 million) had surpassed that of any European socialist country except the USSR. Trade with Czechoslovakia ($83.6 million) was in fourth place (*El Comercio Exterior de Cuba y Sus Tendencias* [Havana: Ministerio de Comercio Exterio, 1967], pp. 73–75).

13. In 1963, under the so-called Hallstein doctrine, the German Federal Republic automatically broke diplomatic relations with any country that recognized the German Democratic Republic, as Cuba had done. "West Germany," Castro said in his speech supporting the invasion of Czechoslovakia, "is simply a pawn of Yankee imperialism. . . ." He knew better, especially since Bonn refused to follow the U.S. lead when the latter broke relations with Cuba in January 1961. Relations between Cuba and West Germany were resumed in early 1975.

In all fairness to Fidel, it must be said that there was an element of sincerity in his analysis, if not in his conclusion. Perhaps in earlier days, when he was promoting "humanism" and castigating old-time Cuban Communists as "Nazi gauleiters,"[14] he might have sympathized with many of the reforms of Dubček and company. But he was now running one of the most tightly controlled, militarized, and personalized dictatorships in the Communist world. His deep aversion for the new Czech model of socialism was thus genuine enough. Still, the aversion was also shared by the Rumanian, Chinese, and Albanian rulers, but this did not prevent them from denouncing the invasion of Czechoslovakia (more about their views shortly).

Familiar Rhetoric

The larger part of Fidel's speech dealt with the "causes" and "factors" that "created the necessity for such a . . . drastic measure," and with lengthy digressions on related topics. To a considerable extent, the speech was an elaborate exercise in public relations aimed at convincing the world, and his own people, that he had not become a puppet of the Russians. Thus, he declared that the blame for the "drastic measure" lay with the "slackening and softening of the revolutionary spirit of the socialist [meaning the Soviet Union and satellites] countries," and the "neglect of communist ideals" such as a "society in which man is no longer slave to money, in which society no longer works for personal gain," and so on—that is to say, the ideals of the Cuban Revolution. It was the familiar rhetoric of Fidel's "cold war" against the Russians, which he had prudently abandoned some months past but which had a special function here. In fact, this was to be his last anti-Soviet "fling."

As he went on in this vein, Fidel paradoxically settled an old score with the Czech system whose restoration by Soviet arms he had just endorsed. In the process, he revealed an ugly skeleton in the socialist closet. The Novotny regime, "plagued with many vices," he said, "sold this country, at high prices, many weapons which were the spoils of war seized from the Nazis. . . . And we have had to pay for them, and we are still paying for them." Furthermore, on "many occasions they sold us very outdated factories," motivated by their "eagerness to sell any old junk," even to a "country which is making a revolution and has to develop." All of this, he declared, was the result of the "economic concepts on which they base their business

14. See my *The Rise and Decline of Fidel Castro* (Berkeley and Los Angeles: University of California Press, 1972), pp. 50 and 153.

transactions,"[15] and of the policy of motivating society through "material incentives and the promises of more consumer goods. . . ." He did not need to add that Cubans were spared these iniquities. As Fidel's argument shaped up, what he was saying, almost in these words, was that the seeds of capitalism, planted in Czechoslovakia by the distorted model of socialism in the Soviet Union, finally sprouted into "liberalism," which is to say, anti-Marxism and counterrevolution.

There was still another matter that troubled Fidel. "We are disturbed," he declared, "that neither the Communist Party nor the Government of the Soviet Union . . . has made any direct accusation against Yankee imperialism for its responsibility in the events in Czechoslovakia." He offered no evidence other than a conviction that Yankee imperialism "is the principal culprit in the world plot and conspiracy against the socialist camp." But at this point Fidel was not concerned with facts. His target was the Soviet policy of "peaceful coexistence," a pet abomination which he had to include among the sins responsible for the deterioration of socialism in Czechoslovakia. This concluded his analysis of the "causes" and "factors" that led to the "necessity" of the invasion. Fidel did not conceal the purpose of his analysis. "The events in Czechoslovakia," he summarized, "only confirm the correctness of the positions and theses that our Revolution and our Party have maintained. . . ."

Finally, Fidel called upon the "Parties of those countries, in line with the decision made in Czechoslovakia," to mend their ways in foreign policy. They should recognize that Tito, "received in Prague as a hero a few weeks ago" (like Rumania's Ceauşescu, which he conveniently failed to mention), plays the role of an "instrument of imperialism," as Cuba has always maintained.[16] They should cease their policy of "rapprochement"

15. It took the Cubans a while to learn that when they were trading with the socialist countries, they were not negotiating with Karl Marx. They were mostly dealing with a host of export-import bureaucracies managed by harassed officials who were required to meet quotas and otherwise satisfy predetermined goals set by the state planning authorities, and subject to penalties for failure to do so. "Caveat emptor," Fidel discovered, applied equally to market and centrally planned economies.

16. Fidel read from hitherto undisclosed documents which purported to show a receptive attitude by the Yugoslav embassy in Mexico to a request by Batista's agents for the purchase of arms in late 1958; and an equivocal attitude by the Yugoslav embassy in Havana in late 1959 to a similar request by Raúl Castro. No deal was closed in either case. At the time of his speech, as noted earlier, Fidel could not foresee that he would later overlook these matters and in general change his mind about Yugoslavia.

toward the Latin American governments that "are accomplices in the imperialist blockade against Cuba." They should renounce the "idyllic hopes of an improvement in relations with the imperialist Government of the United States." As for Cuba, "never under any circumstance" will it make any "concessions to the Yankee imperialists."

Comparative Perspective

Fidel's speech was strained, defensive despite its bluster, and extraordinarily long-winded and repetitious, even judged by his standards. As a response to the invasion of Czechoslovakia, aside from matters of style, the speech was unique among the Communist regimes of the world, although it was similar to their responses in one important respect: all the Communist countries invoked "principle," which, by more than coincidence, corresponds to eminently practical considerations. Thus, for Rumania, Yugoslavia, China, and Albania, resistance to Soviet overlordship, to which they had long been committed, was the prime issue to be faced. The Chinese and Albanians, open enemies of the Kremlin, reiterated their abhorrence of "renegade revisionism," both the Soviet and Czech varieties, but centered their attack on Soviet "imperialism." In the cases of Yugoslavia and Rumania, the precedent set by the invasion was ominous, since they bordered the Soviet Union or its Bulgarian and Hungarian accomplices. Hence, they denounced the "Brezhnev doctrine," but with no provocative excursions into other areas of disagreement.

On the other side, both North Vietnam and North Korea defended the Soviet-led invasion, with no digression that could give offense to the Kremlin. The Vietnamese were critically dependent on Moscow in their war with the United States. Although Kim Il-sung had always been a stickler for independence vis-à-vis both his Russian and Chinese neighbors, North Korean relations with China were at a low ebb at the time of the Czech crisis, while a substantial increase in Soviet economic and military aid had taken place.[17] The Mongolian People's Republic predictably endorsed the invasion, since from the time of its incorporation within the Soviet block it had not had an independent foreign policy. As for the Soviet Union's satellite accomplices, their reasons for violating the sovereignty of Czechoslovakia require no comment.[18]

17. See Ilpyong J. Kim, *Communist Policies in North Korea* (New York: Praeger, 1975), pp. 108–111.

18. For reactions to the invasion by all ruling and nonruling Communist parties, see Richard F. Starr, ed., *Yearbook on International Communist Affairs* 1969 (Stanford, Calif.: Hoover Institution Press, 1970).

An Hypothesis

There is no way to know what went on in Castro's headquarters between the time the news of the invasion reached Havana and the time Fidel went on the air. All the available evidence would indicate that his decision to support the Russians came very late. This would be understandable, for he clearly had far more complex problems to consider than those of the other Communist regimes. Had there been an exchange of views with the Kremlin through the Soviet embassy in Havana? That would be a reasonable hypothesis. Consultation would have been a matter of urgency for both parties. Was a deal, explicit or implicit, worked out? That would be highly plausible, and the terms could be inferred from what transpired soon after: expanded Soviet assistance, including a sizable increase in the supply of petroleum,[19] for completing the ten-million-ton sugar harvest in return for Cuban backing of the "Brezhnev doctrine," as the start for adjusting Cuban foreign policy to conform, or at least not to conflict, with that of the Soviet Union.

Castro also had other requirements that the Soviets could understand. To keep up the momentum of his crash program, he had to maintain the spartan ideology which justified the discipline and sacrifice imposed on the population in order to meet his goal. At the same time, Fidel had to save face with his people and the world, both equally unprepared for his betrayal of Czechoslovak sovereignty and the concomitant support of Soviet-defined "internationalism." Fidel's ideological and other face-saving tirades were probably sharper than the Kremlin anticipated, but here again they could be overlooked. They bolstered Fidel's posture as an uncontaminated idealist, as an unreconcilable enemy of imperialism, as the incorruptible champion of the Third World, and as a dedicated revolutionary, and thus enhanced his support for the invasion.

A Boon for Moscow

At a time when the Soviet Union was condemned by the majority of European Communist parties, including the powerful Italian and French parties, by the Japanese party and even two Latin American parties, the Mexican and Dominican, and by unaffiliated leftists throughout the world,

---

19. In round figures, the petroleum supply increased from 5.3 million tons of crude oil and oil products in 1968 to 5.8 million tons in 1969, and to 6 million tons in 1970 (Arthur Jay Klinghoffer, *The Soviet Union and International Oil Politics* [New York: Columbia University Press, 1977], p. 204).

among them Bertrand Russell and Jean-Paul Sartre;[20] when governments with close ties to the Soviet Union such as India, Egypt, and Algeria preferred to withhold judgment rather than support the Soviet Union;[21] and when troublesome dissidence cropped up in the Soviet Union itself and in other invading states,[22] Castro's unequivocal backing of the invasion was of no small importance to the Kremlin.

Shortly after the first impact of the news of the invasion, Soviet propaganda opened a sustained campaign to reverse the widespread negative reaction. In the first major Soviet publication given international circulation in several languages, a slightly amended version of Fidel's key statement, extracted from the rest of his speech, was prominently displayed: "Czechoslovakia was going toward counterrevolution and capitalism and into the embrace of imperialism. It is our belief that it was absolutely essential to prevent this at all costs in one way or another, and that the socialist camp has every right to do so."[23] It was the first time in several years that Castro had been cited with approbation in the Soviet Union. In the Kremlin there must have been more than a little satisfaction that the first stage in the domestication of their wayward client had been successfully completed.

20. Mastny, *Czechoslovakia*, p. 92.

21. Indian, Egyptian, and Algerian reactions were reported in the *New York Times*, August 27, 1968.

22. See H. Gordon Skilling, *Czechoslovakia's Interrupted Revolution* (Princeton, N.J.: Princeton University Press, 1976), pp. 753–754.

23. *On Events in Czechoslovakia: Facts, Documents, Press Reports, and Eye-witness Accounts*, Russian language edition, Issue No. 1 (Moscow: Press Group of Soviet Journalists, September 14, 1968), p. 154.

39

■

The Tenth Anniversary

The Engineering of a Monster Rally

"SEVERAL CELEBRATIONS of this type have been held during the past few years, but this one certainly seems to be the one in which the greatest number of people have gathered in this Plaza de la Revolución. Not only does this multitude extend over a large area, but there are no empty spaces within that area. And much more important than the size of the crowd is the fact that this is a multitude, a people with an extraordinarily greater political awareness." This was Fidel speaking on January 2, 1969, the tenth anniversary of the Revolution.[1] Also noteworthy, although it was not mentioned, was the fact that there had been more than the customary preparation for this massive assembly of the people.

To promote the "extraordinarily greater political awareness" of which Fidel spoke, there had been an urgent need to "sell" his speech on the Czech crisis to the nation, which was confused by its bizarre reasoning and the unexpected decision to which it led. Hence, extraordinary measures were taken, probably unique since the establishment of Castro's regime. Literally thousands of meetings were organized over a period of weeks throughout the island. As described at the end of August, the "revolutionary organizations of the country—the CDR [Committees for the Defense of the Revolution], the FMC [Federation of Cuban Women], the UJC [Union of Young Communists], the CTC [Confederation of Cuban Labor], and the local and regional sections of the Party—proclaimed their identification with the Cuban Maximum Leader . . . in public demon-

---

1. All citations from the speech are from the text published in *Granma Weekly Review*, January 5, 1969.

strations, messages, and declarations. . . . As the basic mass organization of the country, CDR faithfully polled the solid approval of all Cubans of good will. . . ." What they had approved with one voice was the essence of Fidel's historic speech, which, it was explained, "in an exceptional moment of crisis in the socialist world" was a "valiant" affirmation of the "principles of international solidarity and national autonomy represented by the Revolution."[2] The choice of "principles," incidentally, was not entirely deceptive. It further confirmed the nature of the "deal" concluded between Fidel and the Kremlin.

In the early years of the Revolution, the hundreds of thousands of people who filled the Plaza on these occasions came spontaneously. Gradually attendance became organized, until, by the late 1960s, it had become in effect compulsory for most of those who assembled to hear the Commander-in-Chief. This year the manipulation of the population reached a new level of intensity. As reported in the press, the preparations for the "mobilization directed by the Party, which assigned the [various] tasks to the mass organizations," had been under way "since the middle of November." Meetings were held in work centers "where thousands of workers pledged that they would join the Commander-in-Chief in the Plaza de la Revolución on January 2." It was to be, according to the leader of the Havana region of the CDR, "the most grandiose of any rally, not only in numbers of people, but also in the display of enthusiasm and fighting spirit."

Nothing was left to chance. "Very early in the morning of January 2," it was explained, the blowing of bugles will awaken the population, and the "CDR . . . will go from door to door, calling upon the neighbors to assemble at the designated places. . . . They will then proceed . . . to the Plaza de la Revolución, to participate in the joyous celebration of the Revolution, which is marching onward toward communism. . . . We are convinced that there will be more than one million people in the Plaza."[3]

And so it turned out, as far as numbers were concerned, as Fidel observed at the beginning of his speech, although most of the foreign guests seated on the platform behind him did not suspect why. It was, to be sure, the Tenth Anniversary, reason enough to insure that there would be a record-breaking turnout. Yet, paradoxically there was less for the population to celebrate than at any previous anniversary. Rations were slimmer than

2. *Bohemia*, 35 (August 30, 1968), 55.
3. *Bohemia*, 52 (December 27, 1968), 60.

ever, work was harder, discipline was tighter, and the prospects were for more of the same for another year.[4] Morale was at its lowest point since Fidel took power. Hence, nothing less than massive efforts to mobilize the people of Havana could have filled the Plaza for the ritual of observing what the calendar designated as a landmark anniversary.

A Sober Mood

Except for his projections of prosperity in the future, Fidel's speech was relatively sober, reflecting the austerity of the moment and the arduous labor which still lay ahead in the eighteen months that remained before the completion of the great sugar harvest. "On this anniversary," he said, "there is no military parade. . . . Since the most important thing [is] work, . . . we decided . . . not to use up a single gallon of fuel or to stay away from work one minute longer than was necessary. . . ." This was undoubtedly a matter that pained him, as he half admitted, since what could have been more fitting for the tenth anniversary than a display of the military power which the Revolution had created and which was thus far by all odds its most conspicuous achievement. However, much of Fidel's army was dispersed in the countryside preparing the land for next year's sugar harvest. Very likely, this was the main reason for omitting the parade.

Nor would there be a parade on the following anniversary: "Next January 2, it is quite possible that we will not be able to gather here in this Plaza, since a great many of us will be out in the fields cutting sugarcane. Thus, the next New Year will probably be celebrated on July 1 [1970], while the next Christmas will be celebrated between the first and the 26th of July."

The Rationing of Sugar

There was more bad news. Later in the speech, Fidel explained that consumption of sugar had been rising. To compensate "for our lack of other products," he said, "there are many people who feed sugar to the hogs, give sugar to chickens . . . and cows." He failed to mention that for the same "lack of other products," human consumption of sugar had also increased, sugar being an excellent source of energy. The result, he calculated, is that "we are using 200,000 tons more sugar" (probably some forty to fifty percent

4. *The Economist* (London, December 21–27, 1968, p. 15) estimated that Cuban "rations, even on paper, are considerably lower than British wartime rations. . . ."

above normal consumption). This, he continued, is a "waste" that represents "15 million dollars in foreign exchange." In three years, he added, this would amount to enough money to purchase "3,000 ten-ton trucks, more than what we have [operating] in [our] whole vast program. . . ." Thus, on the less-than-glorious tenth anniversary, the unimaginable occurred: sugar would be rationed for the first time. Fidel "suggested" six pounds per capita per month.[5] "If it's all right with you," he concluded, "this measure will go into effect tomorrow."

In keeping with the mood of the day, Fidel passed quickly over the accomplishments in education and public health during the first decade of his regime, to concentrate on the tasks that lay ahead. "A revolution," he declared, "must base itself upon an economic structure. And it has been precisely in the field of economic structure that our people have faced the most difficult challenge. . . . It was as if overnight all of us, with a vast ignorance of everything, had taken charge of everything and of doing everything with an utter lack of experience." This was, to be sure, a realistic appraisal of the first ten years, although "all of us" were not equally to blame. But it would only be after the great disaster of 1970 that Fidel would accept the major share of the blame.

An Absurd Prediction

Fidel's realism, however, did not extend into the future, for the greater part of his speech was devoted to the phenomenal growth of the Cuban economy that he stubbornly insisted lay immediately ahead. The details need not concern us, since we are already familiar with his propensity for reckless miscalculation, although there was nothing then on record quite so absurd as one of his predictions at this time. We are at the beginning of 1969, he said, "and by 1970, Cuba's agricultural production will be approximately double—twice as much!—what it was before January 1, 1959. This is truly amazing, perhaps even incredible." Indeed, it was, especially since there would actually be less food produced than in 1958. But for Fidel, what was

5. Direct human consumption of sugar in many tropical sugarcane-growing countries, including Cuba, is normally considerably higher than in the United States or Canada. In the Cuban conditions of 1969, Castro's ration probably resulted in a reduction of human, as well as animal, consumption. The surreptitious diversion of food from human to animal consumption has been a familiar one in other socialist countries. In the Soviet Union, for example, during periods of shortages of animal feed, bread has been substituted by private owners of livestock, leaving insufficient supplies in the shops for legitimate customers.

"truly amazing" was the historic dimension of an achievement he took for granted. "Something we can examine," he continued, "in the light of all the studies of the increases in agricultural production in every country and under all circumstances, without finding another case that even remotely resembles this achievement. Because doubling agricultural production in ten years is something that cannot be done even by the so-called developed countries."

It was once again Fidel's way of convincing his people that their sacrifices were about to bear fruit. Yet, as always, he projected the most complete sincerity and confidence, while many, perhaps even most, Cubans—like Sancho Panza, half-doubting and half-believing the visionary Don Quixote—still hoped for the best. And in truth, it would appear that it was not demagogy which consciously motivated Fidel, but conviction born of an enormous capacity for self-deception combined with more than a trace of megalomania.

The New Era Confirmed

What was most important about the speech was the corroboration it provided that a new era in Cuba's international relations had begun. To be sure, there was the familiar attack against the United States, this time focused on the "new tenant in the White House, a Mr. Nixon." Also familiar was the "solidarity and our full support" for the "brother people of Vietnam, who with their blood and sacrifice. . . ," and so on. At the same time, Fidel's praise for the Soviet Union signaled a new departure and again confirmed what lay behind his support of the Russian-led invasion of Czechoslovakia.

There had already been significant evidence of a new attitude before the speech. In sharp contrast to Fidel's personal snubbing of the Kremlin in November 1967, when he sent a low-ranking official to represent Cuba at Moscow's observance of the fiftieth anniversary of the Bolshevik Revolution, an event of much lesser importance a year later was celebrated in Cuba with a new fervor. It was the fiftieth anniversary of the Komsomol, the Soviet Communist youth organization founded in late October 1918. Among the demonstrations of revived mutual admiration was the appearance in Cuba of three hundred members of the Komsomol working side by side in the fields with a contingent of Cuba's Communist youth organization.[6] Then, in mid-November, an East German delegation, headed by

6. *Bohemia*, 44 (November 1, 1968), 65.

the third highest official of the German party, arrived in Havana for a visit that was given top prominence in the Cuban media. This was the first official visit by a delegation on the Politburo level from any East European country, including the Soviet Union, since 1964.[7]

It was therefore not a complete surprise when, toward the end of his speech, Fidel paid tribute to the Soviet Union. "We must say on this occasion," he declared, "how much the solidarity of the socialist camp, and especially the solidarity of the Soviet Union, has meant to us." He gracefully admitted that on "certain occasions we have had differences of opinion on certain matters," but the fact remained that Soviet aid was decisive for the nation:

> The shipments of food to Cuba; at the times when the threats were greatest, the shipment of arms to our country. And bear in mind that these arms are worth more than all the equipment we are using for development. . . . And we have received these weapons at no cost! When we lacked qualified personnel for industrial projects, geological investigation, dam construction, and a thousand other needs, we were able to obtain all of the technicians we needed. . . . [When] we were short of products [to export], . . . this did not affect Cuba's imports. . . . [Their help] enabled us to fulfill our commitments [with capitalist countries] . . . to maintain our credit for purchasing . . . types of equipment which were unavailable in the socialist camp. In short, in all justice we must say that this aid was decisive for us.

From time to time in the past, Castro had publicly acknowledged Soviet military and economic assistance, but in recent years less and less and mostly in a perfunctory manner. Certainly, there had been nothing remotely comparable to this inventory of generosity since the peak of his cordial relations with Khrushchev between mid-1963 and early 1964.

A New Role Projected

No less significant was what Fidel left unsaid in this speech. There was no mention of the remnants of guerrilla bands still struggling against imperialism in Latin America. Conspicuously absent from his summary of the first decade of the Revolution and from his characterization of the spirit that was to animate the second decade was even a single reference to Ché

7. *Le Monde*, November 15, 1968.

Guevara, as if he had never existed.[8] Gone were the ideological heresies that irritated the Kremlin, such as the primacy of moral over material incentives, the pernicious role of money in a socialist economy, the imminent emergence of the "new man," and the simultaneous construction of socialism and communism.

Instead, Fidel spoke of Soviet "international solidarity and economic cooperation with our country," which will provide an "example for the underdeveloped countries of the world, a solution and a road to be followed by those who suffer from hunger, poverty, . . . and exploitation." Although he did not state it explicitly, Fidel left a strong impression that the role of the Cuban Revolution was henceforth to be that of a showcase of socialist economic development, an objective long ago proposed by the Soviet Union. And there was at least a hint that once the ten-million-ton sugar crash program was completed, Cuba would adopt the normal patterns of socialist development exemplified by the Soviet Union.

There remained only the naming of the new year. "If you agree with it," he said, concluding his speech, "we shall hereby baptize[9] this year, 1969, as the Year of the Decisive Endeavor. Patria or muerte, venceremos!"

8. What Castro's speech on the tenth anniversary could mean for the United States was cogently but prematurely argued in a *New York Times* editorial on January 3, 1969: "The key point is that Castroism, as a potential disruptive force in Latin America, has been effectively contained. Now Castro's Cuba is largely a source of minor inconvenience, as when an airliner is hijacked to Havana. Both countries would benefit if their present abnormal, strained and hostile relations were replaced by more rational contact."

9. Castro would occasionally revert to his pre-Marxist vocabulary, using such words as "baptize" and, at other times, "señores" (gentlemen) instead of "compañeros" (comrades).

Epilogue

The Aftermath of Disaster

On May 20, 1970, Fidel Castro publicly conceded that the "super harvest" would fall short of the target. Then, in a memorable speech on July 26, he personally accepted the blame for the fact that not only had Cuba failed to achieve the sacred goal, but the effort had resulted in a disastrous setback for the entire economy and in physically exhausting the population.[1] There have been few, if any, examples in recent history of the head of a government who could survive a crisis of comparable dimensions without resort to drastic measures of repression. But few could match Fidel's extraordinary charisma, political shrewdness, and the unchallenged authority that he has enjoyed since his seizure of power.

Thus, he could begin the task of reconstruction in full control of a docile people. There was now no alternative but to completely abandon his dream of achieving instant prosperity, pure communism, and effective national independence. And with unaccustomed humility, he accepted the conditions of survival offered by the Kremlin: basic conformity with the economic, political, and ideological postulates of the Soviet model of socialism in domestic affairs, and with Soviet foreign policy in international affairs.

The Process of Economic Transformation

The magnitude of the task of overhauling Cuba's economic and political institutions can be judged by the fact that it required six years to complete the transformation and to simultaneously complete the full integration of

---

1. Castro gave a candid account of some of the losses to the economy, mentioning cement, fertilizers, tires, batteries, steel bars, soap, detergents, milk, poul-

the Cuban economy with the Soviet and its satellite economies. The main steps in the process can be summarized as follows:[2]

1. In December 1970, a Cuban-Soviet Commission of Economic, Scientific, and Technical Collaboration was created, in effect an instrument for Soviet supervision of the Cuban economy.

2. In mid-1972, Cuba became a full member of the Council for Mutual Economic Assistance (CMEA or COMECON), the Soviet-bloc organization that coordinates economic relations among the participating states.

3. At the end of 1972, the Soviet Union agreed to a significant increase in technical aid to Cuba; deferred the liquidation of Cuba's accumulated debt to the Soviet Union since 1960, with payments on principal and interest to take place between 1986 and 2011; granted massive new credits, with payments on the new debt also postponed to the period between 1986 and 2011; and subsequently made supportive trade agreements which further insured Cuban economic dependence on the Soviet Union.

4. In November 1973, the thirteenth National Workers' Congress, the first in six years, revived the moribund Cuban trade unions and restored their functions according to patterns long established in the Soviet Union. The "socialist" principle of "from each according to his ability, to each according to his work" was formally endorsed.

5. By the end of 1975, the arduous task of setting up and putting into operation the Soviet-directed "System for Economic Management and Planning" was by and large completed, and Cuba's first five-year economic plan was inaugurated. Among the system's features were the decentralization of many managerial functions on both the national and local levels, the financial autonomy and accountability of state enterprises, and reliance on material incentives (hence inequality of incomes) to increase production. Sugar remained the principal sector of the economy, its growth now subject to calculated allocation of use of the country's resources, as well as to the gradual mechanization of the harvest process and the modernization of the sugar mills. Dependence on "voluntary" labor in the cane fields and else-

---

try, vegetables, fruits, etc. For an analysis of the ten-million-ton episode and its aftermath, see Edward González, *Cuba Under Castro: The Limits of Charisma* (Boston: Houghton Mifflin, 1974), pp. 207–213.

2. For a detailed description and analysis of the process, see Carmelo Mesa-Lago, *Cuba in the 1970s: Pragmatism and Institutionalization*, revised edition (Albuquerque: University of New Mexico Press, 1978).

where was drastically reduced, and crash programs, including Castro's "special plans," disappeared.

6. As one of the few institutions not seriously affected by the "organized chaos" that characterized Cuban planning and administration in general during the 1960s, Cuba's Soviet-trained-and-equipped armed forces underwent less significant change than occurred in the country's economic and political structures. A streamlining process already under way to separate the full-time professional army, reduced to about 100,000 men, from the reserve of between two and three times that number, was completed. Army-directed labor squads, a special feature of the Cuban military system, were retained but were now completely insulated from the regular combat troops.

In a two-stage process (the first in 1973 and the second in 1976), the conventional hierarchy of officer ranks was formally established, doing away with the egalitarian camouflage—and eliminating cumbersome circumventions—by which the top rank had remained that of *comandante*, or major, according to the practice established in Castro's guerrilla army during the campaign against Batista. Thus, the highest rank became that of General of the Army, assumed by Fidel's brother Raúl, while Fidel retained his special noncompetitive rank of Commander-in-Chief. Guerrilla *comandantes* who had permanently drifted into civilian occupations henceforth gave up their uniforms and side arms and received the title of "*comandante* of the Revolution."

A significant innovation in combat training occurred in mid-1975. Apparently in anticipation of large-scale military intervention in Angola, war exercises traditionally focused on defending Cuban territory against external aggression were converted into major preparations for offensive action overseas. At a time when requirements for both external and internal security had notably diminished, the new role of the armed forces, soon reinforced by their exploits in Angola and Ethiopia, assured their continued, and perhaps growing, importance in Cuban affairs.[3]

7. The long-postponed first congress of the Communist Party, held in December 1975, approved a new set of principles and statutes comparable

3. For an exhaustive analysis of the Cuban military establishment and its role in Cuban society since the revolution, consult the relevant sections of Jorge I. Domínguez, *Cuba: Order and Revolution* (Cambridge, Mass.: Belknap Press, 1978). The book is a significant source of information and insight concerning Cuban history in modern times.

to those regulating the functions of the Soviet and Soviet-bloc parties.
Apart from its new image as a responsible, as well as a ruling, party, a significant innovation was the shift from its earlier role of direct involvement,
at almost any level, in the administration of the country's affairs to that of
supervision and control, as practiced in the Soviet Union. The congress
also authorized transforming Cuba's six traditional geographic-political
units into fourteen new provinces corresponding more closely to current
and projected economic and demographic patterns. One important feature
of the party remained unchanged: Fidel and his brother Raúl were elected
first and second secretaries, respectively, of the Central Committee.

8. The draft of a socialist constitution was completed in February
1975; was submitted to months of nationwide closely-guided popular "discussions" and other extraordinary measures of persuasion; was then approved at the first party congress in December; and was finally adopted, essentially unchanged by the "discussions," in a national referendum in
mid-February 1976. Predictably, both voter turnout and affirmative votes
were close to one hundred percent.

Except in minor details, conforming to specific Cuban conditions
and the rhetorical traditions of the Cuban Revolution, the document faithfully reflected both the letter and the spirit of the Soviet and satellite constitutions. The recognition given to the Soviet Union in the constitutions
of all Soviet-bloc countries, with the notable exception of Rumania,
founds its way into the preamble to the Cuban document, which specifically acknowledged the "help and cooperation of the Soviet Union."[4] Similarly, the Communist Party, as the "organized Marxist-Leninist vanguard
of the working class," was declared to be the "highest leading force of the
society and of the state" (Article 5). The constitution provided for a uni-
cameral legislative body closely resembling the Supreme Soviet (exclusive
of the Soviet of Nationalities) but uniquely designated as the "National Assembly of People's Power" (Article 67), in keeping with the more exuberant

---

4. See Lester A. Sobel, ed., *Castro's Cuba in the 1970s* (New York: Facts on
File, 1978), pp. 167 ff., for the complete text in English of the Cuban constitution.
The current Czech, Hungarian, and Polish constitutions, like the Cuban one, refer to the Soviet Union in their respective preambles. In the case of Bulgaria and
the German Democratic Republic, reference to the Soviet Union occurs in the text
of the constitutions (Article 3 and Section 2 of Article 6, respectively). As in
Rumania, no version of the Yugoslav constitution mentions the Soviet Union.
The same is true of the People's Republic of China. I am indebted for this information to my colleague Professor Lenard Cohen, a specialist in Communist systems.

Cuban demagogy.[5] The Presidium of the Supreme Soviet became the Council of State, but here a not surprising innovation was introduced. The President of the Council of State, that is, the head of the state, also assumed the post of President of the Council of Ministers, that is, the head of the government (Article 69).

Thus, at the first session of the National Assembly of People's Power, held in December 1976, when Castro was unanimously elected President of the Council of State, he automatically became President of the Council of Ministers, or what amounted to Prime Minister, thereby becoming the only leader in the Soviet-bloc (to which Yugoslavia can be added) to hold both jobs. Already the First Secretary of the Central Committee of the Communist Party and the Commander-in-Chief of the Armed Forces, Fidel's supremacy was duly solemnized and legitimized. As the French saying goes, "the more things change, the more they remain the same." But not quite, as we shall presently see.

Relations with Latin America

While there was little room for Fidel to display his talents of originality in the restructuring of Cuban institutions on the Soviet model, the reorientation of Cuba's external relations to conform with Soviet foreign policy[6]— and common sense—offered him considerable opportunity to demonstrate his remarkable versatility. With great skill, and accordingly with little loss of face, he transferred his energies from exporting revolution to Latin

5. The more modest term of "People's Chamber" or "People's Assembly" is used in the German Democratic Republic, Czechoslovakia, and Bulgaria.

6. Referring to changes in Cuban policies since 1968, Jorge I. Domínquez notes that the "thrust of these changes does reflect a greater degree of convergence with the foreign policy of the Soviet Union" ("Cuban Foreign Policy," *Foreign Affairs*, 57:1 [Fall 1978], 90). This is an understatement. The record shows, at least as of mid-1980, that in no single instance of any significance has the "convergence" been less than total. A conspicuous demonstration of Cuban loyalty to the Kremlin took place in the UN General Assembly on January 14, 1980, when Cuba backed the USSR in the roll-call vote that condemned the Soviet occupation of Afghanistan, 104 to 18. Cuba's position on this issue was politically costly, since it found itself isolated from its associates in the Non-Aligned Movement to the tune of 59 votes against the USSR and only 8 supporters of the USSR besides Cuba: Afghanistan, Angola, Ethiopia, Grenada, Laos, Mozambique, South Yemen, and Vietnam (*New York Times*, January 15, 1980). Castro had been elected president of the Non-Aligned Movement at the September 1979 summit meeting in Havana. On October 12, 1979, he addressed the 34th session of the General Assembly as the Movement's Official spokesman.

America to developing normal relations with governments professing reformist tendencies and a nationalistic attitude toward the United States.

As a result, with only Mexico having maintained relations with revolutionary Cuba over the years, by the end of 1977 Cuba had established diplomatic relations with Argentina, Colombia, Panama, Peru, and Venezuela, and with the English-speaking Carribbean states of the Bahamas, Barbados, Guyana, Jamaica, and Trinidad and Tobago. Relations were also renewed with Chile in 1970, but were broken off in 1973 after the fall of Allende. In addition, relations on a consular level were negotiated with Costa Rica. Meanwhile, reflecting these changes, sanctions imposed against Cuba by the Organization of American States in 1964 were in effect lifted in mid-1975. These developments represented a successful challenge to American influence and were exploited to the full by Castro's propaganda machine, but they also represented compliance with Soviet policy in the area, which was discreetly overlooked. In addition, the developments held out the prospect of benefits through trade and participation in regional economic projects. For the countries recognizing Castro's government, these changes provided both a sop to internal leftist and nationalist opposition groups and also an independent posture vis-à-vis the United States at a time when uncertainties in American policy toward Latin America precluded retaliation.

Relations with the United States

Among other factors, Castro's success in breaking through the American-inspired isolation of Cuba from the rest of Latin America indicated the need in Washington for a reassessment of policy toward the Castro regime. Simultaneously, Fidel's acceptance of the Soviet policy of détente with the United States, as well as Soviet-style economic rationality, provided him with a new basis for contemplating the normalization of relations with the United States. Predictably, the process was to be slow and cumbersome, at first involving mutually useful agreements such as an antihijacking pact signed in 1973, and then moving on to the removal of travel barriers between the two countries (the resumption of direct commercial flights, cut off in 1962, was delayed until the end of 1978) and the easing of academic, scientific, cultural, and sports relations.

The end of the war in Vietnam and the election of Jimmy Carter facilitated further rapprochement, culminating on September 1, 1977, in the establishment of so-called "interest sections" in the former U.S. embassy in Havana and the former Cuban embassy in Washington. This amounted to the opening of consular relations between the two countries, the first exchange of official representatives in nearly seventeen years. Since then, contacts between citizens of both countries have continued to increase, including visits by members of Congress to Havana and by the Cuban minister of foreign trade to Washington and New York.

Of the two sides, by and large the Cuban showed the greater desire to move on to full normalization, with the obvious encouragement of the Soviet Union. Presumably, both Cuba and the Soviet Union anticipated economic advantage, Cuba through access to the American market and technology, and the Soviet Union through a lessening of the burden of supporting the Cuban economy. For the Soviet Union, the risk of Castro's defection was minimal, while the removal of a potential source of renewed Cuban-American friction would ensure the Soviet presence in the Caribbean without the risk of another confrontation with the United States.

Washington was more reluctant to move on to full relations with Havana, partly because of conflicting views and interests in the policymaking process, and partly because the costs and benefits were more difficult to assess.[7] However, the most conspicuous obstacle was the initial intervention, and then prolonged stay, of two large, highly effective Cuban armies in Africa, one in Angola and the other in Ethiopia, and the potential for further Cuban military involvement in other African countries. Since Cuban operations and objectives in Africa interlocked with those of the Soviet Union, the issue of the Cuban presence transcended purely Cuban-American relations.[8]

7. For a provocative discussion of the problems of assessment as of mid-1978, see Irving Louis Horowitz, "The Cuba Lobby: Supplying Rope to a Mortgaged Revolution," *Washington Review of Strategic and International Studies*, 1:3 (July 1978), 58–71.

8. As of the end of 1978, according to U.S. State Department figures, there were "45,000 Cubans spread throughout 13 African countries. Nearly 7,000 [were] non-military personnel. . . . Cuban soldiers [were] training Rhodesian guerrillas in Zambia and Mozambique. The Cuban military presence represented more than one-quarter of its armed forces and [was] far larger than that of any other foreign nation. Twenty thousand soldiers [were] in Angola alone, and more than 16,000 in Ethiopia" (*New York Times*, November 12, 1978). At one time, there were 36,000 Cuban troops in Angola, as Castro disclosed in a speech on December 27, 1979 (*Province* [Vancouver, British Columbia], February 8, 1980). For detailed analyses of Cuban and Soviet involvement in Africa over a period of two decades, see Jiri Valenta, "The Soviet-Cuban Intervention in Angola, 1975," *Studies in Comparative Communism*, 11:1–2 (Spring–Summer 1978), 3–33; William J. Durch, "The Cuban Military in Africa and the Middle East: From Algeria to Angola," ibid., pp.

Intervention in Africa

While not denying that his troops were supplied with arms and ammunition shipped directly to Africa from the Soviet Union, and that in other respects Cuban and Soviet operations were closely coordinated, Castro insisted from the beginning that Cuban policy was that of an independent and sovereign nation performing its "internationalist" duty on the invitation of legally constituted and internationally recognized governments. From the juridical point of view, he could defend his position and reject American and Chinese claims, among those of other countries, that Cuban troops were "mercenaries" in the service of Moscow.

However, the fact remained that without Cuban troops the Soviet-supported contenders for power would have been quickly defeated in the Angolan civil war, which followed the Portuguese withdrawal in late 1975. Likewise, the revolutionary Ethiopian regime, closely allied with Moscow, would have lost the war against Somalia in 1977, and almost certainly would have disintegrated as a nation. Whatever the future may hold for the dominant position achieved by the Soviet Union in Angola and Ethiopia, the Cuban intervention was decisive in creating a new political, ideological, and strategic balance of power in southern Africa and the Horn.

That Fidel was willing, and even eager, to collaborate with the Russians can readily be assumed. With the collapse of his "profound revolutionary offensive" in Cuba and the abandonment of revolution in Latin America, Africa providentially offered him the opportunity to resume his mission and refurbish his image as the great leader of oppressed mankind, and on a scale that dwarfed all his previous, and futile, efforts to foment revolution in Latin America and Africa. This is not to say that he might not have been moved by additional considerations: the satisfaction of successfully challenging the United States and thwarting South Africa; providing battle experience for his untested military establishment; and earning the gratitude and confidence of his Soviet benefactors. Nevertheless, without his enormous and insatiable hunger for leadership and glory, which, not unlike other inspired rulers of recent unlamented memory, he identi-

34–74; Edward González, "Cuba, the Soviet Union, and Africa," in *Communism in Africa*, ed. David E. Albright (Bloomington: Indiana University Press, 1980), pp. 145–167; and Maurice Halperin, "The Cuban Role in Southern Africa," in *Southern Africa Since the Portuguese Coup*, ed. John Seiler (Boulder, Colorado: Westview Press, 1980), pp. 25–43.

fied with his country's national prestige, it is unlikely that Fidel would have sent Cuban armies on missions which were in no way required by the needs of Cuban security, economic development, or the welfare of the Cuban people, and at the cost of Cuban blood and the bereavement of Cuban families. Castro was understandably sensitive to an unflattering assessment of the motivation, and on occasion he would reveal this sensitivity, as in a speech he delivered in East Berlin (although there he was immune from public disparagement). "There are Cubans working in . . . Africa," he said. "We aren't doing it for national prestige or out of vanity to play a role on the international scene."[9]

Thus it was that Fidel Castro reemerged on the international scene as a foremost champion of the Third World, but this time in complete harmony with Soviet policy. In his own extensive travels, and through Cuba's representatives in international organizations and conferences, he aggressively supported the "new economic order" in Latin America and the Caribbean, black liberation in Africa, the struggle against "Zionist imperialism and racism" in the Middle East, and "international proletarian solidarity" wherever infant Marxist-Leninist regimes needed assistance to survive. And time and again, he and his subordinates stoutly defended the Soviet Union from its detractors in matters of human rights or Marxist-Leninist doctrine and echoed the Kremlin's attack on the Chinese for their sinful repudiation of true Marxism-Leninism and their shameless complicity with imperialism. It would almost appear that with the proverbial zeal of the recent convert in his new role, Fidel had become, as the French put it, "more Catholic than the Pope."

The End of the Revolution

Twenty years after Castro's successful insurrection, there could be little doubt that the revolutionary process which it inaugurated had come to an end. What was known as the Cuban Revolution in fact belonged to the past. In its place, making due allowance for Fidel's still flamboyant presence, there finally emerged a soberly structured regime, of largely predictable behavior, closely patterned on the Russian model, fully integrated with the Soviet-bloc economies, and unavoidably dependent on the Soviet Union for its military security and economic welfare. Cuban dependency on the Soviet Union was already a prominent feature of the Cuban Revolution, but its political and ideological consequences were resisted to one

9. *Granma Weekly Review*, April 17, 1977.

degree or another during the first decade of the Cuban-Soviet relationship. This anomaly having vanished, there was no likelihood that the new harmony would be appreciably disturbed in the foreseeable future. The massive and incessant indoctrination of the Cuban people, on a hitherto unprecedented scale, designed to bind them politically, ideologically, and emotionally to the Soviet Union, gave evidence that the Cuban regime did not remotely contemplate loosening its ties with its powerful ally.

Hence, there was now little of importance to distinguish Cuban socialism from the basic features of the regimented societies of eastern Europe, ruled by self-appointed and self-perpetuating oligarchies legitimated by infallible doctrine. To be sure, the Cuban Revolution had already achieved an approximation of these features. However, whatever promise it once held of a larger measure of civil liberties, of more equal distribution of material goods, and of intellectual and artistic innovation irrevocably disappeared.

The Legacy of the Revolution

The Cuban Revolution, however erratic and frequently destructive its performance, and at an inestimable cost in human misery for its thousands of victims, was not without positive achievements. Leaving aside the value to be attached to the preeminence of its armed forces and its internationally acclaimed professionalized athletes,[10] the extension of public health services and educational opportunities to the entire population was its most notable accomplishment. Here again, some would argue that education

---

10. "Let us keep in mind that Cuba finished second, behind the United States, in the Pan American games held in Mexico in 1975; eighth . . . in the Montreal Olympics of 1976, an event in which more than 90 countries took part; and first in the Central American and Caribbean Games held in Medellín, Colombia, in 1978" (*Granma Weekly Review*, January 7, 1979). This was part of the text under the heading "The Olympic Fruits of the Revolution," which was accompanied by a photo of Cuba's world champion sprinter Alberto Juantorena. As in other socialist countries, and more so than most, there is an elaborate system of selecting, training, and motivating athletes for performance in competitive sports, with an overriding emphasis on "winning." There is a sizable investment in imported equipment, special medical facilities, and coaching staffs (mainly Soviet and East German). In Cuba there is also a conspicuous diversion of nourishing food, in short supply elsewhere, to the training tables, and other perquisites are also provided for athletes. Sports play an important political role, as the above *Granma* text indicates. As for the compatability of this kind of sports enterprise with socialist behavior, that is another question.

was not an unmixed blessing. Along with providing basic and specialized technical skills, it inculcated regimented discipline and blind acceptance of officially imposed dogma. On the other hand, undeniable progress was made in various sectors of the economy, such as the construction of roads and dams; the increase in the production of electric power, cement, synthetic fertilizers, and nickel; the purchase and operation of a modern merchant marine and fishing fleet; the application of artificial insemination in cattle breeding; the large-scale development of export-oriented citrus groves; and the inauguration of a modern building industry. However, little of the social and economic improvements would have been possible without heavy Soviet subsidies, nor could they be sustained without continuing and even larger subsidies.[11]

Perspective on the Future

"The coming years will be marked by effort and hard work. They will continue to be difficult years," Castro warned the Cuban people as the year 1979 was about to begin.[12] This would be particularly true in meeting the desperate housing shortage and improving the Cuban diet. A significant indicator of the latter problem was the slow recovery in the supply of rice, a basic food staple. At the beginning of 1979, the monthly per capita ration of five pounds[13] was still less than the six-pound hardship ration imposed in 1962, although it was higher than the drastically reduced three-pound ration of 1966.

Toward the end of 1979, more serious underlying problems affecting the performance of the regime and the morale of the population were dramatically exposed by Raúl Castro. In a speech delivered on November 4, he sharply criticized the "privileged" members of the higher bureaucracy

11. According to Jon Nordheimer (*New York Times*, January 3, 1979), Moscow's direct and indirect subsidies in the late 1970s (the indirect kind taking the form of premium prices paid for sugar and nickel) were "running as high . . . as $2.8 billion a year."

12. The warning was given in a speech to the fourteenth Congress of the Central Organization of Cuban Trade Unions (CTC) on December 2, 1978 (*Granma Weekly Review*, December 17, 1978). In a speech a year later (December 27, 1979), Castro declared: "We are sailing on a sea of troubles. . . . We have been on this sea for some time, and we shall remain on this sea, sometimes stormier, sometimes calmer, but the shore is far away" (*Province* [Vancouver, British Columbia], February 8, 1980).

13. According to a report from Havana by John Hart over the NBC television network on January 2, 1979. As of mid-1980, the rice ration has not changed.

and the "deficiencies of socialism," and he denounced "irresponsibility, tolerance [of malfeasance], lack of discipline, . . . [and] favoritism" in the party and government, "absenteeism" in industry, etc. The railroads, he said, had operated "more efficiently under capitalism," while some state farms had more white-collar workers than field workers.[14] These were some of the familiar complaints of the 1960s.

Matters came to a head in late December and early January 1980 in a two-stage major reshuffling of the cabinet—the most drastic since 1960, although this time in conformity with constitutional procedure. The changes involved the replacement of a dozen ministers. At the same time, as part of a reallocation of the "duties of supervision and coordination" among the "members of the Executive Committee of the Council of Ministers," according to the official decree, Fidel Castro, assisted by his brother Raúl, took "[direct] charge of the ministries of the armed forces, interior [i.e., the police], public health, and culture [i.e., anti-dissident vigilance]."[15] In addition to the armed forces, already assigned to Fidel's "supervision," the other three ministries were apparently considered the critical areas in which Fidel's prestige, more than operational intervention, was most needed to enforce a "hard line," since the ministers in charge were among Fidel's most experienced and trusted comrades since before 1959.

Nevertheless, despite these setbacks and signs of restlessness in the

14. *Le Monde*, November 6, 1979.

15. *Granma Weekly Review*, December 13, 1979, and January 20, 1980.

16. Among the symptoms were an increase in antigovernment leaflets and graffiti; warnings in the press that internal passports should be carried at all times; more conspicuous police surveillance on the streets, highways, and buses; and a resumption of "embassy-ramming," reminiscent of the 1960s, this time involving two shooting episodes as police tried to prevent asylum-seekers from crashing their vehicles through the roadblocks guarding the entrances to the grounds of the Venezuelan and Peruvian embassies (*Le Monde*, January 12, 19, and 22, 1980). An article in the Book Review section of the *New York Times*, November 11, 1979, documents dissaffection by Cuban writers and poets and the "elaborate system of repression used to silence them." As mentioned earlier (Chapter 20, note 8), there was an invasion in April 1980 of the Peruvian embassy grounds by more than 10,000 would-be Cuban emigrants. This prompted the Italian Communist daily *Unitá*, in rejecting Castro's explanation that these were "antisocial scum," to suggest: "Shouldn't this be the moment for all of us to reflect on the need for socialism to offer something else, something different, which would take into account the profound mutations on the world scene and in the conscience of peoples?" (*Le Monde*, April 11, 1980).

population,[16] the regime appeared to be secure. Under the postrevolutionary order, something approaching a systematic and sustained economic growth clearly would be difficult to achieve, but it could not be ruled out.[17] One could even speculate that before the end of the century, Cuban living standards might be comparable to those of the more comfortable socialist countries, such as Hungary or Czechoslovakia, given Cuba's benign climate, her fertile soil, her large deposits of nickel and other minerals, her geographic location, the heritage of her western culture, and the magnitude of Russian assistance. These standards would not be precisely the consumer standards of the capitalist era, which not a few Cubans once enjoyed and most others hoped to attain, but they would mark a considerable improvement over the deprivations, however evenly distributed, of the Cuban Revolution.

The Role of Fidel Castro

In the postrevolutionary era, what most conspicuously distinguishes the Cuban political scene from that of its East European associates is the presence of Fidel Castro, and this distinction is likely to continue for some time. It does not mean that no change has occurred in his role. From all the evidence, he is no longer the supreme and indispensable authority from whom all decisions flow, or the incessant meddler in all matters that strike his fancy. Although the "institutionalization" of his regime confirms and legitimates the power that he has always wielded, it also creates the

17. Sugar would continue to be the mainstay of the economy for many years. During the late 1970s, production appeared to average better than 7 million tons per year, with a trend toward gradual increase. Some forty percent of the cane harvest was machine-cut in 1978, again with prospects of a gradual increase. Earnings, however, remained vulnerable to price oscillations and quota restrictions in the capitalist markets, which absorbed more than a third of Cuba's sugar sales. Increasing exports of nickel and citrus fruit (raw and processed) toward the end of the 1980s and thereafter could reduce Cuban dependence on sugar. This is the gist of a report by Carlos Serrano, of the University of Paris, entitled "La primauté du sucre dans l'économie [cubaine] demeure écrasante" (*Le Monde*, January 3, 1979). As for the year 1979, the sugar harvest produced just under eight million metric tons, the second largest amount in Cuban history (*Granma Weekly Review*, August 5, 1979). However, toward the end of the year, Raúl Castro declared that "climatic and natural phenomena . . . have recently adversely affected crop yields and have considerably reduced the quantity of cane available for the next sugar harvest, all of which will inevitably be reflected in 1980 and even in 1981" (*Granma Weekly Review*, November 11, 1979).

mechanisms that "routinize" his power, as one writer has put it.[18] Thus, the new bureaucratic rationalism curbs his intervention in the ministries, notably those affecting the economy, which appear to be directed exclusively by fully responsible functionaries and their Soviet advisors. There are also other symptoms of change. In the past, Castro rarely left the country, and only on matters of great urgency. Since the beginning of the 1970s, however, with others now entrusted with "minding the store," he has frequently traveled abroad and remained away for weeks at a time.

Nevertheless, the congenitally irrepressible Fidel has not faded from the domestic and international scene. At home he still exercises his charisma in countless public appearances and speeches, and he continues to dominate the news. In his visits to his Caribbean neighbors, he remains the commanding and grandiloquent figure of earlier days. It is in the conduct of foreign affairs, where his personal control seems to be undiminished, that he completely overshadows the lackluster rulers of the other Soviet-dependent states. He has, in fact, managed to convert Cuba's image from that of a humdrum satellite of Moscow into something like a junior partner.

Meanwhile, with his stately, now somewhat portly figure, his finely chiseled features, ample beard, and piercing eyes, with his long cigar and crumpled olive-green army fatigues, and a pistol dangling from his belt (on very formal occasions replaced by a resplendent uniform), the legend of the guerrilla warrior-hero appears to be indestructible. "Castro's revolutionary image comes right out of Central Casting," a startled American visitor remarked in late 1977, after conversing with the Commander-in-Chief.[19] He is, in truth, the image of a consummate actor, enamored of his role and intent on maintaining the aura of a revolution that has ended.

18. Domínguez, *Cuba: Order and Revolution*, p. 197.
19. Thomas P. O'Neill, III, quoted in the *Boston Globe*, November 9, 1977. I am indebted to my sister-in-law, Ethel Halperin, for this and many other clippings from this source.

About the Author

Maurice Halperin was born in 1906, in Boston, Massachusetts. He was educated at Harvard and the Sorbonne, where he earned a doctorate in comparative literature in 1931.

He was twice forced out of teaching positions in American universities because of his political beliefs. Concerning the second occasion, he wrote in the *Harvard Class of 1927 Fiftieth Anniversary Report*:

> Some of my readers may recall the newspaper accounts of my hassle with a U.S. Senate committee on subversion . . . in 1953, and my subsequent firing from Boston University. This propelled me, accompanied by my steadfast wife, from the sheltered existence of a tenured professor into a series of academic adventures in Mexico, the Soviet Union, Cuba, and finally, in 1968, to end up in the hospitable climate of a Canadian university. . . .
>
> As it happened, what at first appeared to be a misfortune turned out to be a richly rewarding experience, professionally, intellectually, and spiritually. My brother once summed it up for me with a bit of pungency: "You fell into a barrel of [manure] and came up with a handful of diamonds."

During his five years in Mexico, Dr. Halperin lectured at the School of Social and Political Sciences of the National University and was employed as an economist by the Nacional Financiera, the government industrial bank. From 1959 to 1962, he was a visiting professor at the Institute of World Economy and International Affairs, in the Academy of

Sciences of the USSR. From 1962 to 1968, he taught in the Faculty of Geography at the University of Havana. In 1968 he was appointed Professor of Political Science at Simon Fraser University in British Columbia. In 1979 he was named Professor Emeritus.

During World War II, Dr. Halperin was Chief of the Latin America Division of the Office of Strategic Services. After the war, he served as a consultant to the Economic and Social Council of the United Nations in New York and to the government of the State of São Paulo, Brazil. In 1952 he was decorated by the government of Brazil with the Order of the Southern Cross. He was elected Councillor at the XLIII International Congress of Americanists held in Vancouver, British Columbia, in 1979.

Dr. Halperin's published works cover a wide range of topics, from medieval literature to modern developmental economics. His major area of interest has been Latin America—in particular, Mexico, Brazil, and Cuba. His teaching career has included faculty appointments at the University of Oklahoma, the University of Florida, and the University of Paris, and he has also lectured at the University of São Paulo, McGill University, and Tokyo University.

Index

Afghanistan, 329n
Africa, Cuban personnel in, 331n. *See also* Castro, Fidel; Guevara, Ernesto
Afro-Asian Solidarity, Second Economic Seminar of, 125ff
Agnon, Samuel, 248
Alarcón, Ricardo, speech at UN, 246
Alexander, Robert J., 27n, 300n
Alexeiev, Alexandr, 271
Algeria. *See* Ben Bella, Ahmed
Allende, Salvador, 300n
Alliance for Progress, 94
Angola, 332
Arafat, Yasser, decoration of, 253f
Arcocha, Juan, 2n, 82n
Armed struggle, policy of, 188f
Axis, miniature, of Cuba, N. Korea, N. Vietnam, 168f

Baran, Paul, 73
Batista, Fulgencio, 2f
Belfrage, Cedric, 259n
Ben Barka, El Mahdi, 170
Ben Bella, Ahmed, 122
Bettelheim, Charles, controversy with Ché Guevara, 80, 81n
Bolivia. *See* Guevara, Ernesto
Bonachea, Ramón L., 2n
Borrego, Orlando, dismissal of, 228
Boti, Regino, 72, 82, 91
Boumediène, Lahovare, 167n

Bouteflika, Abdelaziz, 167f
Brezhnev, Leonid, 115, 178; "doctrine" of, 312
Bulgaria, 302f
Burnham, Forbes, 249

Caamaño, Deñó, Francisco, eulogy of, 164f
Carmichael, Stokely, 259f
Carpentier, Alejo, 92
Carrillo, Santiago, 295n
Carter, Jimmy, 20, 330
Castro, Fidel: autobiography of, 1ff; initial reform program of, 4ff; and Bay of Pigs, socialism, 6f; adopts Marxism-Leninism, 7; and October missile crisis, 8f, 160; first trip of, to Moscow, 10; second trip of, to Moscow, 11ff; new sugar strategy of, 13ff; USSR foreign policy supported by, 20ff; as witness at trial, 60ff; and centralization, 74; compared with Ché Guevara, 84, 117, 129n; personality of, 86f, 136f, 332f, 337f; offers normalization with U.S., 94ff; and non-intervention in Latin America, 103ff; African strategy of, 121f; interprets Marxism, 156f; condemns invasion of Dominican Republic, 162f; derides peaceful coexistence, 163; confesses heresies, 173f,

276; China polemic of, 187, 199ff;
attacks Trotskyists and *Monthly Review*, 192n, 193; declares China imperialist, fascist, Mao Tse-tung senile, 203, 205ff; and China as
scapegoat, 206; rejects stagnant
Marxism-Leninism, capitalist road,
212f; denies abuse of power, 214ff;
equates dissent with counterrevolution, 220; on revolutionary consciousness, 224ff; on neglect of
consumer needs, 227; conflict of,
with Venezuelan Communist Party,
231ff; denigrates USSR, 235; defends USSR, 250f; challenged by
Prince Norodom Sihanouk, Colonel
Moammar Khadafy, 251f; breaks relations with Israel, 252; defends
USSR invasion of Czechoslovakia,
311; excoriates Novotny regime,
313f; extols USSR aid, 323; accepts
USSR conditions for survival, 325ff;
unconditionally supports USSR for-
eign policy, 329, 332f
Castro, Raúl, 3, 98, 163n, 273f, 327f,
335f
Castro Hidalgo, Orlando, 130n
Cazalis, Segundo, 33, 67
Ceauşescu, Nicolae, 309
Central Intelligence Agency, 164
Ché. *See* Guevara, Ernesto
China, 187, 199ff, 207. *See also* Cas-
tro, Fidel
Chomón, Faure, 30, 32, 34ff, 43f
Church, Frank, 260n
Clissold, Stephen, 205n
Codovilla, Victorio, 209
Cohen, Lenard, 328n
Communist Party, creation of, 172ff;
first congress of, 327f
*Cuba 1968: Supplement to Statistical
Abstract of Latin America*, 197n
Cultural Congress, 257n
Czechoslovakia, crisis in, 295ff; press
coverage of, 307ff; comparative per-
spective on, 315ff. *See also* Castro,
Fidel

Debray, Régis, 116, 130n
Delinquency, juvenile, 287

Directorio Revolucionario, 27ff, 53,
277n
Domínguez, Jorge I., 327n, 329n
Dominican Republic, 162f. *See also*
Castro, Fidel
Don Quixote, 231, 322
Dorticós, Osvaldo, 57ff, 85, 114
Draper, Theodore, 82n
Dubček, Alexander. *See*
Czechoslovakia
Dumont, René, 137
Durch, William J., 331n

Economy: and rationing, 8, 76, 148f;
underdevelopment of, appraised, 12;
and trade with capitalist countries,
23; and exports, 72n; "organized
chaos" of, 75ff; self-financing system
of, 78ff; budgetary system of, 79ff;
"special plans" for, 88ff; and money,
217f; planning of, abandoned, 219;
and milk deficit, 280; and breach of
U.S. boycott, 280f; "mercantilist infrastructure" of, eradicated, 282f;
and neglect of equipment, 289ff;
and absence of labor discipline, 291;
USSR aid to, 293; absurd prediction
on, 321; 1970 disaster of, 325f;
post-1970 re-organization of, 325;
achievements of, 335; new setbacks
to, 335ff. *See also* Petroleum; Rice;
Sugar
Eder, Richard, interview by, 93ff
Education, 7, 80, 229, 230f, 334f
El Purio, community study of, 229f
Emigration, 169ff, 171n
Escalante, Aníbal, 54n, 272n
Escalante, César, 54
Ethiopia, 332

Fain, Tyrus G., 260n
Fanon, Franz, 115
Fernández, Marcelo, 79ff
Fernández Retamar, Roberto, 68n
Franqui, Carlos, 2n, 84n, 129n
Frei, Eduardo, 121
Fulbright, William J., 108

García Buchaca, Edith, 48ff
García Márquez, 131n, 177n

Gerassi, John, 260n
German Democratic Republic, 273, 302f, 322f
German Federal Republic, 312
Goldenberg, Boris, 197n
Goldwater, Barry, 108
González, Edward, 259n, 326n, 332n
Granma, first edition of, 175
Griffith, William E., 164n, 168n
Guantánamo, border incidents at, 95, 98
Guevara, Ernesto (Ché): in Sierra Maestre, 3; as minister of industries, 72; polemic of, on Marxist economics, 79ff; remarks of, concerning Castro, 92, 129n; rejects Castro's thesis, 98; compared with Castro, 117f; addresses UN General Assembly, 118f; and reconnaissance in Africa, 121ff; in Peking, 124f; chastises USSR, 125ff; relations of, with Castro, 128f; Congo compaign of, 129ff; farewell letter to Castro, 177; cult of Ché, 177, 268; letter to Tricontinental, 192; disaster of, in Bolivia, 261ff; Moscow visit of, remembered, 263f; record of failures of, 264ff; Castro's eulogy of, 267f. *See also* Castro, Fidel
Gulf of Tonkin, resolution of, 113

Hagelberg, G. B., 290n, 292n, 293n
Halperin, Ernst, 203n
Halperin, Ethel, 338n
Havana, Sino-Soviet propaganda war in, 202ff
Health, public, 230, 334
Horowitz, Irving Louis, 331n

Ice cream, politics of, 218f
Imperialism, peace with anywhere rejected, 182
International Bank for Reconstruction and Development, *Report on Cuba*, 197n
Internationalism, function of, 154, 166, 213
Israel, 137n, 242ff. *See also* Castro, Fidel

Jackson, D. Bruce, 190n
James, Daniel, 121, 124n, 125n, 130n
Jews, treatment of, 237ff; and Castro's ancestry, 241. *See also* Israel
Jiménez, Guillermo, 30f, 40f
Jiménez, Marta, 29
Johnson, Lyndon B., 23, 105
Journalism, decline of, 67f

Karol, K. S., 25n, 124n, 247
Kennedy, John F., 9, 24
Kennedy, Robert, 108
Khrushchev, Nikita: and missile crisis, 8f; praised by Castro, 25; on overtaking U.S. economy, 80n; warns U.S. on Cuban airspace, 95; disparaged by Castro, 153f; testament of, 161. *See also* Castro, Fidel
Kim, Ilpyong J., 315n
Kim, Il Sung, 168
Klinghoffer, Arthur J., 316n
Koestler, Arthur, 27
Kosygin, Alexei, 125, 178, 247

Latin American and Caribbean Communist Parties, conference of, 207
Latin American Communist Parties, conferences of, 116, 201
Latin American Solidarity Conference, 257ff
Latin and Caribbean America, relations with, in 1970s, 329f
Lenin, V. I., 80, 85, 158
Levav, Shlomo, 240n, 241n, 244n, 245
Lévesque, Jacques, 202n
Lewis, Oscar and Ruth, 141ff
Liberman, E. G., 83n
Liebman, Seymore B., 242n
Lockwood, Lee, 154n

Mah, Feng-hua, 198n
Manley, Michael, 249
Mao Tse-tung, 80, 205f, 285. *See also* Castro, Fidel
Marrero, Leví, 147n, 197n
Marx, Karl: church of, 178; Marxism of, 282; and inter-socialist trade, 314n
Mastny, Vojtech, 308n

Mead, Margaret, x
Mesa, Blanca Mercedes, 42f
Mesa-Lago, Carmelo, 326n
Mezerik, A. G., 308n
Microfaction: purge of, 371ff; depreci-
    ates Castro and Ché Guevara, 274;
    denies sanity of Castro, 275
Mikoyan, Anastas, 5, 9
Military establishment, 327
Mohammed, 17
Money, obsession with, 217f
Monoculture, role of, 72f
Monthly Review, 193n
Mora, Alberto, 82
Morocco, 26; Algerian conflict with,
    122
Morse, Wayne, 299
Mussolini, 17

Nasser, Gamal, advises Ché Guevara,
    123
Neruda, Pablo, complaint by, 68n
New Year's Eve, celebration of, 182ff
Niedergang, Marcel, 189n
Nixon, Richard, 108, 207
Non-aligned countries, summit meet-
    ings of, 114n, 249ff, 255
Novotny, Antonin. *See* Castro, Fidel;
    Czechoslovakia

Oltuski, Enrique, 90ff
O'Neill, Thomas P., III, 338n
Ordoqui, Joaquín, 51f, 65f; arrest and
    release of, 69f
Organization of American States
    (OAS): suspension by, 8; sanctions
    by, 99; sanctions lifted by, 330

Padilla, Heberto, arrest of, 257
Panama, championed by Castro, 18ff
Partido Socialista Popular, 28
Partido Unido de la Revolución So-
    cialista, 28
Pérez, Orlando, 85
Petroleum, 5f, 269f, 270n, 278n, 316n
Pico de Turquino, graduation at, 180ff
Politburo, composition of, 176
Pollitt, B. H., 75n
Prebisch, Raúl, 72
Preston, Thomas, 137n

Prisoners, political, 96, 220
"Profound revolutionary offensive,"
    motivation of, 282ff

Quo, F. Quei, x

Ratliff, William E., 201n, 207n, 259n
Revisionism, Yugoslav and Soviet,
    208ff
Revolution: end of, 333f; legacy of,
    334f
Rice: role of, in economy, 196ff; ra-
    tioning of, 197, 335; imports from
    China, 198f; rice-sugar agreement,
    199ff; technology assessed, 200;
    agreement terminated, 204. *See also*
    Castro, Fidel; China
Rigdon, Susan, 142
Robinson, Joan, 166
Roca, Blas, 28, 67n, 176n
Rodríguez, Carlos Rafael, 52ff; 176n
Rodríguez, Marcos: crime and ordeal
    of, 27ff; chronology of, 69
Rom, Luis Alvarez, 79
Romeo, Carlos, 73
Rumania, 278n
Rusk, Dean, prophecy of, 108
Russell, Bertrand, 317

Sabotage, wave of, 286f
Salon de Mai, 256f
San Martín, Marta. *See* Bonachea,
    Ramón L.
Santa Clara, battle of, 3
Santiago, Declaration of, 105
Sartre, Jean-Paul, 90, 317
Schorr, Daniel, 260n
Shapira, Yoram, 242n
Sierra Maestra, 3
"Siquitrilla." *See* Cazalis, Segundo
Skilling, H. Gordon, 317n
Sloan, John W., 268n
Sobel, Lester A., 212n, 328n
Socialism, concurrent with commu-
    nism, 173
Socialist constitution of 1976, 328f
Soldatov, Alexandr, 271
Soviet Union. *See* USSR
Spain, 93, 113, 312
Sports, political role of, 334n

Stalin, 80, 92, 145, 158, 205
Stevenson, Adlai, 108
Strohl, Michael, 268n
Sugar: 1964 USSR agreement on, 13ff;
 harvesting machine, 15; prices,
 281n; plan obstacles, 287ff; statistics,
 289n, 290n; exports to USSR, 292f;
 political importance of 10-million-
 ton harvest of, 294; consumer rationing of, 320f; failure of super-
 harvest of, 325; perspective for
 1980s, 337n. *See also* Castro, Fidel;
 China; Economy
Sulzberger, Cyrus L., 87n, 153f
Syria, 253
Szulc, Tad, 164

Third World, leadership of, 329n, 333
Tito, 205, 212, 314
Tomic, Rodomiro, 299
Torrijos, Omar, 19f
Touré, Sékou, 249
Tricontinental Conference, 185ff; and
 rivalry among socialist countries,
 190; Trotskyists attacked during, 191;
 Ché Guevara's message to, 192n;
 effectiveness of, assessed, 192ff

Ulam, Adam B., 209n
"Unequal exchange," 18, 126n
United Nations Conference on Trade
 and Development (UNCTAD), 17f
United States: breaks diplomatic relations with Cuba, 6; rejects normalization offers, 107ff; projects new
 flexibility, 298f; "interest sections"
 established in Washington and
 Havana, 330f. *See also* Castro,
 Fidel; USSR
USSR: opens diplomatic relations, 5;
 missile strategy assessed, 8; "vanguard" party recognized, 9f; SAM
 installations, 95; optimism concerning President Johnson, 110; pro-
 motes conference of Latin American
 communist parties, 116; friction over
 Ché Guevara's Congo operation,
 130; pressure on Castro to accept
 atomic missiles revealed, 161; reaction to overthrow of Ben Bella, 168;
 embarrassment at Tricontinental,
 189f; 23rd congress of Communist
 Party of, 208f; relations of, with
 Venezuela, 235; Israel as strategic
 threat to, 254; dilemma in Cuban
 relations, 270f; new ambassador appointed, 271; concerning KGB, 275,
 275n; dollar value of arms donated
 by, 294n; 1968 trade protocol of,
 297, 297n; post-Czech invasion
 propaganda of, 317; 50th anniversary of Komsomol, 322; extraordinary inventory of aid from, 323;
 intervention in Africa, 332. *See also*
 Castro, Fidel; Economy;
 Khrushchev, Nikita; Petroleum;
 Sugar

Valdés Vivó, Raúl, 45f
Valenta, Jiri, 331n
Venezuela, Communist Party of,
 231ff
Ventura, Esteban, 29
Vietnam, 159, 162f, 187, 209
Voisin, André, 134ff

Women, status of, 147f

*Yearbook on International Communist
 Affairs*, 315n
Yugoslavia: polemic with, 209ff; as surrogate target, 210; reconciliation
 with, 212; as instrument of imperialism, 314

Zionism, 244, 248, 253f

DATE DUE